STUDIES IN ISHCHALI DOCUMENTS

Bibliotheca Mesopotamica

Primary sources and interpretive analyses for the study of Mesopotamian civilization and its influences from late prehistory to the end of the cuneiform tradition

Editor: Giorgio Buccellati

Assistant Editors: John L. Hayes, Patricia Oliansky

Volume Nineteen

Published Under the Auspices of
IIMAS
The International Institute for Mesopotamian Area Studies

Studies in Ishchali Documents

by Samuel Greengus

Undena Publications
Malibu 1986

Ishchali is the site of an ancient city, near the junction of the Diyala and Tigris Rivers, which has yielded a sizeable number of documents from the middle of the Old Babylonian period (ca. 1900-1600 B.C.). The site was excavated by the Oriental Institute of the University of Chicago in 1934-35. The Ishchali Tablets supply important new information on society and economy. Ishchali emerges as a microcosm of Mesopotamian civilization encompassing the activities of temple, bureaucracy, royal and local government, scribal education, agricultural management, property, and finance.

Studies in Ishchali Documents is a companion study to the 416 published Ishchali Tablets in North American collections housed at the University of Chicago and the University of California, Berkeley. This work supplies transliterations, translations, of tablets as well as lexical and content notes, corrections, and new autograph collations, indexes of persons and places. The book treats over half of the North American corpus; and in addition presents 19 new Ishchali Tablets recovered from the collection of the Lowie Museum of Anthropology, University of California, Berkeley.

Published with the assistance of the Henry Englander-Eli Mayer Publication Fund, established in their memory by Esther Straus Englander and Jessie Straus Mayer.

Library of Congress Card Number 85-50820
ISBN 0-89003-167-3 (paper)
0-89003-166-5 (cloth)

Undena Publications, P.O.Box 97, Malibu, CA 90265 U.S.A.

In loving memory of my mother,

Thelma Greengus

TABLE OF CONTENTS

PREFACE

This book is the product of a number of years of study on the Old Babylonian Tablets from Ishchali contained in collections housed at the Oriental Institute of the University of Chicago and at the Lowie Museum of Anthropology of the University of California, Berkeley. The work on the Chicago tablets began in 1969 and was essentially completed in 1976. My study of the Berkeley texts began in 1974 and, aided by subsequent visits to that University in 1978 and 1980, was completed in 1981. The manuscript of this book was submitted to the press in July, 1982; it has, thus, not been possible to fully consider or incorporate the findings of studies appearing since that date.

This entire project owes a great deal to the help and encouragement of Thorkild Jacobsen. Prof. Jacobsen was the Director of the Oriental Institute excavations at Ishchali in 1934-35 and was the first scholar to study the collection of Ishchali tablets purchased by Henri Frankfort for the Oriental Institute in 1930. He generously shared with me all of his earlier work on these tablets and was later kind enough to read many parts of the manuscripts relating to the tablets belonging to the Oriental Institute. He has given so much to me as my teacher and friend; and I am pleased to acknowledge my great debt to him.

I also want to thank I. J. Gelb, my teacher, friend, and former Curator of the Oriental Institute Tablet Collections. Prof. Gelb has assisted my work in every possible way and continues to be a valued resource and consultant.

Martin Stol carefully read through all parts of the manuscript; he has offered many suggestions, superb restorations and readings, along with correcting misspelled words and supplying improvements in presentation. Some of his contributions are expressly acknowledged in the text; but they are truly too numerous to enumerate. I want to express my deep thanks to Dr. Stol for his readiness to share his knowledge and for his willingness to improve the works of others.

I want to thank the staff of the Lowie Museum of Anthropology at the University of California, Berkeley for their helpfulness and courtesy, especially Frank Norick, Dave Herod, and Prof. Anne D. Kilmer, Curator of the Tablet Collection. Dr. Kilmer not only encouraged me to collate the tablets in Lutz UCP 10/1 but also generously allowed me access to unpublished tablets in the collection. Her warm support is directly responsible for our being able to uncover the new Ishchali tablets published here in this book.

Dr. Isaac Kikawada lent personal assistance to my work at Berkeley on every one of my visits; I thank him for all of his help including assisting me with some final collations in 1982.

My colleagues at the Hebrew Union College–Jewish Institute of Religion have given me continuous encouragement on this project over the years. I am grateful for their support, their advice and counsel, and particularly for the grant to help defray the cost of publishing this book given by the Publications Committee for the College-Institute.

I wish to thank Miriam November, Bryan Beyer, and Judith Webster for their assistance in typing this manuscript; and Dawne Sarchet for proofreading and corrections.

And finally, I would like to express my appreciation to Undena Publications for undertaking to publish this book; to Prof. Giorgio Buccellati and the fine staff of Undena for their careful work, unfailing courtesy, and helpful suggestions, especially John Hayes, Marie Louise Penchoen, and Ann West.

CHAPTER 1

1. INTRODUCTION

1.1 The Purpose and Scope of the Work

The purpose of the present work is to serve as a companion study to published Ishchali tablets in North American collections. These tablets are found in two publications: *Old Babylonian Tablets from Ishchali and Vicinity*, which was published by the writer in 1979; and *Legal and Economic Documents from Ashjâly*, published by Henry F. Lutz in 1931.[1]

An interval of almost fifty years separates these two publications; accordingly, their companion studies reflect different needs and designs. Review of the documents in OBTIV, which represent fairly recent research, yields us modest gains in perspective and insight. Our strategy here is thus simply to expand and continue our earlier study of selected documents which appeared in OBTIV, pp. 58-77. That section originally was to have been larger but had to be diminished because of publication costs connected with producing that volume. The present work seeks to treat a number of important and interesting texts which were not included before and to provide a wider look at the diversity of materials found at Ishchali. These are contained in Chap. 2.[2] Treatment of these texts is supplemented by a short list of corrections and additions to readings and printings that appear in OBTIV (See Chap. 3).

Much more was gained through the study of the tablets published by Lutz in UCP 10/1. This was a pioneer effort and a good one at that, considering the fact that his work represented the first publication of a new and unfamiliar body of material, mostly written in inelegant and poorly spaced handwriting. But there were deficiencies in his treatment. A number of problems were commented upon by Koschaker in his review in ZA n.f. 9 (1936) 210-211. This led to a doctoral study, *Über die altbabylonischen Rechts-und Wirtschaftsurkunden aus Iščâlî* written in 1938 by Mirjam Seif, a student of Koschaker, Ebeling, and Eheloif.[3] Seif's study is an extremely helpful and useful piece of work since it also contains a new edition of PNs, GNs, etc., plus an index to selected vocabulary terms. But Seif

[1] Samuel Greengus, *Old Babylonian Tablets from Ishchali and Vicinity* (Uitgaven van het Nederlands historisch-archaeologisch Instituut te Istanbul XLIV), 1979–henceforth abbreviated as OBTIV. Lutz's work appears as University of California Publications in Semitic Philology Vol. 10, No. 1, pp. 1-184, University of California Press, Berkeley, California, 1931. This work will henceforth be cited as UCP 10/1 followed by the text number or page number (when appropriate). For pertinent details relating to the discovery and publication of the Ishchali tablets, see the discussion in OBTIV, pp. 1-8. The discussion points out that Ishchali tablets–many unpublished–are also to be found in museum collections at Baghdad and Geneva. Recently, yet another group turned up in the collection of the Free Library of Philadelphia. A preliminary description of these texts was given by Maria de J. Ellis in a paper "The Archives of the *šangû* of the Old Babylonian *Kitītum* Temple at Ishchali" delivered on April 16, 1980 at the meeting of the American Oriental Society in San Francisco.

[2] OBTIV also contains 21 tablets from Khafaje of a period later than the tablets from Ishchali (cf. the date formulas in OBTIV, p. 35). These Khafaje texts will be the subject of a separate study.

[3] The work by Seif was published as an "Inaugural-Dissertation" of the "Friedrich-Wilhelms-Universität zu Berlin." This work will henceforth be referred to as "Seif" followed by page numbers.

was unable to obtain photographs of the tablets and had to work on the basis of lexicography and surmise. We were fortunate to have the opportunity to re-study all of the texts published by Lutz in UCP 10/1. We discovered that there were many passages that could be clarified, as well as missing lines, omitted signs, signs read in error, etc. We have attempted to check and read through all doubtful and difficult passages; the results of these efforts are contained in Chaps. 4 and 8, Sec. 1.

The Ishchali tablets published by Lutz are part of a larger group of over 750 tablets in the collection of the Lowie Museum of Anthropology of the University of California, Berkeley. This larger group, now labeled as the Lutz-Kohlberg Collection,[4] consists of tablets mainly from the Old Babylonian Period; but there are numerous texts from both earlier and later times and sites other than Ishchali.[5] Lutz published 110 of the Ishchali tablets in UCP 10/1 but there were others that he did not include. He mentions "some seventy additional tablets, tablet fragments, and envelope fragments" which he "omitted, as adding nothing new to the selected material. . . ."[6] No list of museum numbers has been perserved so it is impossible to identify the specific items that Lutz excluded. We were not able to examine all of the tablets in the Lutz-Kohlberg Collection in detail; however, consultation of museum catalogue notes along with cursory visual impressions of physical characteristics of the tablets and their scripts has enabled identification of some seventeen additional Ishchali tablets plus two envelope fragments. These appear in Chap. 5 and Chap. 8, Sec. 2. Also included are two important date formulas belonging to the Kings of Eshnunna which are found on tablets coming from the Diyala region but which still lack specific links to the known Ishchali corpus.[7] There certainly must be others but they are yet to be identified.[8]

[4] For details on the acquisition of Lutz-Kohlberg Collection, see OBTIV, p. 2[9].

[5] In OBTIV, p. 2 we noted that the "Frankfort Collection" of the Oriental Institute, which contained the Ishchali tablets, also included tablets from other periods and places. There was no basis upon which to extract the Ishchali corpus except by looking at each tablet and establishing its content. We have no record of how Lutz came to isolate his Ishchali tablets out of the larger Lutz-Kohlberg Collection. We must observe in this connection that UCP 10/1 36 does not appear similar to the other Ishchali tablets; it is a light buff color (now that it is baked) and much lighter in color than the rest of the group. It is written in an archaic script. This tablet could have been preserved in an ancient archive at Ishchali but it appears to have been written at a different locale.

[6] UCP 10/1, p. 1.

[7] The two date formulas are UCLMA 9/2828 and 2859; yet a third date formula may be present in UCLMA 9/2906:25f. Links to the published Ishchali tablets are established through prosopography (see the discussion in OBTIV, p. 3). UCLMA 9/2826, 2858 + 2863, 2860, 2862, 2866, 2895, 2958, 3019, 3030 belong to the archive of Ilšu-naṣir (cf. OBTIV, pp. 6ff). UCLMA 9/2957 contains the seal of Ilšu-naṣir. UCLMA 9/2827, 2831, 2864, 2906, 2942 belong to the archive of Bur-Sin, father of Ilšu-naṣir, which is discussed in more detail *infra*. UCLMA 9/2878 is linked via Ipiqšina s. of Ilum-abum. UCLMA 9/2889a-c is a tablet similar in format to UCP 10/1 110 and contains many of the same persons: *mār* Iškun-Sin, Sin-muballiṭ LÚ.TÚG, Šitani, Naramtum LUKUR, Nidnuša, and Rabut-Sin. UCLMA 9/2892 and 2943 are included because they mention Neribtum and Dur-Rimuš (respectively).

[8] At the end of our last visit to Berkeley, we found two additional fragments, which we had no time to copy and therefore did not include in this present study. They are UCLMA 9/2904 and 2957; these also belong to the Ishchali corpus.

1.2 Notes on the Writing and Language of the Ishchali Documents

1.2.1 Syllabary

If one uses, as is customary, von Soden's *Syllabar* (3rd ed.—with W. Röllig) as the standard reference point, one discovers, in the Ishchali texts, a number of significant readings. Some of these are not attested in OB contexts; others are listed here because the *Syllabar* lists them as rare although attested in OB contexts. It is not our intention, for the unattested readings, to argue for their assumption as "standard values." For it is possible that we are dealing with scribal vagaries or errors. We offer them simply as new data, to be included when one comes to re-evaluate the total syllabary. The numbers preceeding each value are the same as the numbers appearing in von Soden's *Syllabar*.

(1) *rim*$_5$ (AŠ), *ne-eš*$_{15}$*-r*[*im*$_5$] OBTIV 114:2. Already attested but rare.

(63) *nu*$_6$ (NUN), ⸢É-*it*⸣ *ku-nu*$_6$*-ki-i*[*a*] *pí-te-ma* OBTIV 13:6f (to be compared with parallel passages É-*it ku-nu-*⸢*ki*⸣*i-ia pí-te-ma* in OBTIV 20:7f). This value is not attested in the *Syllabar* for OB contexts.

(97) *US*$_4$ (AZ); this is posited on the basis of the PN *I-gu-us*$_x$*-su-um* UCP 10/1 89:5, 25. However, note the writing of SU for /ṣu/ in *uš-te-e-*SU*-ni-in-ni*, CT 52 186:3 (OB). Should one instead perhaps read *I-gu-uṣ-ṣu*$_x$*-um* here? The values of AZ as *uṣ*$_4$, *uz*$_4$ are already attested in the OB syllabary.

(135) *túm* (DU), 1 *li-li túm* (*lillittum*) OBTIV 119:3. Already attested but rare.

(137) *tu*$_4$ (TUM), [*wa*] *-ta-ra-am iṣ-ba-tu*$_4$ OBTIV 123:4; *i-na* UDU.ḪI.A *ša i-ṣa-ba-tu*$_4$ UCP 10/1 58:9. In addition, in OBTIV 238:2, 266:5, UCP 10/1 70:2, 12, 14, 19, 22, 24, there are instances of numbers + things counted where it would be preferable to read *-tu*$_4$ in place of *-tum*. This value is not attested in the Syllabar for the OB period.

(156) *iš*$_6$ (GIŠ), *Ni-iš*$_6$-30. UCP 10/1 98:16. Attested but rare.

(233) *bì* (PI), q[í]-bì-ma OBTIV 12:2. Attested but rare.

(238) *ar*$_x$ (ḪAR), *Na-ma-ar*$_x$*-lu-mu-u*[*r*] OBTIV 270:10. This value is not otherwise attested.

(283) *túl* (TÚL), *Ú-túl*-EŠ$_4$.DAR OBTIV 79:5, 162:1, 181:2 and 305:11 (Khafaje). Attested but rare.

(287) *mì* (ME), ^{d}EN.ZU*-i-mì-ti* OBTIV 32:10. Attested but rare.

(298) *mim* (SAL), *na-aš-ku-un ri-ig-mim* OBTIV 278 Obv. col. iii 1′, 2′. This value is not otherwise attested in OB contexts.

1.2.2 Phonetic Sumerian

There are passages in the Ishchali documents where scribes appear to have written in Sumerian phrases out of aural memory rather than reproducing more traditional writings. This practice is not all that unusual in OB "school" Sumerian; but this phenomenon is not often the subject of systematic analysis. Here again the few Ishchali examples are insufficient in themselves; this data will become more useful when it can be incorporated into a larger study.

1) ŠEŠ.PA.TUK (read *Aḫam-arši*) for ŠEŠ.BA.TUK, OBTIV 241:15.[9]

2) IN.NA.AL.LAL for IN.NA.AN.LAL, UCP 10/1 11:11, 22:11, 52:11, 90:10.[10]

3) KI LÚ SILA.MA.DAM Ù LÚ.GI.NA.DAM for KI LÚ SILIM.MA.TA.ÀM etc., UCP 10/1 28:9f.

4) DA.ÀM for TA.ÀM, UCP 10/1 33:1.

1.2.3 Abbreviated Writings

There appear to be a few cases of abbreviated writings in the Ishchali documents. The first is the writing MAŠ.EN for MAŠ.KAK.EN (also written MAŠ.EN.KAK). See OBTIV Index pp. 95f for examples. A possible second example is the writing of NU perhaps for NU.GIŠ.SAR in UCP 10/1 89:32.

1.2.4 Assyrianisms

The language of the Ishchali texts is the Old Babylonian dialect. However, there are instances where forms more typical of the Assyrian dialect occur.

1) In OBTIV 130:5f we find: 1 (GUR) 1 (PI) 4 (BÁN) ŠE *A-ḫa-tum* DAM *Li-w[i-ra-šum]* ŠÀ.BA 3 (BÁN) ŠE *a-na ti-šu-up-ku-tim ḫa-ri-iṣ*. *Tišupkūtim* appears to be a pl. of *šapākum*, Gt inf. with metathesis and vowel harmony i.e., *šitapkum* > *tišapkum, tišapkūtim* > *tišupkūtim*. For the metathesis of t and š (so far only in OA), see GAG § 36a. For *šitapkum* see AHw 1168b; according to von Soden, the meaning of 11.5f should be: "1.1.4 (kors) barley, Aḫatum wife of Liwiraššum, including 0.0.3 (kor) barley, deducted for (earlier) deposits."

2) OBTIV 233:1-3: 1 ŠEN[x] *a-na* É [d][EN.ZU] (?) *a-na ša-ku-lim*. *Šākulu* appears to be an Assyrianism occurring in place of expected *šūkulu*; these lines apparently state: "1 . . . cauldron to the Temple of Sin for steeping;" for the meaning "steep in a liquid" see CAD A/1 258a. The unread sign [x] is not DILIM or TAB; perhaps

[9] Falkenstein *Das Sumerische* p. 27 notes the apparent interchangability of /p/ and /b/ in OB writing of Sumerian.

[10] The assimilation of n > l before l was noted by Poebel GSG § 55.

it can be read IGI; one may compare GAL.LIM/IGI in OBTIV 236:1. For GAL (*rabītum*) see AHw 936a.

3) UCLMA 9/2864:1f, 2906:1f (and TIM 3 124:2–probably Ishchali): KÙ.BABBAR TAB.BA *a-na ba-ab* KASKAL. This phrase is so far only attested in OA contexts; see notes to these texts, below.

1.3 The Archive of Bur-Sin

In OBTIV pp. 4-13, we were able to detail a number of archives among the Ishchali tablets. With the help of data from Ishchali texts belonging to the Lutz-Kohlberg Collection of the Lowie Museum of Anthropology, the University of California, Berkeley, we are able to identify an additional archive: that of Bur-Sin, father of Ilšu-naṣir.

Bur-Sin appears repeatedly as a lender of silver; at MÁŠ ^{d}UTU,[11] in *ḫubuttātum* loans,[12] and for trading ventures.[13] The amounts lent are substantial: the smallest is 11 shekels and the rest range from 1/2 to 4 minas.[14] From a number of texts we learn that Bur-Sin was the son of Ibbi-Tišpak and an overseer of merchants.[15]

The year date formulas appearing in the Bur-Sin tablets almost all belong to the reign of a single ruler: Sin-abušu.[16] The only other king mentioned is Ipiq-Adad.[17] The time frame of the Bur-Sin archive fits in with what has already been suggested concerning the reign of Sin-abušu, namely that Sin-abušu must have preceded the sequence of rulers at Eshnunna and Ishchali which included: Ibalpiel I–Ipiq-Adad II–Naram-Sin–Daduša–Ibalpiel II.[18] Bur-Sin tablets are dated to the time of Sin-abušu and Ipiq-Adad; the extensive archive of

[11] See excursus on MÁŠ ^{d}UTU on pp. 194 ff. He lends at MÁŠ ^{d}UTU in OBTIV 43, 44, UCP 10/1 80, UCLMA 9/2827, 2831, 2942, TIM 3 125.

[12] UCP 10/1 2, 61 are *ḫubuttātum* loans of Bur-Sin.

[13] UCLMA 9/2864, 2906 are trading venture loans; it is likely that TIM 3 124 is another such loan by Bur-Sin; his name is, however, almost all obliterated in line 3. This text is from Ishchali, to judge from the name of one of the witnesses–Bur-Sin s. of Imgur-Sin in lines 18f.

[14] UCLMA 9/2831 is for 11 shekels; 2942 and 2827 are for 1/2 and 2/3 mina; OBTIV 43, 44, UCP 10/1 2, UCLMA 9/2864, TIM 3 125 are for 1 mina each; UCP 10/1 80 is for 1 1/2 minas; UCP 10/1 61 is for 4 minas. So is TIM 3 124 (which may be from Bur-Sin). UCLMA 9/2906 is for some fraction or multiple of minas.

[15] Ibbi-Tišpak's name appears in UCLMA 9/2827, 2831 and may be restored in OBTIV 29, Seal Legend. Bur-Sin is identified as an UGULA DAM.QAR in OBTIV 29:9. Perhaps he is the same individual mentioned in OBTIV 21:29.

[16] See *sub* year date formulas cited in OBTIV pp. 23-35: No. 5 (OBTIV 43, 44); No. 13 (UCLMA 9/2831); No. 18 (UCP 10/1 61); No. 38 (UCP 10/1 2); No. 39 (UCLMA 9/2827); No. 60 (TIM 3 125); No. 61 (UCMLA 9/2864, 2942). All of these formulas belong to the reign of Sin-abušu, as does the formula MU ^{d}EN.ZU-*a-bu-šu* GIŠ.GU.ZA IN.DAB$_{5}$ (Reschid, *Nuršamaš* [s]) which occurs in TIM 3 124 (see note 14 above). The name of Sin-abušu also appears in the fragmentary formulas in UCP 10/1 80 (see OBTIV p. 34[72]) and in UCLMA 9/2906.

[17] Ipiq-Adad appears in OBTIV 29, which is year date formula no. 43 (OBTIV p. 32); this king is of course Ipiq-Adad II; cf. in this connection the discussion in Jacobsen OIP 43 127.

[18] See OBTIV pp. 21f. It is of course possible that the reign of Sin-abušu at Ishchali and elsewhere may have overlapped the reign of Ibalpiel I at Eshnunna since there is no certain evidence that the latter in fact ever ruled at Ishchali. All of the Ibalpiel year date formulas belong to Ibalpiel II (cf. OBTIV p. 14[59],

his son Ilšu-nasir shows evidence of the reigns of Daduša[19] and Ipalpiel II.[20] No other rulers can be identified in the archive. Accordingly, the sequence Bur-Sin and his son Ilšu-naṣir incorporates the priority in time of Sin-abušu and Ipiq-Adad II to Daduša and Ipalpiel II.[21]

16[83]). However, his successor Ipiq-Adad II did rule at Ishchali (cf. OBTIV pp. 14, 19). So Sin-abušu must have completed his reign before or during the time of Ipiq-Adad II.

[19] Daduša year date formulas occuring in the Ilšu-naṣir archive are (OBTIV pp. 23ff) No. 8 (TIM 3 127), No. 32 (UCP 10/1 50), No. 47 (UCP 10/1 7), No. 52 (UCP 10/1 4).

[20] In the Ilšu-naṣir archives, year date formulas which specifically mention Ipalpiel are (OBTIV pp. 23ff), No. 19 (UCP 10/1 44), No. 21 (UCP 10/1 21), No. 25 (UCP 10/1 58), No. 59 (UCP 10/1 5), No. 69a (UCP 10/1 42).

Other Ibalpiel formulas, which do not mention the royal name, are No. 1 (UCP 10/1 59), No. 25 (UCP 10/1 23), No. 30 (UCP 10/1 45, 63, 103), No. 46 (UCP 10/1 38, 68), No. 59 (UCP 10/1 5, 6, 74). In addition, oaths are sworn by Ipalpiel in UCP 10/1 11, 14, 15, 22, 52, 90, and TIM 5 21.

[21] Note too, the fact that the Ibalpiel dates are more numerous than those of Daduša. The seal of Bur-Sin which is partially preserved on OBTIV 29 appears in the third line to read: [AR]AD *D*[*a* . . . . .]; since the document itself is dated to the reign of Ipiq-Adad, one cannot hope to read *D*[*a-du-ša*] here. Daduša is the grandson of Ipiq-Adad II.

CHAPTER 2

SELECTED DOCUMENTS,
OLD BABYLONIAN TABLETS FROM ISHCHALI AND VICINTY
(OBTIV)

OBTIV contains 305 tablets from Ishchali plus 21 from Khafaje. In this volume we focus only on the Ishchali portion and leave the Khafaje tablets for future, separate treatment. In OBTIV, only a small number of the Ishchali tablets were accompanied by transliteration and translation. Our purpose in this section is to augment that presentation in order to further bring out both the variety of genres and interesting data found in the Ishchali tablets.

In the process of working on the Ishchali tablets we of course prepared a working transliteration and translation for every text in the corpus. But we have refrained from publishing all of this material for a number of reasons: the enormous size of the total manuscript; the fact that there are many texts which differ only a little from each other; the presence of many conventional texts that can be read and understood without difficulty, given the catalogue and indexes in OBTIV; and the persistance in some places of unresolved readings and problems which render our treatment insufficient.

Some texts are given with full transliteration and translation; these are selected because of their intrinsic importance, e.g. most of the letters in the collection, or because they are representative of a series of similar texts in the collection. For these similar texts, we have included more limited treatment of excerpted selections where we encounter variant, less typical language or where we offer suggestions for reading a broken or unclear passage. And in a few instances, we confine our treatment simply to a brief note on a line in a given text. A large number of texts are given only in transliteration; these are usually lists which can be readily handled with the aid of indexes, dictionary, and notes appended to our transliteration.

LIST OF SELECTED TEXTS FROM OBTIV

2
3
4
5 (OBTIV)
6
8
9 (OBTIV)
11
13
14
15
16
17
18
20
21 (OBTIV)
23 (OBTIV)
24
25 (OBTIV)
26 (T)
27
28
29
30
31
34 (OBTIV)
42
44
47 (P)
50 (T,P)
54 (T,P)
57 (N)
58 (T)
60 (N)
63 (N)
66 (P)
70 (N)
74 (N)
77
78
80 (T)
82 (N)
83 (N)
85 (P)
86
90 (T)
91 (OBTIV)
92 (T)
93 (P)
94
95
98
99
103 (T)
106
107 (T)
111
113
114 (T)
115 (T)
117
119
120
121
122 (T)
123 (T)
124 (T)
128
134 (T)
135 (N)
136 (T)
138 (T)
142 (T)
143 (T)
145 (T)
151 (T)
152 (T)
154 (T)
163 (T)
164 (T)
165 (T)
167 (T)
168 (N)
169 (T,P)
174 (T)
176 (T)
177 (T)
182 (T)
187 (T)
189 (T)
119 (T)
197 (T)
205 (T)
218 (T)
225 (T)
227
228
247 (T)
248 (T)
251 (T)
253 (T)
254
255 (T)
257 (T)
259 (T)
260 (T)
261 (OBTIV)
262 (T)
263 (T)
265 (T)
266 (T)
281 (T)
284 (T)
287 (T)
288 (T)
290 (T)
292 (T)
304 (T)
326 (OBTIV)

Texts accompanied by transliteration and translation are simply lsited by numbers; (OBTIV) indicates that these appear on pp. 58-77 in that volume. The symbol (T) indicates transliteration only; (P) records partial treatment only, i.e. on a portion of the text; (N) indicates notes only.

OBTIV 2

A7704

Letter: Abizum SANGA to . . .

Obv.	*[a-na] ⸢x x x x⸣*	Unto . . .
	[qí]-bí-ma	[sp]eak;
	⸢um-ma A⸣-bi-zu-⸢um SANGA*-ma⸣*	thus says Abizum the head priest:
	⸢ša ma-ḫar⸣ ^{d}*Ki-t[i-tum]*	who before Kititum
	ik-ta-na-ra-ba-[ak-kum]	continuously prays for you:
	ṭup-pa-ka ša tu-ša-bi-lam eš-mi	"Your tablet that you sent me, I have heard;
	a-na ša ṭup-pa-am ub-lam	to the person who brought me the tablet
	5 MUNUS.KISAL.LUḪ.MEŠ 1 GURUŠ *id-di-nu-šum-ma*	they gave 5 charwomen (and) one male worker;
	ku-up-ra-am iš-tu Ú-pí-i^{KI}	they took on pitch from Upu
	iš-šu-ú-ma it-ta-al-ku-nim	and went off.
	at-ta ti-di ši-ip-rum an-num	You know, this work –
L.E.	*a-na nu-qi it-tim*	to pour pitch –
	ša ma-tim ka-li-šu	(belongs) to the country (as a whole).
	za-ba-lim	(To) carry all of it
Rev.	*ú-ul ka-aš-[da]*	they are not able.
	ṭup-pi ki-ma še-⸢me-e⸣-im ar-⸢ḫi-iš⸣	Upon hearing my tablet, quickly
	li-⸢iṭ-ru⸣-du-ni-ši-na-ti	let them send them back;
	la ik-ka-al-la-nim	let them not be delayed."

NOTES

(1) Traces at the end of this line would support reading ⸢*ša* DINGIR.MEŠ⸣.

OBTIV 3

Letter: the head priest (SANGA) to Šum . . .

A7729

Obv.	*a-na Šu*[*m*]-⸢x x x⸣	To Šum . . ;
	q[*i*]-*b*[*i-m*]*a*	speak;
	um-ma SANGA-*ma*	thus says the head priest:
	aš-šum 10 UDU.NITA$_2$.Ḫ[I.A *š*]*a* *aš-pu-ra-*⸢*am*⸣	"Concerning the ten male sheep about which I wrote–
	la ta-na-d[*i-i*]n	do not give them out.
L.E.	*a-nu-um-ma*	Now,
	7 UDU.NITA$_2$.ḪI.A	seven sheep
Rev.	*it-ti* ⸢*ku*⸣*-ru-uš-te-e*	with the feeders
	ša É.GAL-*lim*	of the palace
	uš-⸢*ta*⸣*-ri-a-am*	I have sent up.
	3 UDU.NITA$_2$ *ki-ma ka-ia-ma-an-ti-ka*	Three sheep as your regular (delivery)
	≪*aš*≫ *ta-aš-pi-iṭ* 10 UDU.NITA$_2$.ḪI.A	you have been responsible for; (these) ten sheep
	a-na d(!)UTU-*na-ṣir*	to Šamaš-naṣir
Edge	*i-di-in-ma*	give (them now) and
	a-na UD.KIB.⸢NUN⸣.NA.KI	unto Sippar
	li-il-li-ik	let him go.

NOTES

(12) Translation assumes G preterit of *šapāṭu*(i/i) following the remarks of M. Stol BiOr XXIX (1972), 276. The ≪*aš*≫ is written over an erasure; it is perhaps also part of the erased sign.

OBTIV 4

A21923

Letter: . . . to the head priest (*ana šaggīm*)

Obv.	(1)	*a-na ša-⸢gi⸣-im qí-bí-ma*	(1)	Unto the head priest speak;
		um-ma ⸢x x x *-ma*⸣		thus says . . . :
		^{d}UTU *ù* ^{d}⸢INNIN⸣ ⸢*da-ri-iš* u_4*-mi*⸣	3)	"May Šamas and Ištar cause you to
		⸢*li-ba-al*⸣-[*li-ṭú*]-⸢*ka*⸣	4)	live (for) a long life
	(5)	[ ] ⸢x x (x) x⸣	(5)	. . .
		⸢x⸣ [ ] ⸢x x x x⸣		. . .
		⸢NE NA ḪA-*ti*⸣*-ku-nu ša it-ti*		. . . your . . . which
		É.GAL-lim *ša* KI *ik-ka-ri*		the palace has, (that) which the farm supervisors have,
L.E.		*ša it-ti ri-i tu-ra-am*		(that) which the shepherds have. Come back here;
	(10)	*be-lí it-ti-ku-nu*	(10)	my lord will make the journey
		gi-ir-ra-am i-la-ak		together with you.
Rev.		*a-na* KA *i-gi-sá-ku-nu*		In (proportion to the amount of) your temple tax
		ṣa-ba-am i-pa-qí-du-ku-nu-ti		they are supplying you with workers–
		⸢70 GURUŠ⸣.MEŠ *ša* ⸢*ka*⸣*-ru-*⸢*ú-ma*$^{(?)}$⸣		70 young men who are (too) short–
	(15)	*ba-lu-um ša-*⸢*al*⸣ *ša bi-ti-im*	(15)	without asking the palace steward!
		ú(?)-ma-am ⸢*šar(?)*⸣*-rum be-el* ⸢*ma*⸣*-ti-i-šu*		Is the king today lord of his land?
		a-na KA *i-gi-sá i-pa-qí-du-na-ti*		They are (also) supplying us (with men) according to the temple tax.
		a-wi-li-e ṭu-ur-⸢*dam*⸣*-ma*		Send (those) men back here
		ù 1 GURUŠ*-ku-nu it-ti-šu-nu*	19)	and let one of your young men
U.E.	(20)	*li-li-*⸢*kam*⸣*-ma a-na ša bi-ti-*⸢*im*⸣	20)	come here with them and let
		⸢*ù*⸣ *lu a-*⸢*na*⸣ *šar-ri-im*	21)	him speak to the palace steward
		*li-iq-bi-i-ma (*ERASURE)	22)	or (even) to the king and
		li-wa-še-ru-ni ku-šu-nu-ti-i-ma		let them release them for you (i.e. discharge the 70 men assigned to you).
	24)	*ki-i-ma* ≪ *i-ma* ≫ *i-na* ⸢GURUŠ⸣(?)	24)	So that they do not pester (you)
Edge	(25)	⸢*ša*⸣*-ni-im la ud-*⸢*da-ab-ba*⸣*-bu*	(25)	about another man
		a-wi-li ṭú-ur-⸢*dam*⸣ ⸢*la*⸣ *ta-ka-*⸢*la*⸣		send (these) men back; do not hold (them).

OBTIV 6

A7703

Letter: Izi-Sumu to E.GI$_4$.A É

Obv.	*a-na* É.GI$_4$.A É	To the daughter-in-law of the house
	qí-bí-ma	speak;
	um-ma I-zi-Su-mu-ú-ma	thus (says) Izi-Sumu:
	ši(!)-⌈*ra*⌉-*am ša* AN.ZA.QAR.MEŠ	"The meat of the districts –
	a-na ṣé-ri-ki li-it-ba-lu-ni-ki-im	let them bring to you.
	ma-ar-ṣu-tim	6) (As for) those sick ones, all
	a-nu-um-mu-tim ša ki-ma	7) whose
	pa-nu-šu-nu ú-ḫa-šu-ú	faces *were growing dark*,
	i-na AN.ZA.QAR *ma-aḫ-ri-ki*	in the district, under your supervision
Rev.	ITU.5.KAM *a-di* ŠE.GUR$_{10}$(!).KUD	(from) the fifth month until harvest
	a-di i-ba-lu-ṭú-ú	(or) until they get well.
	li-iš-bu-ú ù a-na a-wi-lim	let them dwell (there). And as for that
	a-nu-um-mi-im la te-gi ≪NE≫	man, do not be neglectful;
	ù šu it-ti-šu-nu	moreover, let him eat
	li-ku-ul ŠE *e-zu-ub*	with them. (Additional) grain, apart from
	ŠE.⌈BA-*šu*⌉-*nu a-na a-ka-li-šu-nu*	their grain ration, for their food
	⌈*i-na*⌉-*di-nu-ni-ki*	they will give you.

NOTES

(7) For *ša kīma* followed by subjunctive cf. Finet, *L'Akkadien* 235, Stola WZKM 63/64 (1972) 102ff.

(8) We are uncertain about the exact meaning of *uḫaššū*. The proposed, tentative, translation implying that darkness of face is an expression for sickness is suggested by the following: (1) *ḫašû* adj. "dark" CAD Ḫ 143b and G 154a (2) a possible relationship of our verb with (*ḫ*)*ašû* "a disease" CAD A/2 476b, which AHw 259b and CAD E 378b connect with *ešû*, which has the meaning "to veil, to confuse" in the G stem and "to bring together in confusion" in the D (3) *ḫašû* VI AHw 335b and *ḫašû* B verb CAD Ḫ 145b "to be darkened" (only G attested). In this last connection, Landsberger WO 3 61[52] interprets *šumma* IGI.MEŠ-*šu ḫa-šu-ú*, Kraus, *Texte* 13:16 cited by CAD Ḫ 145f sub *ḫašû* D (verb), to refer to "face" and not "eyes." There is a problem in the absence of a D form of *ḫašû* "to be dark;" our tentative translation assumes a possible similarity in usage between our form here and D forms of the verb *ekēlu* "to be dark" which are used with *zīmu* and *panû* (CAD E 64b).

(10) One might also consider reading *a-di* <ITU> ŠE.GUR$_{10}$(!).KUD; however, the month name Addarum does not otherwise occur in the Ishchali texts.

(13) The sign at the end of this line is clearly NE.

OBTIV 8

A7758

Letter: Izi-Sumu to Aḫi-ša-kimi

Obv.	*a-na A-ḫi-ša-ki-mi*	To Aḫi-ša-kimi
	qí-bí-ma	speak;
	um-ma I-zi-Su-mu-ú-ma	thus (says) Izi-Sumu:
	a-nu-um-<*ma*> *ṭup-pa-am*	Now, a tablet (written)
	a-na ARAD.^{d}MAR.TU	to Warad-Amurrim
	aš-šum [SÍG].ḪI.A *uš-ta-bi-lam*	concerning wool I have sent along;
	a-li-ik-ma	go and
	ṭup-pa-am bi-il-šum	take the tablet to him.
	SÍG.ḪI.A *ša i-na-di-na-kum*	The wool (parcels) which he will give you,
Rev.	*ku-nu-uk ki-i* ⸢*qà(?)-ta-tum*⸣	seal (them) up in safekeeping) like (as if they were being held) *as securities*;
	a-di u$_4$*-um* ⸢*a-la*⸣*-kam*	until the day I arrive,
	la ⸢*ip-pí-it-tu-ú*⸣	let them not be opened up.
	ù ki-a-am ⸢*qí-bi*⸣*-šum*	And tell him as follows:
	um-ma at-⸢*ta-a-ma*⸣	Thus you (should say):
	an-⸢*na*⸣ *i-na* ⸢x x x (x) x⸣	Indeed, into . . .
	ša bi-il-t[*i-im*]	receive
U.E.	*mu-ḫu-ur*	the porter (who comes with the goods)!
	6 GÚ SÍG.ḪI.A	(He brings) six parcels of wool,
	ṭe$_4$*-ri-du(?)-su*	his *assigned portion*,
Edge	*ù* ÁB.AL *ša* ^{d}UTU*-ma-ti*	and the heifer of Šamaš-mati (which)
	tu-ra-a-am-ma(?) ⸢*pu-ur*⸣*-tam*	you dote upon – the heifer
	tu-ra-am ša aq-bi-⸢*a-kum*⸣	you dote upon, which I promised to you.

NOTES

(10) Our translation assumes our form to be *qātātum* (AHw 910f), in the locative-adverbial case.

(16) *Ša-pi-il-ti* [ ] ⸢x⸣ is also possible.

(19) The signs *-du*(?)*-su* are as copied; translation is very conjectural and assumes a form **ṭeridūtum* (*ṭaridūtum* ?) from *ṭarādum*.

OBTIV 11

A7763

Letter: Ḫannabnatum to Wir-banišu

Obv.	(1)	*⸢a-na Wi⸣-ir-ba-ni-šu ⸢qi-bi⸣-[ma]*	(1)	Unto Wir-banišu speak;
		um-ma Ḫa-an-na-ab-na-tum-ma		Thus (says) Ḫannabnatum:
		be-lí ù be-el-ti		May my Lord and Lady
		li-ba-al-li-ṭú-ka		keep you well.
	(5)	*an-nu-um da-mi-iq*	(5)	This is (a) fine (thing)!
		ri-bu-um ITU *an-nu-um*		This is the fourth month (since you said):
		a-ma-tim	7)	"I sent (you)
		aṭ-ru-dam-ma	8)	slave women."
		a-ma-tum		(But) the slave women
L.E.	(10)	*wa-aš-ba-ma*	(10)	are sitting (there) and you (people)
		ú-ul ṭa-tà-ra-da-nim		do not send (them) to me.
Rev.		*ma-ak* DUMU.SAL *ši-ip-ri*		The lack of (having) a female messenger
		a-na li-bi-ia	13)	troubles
		i-⸢te⸣-ru-ub	14)	my heart.
	(15)	*ma-⸢an⸣-ma-an*	15)	I have no one
		ša ⸢GIŠ⸣ *a-na a-bi-ia*	16)	who can
		i-⸢ta⸣-ba-ka-am	17)	transport wood
		ú-u[l] i-šu	18)	unto my father.
		⸢an-nu⸣-um da-mi-iq		This is (a) fine (thing)!
	(20)	[ ] ⸢*a*⸣ [ ] ⸢UD⸣	(20)	. . .
		[ ] ⸢x x x⸣ [ ]		. . .
U.E.		*⸢a-ša⸣-pa-ra-am*		. . . I write (to you)
		⸢ù at⸣-ta		and you
Edge		*ta-na-ṭà-al-ši-na-ti-[ma]*		(just) look at them and
	(25)	*ú-ul ta-ṭà-ra-da-ši-na-ti*	(25)	do not send them.
		na-[ ] ⸢x x-*na*⸣ *li-ik-šu-da-ni-ni*		. . . let them get here to me!

—indistinct three line seal legend on envelope fragment—

OBTIV 13

A7661

Letter: Sin-eribam to Sin-rimenni

Obv.

⸢*a-na*⸣ ^{d}EN.ZU-*ri-me-n*[*i*]	Unto Sin-rimenni
qí-bí-ma	speak;
um-ma ^{d}E[N.ZU]-⸢*e*⸣-*ri-ba-am-ma*	thus says Sin-eribam
a-ḫu-[ka(?)]-*a-ma*	your brother:
ṭup-pí an-ni <-*am i-na*> *a-ma-ri-im*	upon seeing my tablet
[E-*it*] *ku-*nu_6*-ki-i*[*a*]	my locked storeroom
[*pí*]-*te-ma*	unlock and
10 GUR ŠE.BABBAR	10 kors . . . barley
a-na [*it*]-*ta*(!)-*ti*(ERASURE)-*ia*	for the collection notices against me
a-na ^{d}EN.ZU-*ba-ni*	unto the Sin-bani
[ ] [x x]	. . .
—rest destroyed—	

NOTES

(5) Ll. 5-8 have a parallel in OBTIV 20:5-9: *ṭup-pí an-ni-am i-na a-ma-ri-im* É-*it ku-nu-ki-ia pí-te-ma* 10 GUR ŠE.BABBAR. The writing here of *nun*/nu_6 for *nu* is most unique. Ll. 5-8 here and 20:5-9 are strikingly similar to a passage which appears in four other OB letters, discussed by Kraus, JEOL 16 (1959-1962) 20f. The four texts are two groups of nearly identical twins; and all four contain the phrase *ṭuppī*/*kunukkī anniam ina amārim*/*amārika* É/*bi-it kunukkija pitēma* followed by a list of cereal items to be given out. The occurrence of these and other similar or identical passages in other OB letters led Kraus to conclude that these duplicates and near-duplicates were in fact school exercises rather than letters actually sent. Nos. 13 and 20 are not full duplicates; one can therefore not come to a definite decision concerning their possible identity as school texts. But the possibility certainly exists. See further note to OBTIV 20:17.

(9) This translation of *ittātija* considers the form to be a plural of *ittu* CAD I/J 308f, the pl., however, is not otherwise attested. Another possibility is to read *á-ḫu*(!)-*ti-ia* "out of my brotherly consideration." The sign, however, has more elements than a normal ḪU.

OBTIV 14

A7678

Letter: Sin-eribam to his father (*ana abîja*)

Obv.	(1)	*a-na a-bi-ia qí-bí-ma*	(1)	Unto my father speak;
		um-ma ^{d}EN.ZU-*e-ri-ba ma-ru-k*[*a-*<*ma*>]		Thus (says) Sin-eriba(m) your son:
		^{d}UTU ^{d}⸢TIŠPAK⸣ *ù* ^{d}Ki-ti-tum		May Šamaš, Tišpak, and Kititum
		ša ⸢*pa-ni*⸣-*ša tu-la-pa-tu*		whose countenance you may touch
	(5)	*aš-*[*šu*]*-mi-ia da-ri-iš u*$_4$*-mi*	(5)	for my sake forever
		li-ba-al-li-ṭú-ka		keep you well.
		aš-šum ṭe$_4$*-em a-*⸢*ḫi*⸣ *ša Ḫa-*⸢*li-wu-um*⸣		Concerning the instruction on Ḫaliwum's brother
		ša ta-aš-pu-ra-am a-na-ku a-na ⸢*ša-šu*⸣*-ma*		which you sent: unto him I
		aq-bi-ma ⸢*el*⸣*-te-qí-*⸢*šu-ma*⸣		spoke and I took him and
	(10)	*be-lu-sú* ⸢*a-al-la-ak-ma*⸣	(10)	I *took charge of him*; and
		⸢*a*⸣*-nu-um-m*[*a*]		now, . . .
Rev.	(1′)	[ ] ⸢*ḫa-ru*⸣ [ ]	(1′)	. . .
		[*a*]*-na* ⸢*gi-ir-ri*⸣*-im it-t*[*a-la-ku*]		when he has gone on (his) journey
		⸢*a*⸣*-al-la-kam*		I will come.
		ša-ni-tam aš-šum TÚG *tu-*⸢*ma-ri-im*⸣		Secondly, concerning the *tumarum* garment:
	(5′)	^{I}*Ḫa-li-wu-um* [*aš*]*-*⸢*pu-ra*⸣*-kum-ma*	(5′)	I sent Ḫaliwum to you and
		UD.3.KAM *wa-ar-*[*ki*] *it-ta-la-ak-ma*		the third day thereafter he left and
		ú-ul ta-⸢*pu*⸣*-ul-šu*		you did not pay him.
		i-na-na TÚG *tu-ma-ra-am šu-bi-*[*l*]*-am-ma*		Now, send me the *tumarum* garment and
		a-na Ku-tu-ú^{KI} *lu-ša-bi-il-šu-ma*		I will send it to Kutha and
	(10′)	KÙ.BABBAR-*šu ù lu-ú* 1 MA.NA *ù lu-*⸢*ú*⸣ 1/2 MA.NA	(10′)	its price–either one mina or one-half mina–
		li-il-qú-nim-ma ku-ú-⸢*um*⸣*-ma*		let them get for it. And as for your (stuff),
		šum-ma la il-qú-ú uš-te-pí-la-kum(!)		if they have not already taken (it), then it will be replaced for you.
		KÙ.BABBAR-*ka ù* KÙ.BABBAR *za-zu-um zi-iz-*⸢*zu*⸣		Your silver and (that) silver are being kept carefully separate.
		a-na-ku TÚG *tu-ma-ra*<*-am*> *ša-a-*⸢*tu* x x⸣	14′)	I will not continually keep asking you for that
U.E.	(15′)	*a-na ḫi-il-la-ti-ia a*	15′)	*tumarum* garment . . .
		i-te-ne-er-ri-iš-ka	16′)	(or) for my *wraps*.

NOTES

Obv.

(1) Cf. for similarity of style the Ishchali letter TIM 2 42: (1) *a-na* SANGA *a-b[i-ia]* (2) *qı-bí- ma* (3) *um-ma I-zi-Na-bu[ú]* (4) *ma-ru-ka-a-m[a* (5) ^{d}UTU *ù* ^{d}*Ki-ti-[tum]* (6) *aš-šu-mi-ia* . . . . Is it possible that Sin-eribam in our letter is likewise writing to the SANGA of Kititum, seeing how that deity is especially invoked in lines 3-4?

(4) Alternatively, "before whom you play (music)"

(10) Cf. *belūtam alākum* CAD A/1 315, B 205a, AHw 121b.

Rev.

(4′) For this garment cf. MSL 10 132 (Hh XIX) 172; it appears in a context of costly clothing.

(12′) Gt pres. *šupēlum* GAG § 109k.

(15′) For *ḫillātum* cf. AHw 345b sub *ḫillu*.

(15′) For *a* written in place of *a-a*, *a-ia*, a-i, etc. cf. CAD A/1 218a and add VAS 1 32 i 17.

OBTIV 15

A7761

Letter: Aḫat-waqrat to Sin-eribam

Obv.	*a-na* ^{d}EN.ZU-*e-ri-ba-am*	To Sin-eribam
	qí-bí-ma	speak;
	um-ma A-ḫa-at-wa-aq-ra-at-ma	thus (says) Aḫat-waqrat:
	i-na sú-[qí]-im na-ás-ḫa-a-ta	Have you been moved away from (your) street?
	a-di ma-ti ú-ul a-ša-ri-iš	How long (will it be)? Don't you
	wa-aš-ba-a-ta-a-ma	live there (still)?
	an-ni-ki-a-am bi-tum i-na bu-bu-tim	Here, the house with hunger
	i-na-ap-pu-uḫ an-ni-ki-a-am	breaks out; here,
	še-um ša it-ti ^{1}*Im-[di]-um*	the barley that is (stored) with Imdijum
	ú-ul šu-ud-du-un	has not been collected.
	i-na bi-tim ra-ap-ši-im	In (this) expansive house
L.E.	*še-um su-lu-uḫ*	the (supply of) barley has become a trickle;
	ú-ul i-ba-aš-ši	there is nothing (here).
Rev.	*ša i-na te-ri-ti-šu-nu nu-uš-šu*	Those persons, who according to their instructions were made to move,
	i-na [Èš]-nun-na-ak-ma	are being settled

	[*uš-ta-aš-ša-a*]-*bu-ú-ma wa-ar-ka-at*	in Eshnunna but the disposition
	[*bi-ta-a-ti-šu*]-[*nu*] *ú-ul i-pa-ar-ra-su*	of their property they are not deciding.
	[ ] [*ki-i*] *is-qú-ša* 5 *si-im-da-a-tum*	. . . that *her shares* (are) 5 teams
	[*š*]*a* ^{d}UTU	. . . of Šamaš
	[ ] [x] *ta-aš-pu-ra-am*	. . . you sent
	[*š*]*u*(?) *da*	– remainder unintelligible–
	[ ]*it ù* [*bi-im*]	
	[ ] [x] *e-ma*	
U.E.	[ ] [x x]	
	[ ]*ma-aḫ*-[x x x]	
	[ ] [x] *ú-ul*	

OBTIV 16

A21901

Letter: Sin-iddinam to Isim-ilu

Obv.	*a-na I-si-mi*-[*lu*]*(?)*	Unto Isim-ilu
	qí-bí-ma	speak;
	um-ma ^{d}EN.ZU-*i-din-nam*	thus says Sin-iddinam:
	lu nu-ba-ta-am	Either in the evening
	ù lu ú-ra-am i-[*na*] *ka-ṣa-tim(?)*	or tomorrow early in the morning
	a-di ṣé-ri-ia	come to
	al-ka-am	me here.
	ṣi-[*bu*]-*ut-ka*	Your need
	[*ma-la*] *i-šu-ú*	—as much as there is—
	[*ku-uš*]-⌜*da*⌝-*am*	satisfy.
L.E.	[*i-na*] ⌜*pa*⌝-*ni-ka*	At your place—
Rev.	[GURUŠ *t*]*a*-⌜*ak*⌝-*la-am*	reliable worker(s)
	⌜*ù*⌝ MAŠ.EN.KAK	and villein(s)
	ma-la 30-*ša-me*-[*i*]	as many as Sin-šame
	ú-ka-la-mu-ka	will produce for you—
	i-na pa-ni-ka	at your place
	la ti-zi-ba-am	do not leave (them behind).
	ta-ra-a-am	Get (them) here!
	ap-pu-tum	Please!

NOTES

(17) On *ezēbu* + ventive, cf. OBTIV 9 pp. 59f, note to lines 15 and 17.

OBTIV 17

A7870

Letter: Sin-iddinam to his lord (*ana bēlija*)

Obv.	*[a-na] be-lí-i[a]*	Unto my lord
	[qí-b]í-ma	speak;
	[um-ma] ^{d}EN.ZU-*i-din-nam-ma*	thus says Sin-iddinam:
	[i-na] ⸢u_4⸣-*mi*-⸢*im*⸣ *sa eṭ-ḫa-am*	On the day I came over,
	[bi-it-qum š]a i-na a-ga-am-mi-im	the sluice which is in
	[i-ba]-aš-šu-ú	the marsh
	[up-ta-ši-i]q-ma i-na ša-ni-im u_4-*mi-im*	got clogged up and so on the second day
	[pu-uš]-šu-qí-im ba-ta-qí-im	I set my hand to
	[qa]-ti aš-ku-un	opening up the obstructed area;
	[mu-ú š]a i-na bi-it-qi-im	but the water (coming) through the sluice
	[a-na ša-qi]-im 30 *pa-ta-tim iṣ-ṣú*	is to meagre to feed 30 irrigation canals.
	[a-na b]e-el-šu-nu	Unto their owner
	[ki-a-am] aš-pu-ur um-ma a-na-ku-⸢*ma*⸣	I wrote as follows: thus I (said):
	[mu-ú š]a i-na bi-it-qa(!)-⸢*tim*⸣	The water which is (coming) through the sluices
	[a-na ša-qí]-⸢*im*⸣ 30 *pa-ta-tim iṣ-ṣú*	is to meagre for feeding 30 irrigation canals;
	[ERÍN].⸢ḪI.A⸣ *a-na ab-ni* LUGAL	let them send workers
	[li-iš-š]a-ap-pa-ru-ú	(to fetch) the king's stones;
	[a-na ma-a]ḫ-ri-i[a]	unto me
	[li-iš-šu-nim] 30 *pa(?)*-⸢*ta(?)-a-tim*⸣	let them bring (them). The thirty canals
	[ ] ⸢x x⸣ [ ]	. . .
Rev.	[ ]*-ma*	— Rev. too fragmentary for translation —
	[*b]i-ma*	
	[ ] ⸢x x x⸣ [ ] ⸢x⸣ *bi-ku-tam*	
	[*ša e-l]i-ka-ma ṭà-bu*	
	[ ] ⸢x⸣	
	[ ] ⸢x x⸣ [ ] ⸢x⸣ *šu-um-ma*	
	[ ] ⸢x⸣	
	[ ]	
	[ ] ⸢*ma*⸣	
	[ ] ⸢x x⸣ [ ]	
	[ ] ⸢*ru*⸣-*na-m[a]*	
	[Š]À ⸢x x⸣ [ ]	
	[*pa]-ta-tim ma*⸢x⸣ [ ]	
	[ ] ⸢*iš*⸣-*ta-na-ap-pa*⸢*ru*⸣-*[ú]*	
	[ ] ⸢x⸣-*bi*	
	[ ] ⸢x-*bi-ma*⸣*(?)*	
	[ ] ⸢*za-ba-la*⸣*(?)*	
	[ ] ⸢*i*⸣-*na-aš ta-aš*-⸢x⸣	

	[	] ⸢x x⸣*di*
(20)	[	] ⸢x-*ia*⸣
	[	] ⸢x⸣

– rest destroyed – 2-3 more lines –

NOTES

(1) The identity of the addressee is unknown. There are a number of letters similarly addressed (*ana bēlija*) written by Abizum; see OBTIV 4. One should also note TIM 2 4, a letter written by Abizum SANGA which, like the present text, also deals with the clearing of silted canals (cf. OBTIV 5[18]). A certain Sin-iddinam is known to have been a SANGA at Ishchali according to UCP 10/1 75:8 and 79:8.

(12) Alternatively, the PN Belšunu; this PN is amply attested in the Ishchali corpus.

OBTIV 18

A21933

Letter: Apil-Sin . . .-Sin and Anum-pi-Ištar

Obv.	(1)	[*a-na*] ⸢x⸣-^{d}EN.ZU	(1)	[Unto]. . . .-Sin
		[*ù* AN]-⸢KA⸣-EŠ$_4$.DAR		[and] Anum-pi-Ištar
		[*q*]*í-bí-ma*		speak;
		[*u*]*m-ma A-pil-*^{d}EN.ZU-*ma*		thus (says) Apil-Sin
	(5)	[*a-ḫ*]*u-ka-a-ma*	(5)	your brother:
		[*bi*]-⸢*it*⸣-*ku-nu a-bu-ka*		your household, your father,
		um-ma-ka a-ḫa-a[*t-ka*]		your mother, your sister,
		⸢*at-ta*⸣-*a*		you
		ù ni-šu-ka		and your kinfolk–
	(10)	*ša-al-ma-tu-nu*	(10)	are you (all) well?
		li-ba-li-iṭ-ku-nu-ti	11)	May Ištar keep you
		EŠ$_4$.DAR ^{d}MAR.TU ^{d}EN.[ZU] (?)	12)	well; may Amurru, Sin(?)
		ù ^{d}*I-šar-ki-di-su*		and Išarkidisu
		a-na šu-ul-lu-mi-ku-nu	14)	be attentive to
	(15)	⸢*lu*⸣-*wa-qù-ú*	(15)	making you well.
		li-ba-ka		Let your heart
		mi-im-ma	17)	not
L.E.		⸢*la*⸣ *i-ma-ra-aṣ*	18)	grieve any.

		⸢ÁB⸣(?) *ar-*⸢*ḫi-iš*⸣	19) I did not promptly give
Rev.	(20)	⸢*la*⸣ *a-*⸢*ap-qí*⸣*-da-ka*	20) over the cow to you
		a-na 30*-ta-*⸢*a*⸣*-ia-ar*	21) (because) I offered (it)
		ú-ki-il-⸢*ma*⸣	22) to Sin-tajjar
		ú-ul im-[*ḫu-ra-an-ni*]	but he did not approach me (to accept it).
		ki-i-ma a-da-⸢*num*⸣ [*e-te-qu*]	When the term (for the offer) has expired–
	(25)	^{d}UTU ⸢*ù* EŠ$_4$.DAR⸣ [ ]	(25) may Šamaš and Ištar
		li-ba-⸢*al-lí*⸣*-*[*ṭú-ka*]	keep you well (until that time)–
		⸢*ù ka-a-*x⸣ [ ]	and then . . .
		[ ] ⸢x x x⸣	. . . .
		– break of about 7 lines –	– lines 29-41′ are missing or too broken for translation –
U.E.	(36′)	[ ] ⸢*za ni*⸣ [ ]	
	(37′)	[ ] ⸢x⸣ *te*(?)*-en-*[ ]	
	(38′)	[ ] ⸢x bi⸣ [ ]	
		– break of 3 lines –	
Edge	(42′)	*ša ṭú-up-*(ERASURE)*pa-am*	42′) (as far as) the one (by) whom you
	(43′)	*tu-ša-bi-la-am*	43′) have sent the tablet
	(44′)	⸢x x *bi la* x x⸣	44′) . . . .

NOTES

(15) For another reading see AHw 1456a *sub wagûm*.

OBTIV 20

A7672

Letter: Abu-waqar to Eribam

Obv.	(1)	[*a-n*]*a E-ri-ba-am*	(1) Unto Eribam
		[*q*]*í-bí-ma*	speak;
		um-ma A-bu-wa(!)-qar	thus says Abu-waqar
		a-ḫu-ka-ma	your brother:
	(5)	*ṭup-pí an-ni-am*	5) upon seeing
		i-na a-ma-ri-im	6) my tablet,
		É*-it ku-nu-*[*ki*]*-ia*	my locked storeroom
		pí-te-ma	unlock and

	10 GUR ŠE.BABBAR	10 kors ripe barley
	⸢10⸣ GUR ZÍZ	10 kors emmer
Rev.	⸢2⸣ GUR GÚ.GAL	2 kors chick peas
	⸢10⸣ GUR GÚ.TUR	10 kors lentils
	a-na ŠU 30-*i-*[*qí*]-*ša-am*	into the hand of Sin-iqišam
	⸢*mu*⸣-*du-ud*	measure out.
	ap-pu-tum	Please
	la te-gi	do not neglect (my orders).
	PAB	FINIS
	Ma-nu-um DUB.SAR	Mannum the scribe

NOTES

(5) Ll. 5-9 have an exact parallel in OBTIV 13:5-8; see also the note there.

(13) The reading of the PN in line 13 is equivocal in that one could also read a PN Šu-Sin-iqišam.

(17) The occurrence of PAB between ll.16-18 and the inclusion of the scribe's name raise the question whether this document is a school letter. PAB plus a scribe's name also occur in OBTIV 12:20; and this text contains other features suggestive of its perhaps being a school letter. For these other features see note to OBTIV 13:5.

OBTIV 24

A7695

Letter:

Obv.	[ ]	Unto . . .
	q[*í-bí-ma*]	speak;
	a-⸢*nu-um*⸣-[*ma*]	Now, . . .
	ša ^{d}EN.Z[U]x[ ]	which Sin- . . . .
	iš-ti-iš-šu sǎ-a[*m-ša-ti*]*m*	First, concerning the sun-disc ornaments
	ša ì-lí-ia e-li-⸢*ia*⸣	of my god he
	i-di iš-ni-ma	accused me. Second,
	ši-ib-ši ša É.GAL	about the rent (due) the palace
	e-li-ia i-di	he accused me.
	iš-lu-uš-ma	Third,
	a-na DUMU *a-wi-li*	he said: "Go to the

	a-lik LUGAL *mu-ḫ*[*u-u*]*r*	citizens! Appeal to the king
	iq-bi	(in this matter)!"
	ir-bu-ma qa-ti	Fourth, the hand of
	GÌ[R.NIT]A_2 ⸢*iṣ-ba*⸣-*a*[*t-m*]*a*	the military governor he grasped and
	a-na š[*e-pi-šu*]	before his feet
Rev.	*ù I-ku-*[*pí-*^{d}EN.ZU]	and (before) Ikuppi-Sin
	ú-ša-am-qí-it-[*an-ni*]	he had me fall.
	iḫ-mu-uš-ma qa-ti	Fifth, the hand of
	DUMU *A-da-a-a iṣ-ba-at-ma*	the son of Adaja he grasped and
	a-na I-ku-pí-^{d}EN.ZU	unto Ikuppi-Sin
	ú-⸢*ṭe*$_4$*-eḫ(?)*⸣*-ḫi ù ki-ma*	be brought (him) near; and that
	e-⸢*es*⸣*-re-ku ti-di*	I was confined (in prison) you know.
	a-na-ku a-na ÁŠ.NUN.NA^{KI}	I came here to Eshnunna but
	al-li-⸢*kam*⸣*-ma ú-ma-am*	today I did not
	⸢*la*⸣*eṭ-ḫi-am-*⸢*me*-x x⸣	draw near . . .
	⸢x x x⸣-*ma*(?)	. . .
	uš-ta-ri-aš-šum	I had led unto him.
	me-eḫ-ri-it-tum ⸢x⸣	On the opposite side . . .
	ḫu-tu-[*me*]*-su ša*⸢x⸣ [ ]	. . .
	ša[ ]	. . .
Edge	*ú-ṭe*$_4$*-ḫi*	he brought near
	ù ka-ar-ṣi-ia i-ku-ul	and he slandered me.
	⸢*ù*⸣ *i-nu-ma am-ta-na-ḫa-ru-ku-nu-ti*	Moreover, when I continuously appeal to you
	a-na ia-ši-im-ma tu-ka-ma-ra-nim	you heap up (excuses) for me.
	a-di ma-ti i-ṣí-da-ni	How long will he mow me down?

NOTES

(6) Ll. 6-21 are translated by CAD Ḫ 61. Some minor corrections are required; for 1.6 the reading *ša ta-am-*[x x] is incorrect. CAD takes *i-lí-ia* as a PN; but this PN is otherwise unattested in the Ishchali texts.

(16) CAD Ḫ, 61 reads *qāti* PN *i*[*ṣbatma*]; a PN is unlikely in view of traces which support GÌ[R.NIT]A_2 but ⸢*iṣ-ba*⸣*-a*[*t-m*]*a* is possible and tentatively acceptable.

(37) Translation derives verb from *eṣēdum*, "to harvest;" for the use of this verb in transferred meanings, other than cutting grain, cf. AHw 251a.

OBTIV 26

A21957

Court Record

Obv.

^{1}LÚ-⸢^{d}MAR⸣.TU
ù ARAD-*ì-lí-šu*
i-di-nu-ma DI.KU$_5$.MEŠ
di-nam KÁ ^{d}EN.ZU
⸢*ša Ka(?)*⸣-*ma-nim*
[*ú-ša-ḫi*]-⸢*zu-šu-nu-ti*⸣
– rest of Obv. destroyed –

Rev.

[1]*i-mu*
[*di-na*]*m ú-šà-ḫi-zu*
^{d}⸢*I-šar*⸣-[*ki-di-su*]

Seal Legend

LUGAL.A.NI.[IR]
I-ku-un-KA-^{d}EN.ZU
– no more lines preserved –

NOTES

Seal Legend: It is possible that Ikun-pi-Sin on this seal (cf. also OBTIV 300) is the same person as Ikun-pi-Sin who is elsewhere attested at Ishchali as a ruler. Ish. 34-T.72 is a jar cover which bears a seal impression: *Be-la-nu-um* DUMU *E-te-el-lum* ARAD ⸢*I-ku-un*-KA-^{d}EN.ZU⸣. For this ruler, see the discussion in OBTIV pp. 19, 21[103], and R. Harris JCS 9 (1955) 55.

OBTIV 27

A21886

Court Record

Obv.	– beginning missing –	
	[ ] ⸢*me*⸣-*e ú-su*-⸢x⸣ [ ]	. . .
	⸢x⸣ ^{d}*Ú-mu-u*[*m*]	. . . the Storm symbol
	ša ^{d}*Be-el-ga-še-e*[*r*]	of Belgašer
	ù ^{d}*Šu-ku-ru-um*	and the Lance
	ša ^{d}*Wi-ir*	of Wir
	im-ta-ag-ru	they agreed.
L.E.	*ni-iš* ^{d}EN.ZU	(With) an oath by Sin
	ù Su-mu-a-bi-ia-ri-i[*m*]	and Sumu-abi-iarim

Rev.		ba-ab-tum É [^{d}] [EN.Z]U		at the gate of the Temple of Sin
	(10′)	⸢*im*⸣-*ta-ag-ru-m*[*a*]	10′)	they agreed; and
		⸢*ma-ma-an a*⸣-*na wa-ar-ki-it*		whoever in the future
		[u_4-*mi-i*]*m* ⸢*ša i-ra-ga-mu*⸣		will raise claim
		[ ] ⸢x⸣ [ ] ⸢x⸣ [ ]		. . .
		– remainder lost –		

NOTES

(1′) One might consider restoring a PN [*I-na-ša-m*]*a-ú-su-u*[*m*]; but there seems to be room for only two more signs before the ME. One might also consider restoring an emblem of another deity in line 1′ and in the gap preceeding, reading [*ù*] at the beginning of line 2′.

(2′) If one restores a PN in line 1′, then one would expect to read [*ma-ḫa*]*r* in line 2′; thus, "before the storm symbol of DN$_1$ and the lance of DN$_2$ they agreed." However, the terms for the emblems are in the nominative case and not in the genitive as would be expected after *maḫar*. One may wonder whether the terms for the divine emblems could be taken as proper names and thus not be put into the genitive case.

(3′) For the deities cf. Simmons JCS 14 (1960) 26 no. 53 Seal: ^{d}*Be-el-ga-ši-ir* LUGAL *Ša-du-pé-e*^{KI}; cf. also Goetze, Sumer 14 (1958) 9, who cites IM 51458 (unpub.), a barley loan "from the god Wer *ša Ka-ku(?)-la-tim*^{KI}." These deities were gods of neighboring cities who were also venerated at Ishchali.

(9′) Alternatively: (1) "the city quarter (residents) at the temple of Sin agreed;" (2) *babtum ip-ḫ*[*u-ur-m*]*a* "the city quarter assembled;" (3) *ip-ḫ*[*u-ru-m*]*a imtagrūma* "(the city quarter (residents)) assembled and agreed."

OBTIV 28

A21956

Letter Fragment

Obv.	(1′)	[ ] ⸢x x⸣ [ ]	(1′)	. . .
		[*lu t*]*i-*[*di ša*]		You indeed know that
		[*ki-a*]*-am la* ⸢*aq*⸣-*bu-šum*		I did not tell him thus.
		[*i-nu*]-*ma*		When
	(5′)	[^{d}EN.ZU]-⸢*e*⸣-*ri-ba-am*	(5′)	Sin-eribam
		[*ŠE-šu*] ⸢*i*⸣-*na* É		his barley into the house
		[^{d}EN.ZU-*we-de-k*]*u*		Sin-wedeku
Rev.		[*iš*]-⸢*pu-ku*⸣-*ma*		stored; but
		^{d}EN.ZU-*e-ri-ba-am*		Sin-eribam

(10′)	[*p*]*i-ti-ma li-qí*	(10′)	"Open, take (some of it)"
	[*a-na*] ^{d}EN.ZU-*we-de-ku*		unto Sin-wedeku
	[*la i*]*q-bu-ú*		did not say;
	[*ù ba-l*]*um ša-al*		and so (it was) without asking
	[^{d}EN.ZU]-*e-ri-ba-am*		Sin-eribam
(15′)	[ŠE *iḫ-bu*]-[*tu*]-*ma*	(15′)	(that) he borrowed barley.
	– remainder lost –		– remainder lost –

NOTES

The identification of this text as a letter is based upon the restoration of line 2; otherwise, it may be a court record as suggested in OBTIV 37.

OBTIV 29

A7716

Settlement of Account by *kārum*

Obv.	(1)	3 GUR ŠE KÙ.BABBAR	(1)	3 kors barley, (equivalent of) silver,
		ni-ka-sú-šu		are his accounts;
		i-na KÁ ^{d}TIŠP[AK]		in the Gate of Tišpak
		ka-ru-um		the mercantile guild
	(5)	*i-pu-uš-ma*	(5)	figured (them); and
		še-um an-nu-um		this barley
Rev.		KI *Li-wi-ra-šum*	7)	is owed
		Ì.GÁL	8)	by Liwiraššum.
		IGI *Bur*-^{d}EN.ZU UGULA DAM.QA[R]		Witnessed by Bur-Sin, the overseer of merchants
	(10)	IGI EN.ZU-*i*-⸢*qí*⸣-*š*[*a-am*]	(10)	Witnessed by Sin-iqišam
		IGI *En-nam*-^{d}EN.[ZU] (?)		Witnessed by Ennam-Sin
		ù ka-ru-u[*m*]		and the mercantile guild
		ša ⸢*Ne-ri-ib-tim*⸣ [KI] (?)		of Neribtum.
		ITU ⸢^{d}*Ma-mi* UD.10+⸣.[KAM]		Month of Mami, . . .-th day,
U.E.	(15)	⸢MU x⸣ [ ]^{d}*I-pi-iq*-⸢^{d}IM⸣	(15)	The year the . . . (called) "Ipiq-Adad
Edge		KALAM.⸢MA⸣ DI[ ]		of the country . . ."
		^{d}⸢*I*⸣-*pi-iq*- ⸢IM BA.DÍM.DÍM⸣.⸢MA⸣		Ipiq-Adad built.

Env.		⸢*ka-ru*⸣-[*um*]
Variants	(5)	*i-pu-uš*-[*ma*]
		⸢*še-um an*⸣-[*um*]
Seal Legend		

Bur-^{d}EN.Z[U]	Bur-Sin
[DUMU] [*I*]*bi*-^{d}T[IŠPAK]	son of Ibbi-Tišpak
[AR]AD *D*[*a* . . . .]	servant of Da . . .

NOTES

(7) For KI PN *bašû*, implying obligation to repay, see note to OBTIV 78:3, below.

(15) For this year date formula see OBTIV p. 32 no. 43.

OBTIV 30

A21952

Sale of House

Obv.	2/3 SAR 15 ŠE É.DÙ.A	A 2/3 *sar* 15 *še* built-up plot
	DA É *I-ku-un*-KA-^{d}IM	adjoining the house of Ikun-pi-Adad
	ù DA É 30-*i-qi-ša-am*	and adjoining the house of Sin-iqišam
	KI ^{d}EN.ZU-*mu-ba-li-iṭ*	from Sin-muballiṭ
	ù A-pil-^{d}EN.ZU *ù* ŠEŠ.A.NI	and Apil-Sin and his brother
	^{l}*Ku-ri-tum* LUKUR ^{d}UTU	Kuritum the *nadītu* of Šamaš,
	DUMU.SAL *Be-la-ia*	daughter of Belaja,
	IN.ŠI.ŠÁM	purchased.
	ŠÁM.TIL.LA.BI.ŠÈ	For its complete purchase price
L.E.	ŠÀG.GA.A.NI Ì.DÙG	she satisfied him;
	INIM.BI AL.TIL	the transaction is concluded;
Rev.	GIŠ.GAN.NA IB.TA.BAL(!)	they passed the pestle.
	U$_4$.KÚR.ŠÈ LÚ.ŠÈ	In the future, one party with another
	NU.MU.UN.GI$_4$.GI$_4$	shall not contest.
	MU NU(?) LUGAL PÀD	(They) swore by the name of the king.
	IGI *Ri-iš*-^{d}IM DUMU *E-ta-na*	Witnessed by Riš-Adad son of Etana
	IGI 30-*ki-ì-li-ia* DUMU *Ar-ši-tum*	Witnessed by Sin-ki-ilija son or Aršitum
	IGI BA.EŠ$_4$.DAR DUMU *Mu-na-wi-rum*	Witnessed by Iqiš-Ištar son of Munawwirum
	IGI *Nu-úr-Ku-bi* DUMU *I-lu-šu-nu*	Witnessed by Nur-Kubi son of Ilušunu
	IGI *Ib-ni*-^{d}IM DUMU *Na-bi*-DINGIR-*šu*	Witnessed by Ibni-Adad son of Nabi-ilišu

	IGI *Mu-na-wi-rum* DUMU *I(?)-k[u-u]n*-KA-*ì-lí*	Witnessed by Munawwirum son of Ikun-pi-ili
	IGI ARAD-*sà* DUB.SAR	Witnessed by Warassa the scribe
U.E.	DUMU ARAD.^{d}EN.LÍL.LA	son of Warad-Enlil
	IGI *Im-gur*-^{d}UTU DUMU ^{d}UTU [x x]	Witnessed by Imgur-Šamaš son of Šamaš-. . .

Envelope Variants

(1)	DUB 2/3 SAR *etc.*	(1)	tablet of 2/3 *sar* etc.
(2)	*I-ku-pí*-^{d}I[M]	(2)	Ikuppi-Adad
(3)	^{d}EN.ZU-*i-qí-š*[*a-am*]		
(20)	*Na-bi-ì-lí-šu*		
(21)	*I-ku-un*-KA-*ì-lí*		
(24)	^{d}SEŠ.KI⌜x⌝ [ ]	(24)	[Img]ur-Šamaš son of Nanna . . . (!)

Seal Legends

A	^{d}*A-a*	A	Aja
B	*Li-pí-it*-EŠ$_4$.DAR DUMU *Mu-na-wi-ru-um*	B	Lipit-Ištar son of Munawwirum

NOTES

(8) ŠÁM is written the same way on both the tablet and envelope.

(12) This line is not preserved on the envelope.

(15) Envelope has only [LU]GAL PÀD preserved.

(18) The value BA is normally understood as a form of the verb *qâšu*; cf. AHw 919 for references; it is therefore surprising to encounter the PN *Li-pí-it*-EŠ$_4$.DAR DUMU *Mu-na-wi-ru-um* in Seal Legend B of our text. There is no Lipit-Ištar listed among the witnesses but there is one BA.EŠ$_4$.DAR DUMU *Mu-na-wi-rum* in line 18. Is it possible that there is some confusion here with BA written for Lipit? R. Whiting has called my attention to the equation BA=*li-bit*= *libittu* cited by ŠL 5, 7; he suggests that the scribe wrote BA=*libit(u)* as a "phonogram" for *lipit*. This is an attractive suggestion; but it requires us to so also interpret other PNs using BA which occur in the Diyala texts: e.g., BA.^{d}EN.ZU, OBTIV 47:18 from Ishchali; BA.^{d}INNIN (Ellis JCS 24 [1972] p. 63 56:17); and BA.^{d}TIŠPAK (Goetze Sumer 14 [1958] p. 65 41:1) from Harmal. Another possibility is that two persons, perhaps brothers, are using the same seal, i.e., Iqiš-Ištar and Lipit-Ištar both use the seal of Lipit-Ištar. The situation suggested here might be similar to the one encountered in UCP 10/1 where Munawwirum DUB.SAR apparently used the seal of Munanum DUB.SAR in text nos. 11 and 107 (as well as in TIM 5 21). UCP 10/1 42:5ff attests that Munanum is a son of Gullubija; and the seal legends attest the same for Munawwirum (the suggestion of Seif loc. cit. 63[167] that they are the same person is thus unnecessary). They are apparently brothers.

(24) The envelope reads [*Im*]-⌜*gur*-^{d}⌝UTU DUMU ^{d}ŠEŠ.KI ⌜x⌝ [ ] while the tablet has *Im-gur*-^{d}UTU DUMU ^{d}UTU [x x]; this juxtaposition seems to be due to some confusion or error.

OBTIV 31

A21912

Sale of Field

	Transliteration	Translation
Obv.	⌈1 EŠE⌉ 3 GÁN ⌈A⌉.[ŠÀ]	900 sar field
	i-na a-ga-⌈*am-mi-im*⌉	in the marsh
	DA ^{d}IM-*ra-bi*	next to (the field of) Adad-rabi,
	KI *A-da-a-a* DUMU ⌈*Ṭà*⌉-*ab-ṣíl-*⌈*la-šu*⌉	from Adaja son of Ṭab-ṣillašu
	ù ^{d}EN.ZU-*ba-ni* DUMU.NI	and Sin-bani his son
	^{Id}EN.ZU-*še-mi*	Sin-šemi
	IN-ŠI.⌈ŠÁM⌉	bought.
	ŠÁM.TIL.LA.NI.ŠÈ	For its complete price
	5/6 MA.NA 5 1/2 GÍN KÙ.[BABBA]R	5/6 mina, 5 1/2 shekels silver
	IN.NA.LAL	he paid him.
	GIŠ.GAN.NA ÍB.TA.BAL	He passed over the pestle;
	ŠÀ.GA.NE.NE Ì.DÙG	he satisfied them;
	INIM.BI.NE AL.TIL	their transaction is concluded.
	U_4.KÚR.ŠÈ LÚ.LÚ.ŠÈ	In the future one party with another
	NU.MU.UN.GI_4.GI_4.DAM	shall not contest.
	MU.L[UGAL].BI IN.PAD.DÈ.EŠ(?)	They swore to it by the name of the king.
	I[GI] *am-mu-*⌈*šu* x⌉	Witnessed by . . .
	– the text is broken for several lines –	– the text is broken for several lines –
Rev.	[ ] ⌈EN⌉ [ ]	. . .
	IGI ARA[D]	Witnessed by Warad- . . .
	IGI ARA[D]	Witnessed by Warad- . . .
	DUMU ^{d}EN.⌈ZU x⌉ [ ]	son of Sin- . . .
	IGI *A-na-*^{d}UTU-*ták-*[*la-ku*]	Witnessed by Ana-Šamaš-taklaku
	DUMU [*Mu-ta*]-*a-*⌈*a*⌉	son of Mut-Aja
	IGI ^{d}EN.ZU-*e-ri-ba-am*	Witnessed by Sin-eribam
	DUMU ^{d}EN.ZU-*en-nam*	son of Sin-ennam
	IGI *A-ḫa-am-nu-ta*	Witnessed by Aḫam-nuta
	DUMU INIM.^{d}EN.LÍL.LA	son of Awat-Enlil
	IGI DINGIR-*šu-ba-ni*	Witnessed by Ilšu-bani
	DUMU *A-da-a-a*	son of Adaja
	IGI *La-ṭà-bu-um* LÚ.⌈$BAPPIR_2$⌉	Witnessed by La-ṭabum the brewer
	IGI *E-ri-bu-u*[*m*]	Witnessed by Eribum
	DUMU *En-num-*^{d}EN.ZU	son of Ennum-Sin
	ù ARAD.^{d}TIŠPAK DUB.SAR	and (by) Warad-Tišpak the scribe.
	[MU] *Ḫu-ri-ib-šum*^{KI}	The year he
	[MU.U]N.DÙ	built Ḫuribšum

NOTES

Rev. (6) The last sign [*a*] is not really "visible" on the tablet; but the break is very clean and straight and there is a good deal of space left open between the first *-a-* and the right margin of the tablet.

(17) For this year date formula see OBTIV p. 25 no. 14.

OBTIV 42

A7687

Rental of Commercial Premises

	Transliteration	Translation
Obv.	É *ma-ḫi-ri ša Im-gur-*^{d}⸢EN.LÍL⸣	The commercial premises belonging to Imgur-Enlil
	KI *Im-gur-*^{d}EN.LÍL	from Ingur-Enlil
	^{Id}EN.ZU-*ma-*⸢DINGIR⸣	Sin-ma-ilum
	a-na MU.1.⸢KAM⸣	for one year
	i-[*g*]*u-ur*	rented.
	4 GÍN KÙ.BABBAR *ki-iṣ-ru-*⸢*šu*⸣	Four shekels silver is his rent;
	⸢*i-na* ŠÀ⸣.BI 2 ⸢IGI.4.GAL KÙ.BABBAR⸣	out of that (amount) 2 1/4 (shekels) silver
Rev.	*ma-ḫi-ir* MU.1.KAM	has been received. When the year
	i-ma-ša-al-ma ⸢*ši-ta-at*⸣ KÙ.[BA]BBAR	is half [over], then the rest of the silver
	Ì.LAL.E	he shall pay.
	IGI ^{d}UTU-⸢*ḫa-zi-ir*⸣	Witnessed by Šamaš-ḫazir
	[DU]MU ⸢^{d}EN.ZU⸣*-mu-ba-li-*⸢*iṭ*⸣	son of Sin-muballiṭ
	^{I}*I-li-ù-*^{d}UTU	Ili-u-Šamaš
	DUMU LÚ.^{d}ŠEŠ.KI	son of Lu.Nanna
	^{Id}E[N ZU]-⸢*e*⸣*-ri-ba-am*	Sin-eribam
	DUMU ^{d}EN.Z[U-*i*]*-qí-ša-a*[*m*]	son of Sin-iqišam
U.E.	[^{I}]^{d}EN.⸢ZU-*ma-gir*⸣	Sin-magir
	[LÚ(?) ⸢x⸣ [ ] [x x x]	. . .
L.E.	⸢ITU.DIRI *ša*⸣ *Ki-in-kum* UD.1.KAM	**Edge** The intercalary month of Kinkum, the first day,
	⸢MU X X⸣ NA KI	The year . . .

Seal Legends

	Transliteration	Translation
A.	[DUMU] [ ]	A. . . .
	ARAD ⸢x⸣ [ ]	son of . . .
		servant of . . .
B.	[ ] DINGIR [ ]	B. . . .
	⸢x⸣ DINGIR [ ]	
	⸢x⸣ [ ]	

NOTES

(6) *Ki-iṣ-ru-šu* also occurs in TA 1930-T.500:13 (tablet and env.); the reference to this unpublished text comes from Robert Whiting.

(20) For this year date formula see OBTIV 35 no. 63.

Seal Legends: It is not certain whether we have traces of one or two seal legends.

OBTIV 44

A7633

Silver Loan with Interest (MÁŠ ^{d}UTU)

Obv.	1 MA.NA KÙ.BABBAR	1 mina silver –
	MÁŠ ^{d}UTU *ú-sa-ab*	he will add the interest of Šamaš –
	⸢KI⸣ *Bur-*^{d}EN.ZU	from Bur-Sin
	^{1}INIM-^{d}EN.LÍL.LÁ	Awat-Enlil
	DUMU *Nu-⸢úr-ì⸣-li-šu*	son of Nur-ilišu
	ŠU.BA.AN.TI	borrowed.
	a-na Na-ab-⸢ri⸣-i	In (the month of) Nabru
	KÙ.BABBAR *ù* MÁŠ.BI	silver and its interest
	Ì.LAL.[E]	he will repay.
Rev.	IGI *⸢Ṣí⸣-iṣ-⸢ṣú-na-wi⸣-ra-at*	Witnessed by Ṣiṣṣu-nawirat
	DUMU ^{d}EN.ZU-*ri-me-ni*	son of Sin-rimenni
	IGI *É-a-ma-tum*	Witnessed by Ea-matum
	DUMU *É-a-ra-bi*	son of Ea-rabi
	IGI ^{d}UTU-*a-bi-⸢li⸣*	Witnessed by Šamaš-ab-ili
	DUMU *Ba-⸢di⸣-ia*	son of Badija
	IGI *Nu-úr-*^{d}UTU	Witnessed by Nur-Šamaš
	DUMU *Ú-ṣur-*KA-EŠ$_{4}$.DAR	son of Uṣur-pi-Ištar
	IGI *U-bar-*^{d}UTU	Witnessed by Ubar-Šamaš
	DUMU *Im-di-*^{d}E[N.ZU]	son of Imdi-Sin.
	MU ⸢ALAM.MEŠ *a-na* É <d> INNIN⸣	The year Sin-abušu brought in
	[^{1}30-*a-bu-šu ú(?)-še(?)-ri-bu(?)-ú(?)*]	the statues into the Temple of Ištar

NOTES

This tablet and envelope are now missing from the Oriental Institute Collection and were not available for further study.

(2) See the excursus, p. 194ff., for a discussion of the term MAS ^{d}UTU.

(10) Reading of this PN follows unpublished notes of S. Feigin, who apparently was able to read more than our hand-copy shows.

OBTIV 47

A7699

Silver Loan with Interest (MÁŠ ^{d}UTU)

Obv.		. . .		. . .
	(8)	*[a-n]a maš-kán-nim*	(8)	At threshing time
		[is-te-en]-šu-nu		individually
L.E.	(10)	⸢*ša-ni*⸣*-šu-nu*	(10)	or jointly.
Rev.		KÙ.BABBAR *ù* MÁŠ.BI		the silver and its interest
		Ì.LAL.E.MEŠ		they will repay
		. . .		. . .

OBTIV 50

A21963

Silver Loan with Interest (MÁŠ ^{d}UTU)

Obv. (1) 3 GÍN ⸢KÙ.BABBAR⸣

MÁS.BI ^{d}UTU

ú-sa-ab

. . .

NOTES

(2) "Its interest (according) to Šamaš he will add."

OBTIV 54

A7778

Barley Loan with Interest

. . .

(10) IGI ⸢ARAD-*Ku-bi* x⸣

. . .

NOTES

(10) For the last sign, consider perhaps IŠ=*kizû*, "groom" (CAD K 477f).

OBTIV 57

A7864

Barley *ḫubullu* Loan

(2) A.TA.AN written for TA.A.AN (ÀM); this identical transposition is found in another Diyala text, BIN 7 75:2 (=Simmons JCS 13 [1959] pp. 114f. no. 29). Cf. further OBTIV 56:11, Ì.E.ÁG for Ì.ÁG.E.

OBTIV 58

A7884

Barley *ḫubullu* Loan

Obv.
4 (GUR) 2 (PI) 4 (BÁN) GUR
ŠE UR$_5$.RA
1 GUR-um 1 (PI) 4 (BÁN) ŠE
MÁŠ *ú-ṣa-ab*
KI *Im-gur-*^{d}EN.LÍL
^{1}*Ku-ru-um* NAGAR

L.E.
ŠU.BA.AN.TI

Rev.
[*a-na maš-k*]*án-nim*
⸢ŠE *ù* MÁŠ.BI⸣
[Ì].ÁG.E
IGI·*I-din*-DINGIR DUMU
ARAD-*ì-lí-šu*
IGI *Ma-*[*š*]*um* DUMU *Bur*-30
IGI *Ṣíl-lí-*^{d}⸢INNIN⸣

U.E.
DUMU *Im-gu-rum*
MU KÁ.GAL KI(!).KÚR

Envelope Variants

(4) KI *Im-gu*[*r*]
(4a) ⸢DUMU⸣ EN.LÍL-*a-bu-um*
(5) [^{1}*K*]*u-*⸢*ru-um*⸣ [NAGAR]
(5a) [DUMU]
(6) ŠU.[BA.AN.TI]
(7) *a-n*[*a maš-k*]*án-nim*
(8) ŠE ⸢*ù*⸣ MÁŠ.BI
(9) Ì.ÁG.E
(10) IGI *I-din*-DINGIR
(10a) DUMU A[RAD]-⸢*ì*⸣-*lí-šu*
(11) IGI *Ma-*⸢*šum*⸣ DUMU *Bur*-30
(11a) IGI ^{d}EN.ZU-*mu-ba-li-iṭ*

(11b) DUMU *U-bar-*^{d}UTU
(12) IGI *Ṣíl-lí-*^{d}⸢INNIN⸣
(13) DUMU *Im-gur-rum*
(13a) IGI ⸢*Ip-qú-ša*(?)⸣ DUMU BUR-30
(14) MU ⸢KÁ.GAL KI.⸣KÚR

NOTES

There are two pictorial seal impressions on the envelope, reverse side; one of them has ^{d}UTU within the pictorial composition.

(10) Lines 10-10a on the envelope are included in line 10 of the tablet.

OBTIV 60

A7723

Barley *ḫubullu* Loan

(13) Perhaps *Na-an-na-*≪*an*≫*-tum*; cf. Nannatum s. of Sin-magir in OBTIV 57:11; and see also OBTIV 56:16.

OBTIV 63

A7692

Barley *ḫubullu* Loan

(8) Lines 8-10 state "(At) harvest time, he will repay the barley together with its interest." Cf. mu.un.DU še = *šu-ru-bu-tum še-im* "the bringing in of the barley." Hh I 161 (MSL 5 20). Cf. further mu.DU EBUR.šè OBTIV 72:7, mu.un.DU EBUR.šè = *a-na šu-ru-ub-ti e-bu-ri* Hh I 156 (MSL 5 19), and similar forms cited by CAD E 18a.

OBTIV 66

A7727

Silver *ḫubuttātum* Loan

Transliteration	Translation
. . .	. . .
(6) *e-zu-⸢ub⸣ pí-⸢i⸣ ⸢ṭú⸣-pí* [*pa*]-[*ni*]-[*im*](?)	(6) Apart from (any) amount recorded in any previous tablet.
. . .	. . .

OBTIV 70

A7718

Barley *ḫubuttātum* Loan

(10) The PNs in 11.10-13 are identical with those listed in UCP 10/1 59:11-14. For the PN *Ra-šum*-É, cf. also OBTIV 262:6 *Ra-šu-bi-tum*.

OBTIV 74

A7632

Barley *ḫubuttātum* Loan

. . .

(5) *a-⸢na* ITU *Ša-ad⸣*-[*du*]-*tim*
⸢*še*⸣-*a*-[*am*] Ì.[ÁG.E]

. . .

NOTES

(5) For restoration compare OBTIV 81:7 for another loan negotiated in Kinkum and payable in Šadduttum.

OBTIV 77

A21953

Silver Loan Without Interest

Obv.	6 GÍN KÙ.BABBAR	6 shekels silver,
	iš-tu MU.3.KAM	three years ago
	^{I}*I-li-qa-ti-ṣa-ba-at*	Ili-qati-ṣabat
	DUMU ^{d}EN.ZU-*e-ri-ba-am*	son of Sin-eribam
	ù Ta-ra-am-^{d}IM	and Taram-Adad
	ŠU.BA.AN.TI.MEŠ	borrowed.
	ša ^{d}*A-a-be-li-*⸢*it-ma-tim*(?)⸣	It is (a loan) due to Aja-belit-matim
L.E.	DUMU (sic) PUZUR$_4$-^{d}UTU NAGAR	daughter of Puzur-Šamaš, the carpenter,
	na-di-tum ša ^{d}UTU	*nadītu* of Šamaš.
Rev.	ỊGI ^{d}UTU	Witnessed by Šamaš,
	^{Id}*A-a*	Aja,
	^{Id}*Ki-*⸢*ti-tum*⸣	Kititum,
	^{Id}*I-šar-ki-di-su*	Išarkidisu,
	ši-bu-su	his(?) witnesses.
	IGI *I-pí-iq*-EŠ$_4$.DAR	Witnessed by Ipiq-Ištar
	IGI ^{d}EN.ZU-*a-bu-šu*	Witnessed by Sin-abušu,
	ši-bu-šu	his witnesses.

NOTES

(14) As written, this line has *šibūssu*, "his witnesses"; note the different plural form in line 17. One would expect, however, in view of the lender being a *nadītu* and Šamaš and Aja being witnesses, that all of the divine witnesses in lines 11-13 would have been "her witnesses," while the persons in lines 15-16 would be the witnesses of the borrower. Even if this could be true, one is still puzzled as to how to explain the labelling of witnesses in a loan transaction. This feature is more suggestive of a court appearance, where each party comes with witnesses to testify. The *iš-tu* MU.3.KAM in line 2 suggests that this document could have been written to re-establish a previous loan, perhaps because the original document was lost. Do the divine witnesses reflect the taking of an oath? Not necessarily, to judge from the appearance of divine witnesses in more "normal" loan documents; for these, see p. 196 above.

OBTIV 78

A7711

Barley Loan from the Storehouse of Šamaš

Obv.	(1)	12(GUR) 3(PI) 2(BÁN) GUR ŠE É.DUB	(1)	12.3.2 kors, barley (of) the storehouse
		ša ^{d}UTU		of Šamaš,
		KI *A-gi-gu-ur*(?)	3)	is being held
		i-ba-aš-ši	4)	by Agigur.
	(5)	*i-na maš-kán-nim*	(5)	At threshing time,
		še-a-am a-na É.DUB-⌈*šu*⌉		the grain to its storehouse
Rev.		*ú-ta-ar*		he will return.
		IGI SIG.EŠ$_4$.DAR		Witnessed by Ipiq-Ištar
		^{1}30-*ma-gir*		Sin-magir
	(10)	ù 30-*a-ḫi-i-din-nam*	(10)	and Sin-aḫi-iddinam.
		ITU *Ki-in-*⌈*kum*⌉		The month of Kinkum,
U.E.		UD.11.KAM	(12)	the 11th day,
		MU TÚG.^{d}EN.LÍL.BI.TA		The year the rainment of Enlil together with (the statue).

NOTES

(3) The expression KI PN *bašû* indicates that grain is being held in the possession of PN; it seems to suggest obligation, since the grain being held must be returned or paid back at threshing time. In this respect, the situation seems to be the same as in YOS 14 6:4-6, an OB Diyala text, wherein a sum of silver–KI PN *ibašši*–must be returned at harvest time or else interest is to be added. Accordingly, despite the use of different language to express obligation, OBTIV 78 appears to be a loan very similar to others at Ishchali. At the same time, one must observe that the phrase KI PN *bašû* (alternatively Ì.GÁL) is also found at Ishchali in administrative texts where no provision of repayment is stated; this is the case in OBTIV 29 (a letter), 142, 144, and UCP 10/1 65. The expression of KI PN, which occurs in the administrative texts OBTIV 236, 250, 251 apparently conveys the same idea as KI PN *bašû*; similar, also, must be *ina* ŠU PN in OBTIV 252:6, another administrative text. The question arises, therefore, whether KI PN *bašû* actually indicates a formal loan or whether it essentially conveys the location of given items used by or stored with PN. The latter notion perhaps fits better in contexts like OBTIV 235 where PN is holding oxen and is required to return them to where he got them. Loan in the formal sense cannot be operating in YOS 14 9, where KI PN *ibaššû* is said of harvest workers that the "holding party" must produce at harvest time or else suffer a penalty (*ṣimdat šarrim*). We have placed OBTIV 78 in the category of "legal documents" because, except for the phrase KI PN *ibašši*, it reads very much like a loan. However, as we have noted, there are valid reasons for questioning its place here and for shifting it to the category of "administrative documents".

(13) Our translation of this year date formula assumed that the scribe, for reasons of space, omitted a word (or phrase) like ALAM between TÚG and EN.LÍL.BI.TA. This formula is OBTIV p. 34 no. 58.

OBTIV 80

A7728

Barley Loan from Ištar and the ŠA.TÀM.MEŠ

Obv. (1) 1 GUR Š[E] ^{d}EN.ZU-*a-bu-šu* DUMU
Iš-me-⸢^{d}IM⸣
1 GUR *Pu-ḫu-um* DUMU
⸢*Qa-šu*⸣*-ub-tum*
1(GUR) ^{d}EN.ZU-*a-ḫi-i-din-nam* DUMU
⸢*Ia-an-ti*⸣*-num*
1(GUR) 3(BÁN) ^{d}EN.ZU-*mu-ba-lí-iṭ* ŠU.ḪA
(5) ŠU.NIGIN$_2$ 4 GUR 3(BÁN) GUR.ŠE
e-zu-ub ka(?)-ra-áš-ti-šu-nu
Rev. KI ⸢ES$_4$.DAR⸣
ù ŠÀ.⸢TÀM(?).MEŠ⸣
ŠU.BA.AN.TI.MEŠ
(10) IGI ^{d}EN.ZU
IGI ^{d}UTU
IGI ^{d}IM
(13) *ù* ARAD.^{d}IM

NOTES

This document lacks a notice about repayment; one may thus question whether it is rightfully a legal document; like OBTIV 78 above, it could very well be an administrative record.

(6) There is a small wedge in front of the *ka*(?) but it is not large enough to be read as the numeral 10.

(8) Ish. 34-T.144 (unpub.) is a loan of ŠE UR$_5$.RA from ^{d}*Ki-ti-tum* *ù* ŠÀ.TAM.MEŠ, similarly witnessed by Sin, Šamaš, and Adad.

OBTIV 82

A7720

Barley Loan Without Interest

This document is similar to many of the *ḫubuttātum* loans except for the fact that it is not labelled as a particular kind of loan.

(1) Šamaš-naṣir GÌR.NITÁ$_2$ borrowed a large quantity of barley from Ilšu-naṣir in UCP 10/1 8.

(2) In OBTIV 71:2, *Ḫu-za-lum* DUMU ARAD.^{d}UTU borrowed barley from Ilšu-naṣir.

OBTIV 83

A21960

Guaranty for a Slave

		. . .
Rev.	(12)	IGI Ú.TU.I[ ]
		. . .

NOTES

(12) Perhaps a Sumerogram (Ú for Ù) for a PN like *Ulid-i-*[*lí*].

OBTIV 85

A7891

Settlement of Litigation

Obv.	(1)	[ ]+4 MA.NA [K]Ù.BABBAR	(1)	(As to) the 4 minas silver
		[*š*]*a šar-ru-um*		which the king
		⌜^{I}Ú⌝-*še-pí*	4)	fined
		i-mu(?)-*du*	3)	Ušepi,
	(5)	*li-*⌜*ib-bi* ^{d}⌝*La-qí-pu-um*	(5)	the hearts of (the deity) Laqipum
		ù Ad-m[*a-a*]*t-ì-lí* ŠA.TAM		and Ad-mati-ili, the temple administrator
		ṭà-ab-bi		are satisfied.
		. . .		. . .

NOTES

(7) We take *ṭābi* to be an "i-modus" form of *ṭāb*; cf. the discussion of similar stative forms in OB usage by Kraus, *Symbolae Böhl,* 253-265.

OBTIV 86

A21964

Assignment of Responsibility for Grain Missing from a Storehouse

	Transliteration	Translation
Obv.	300+5 [GUR] [ ]	305 kors . . .
	na-aš-pa-k⌜*um*⌝	a storehouse loan
	ša ^{d}UTU	of Šamaš;
	a-na mu-ṭe$_4$-⌜*šu*⌝	for its shortage
	LÚ.^{d}ŠEŠ.KI	Lu.Nanna
	iz-za-⌜*âz*⌝	will stand (responsible).
Rev.	IGI ^{d}EN.ZU	Witnessed by Sin
	IGI *Ib-ni-*^{d}EN.LÍL.L[Á]	Witnessed by Ibni-Enlil
	I[GI]*-bu-um*	Witnessed by . . . bum,
	[LÚ *A-wa*]-⌜*al*^{KI}⌝	a citizen of Awal.

NOTES

See the excursus, p. 196ff., for a discussion of administrative documents in general, and of the difference between private and administrative archives.

(4) For *muṭûm "Fehlbetrag"* said of a variety of agricultural products, (OA and OB), see AHw 691b.

(6) For *uzuzzum* as a term of guaranty, see Koschaker, *Bürgschaftsrecht* 174[1].

(10) For restoration of line 10, cf. OBTIV p. 97a, Index of Place Names, *sub A-wa-al*^{KI}. One can also restore *A-wa-*⌜*al*⌝^{KI} in the Harmal Geographical List col. v 203 in the line following Diniktum, a recognized Diyala city; see MSL 11 59 and S. Levy, Sumer 3 78.

OBTIV 90

A7667

Jewelry, Ornaments, Garments; Record of Income

Obv.	1 ŠU.GUR 5/6 GÍN 20 ŠE
	KÙ.BABBAR DAM *Mu-uḫ-ra-am-mu*
	⌜1⌝ ŠU.GUR 5/6 GÍN 15 ŠE
	Du-šu-up-tum
	1 ŠU.GUR 1/2 ⌜GÍN⌝ *Ib-ni-*^{d}IM
	1 *ri-mu* 1 GÍN ⌜*Ḫu*⌝*-um-ta-ni*
	1 *ri-mu* IGI.6.GÁL *La-m*[*a*]*-sí*
	ŠU.NIGIN$_2$ 3 1/2 GÍN 5 ŠE
	KÙ.BAB[BAR]

1 *šu-úr-bu-um Ìs-ḫu-na-tum*
1 [TÚ]G.⸢SÍ⸣.SÁ *E-til*-KA-^{d}UTU
Rev. 12 TÚG.BAR.SI.MEŠ
ŠU.NIGIN$_2$ 2 1/2 GÍN 6 ŠE
KÙ.BABBAR
M[U].TÚM PUZUR$_4$-^{d}*Ki-t*[*i*]*-tum*
NÍG.ŠU *In-bu-ša* SANGA
ù Ib-bi-ta-pí-šu
ITU ^{d}DUMU.ZI
UD.30.KAM
MU Da-du-sǎ LUGAL

OBTIV 92

A7706

Jewelry, Ornaments, Garments; Record of Income

Obv. IGI.4.GÁL.LA 5 ŠE KÙ.G[I]
NÍG.RA.AB DAM ^{d}UTU-*pa-ti*
1 ŠU.GUR 5/6 GÍN [10] ŠE
KÙ.BABBAR
In-ba-tum
6 GÍN KÙ.BABBAR *pí-iṭ-rum*
DAM *An-um*-KA-^{d}EN.LÍL
1 *ri-mu* 20 ŠE *Ta-ri-iš-ma-tum*
1/2 GÍN *pi-iṭ-rum*
7 1/2 GÍN KÙ.BABBAR
Rev. 1 TÚG *ša-qu-bu-ri* 30-*mu-ba-lı-iṭ*
⸢1 TÚG *ša(?)-me-e*⸣ *Ma-nu-um-da-mi-iq*
[T]ÚG.BAR.SI.MEŠ
⸢MU.TÚM PUZUR$_4$⸣-^{d}*Ki-ti-tim*
NÍG.ŠU *In-bu-ša* SANGA
ù Ib-bi-TAB.BA-*e-šu*
ITU *Ma-*⸢*ag*⸣*-ra-tum*
UD.⸢20⸣.KAM
U.E. [MU GIŠ.GIGIR NU].⸢SÁ KÙ.⸣GI
^{d}UTU

NOTES

(2) Translation of NÍG.RA.AB as "hoop(?)" is based on conjectued relationship with GÍS.RAB = *rappu*; see AHw 956b for references. Cf. further GIŠ.RAB.GAL, GIŠ.RAB.TUR.TUR = *ma-luṭ-ṭu*, MSL 5 154 (Hh IV) 56-57, among other lexical references cited in CAD M/I 189b *sub maluttu*.

OBTIV 93

A7668

Silver; Record

Transliteration	Translation
. . .	. . .
ŠU.NIGIN$_2$ 1/2 MA.NA 3 GÍN. KÙ.BABBAR	Total: 1/2 mina 3 shekels silver
ša a-na Ì.BA É	which are for the oil ration of the Temple
ša Na-ab-ri-i	for the Nabru (festival)
ù ta-ad-ni-in-ti É	and (for other) distributions (by) the Temple.
. . .	. . .

NOTES

(8) AHw 1300b and CAD D 83-86 derive *tadnintu* from *dunnunu* "to deliver", said of oil, grain, and clothing rations.

OBTIV 94

A7647

Silver; ŠU.TI.A

	Transliteration	Translation
Obv.	8 2/3 GÍN KÙ.BABBAR	8 2/3 shekels silver
	ŠÁM GUD.ŠE	price of a fattened bull
	ša KI DINGIR-*šu-na-ṣir*	which from Ilšu-naṣir
	ù ^{d}*Kab-ta*-ILLAT-*su*	and (from) Kabta-illassu
	iš-ša-mu-ú	was purchased.
	⌈1⌉ GÍN IGI.6.GÁL.LA KÙ.BABBAR	1 1/6 shekels silver
	ŠÁM 1 UDU.NITA$_2$	price of one ram
	ša KI ^{d}EN.ZU-*ma-gir*	which from Sin-magir
	DUMU I-*pí-iq*-^{d}IM	son of Ipiq-Adad
	iš-ša-mu-ú	was purchased.
	1/3 GÍN *a-na* ^{d}EN.ZU-*se-mi*	1/3 shekel for Sin-šemi
	LÚ.KÚ$_6$.US.SA	a . . .
L.E.	*i-nu-ma ta-ba*(?)-*qi-im*	at the time of . . .
Rev.	4 GÍN KÙ.BABBAR *ša* KI *An-um*-KA-^{d}UTU	4 shekels silver which from Anum-pi-Šamaš
	il-li-qú-ma	was taken
	a-na i-di-ia	(and which) for my wages
	in-na-ad-nu	was given.
	2 GÍN *a-na* SÍG	2 shekels for wool
	ša i-nu-ma a-na Il-ba-ba-nim	which, when he went to Ilbabanum,

	(20)	*⌈il-li⌉-ku-ma la iš-ša-ma*	(20)	was not purchased.
		16 GÍN *ša a-na* ^{d}EN.ZU-*e-ri-ba-am*		16 shekels which unto Sin-eribam
		in-na-ad-nu		was given.
		e-zu-ub 1/3 MA.NA ⌈5 GÍN⌉ KÙ.BABBAR		apart from the 1/3 mina 5 shekels silver
		ša ^{d}UTU		belonging to Šamaš
	(25)	[*ù*]. 1/3 MA.NA	(25)	(and) the 1/3 mina
U.E.		[*ša*] ^{d}GÌR(?) ḪAL(?)		belonging to . . . .
Edge		ŠU.NIGIN$_2$ 1/2 MA.NA 2 ⌈GÍN⌉ IGI.6.GÁL.LA KÙ.BABBAR	L.E.	Total: 1/2 mina 2 1/6 shekels silver
		ŠU.TI.A ^{I}*A-ḫi-ia*	(28)	– a *melqētum* of Aḫija

NOTES

(28) For *melqētum*, see AHw 643b, Edzard, *Tell ed Dēr* 149-150. ŠU.TI.A is *melqētum* and is not the same as *namḫartum*, as Edzard suggests; the separateness of these terms can be seen in OBTIV 131-132, where both ŠU.TI.A and *namḫartum* occur side by side. We take *namḫartum* to represent the actual recipient and ŠU.TI.A. to indicate the person legally responsible, along the lines of Edzard, *op. cit.* 29, who makes this distinction for *maḫārum* and *leqûm*. So, too, in our text here as well, the actual recipients of the silver are not the same as Aḫija, the person who is responsible overall. ŠU.TI.A. occurs as a term for loan in Kraus, *Edikt* (of Ammiṣaduqa) §§ 4,7 (i 8′-17′, ii 27-31) juxtaposed with *ḫubullum* and interest bearing loans which are to be cancelled by the *seisactheia*. We are not inclined to agree with Edzard (pp. 149f) who wonders if *melqētum* and *ḫubullum* are one and the same; the spacing of elements in § 4 of the Edikt suggests that *ḫubullum* and *melqētum* are not the only two categories of loans enumerated; *ḫubullum* and *melqētum* would thus not be a kind of hendiadys for *ḫubullum*. The evidence for ŠU.TI.A in texts like OBTIV 94-96, 127, 231-234 would seem to suggest that it was a type of loan, although it is not clear whether it was interest bearing or not. The ŠU.TI.A. transactions are not witnessed as are conventional loans like *ḫubullum*, *ḫubuttātum*, and others (except for OBTIV 127). They seem to be administrative transactions rather than personal, since the lender is usually not explicitly mentioned by name (except in OBTIV 127—a granary and not a person!). The recording of ŠU.TI.A transactions in administrative documents appears to have been a kind of "banker's notebook loan" and as such may have only been recorded there. The situation may be compared to one found in ancient Greece and Rome where a banker's account records were highly reputed to an extent that "these accounts, when introduced as evidence, were accepted by the courts as *prima facie* evidence of the transactions therein entered" (cited from George Calhoun, *The Business Life of Ancient Athens*, Chicago (1926) 97 *apud* Ernst Posner, *Archives of the Ancient World*, Cambridge (1972) 116). Cf. further the statement of Posner on loans in Ptolemaic and Roman Egypt (*op. cit.* p. 143): "Originally of a purely private character, it (the document prepared by the owner of a bank) acquired increased legal value. . . . The text of a transaction entered in the bank's register was considered the original." Cf. also the comments of H. F. Jolowicz in his *Historical Introduction to the Study of Roman Law*, Cambridge (1954) 295-297 on literal contract. We suggest that ŠU.TI.A/*melqētum* was in fact a kind of account book loan, involving goods which were to be paid back on terms and conditions not specified in the account entry but which were apparently well known to the ancient Babylonians. The loans were issued by the temple and were recorded into the temple administrative records. The "wholesale" level of ŠU.TI.A. transactions and the presence of "running accounts" is further suggested by OBTIV 147:1-2, where the borrowers are two cities. Edzard (*op. cit.* p. 29) raises a very interesting point concerning the relationship of ŠU.TI.A and ŠU.BA.AN.TI, the phrase which occurs in so many conventional loans. Perhaps ŠU.TI.A/*melqētum* is simply the common term for "loan." In any case, texts like OBTIV 94-96, 127, 147:1-2, 231-234 should also be considered when discussing loans at Ishchali. See further, in connection

with administrative account book loans, the note to OBTIV 78:3 above. ŠU.BA.AN.TI occurs in OBTIV 248:11 and describes there a simple loan of implements, with interest apparently not a consideration at all. The use of the term ŠU . . . TI, however, indicates that there is an expectation of return, which would not necessarily have been the case had it been stated with *maḫāru/namḫartum*.

OBTIV 95

A7649

Silver; ŠU.TI.A

Obv.	(1)	5 GÍN KÙ.BABBAR	(1)	5 shekels silver
		5/6 GÍN *na-aḫ-ra-mu*		5/6 shekel (for a . . . (garment)
		2 GÍN KÙ.BABBAR *a-na* Ì.GIŠ		2 shekels silver for sesame oil
		A-lí-ba-ni-šu		(bought from) Ali-banišu
	(5)	GÌR 30-*i-qí-ša-am*	(5)	(Under the) authority of Sin-iqišam
		ŠU.TI.A ^{d}ŠEŠ.KI.ARḪUŠ		(It is) a *melqētum* of Nanna.arḫuš
Rev.		ŠU.TI.A		(and also) a *melqētum*
		^{1}*I-zi-Na-bu-ú*		Izi-Nabu.
		ITU *Ki-ìs-ki-si*		The month of Kiskissu,
		UD.27.KAM		the 27th day,
	(10)	MU ^{d}UTU-^{d}IM BA.UG$_{x}$(TIL)	(10)	The year Šamši-Adad died

NOTES

(4) The role of this person in this transaction is unclear, unless we posit a construct between Ì.GIŠ and the PN; the suggestion of a construct relationship is also supported by the slight indentation at the beginning of line 4.

OBTIV 98

A21910

Gold; Record of Obligation

Obv.	(1)	⸢6 1/2⸣ GÍN KÙ.GI	(1)	6 1/2 shekel gold
		ša a-na ŠE.BAR[KÙ].GI.TUR	2)	which was worked into (the shape of)
		in-ne-ep-p[*í-eš*]	3)	a small thornbush
		⸢x x⸣ [ ]		. . .
	(5)	[ ] ⸢x x⸣	(5)	. . .

Rev.	(1′)	[ ] ⸢x⸣ KÙ.GI	(1′)	. . . gold
		⸢*ša*⸣ *iš-tu* É *Ku-nu-*⸢*um*⸣	2′)	which was lost
		in-na-aš-⸢*ru*⸣	3′)	from the house of Kunum
		⸢*ù*⸣ *Li-wi-ra-šum*		and (which) Liwwiraššum
	(5′)	⸢*i-ša*⸣*-mu*	(5′)	will purchase (its replacement).
U.E.		[ITU] MÁ.AN(!).NA UD.⸢25⸣.[KAM]		The month of Mana, the 25th day
		[MU] ÍD ŠÀ URU^{KI} [i]p-		The year the canal in the city
		pí-tu-ú		was opened.

NOTES

(2) Cf. ŠL 367,62 and 64 = MSL 7 169 (Hh XII) 345 ŠE.BAR.KÙ.GI = *eṭ-ṭe-tum* AHw 266a (*eṭṭeṭṭum*) and CAD E 23 (sub *eddetu*).

(3′) Cf. Edzard, *Tell ed Dēr* 215:4, for this same verbal form.

(6′) For this month name (written MÁ.AN.NA) cf. TIM 5 61:6; it also occurs in Ish. 34-T.68. It is not clear whether there is any relationship between the MN MÁ.AN.NA and ITU *Ma-na*, found in tablets from Tell al Rimah, Chagar Bazar, and in Mari letters. For references to ITU *Ma-na* cf. OBT Tell Rimah nos. 195:7, 201:8; Gadd Iraq 7 (1940) 59; ARM 9 4-5.

(7′) For this year date formula cf. OBTIV p. 31 no. 39.

OBTIV 99

A21881

Silver; Memo of Obligation

Obv.	(1)	2/3 MA.NA 2 GÍ[N K]Ù.BABBAR
		ša ⸢*a-na*⸣ ŠE(!).GIŠ.Ì
	(3)	Ì.LAL.E
		– Rev. uninscribed –

NOTES

The memo states: "2/3 mina shekels silver which he will pay out for sesame".

(2) The ŠE is written over an unerased TAB.

OBTIV 103

A21900

Garments; Record of Wool Rations

	(1)	⸢x x⸣ [ ] ⸢x⸣ [ ] ⸢x⸣
		⸢x x x x x⸣
		⸢1 TÚG ARAD.^{d}⸣UTU
		⸢1 TÚG ARAD.^{d}IM⸣
	(5)	1 ⸢TÚG *Šum-ru*⸣-*ṣa*-⸢*a-ku*⸣
		1 ⸢TÚG⸣ *Ka*-⸢*lu*⸣-*mi*-DINGIR
		[1] [⸢TÚG *Su-mu*-^{d}IM⸣
Rev.		ŠU.NIGIN$_2$(?) ⸢6⸣ TÚG(?) *ku-ša-tum*
		KI.LAL.BI ⸢30⸣ MA.NA SÍG
	(10)	SÍG.BA-*šu-nu*
		NÍG.ŠU *A-ia-a*
		⸢28⸣
	(13)	⸢MU 1 ALAM UD.KA⸣.[BAR]

NOTES

(8) Lines 8-11 read: "Total: 6 *kuššatu* garments, their weight being 30 minas of wool, as their wool rations (did the aforementioned individuals receive) under the control of Ajaja." The number of garments in line 8 can be ⸢7⸣ as well as ⸢6⸣, particularly if one expects garments and PNs in lines 1-2. The number 6 is more readily divisible into the 30 minas weight in line 9 than in 7. This reference to *kuššatu* should be added to CAD K 600b, which cites no other OB occurrence.

(12) This tabulation appears intrusive and may represent a preliminary tally of the weight of the wool which is finally recorded in 1. 9.

(13) For this year date formula, "The year one bronze statue," cf. OBTIV p. 24 no. 102.

OBTIV 106

A21998

Gems, Jewelry, Precious Items; List of Objects, Some Persons

Obv.	(1)	[2] NU.ÚR.M[A K]Ù.⸢GI⸣	(1)	2 golden pomegranates
		16 NA$_4$.NIR$_x$(ZA.MIR)] IGI		16 "eye-*ḫulalu* stones"
		28 NA$_4$.NIR$_x$(ZA.MIR).ZA.⸢AZ⸣		28 . . . stones
		490 NA$_4$.ŠID.KIŠIB NIR$_x$(ZA.MIR)		490 cylinder seals of *ḫulalu* stone
	(5)	335 NA$_4$ GUG(ZA.GUL)	(5)	335 carnelian beads
		610 *ḫi-iṣ-bu-um* NA$_4$.GUG(ZA.GUL)		610 carnelian chips

	Transliteration	Translation
	730 *ḫi-is-bu* NA$_4$.GUG(ZA.GUL) KÙ.GI GAR.RA	730 carnelian chips mounted in gold
	490 NA$_4$.NIR$_x$(ZA.MIR) ZA.A[Z.BA]BBAR.BABBAR.DILI KÙ.GI GAR.RA	490 white flecked(?) *ḫulalu* stones mounted in gold
	1 NA$_4$.NIR$_x$(ZA.MIR).IGI KÙ.GI GAR.RA	1 eye-*ḫulalu* stone mounted in gold
	1 SIM KÙ.GI	1 golden swallow
	2 *Ša-am-mu-um* KÙ.GI	2 *šammu* stones
	⸢2⸣ [ ] ⸢x⸣ KÙ.[G]I	2 gold . . .
	3 NA$_4$.[N]IR$_x$([ZA.M]IR) *a-la-lum* KÙ.GI GAR.RA	3 *elallu* stones mounted in gold
	1 NA$_4$ GIŠ.DUB NIR$_x$(ZA.MIR) KÙ.GI GAR.RA	1 plaque of *ḫulalu* stone mounted in gold
	2 NA$_4$.NIR$_x$(ZA.MIR) MAR.ḪA.LUM KÙ.GI GAR.RA	2 *marḫallum* stones mounted in gold
	1 NA$_4$.NIR$_x$(ZA.MIR) MAR.ḪA.LUM	1 *marḫallum* stones
	3 NA$_4$.NIR$_x$(ZA.MIR) BABBAR.BABBAR.DILI	3 *(nir)pappardilu* stones
	[1] NA$_4$ *ḫi-iṣ-bu-um* GUG(ZA.GUL).TUR	1 small chip of carnelian
	[ ] NA$_4$ *mu-ša-ar* GUG(ZA.GUL)	. . . *muššārum* stone(s)
Rev.	[N]A$_4$ ma-áš-ka-tum ⸢KÙ.GI GAR.RA⸣	. . . stones mounted in gold
	1 GIŠ.PA KÙ.GI GAR.RA	1 staff mounted in gold
	1 GAL KÙ.BABBAR KI.LAL.BI	1 goblet of gold, its weight
	8 2/3 GÍN KÙ.BABBAR *šà Be-lí-ba-ni*	8 2/3 shekels silver–belonging to Beli-bani
	1 *an-ṣa-ab* UD.KA.BAR	1 earring of bronze
	šà ARAD.^{d}TIŠPAK	belonging to Warad-Tišpak
	⸢1 x x⸣ UD.KA.BAR	1 . . . of bronze
	šà Ták-la-ak-šum	belonging to Taklakšum
	1 ZAG.DU$_8$ UD.KA.BAR	1 doorstep of bronze
	KIŠIB NA$_4$ *si-du-ru-um* *šà* ^{d}NIN.ŠUBUR	A record of gem stones of (the deity) Ilaprat.
	^{I}ARAD.^{d}NIN.ŠUBUR	Warad-Ilaprat,
	šà DINGIR.MA.AN.SUM	representing(?) Dingir-mansum;
	^{I}*Ma-ti-ì-lí*	Mati-ili,
	šà [^{d}EN.ZU-AN.DÙL]-*lí*	representing (?) Sin-andulli
	⸢*a* x x *um*⸣	. . .
	⸢x x x *ti*⸣	. . .
	⸢EN(?) ^{d}NIN⸣.ŠUBUR	the high priest of Ilaprat
	KI ⸢x x *mu*⸣-*da-ni-iq*	from . . . mudanniq(?)
	[IT]U [*Tám*]-*ḫi-ri-i*	The month of Tamḫiru,
	⸢MU(?) *A-li-e-ši*(?)⸣	The year(?) Alieši(?)

NOTES

(2) CAD Ḫ 226b *sub ḫulal īni,* lex. sec.; NIR_x is apparently a variant of NÍR.

(3) Perhaps to be connected with NA_4.NÍR.ZIZ = *sa-a-su, s[a-a]-zu* Hh XVI 144 and RS Rec. 106 (MSL X 8, 106), AHw 1032b.

(4) According to CAD K 543b, NA_4.ŠID and NA_4 KIŠIB should be mutually exclusive replacives.

(5) CAD G 156b (additions to *ḫiṣbu*) reads 10 in l. 6 and 12 in l. 7; yet ll. 4-5 show that larger numbers are intended; moreover, there is no other way to incorporate the second, smaller *Winkelhaken* in ll. 6-8.

(8) For *papparūm, pappardilûm,* cf. AHw 824a; for ZA.AZ cf. note to l. 3.

(11) Cf. Hh XVI 399 (MSL X 15) NA_4.Ú (NA_4.Ú.Ú^{u}) = *ša-mu, [ša]m-mu.*

(13) Cf. CAD E 74b f, NA_4.NÍR.A.LAL.LUM, MSL X 41 112.

(14) Cf. GIŠ.DUB = *gištuppu* AD E 109f.

(15) For *marḫallum* cf. CAD M/1 279 *sub marḫallu,* lex. section.

(17) Cf. AHw 793b and MSL X 9 (Hh XVI) 151.

(19) Cf. AHw 685a and MSL X 19, note to Hh XVI 149.

(29) Translation "gemstones" is a conjecture based on AHw 1053a *sudduru, sudūru.* Not all of the objects in lines 1-28 are gemstones; cf. e.g. the items of bronze in lines 24, 26, 28. But they are all valuable objects. Lines 29-36 seem to be a description, identifying the objects in the list as "belonging" to the deity Ilaprat. The objects in ll. 23-27 could be private items left for safekeeping in the temple treasury. This text was excavated in a room placed behind the wall of the northeast sanctuary of the Kititum Temple (see OBTIV p. 13[54]); perhaps one of the two smaller sanctuaries at Ishchali was devoted to this deity (cf. the discussion in OBTIV pp. 12-13). If the list was, as has been suggested, a list of items in the safekeeping of the temple, the mention of the high priest of Ilaprat in line 36 seems to fit. But the role of the persons in lines 30-33 are unclear; whom do they *represent*? The idea of trustees or auditors come to mind; but this can only be a conjecture, lacking further evidence about the roles of these individuals at Ishchali.

(39) For this year date formula see OBTIV p. 35 No. 62.

OBTIV 107

A21915

Gems, Jewelry, Ornaments; List of Objects and Persons

Obv. col. i

(1) [ ] ⌈NA_4 x *ka*(?) x x x⌉
30 *kam-kam-ma-tum*⌉ KÙ.GI[ ]
KI.LAL.BI ⌈10⌉ GÍN LÚ[ ]
[ ] ⌈x x⌉ KÙ.GI

[K]I.LAL.BI ⸢x⸣ GÍN 20 ŠE
⸢Nu⸣-ṭú-up-tum
[ ] ⸢KÙ x x x⸣ [ ]
[ ] ⸢x x⸣ [ ]
[ ] ⸢x x⸣ [ ] ⸢x x⸣ [ ]
[ ] ⸢IGI.5.GÁL 4 ŠE⸣
⸢DUMU.SAL ^{d}A- x x x⸣
[ ] ⸢x⸣ 1 ⸢x⸣ DA ⸢x x⸣
1 ⸢GÍN⸣(?) 10 ŠE *Uš-⸢tap⸣(?)-pí(?)-ru*
1 *kam-kam-⸢ma-tum⸣* IGI.6.GÁL 10 ŠE
Ma-ki-ia-tum
1 *kam-kam-ma-tum* IGI.4.GÁL
Il-ta-ni
1 *kam-kam-ma-tum* 1/2 GÍN
⸢Mu⸣-ḫa-⸢di⸣-tum
1 *kam-kam-ma-tum* ⸢IGI.4⸣.GÁL 10 ŠE
Ku-ur-[ku-ú]r-ru-um
1 kam-kam-ma-tum [ ] ⸢x⸣ GÍN
Ḫu-[ ]-tum
1 ŠU.GUR IGI.⸢4⸣.GÁL 10 ŠE
SAL⸢x⸣ [EŠ].NUN.NA^{KI}
1 KISIM(?) ⸢1/2⸣ GÍN 15 ŠE
⸢La⸣-ma-sí
1 KISIM(?) 1/3 GÍN *⸢Ú-ta⸣-tum*
⸢3⸣ *in-⸢bu⸣* IGI.6.GÁL
^{d}Wi-ir-da-ia-an
1 *tu-di-tum* IGI.6.GÁL
Ši-ma-sà
ŠU.NIGIN$_2$ ⸢47⸣ GÍN IGI.4.GÁL 5 ŠE
1 *an-ḫu* ⸢x⸣ [ ]PI PI *ša pa-ar-zi-⸢lum⸣*
Nu-ṭú-up-tum
1 *iš-p[u(?) š]a* NA$_4$.BABBAR.BABBAR.DIL
⸢x⸣ [ ] ⸢x⸣ SAL *Ru-bi-um* (?)
2 NA$_4$.LAGAB [ ] ⸢x⸣ *ka(?)-súm I-tu-li*
[ ] NA$_4$.LAGAB [ ] ⸢x⸣ *ka(?)-súm*
Mu-ḫa-di-tum
[N]A$_4$.LAGAB [ ] ⸢x⸣ *ka(?)-súm*
I-din-DINGIR
[N]A$_4$.LAGAB [ ] ⸢x⸣ *ka(?)-súm*
DAM *Nu-⸢úr⸣-*^{d}UTU
[ ] *⸢ka⸣-súm*
⸢Ma⸣ [ ]

col. ii
[ ]*tum*
[ ]*tum*
[ ] ⸢x x⸣ [ ]
[ ] ⸢x x⸣ [ ]
[ ] ⸢x x⸣ [ ]
[ ] ⸢NA$_4$⸣ LA[GAB(?)] ⸢x⸣ [ ] ⸢x⸣
[ ]LÚ BÀD ⸢x⸣ [ ]
⸢1⸣ NA$_4$ L[AGAB IG]I ⸢4⸣.GÁL
BABBAR.BABBAR.DIL
[ ] ⸢*Qà-aš-tum*⸣ (?)
1 N[A$_4$] ⸢x⸣ [ ] ⸢x⸣
[ ] ⸢x⸣
[ ] ⸢AT⸣
2 N[A$_4$]
1 NA [ ] ⸢x x⸣
Ki-⸢x⸣ [ ] ⸢x x⸣
1 *iš-ša*-⸢x⸣ [ ] ⸢x⸣
[ ]-⸢*tum*⸣
1 NA$_4$ GA[B] ⸢x x⸣
1 NA$_4$ ZI-⸢x x⸣ ZA.GÌN
DUMU *Ì-lí*-⸢x x⸣-*ma-am*
1 NA$_4$ ⸢ZI x x⸣ *ša ḫa-aš-ma-ni*
⸢*La-ma*⸣-*sí*
1 NA$_4$ ŠU.BABBAR.BABBAR.DIL DUMU.SAL
⸢*Ku*⸣-*nu-ub-tam*
1 NA$_4$ GIŠ.AB BABBAR.BABBAR.DIL
DUMU.SAL ⸢*Ta-ab*⸣-*ni*-DINGIR
2 NA$_4$ *mu*-⸢*ta-tum*⸣(?) BABBAR.BABBAR.DIL
DAM AN.KA.EŠ$_4$.DAR

OBTIV 111

A7666

Silver; Short List of Amount and Persons

Obv. 16 ŠE KÙ.BI 120 MUŠEN.MEŠ(!)	16 grains silver (for) 120 birds
Šu-mi-a-bi-ia	*Šumi-abija*
12 ŠE KÙ.BI KU$_6$	12 grains silver (for) fish
^{d}UTU-*id(?)-na-an-ni*	*Šamaš-idnani*

Rev.	15 ŠE KÙ.BI 120 KU_6	15 grains silver (for) 120 fish
	u_4-*mi* 15.KAM	the fifteenth day
	Šu-mi-a-bi-ia	*Šumi-abija*

NOTES

(3) L. 3 has no numeral before KU_6 while l. 5 has the number 120 (2 x 60); the figures of l. 5 suggest a price of .125 grains of silver per fish which agrees with the figures obtained by Curtis and Hallo, HUCA 30 1959 110,130, generally .1 - .2 grains per fish. Should we restore <120> in l. 3 in order to obtain there a figure of .1 grain per fish?

(4) In OBTIV 91, Index of Personal Names, we read this PN as ^{d}*Šamaš-id*(!)*-na-an-ni*. This is still a possible reading. However, *-iš*(!)*-na-an-ni* for *-išnī'anni* > *išnânni* is also possible. Cf. the PN *Išnī-ilī* and Uštašni-ilum cited by Stamm, *Namengebung* 146. Our PN here could thus be interpreted "Šamaš has repeatedly given me (offspring)".

OBTIV 113

A7674

Sheep; Record of Receipt for Fattening

Obv.	21+[ ] UDU.NIM *a-na* ŠA.GÀL *ù* ŠE.BAL	21+ . . . spring lambs for fattening and feed;
	⌜*nam-ḫa-ar-ti*⌝ ⌜*Ab-du*⌝*-e-ra-aḫ*	items received by Abdu-eraḫ
	⌜ŠÀ É.DUB *aš-lu*⌝*-ka-tim*	in the long storehouse.
Rev.	ITU *Ki-nu-nu* UD.9.KAM	The month of Kinunu, the 9th day,
	MU GUD.APIN KÙ.GI	The year the golden plow-ox

NOTES

(1) For UDU.NIM, cf. CAD Ḫ, *ḫurapu*, 245a. For ŠE.BAL see Salonen, *Agricultura* 392,408: grain (or husk material) washed off of seed corn and given to oxen for feed; also as a term describing grain fallen off in transport. See further note to UCP 10/1 75:6 below.

(4) For É.DUB *aš-lu-ka-tim* cf. UCP 10/1 87:16 and CAD A/2 450.

(5) For this year date formula, see OBTIV p. 30 no. 33.

OBTIV 114

A7836

Sheep, Record of Missing Animal

Obv. 1 *pu-ḫa-du*
a-na ne-eš$_{15}$(?)-ri[*m$_{5}$*](?)
NA.QÀD(!) *Ì-lí-*⸢*ki*⸣*-a-bi*
Rev. ITU *Ki-in-kum*
UD.⸢6⸣.KAM
MU ⸢É ^{d}EN.LÍL BA.DÍM⸣

Seal Legend [*A-bi-zum*]
[SAN]GA ⸢^{d}*Ki-ti*⸣*-t*[*um*]
DUMU *Ig-mil-*^{d}EN.ZU
⸢ARAD *I*⸣*-ba-al-pi-*⸢*el*⸣

NOTES

Lines 1-6 state: "1 lamb (to be recorded) as loss; Ili-ki-abi, the shepherd. The month of Kinkum; the 6th day; the year he built the Temple of Enlil."

(2) For *nišrum* cf. AHw 796b, CAD N/2 2826 and also OBTIV 134:2, 136:7, 137:12.

OBTIV 115

A7777

Goats; Record of Dead Animals

Obv. ⸢11 SAL⸣.Á[Š.GAR(ZEḪ)]
RI.RI.[GA]
NA.QÀD *Šum-*[*ma*]*-li-ib-bi-ì-lí*
Rev. ITU ^{d}*Ma-mi*
UD.17.KAM
MU ERÍN SU.BIR$_{4}$(?)⸢KI⸣

Seal Legend [A]-⸢*bi*⸣-[*zum*]
⸢SANGA⸣ ^{d}*Ki-ti-tum*
[DUM]U *Ig-mil-*^{d}EN.ZU
⸢ARAD *I-ba-al-pi-el*⸣

NOTES

(1) Lines 1-3 state: "11 young female goats, fallen dead; shepherd: Šumma-libbi-ili." The PN is more typical of OA and Kassite texts, according to Stamm, *Namengebung* 197.

OBTIV 117

A7725

Sheep; Record of Dead Animal

Obv.	(1)	1 UDU.⸢NITA$_2$ KU.A⸣	(1)	1 . . . sheep
		tu-bu-⸢*uḫ-tum*⸣		slaughtered
		⸢NA.QÀD⸣ *Ì-lí-ma-a-bi*		Herdsman: Ili-ma-abi
Rev.		ITU ⸢^{d}DUMU.ZI⸣		The month of Tammuz,
	(5)	UD.13.KAM	(5)	the 13th day
		[M]U É ^{d}EN.LÍL		the year of the Temple of Enlil
Seal Legend		[*A*]-⸢*bi-zu*⸣-[*ùm*]		
		SANGA ^{d}*Ki-ti-*[*tum*]		

NOTES

(1) For KU.A as a type of livestock, cf. OBTIV 116:1, ÙZ KU.A; cf. also MAD 4 19:5, 14 ÙZ.KU.

OBTIV 119

A21906

Sheep; Record of Dead Animals

Obv.	(1)	2 UDU.NITA$_2$	(1)	2 male sheep
		3 U$_8$.A		3 ewes
		1 *li-li-túm* SAL		1 sexually mature sheep, female –
		UDU RI.RI.GA		fallen sheep
Rev.	(5)	⸢*pí*⸣*-qí-ti*	(5)	in the charge of
		^{1}ARAD-*sà*		Warassa.
		ITU *Na-ab-ri*		The month of Nabru.

NOTES

(2) U$_8$.A may be taken as an irregular writing for U$_8$; CAD L 42a (lex. sec. sub *laḫru*) lists a number of passages where U$_8$ is glossed ú-a, ú-ia as well as ú.

(3) For *lillittum* see note to OBTIV 122:5.

OBTIV 120

A21909

Cattle: Memo on Loss

Obv.	(1)	UD.3.KAM	(1)	The third day
		ITU *Kir-ri-*⸢*tim*⸣		of the month of Kirritum
		i(?)-li-ik-ma		went by and
		GUD.MEŠ ŠÀ.GAL *iṣ-ba-tu*		they seized cattle, fodder;
	(5)	*ša A-du-ur-ba-la-*⸢*ia*⸣ (?)	(5)	(they were) from Adurbalaja;
Rev.		*ša qa(?)-ti DA(?)-*⸢*qum*⸣		(the cattle) were under the control of Daqqum.

NOTES

(3) The first sign is a clear DUMU and not I.

(5) The GN Adurbalaja is variously written. It occurs as here in Goetze Sumer 14 (1958) 10:11 (p. 28 and pl. 7); as *A-du-ur-ba-lu* in no. 7:25 (p. 25 and pl. 5) there; and as *A-du-ur-be-lu-um* in Simmons JCS 15 (1961) 81 no. 138:10. Goetze (*op. cit.* p. 29) calls attention to AN.ZA. QAR-*ba-la-ia* in the Harmal Geographical list 171 (MSL XI p. 59).

OBTIV 121

A21883

Fowl; Perforated Tag Bearing Record of Outlay for Food

Obv.	(1)	⸢1 MUŠEN⸣	(1)	1 bird
		a-⸢*na*⸣ ŠUK		for food allotment
		i-nu-⸢*ú*⸣*-ma*		when
Rev.		⸢*iš*⸣*-tu Maš-kán-Bar-mi*^{KI}	4)	you came in from
	(5)	*te-*⸢*ru-ba*⸣*-am*(?)	5)	Maškan-Barmi.
U.E.		⸢ITU⸣ AN ZI⸢x⸣		The month of . . .
		UD.8.KÁM		the 8th day.
Seal Legend		⸢*Iš*⸣*-bi-*^{d}⸢TIŠPAK⸣		Išbi-Tišpak
		⸢KA.KI⸣		*kakikkum*
		⸢DUMU⸣ *Ib-ni-Ir-r*[*a*]		son of Ibni-Irra

NOTES

(6) in OBTIV p. 99 this line was read as ⸢ITU⸣ ^{d}<DUMU>.ZI; and the end of the line was not considered as a legibly meaningful element. This reading is still a possibility; the MN is otherwise an unknown one.

(7) For this seal see OBTIV 125

OBTIV 122

A7669

Sheep and Goats; Tally of Animals Assigned for Fattening

Obv. 6 UDU.NITA$_2$
14 MÁŠ.TUR
7 ZEḪ(SAL.ÁŠ.GÀR)
2 U$_8$
2 *li-li-du*
2 *li-li-da-tum*
Rev. ŠU.NIGIN$_2$ 33 UDU.ḪI.A
ku-ru-uš-tu

NOTES

(2) MÁŠ.TUR = *lalium* "kid"; cf. CAD L. 51f.

(3) ZEḪ = *unīqu* "young kid"; cf. MSL 8/1 40 (Hh XIII) 276; ŠL 554,62.

(4) U$_8$ = *laḫru* "ewe"; cf. CAD L. 42ff.

(5) For *lillidu, lillittu* "(sexually) mature male, female sheep/goats'; cf. CAD L 188ff.

(7) For *kuruštû* "(for) fattening"; see CAD K 582; for another OB reference cf. also OBTIV 3:7-10.

OBTIV 123

A7792

Cattle; Record

Obv. ITU *Kir-ri-tim*
UD.10.KAM
3 GU *ta-am-*⸢*ša*(?)*-ra-tim*⸣
ša(?) GA PI ⸢x x⸣
Rev. *i-in-*⸢*nu*⸣
4(PI) 1(BÁN) ŠÀ.GAL
⸢*wa*⸣*-ta-ra-am*
iṣ-ba-tu$_4$
MU ALAM KÙ.GI
U.E. ⸢*i*⸣*-ma-ḫa-tu*

Seal Legend AN.K[A]
DUMU *A-*⸢*mur*⸣*-na-ar-bi-*[*šu*]
ARAD *I-pí-iq-*^{d}⸢IM⸣

NOTES

(2) *Tamšaru* is masc. in form but fem. in gender as seen by the pl. form here and in OBTIV 248:3 cf. GAG §§60a, 61n for similar forms. These references from Ishchali should be added to AHw 1316b along with the reference to GUD *ta-am-ša-ru* in YOS 13 380:1.

The reading of the continuation of line 2 is uncertain. One possibility is to read a PN, *Ta-pí-we-d*[*e-k*]*u* (in preference to *-we-d*[*i-m*]*a* in OBTIV p. 926). But the verbs in ll. 3-4 are apparently both plural. One might consider translating ll.2-3: "They removed 3 oxen, trained to the whip (belonging to) Tappi-wedeku."

(3) This reading is not final; one could consider a Sumerian form I.IN.⸢ŠI⸣.⸢ŠÁM⸣; such a form could be read with a sg. subject—a PN like *Tappī-wedēku*. Yet here again, one is left with the problem of no subject for the pl. verb in line 4.

(4) For *wattaru* cf. CAD A/2 511a. Here, too, the reading is not final; one cannot exclude the possibility of reading [*ut*]*-ta-ra-am*.

The writing of tu_4 for /*tu*/ is found elsewhere in Ishchali texts in forms of this same verb; cf. UCP 10/1 7:18, 58:9.

Seal Legend For a more complete copy of this seal impression see OBTIV 205.

OBTIV 124

A21890

Fowl; List of Offerings

Obv.	(1)	1 UZ.TUR.MUŠEN		⸢^{d}IŠKUR.RA⸣
		1		⸢^{d}⸣EN.ZU
		⸢1⸣	d	UTU
		[ ]		AMAR.[UTU]
	(5)	[ ]		⸢x⸣
		[ ]	·	⸢x⸣
		– Rev. destroyed –		

NOTES

(1) Lines 1-3 read: "1 duckling (for) Adad, 1 (for) Sin, 1 (for) Šamaš." Note the separation of signs in line 3.

(4) If Marduk is indeed the recipient, then the DINGIR must be restored, unless the sign in line 3 is meant also to serve for the lines that follow.

OBTIV 128

A7825

Barley; ŠU.TI.A

Obv.	(1)	3 GUR ŠE	(1)	3 kors barley
		Á.BI GIŠ.MÁ.ḪI.A		hire of boats–
		ŠU.TI.A *Nu-úr-*^{d}TIŠPAK		taken as a *melqētum* by Nur-Tišpak
		ma-la-ḫi-im		the boatman–
L.E.	(5)	*ša šu-ra-am*	5)	which carried
Rev.		*a-na ki-ri-a-tim*	6)	reeds
		iz-bi-la-nim	7)	for baskets
		ITU *E-lu-num*		The month of Elunum,
		UD.18.⸢KAM⸣		the 18th day,
U.E.	(9)	MU ⸢*Ra-pi-qum*⸣	9)	The year Rapiqum (was destroyed).

NOTES

(5) Cf. *šūru* "reed," AHw 1287a; for *kirītu* "basket" cf. CAD K 408a.

(9) For the year date formula see OBTIV p. 33 no. 53.

OBTIV 134

A7789

Barley; Record of Withdrawal for Cattle Feed

Obv.	(1)	10(GUR) 5(BÁN) GUR ŠE
		A.RÁ.1.KAM
	(2)	5 GUR A.RÁ.2.KAM
		15(GUR) 5(BÁN) GUR *še-ù*
L.E.		*ni-iš-rum*
Rev.	(5)	*a-na* ŠA.GÀL GUD.ḪI.A
		ITU *Za-ḫa-ra-tum*
		UD.24.KAM
		MU ALAM KÙ.GI
U.E.	(8)	⸢x⸣ *Ši-ma-ḫa-tu*

NOTES

(1) Lines 1-5 state: "10.0.5 kors barley, on one occasion, 5.0.0 kors on a second occasion–(total:) 15.0.5 kors barley; withdrawal for cattle feed".

(7) "The year the golden statue (and) Šimaḫatu;" for this year date formula see OBTIV p. 23 no. 4.

OBTIV 135

A7770

Barley; List of Withdrawals

This document appears to be a "List" of withdrawals rather than a "Record" as claimed in OBTIV p. 40.

OBTIV 136

A7701

Barley; Record of Withdrawal

Obv. 25 GUR ŠE ⸢*a-na ša* x x⸣
1 GUR *A-te-šu-mi-i*
1 GUR *Nu-ur-*^{d}SAG.KUD
1(PI) 30-*it-*⸢*ba-ru*⸣
2(PI) ZI.GA
ú ma-aš-ti-tum
L.E. ŠU.NIGIN$_2$ 27(GUR) 3(PI) GUR ⸢ŠE⸣
ni-iš-rum
A.RÁ.1.KAM
Rev. ⸢52⸣(GUR) 3(PI) GUR ŠE
a-na ša ⸢x x x⸣
⸢3(BÁN) 3⸣ SILA$_3$ ZI.GA
ŠU.NIGIN$_2$ 52(GUR) 3(PI) 3(BÁN)
GUR 3(!) SIL[A$_3$ Š]E
ni-iš-rum
≪UD≫ A.RÁ.2.KAM
U.E. ŠU.NIGIN$_2$ ⸢ŠU⸣.NIGIN$_2$ 80(GUR) 1(PI)
3(BÁN) GUR 3 SILA$_3$ ŠE
na-aš-pa-a[*k*]
Edge ⸢*Ú*⸣*-pí-i le-qú-ú*
[ITU *N*]*ig-gal-lim* [UD].⸢4⸣.K[AM]
MU *Ra-p*[*í-qu*]*m*

NOTES

(1) For the last two signs cf. line 9; the last sign in line 1 could be GÁL as could be the one before the last in line 9, followed there by *-lim*.

(5) "0.2.0 kor (for) expenditure and drink-ration.".

(13) Lines 13-15 state: "grand total: 80.1.3; 3 kors barley, taken (from) the granary of Upu". This sum is the total of withdrawals (*nišrum*) in lines 7 and 11.

(17) "The year Rapiqum;" for this year date formula see OBTIV p. 33 no. 53.

OBTIV 138

A7686

Barley; Record of Rent Collections

Obv. 17(GUR) 2(PI) GUR ŠE ⸢*šà*⸣
6 GÁN(?) A.ŠA
ši-ib-šu še-e me-ri-ši
2⸢4⸣(GUR) 1(PI) 3(BÁN) GUR ZÍZ
ša ⸢*qa*⸣*-at Ta-*⸢*pi-pu*⸣
ši-ib-šu ša me-ri-ši
3(GUR) 1(PI) GUR ZÍZ *ša*
DUMU.MEŠ *A-ka-di*
L.E. *ši-ib-šu ša me-ri-ši*
Rev. ŠU.NIGIN$_2$ 17(GUR) [2](PI) [ŠE]
ù 27(GUR) 2(PI) 3(BÁN) GUR ZÍZ
ša i-na Ḫa-aš-ḫu-ur
i-na me-ri-ši i[*l*]*-le-qú*
ITU *Zi-*⸢*ib*⸣*-num*
UD.10.KAM
MU *Ra-pí-qum* BA.GUL^{UL}

OBTIV 142

A7645

Barley; Record of Loan

Obv. 2 ŠU.ŠI
ŠE.IN.NU.DA
KI ^{I}30-DINGIR
L.E. *i-ba-aš-ši*
Rev. *a-na* ^{d}UTU*-mu-*⸢*uš*⸣*-te-pí-iš*
i-na-di-in
—surface bears traces of seal impressions—

NOTES

For the categorization of this text as an administrative document, see p. 37 above.

(1) ŠU.ŠI probably refers to a unit of 60 GUR; cf. UCP 10/1 30:1 1 ŠU.ŠI 8(GUR) 1(PI) 1(BÁN) GUR ŠE ⸢x⸣.

(2) Cf. ŠL 367, 98 for ŠE.IN.NU; for IN.NU.DA = IN.NU = *tibnu*, cf. ŠL 148, 18 and Kraus RA 64 143^{2}. ŠL 367, 100 has ŠE.IN.NU.DA = "straw (Boghazkoy)."

(3) For the expression KÌ PN Ì.GAL see note to OBTIV 78:3.

OBTIV 143

A7689

Barley; partially Tallied List

Obv. 2(GUR) 2(PI) 3(BÁN) GUR ŠÀ
1(GUR) 1(PI) 4(BÁN) TA.À[M]
5(GUR) 2(PI) 3(BÁN) GUR
ḫu-bu-ta-tum
[1]*Ri-iš*-DINGIR
2 GUR *A-bi-sa-ma*-SU
4(PI) GUR PUZUR$_4$.^{d}UTU
ŠU.NIGIN$_2$ 10(GUR) 4(PI) ŠE
i-na ma-⌈x x⌉
ša i-na Ma-an-⌈*ḫa-tim*⌉^{KI}
i-ba-aš-ši

Rev. 2 GUR *Im-gur-r*[*um*]
5 GUR 1 UDU.NITA$_2$ 1 GUR
GÚ.⌈GAL⌉
ša a-na Sú-be-lim (?)
in-na-ad-na-a
a-na ni-iš DINGIR

NOTES

(1) Lines 1-3 state: "2.2.3 kors (barley)—out of which, per each kor, 0.1.4 kor (will be interest)—(and) 5.2.3 kors (barley)—as a *ḫubuttātum* loan—were given to) Riš-ilum". In other words he received 2 amounts of grain, one as an interest-bearing loan; the other as a *ḫubuttātum*.

(2) Cf. *A-bi-sa-ma-ku*, YOS 14 25:15 and *A-bi-sa-ma-ta*, TIM 7 120:4 (references courtesy of M. Stol); accordingly one may wish to read *-sa-ma-ku*(!) or perhaps *-sa-ma-at*(!) here.

(5) Note the writing 4(PI) with GUR sign.

(7) The line reads: "which is in Manḫatum."

(9) Lines 9-12 state: "5 kors, 1 ram, 1 kor chick-peas which were given to PN (to pay) for taking an oath by the deity." For the assignment of foodstuffs *ana nīš ilim* cf. Birot, ARMT 9, p. 289.

OBTIV 145

A7691

Barley; Record of Storage

Obv. 21(GUR) 3(PI) GUR ŠE GIŠ.PA
24(GUR) 3(PI) [G]UR ŠE EGIR
ŠU.NIGIN$_2$ 46 GUR 1(PI) ŠE
GIŠ.PA *ù* ŠE EGIR
ša Mu-na-nu-um
L.E. *im-du-du-ma*
Rev. *a-na na-aš-pa-ak*
^{I}DINGIR-*šu-na-ṣir*
iš-ša-ap-ku
ITU *Ki-nu-nu* UD.1.KAM
MU *ma-at Ma-ḫa-zum*

NOTES

(3) Lines 3-8 state: "Total: 46.1.0 kors . . . barley and 'late' barley which Munanum measured out and which were poured into the storage unit of Ilšu-naṣir." The meaning of ŠE.GIŠ.PA is uncertain: it also occurs in OBTIV 159:1-2 and 160:4. Also uncertain is any relationship between ŠE.GIŠ.PA and the agricultural harvest operation še.giš.PA.ná.a = *še-im ša ina* GIŠ.PA *šu-nu-lu*, Hh XXIV 175 (MSL 11 p. 84), which involved a "stick." The exact nature of this agricultural operation is also uncertain; cf. CAD H 154a and Salonen, *Agricultura Mesopotamica* pp. 211 (line 105), 266; these translations reflect possibilities earlier raised by Landsberger, MSL 1 173ff. The juxtaposition with EGIR is suggestive: CT 8 38c:20-22 speaks of ŠE.GUR GIŠ.BAR ^{d}UTU *ma-aḫ-ri-am ù ar-ki-am*, which CAD A/2 287f takes as "early and late deliveries." Based on this, the ŠE.GIŠ.PA would seem to describe freshly harvested barley.

(1) "The year Maḫazum"; for this year date formula see OBTIV p. 33 no. 48.

OBTIV 151

A21950

Personnel; List of Overseers

Obv. (1′) ⌜UGULA⌝ [ ]
DUM[U]
(2′) UGULA 10 30-[ ]
DUM[U]

(3′) UGULA 10 *I*[*a-*]
UGULA 10 *Ka-ad-ri-ia*
DUMU *Za-bu-lum*
(5′) UGULA 6 *Maš-pa-lum*
DUMU *Za-bu-lum*
UGULA 12 *Qí-iš-ì-lí-šu*
DUMU *Iš-ḫi*-DINGIR-*ma*
UGULA 10 *Ḫa-zi-ru-um*
DUMU *Na-ar-ba-num*
UGULA 11 *A*[*r*]-*ki*-DINGIR-*ma*
L.E. DUMU *Ḫa-ab-du*-DING[IR]
Rev. ⸢UGULA 10⸣ *Pu-ḫa-nu-u*[*m*]
DUMU *Ku-nu-um*
(10′) ⸢UGULA 10 *Ia*⸣-*aḫ-su-uk*-DINGIR
[DUMU ^{d}E]N.ZU-*en-nam*
UGULA ⸢14⸣ [ ]-⸢x⸣-*ru*
[DUMU]-*bi-ru-um*
– space –
[ ] UGULA 10 ⸢TA.ÀM⸣ (?)
⸢*ša*⸣ [ ] ⸢17⸣ ERIN$_2$
LÚ [*z*]*a-am-ḫa-tum*^{KI}
(15′) *ša aš-šum ma-*[ ]
KÁ.GAL ⸢ME⸣ (?) [ ]

NOTES

(1′) Lines 1′-11′ contain the names of individuals who are overseers of units ranging in size from 6 to 14 persons. Cf. for varying size units UGULA NAM 5, 10, 15, 20 etc., MSL 12 39 (OB Proto-LÚ) ll. 173-178; 119 (LÚ = *ša* II iii) 2-9. Cf. further NAM 10, CT 6 17 v 27f; Birot, *Tablettes* 62:13 (NAM 12 ERIN$_2$.MEŠ), 63:13 (NAM 16 ERIN$_2$.MEŠ) and CAD A/1 279 *sub aklu*.

(8′) The sign KI is clear; it cannot be read DI without emendation.

(12′) Lines 12′-13′ may perhaps be restored: (12′) [ŠU.NIGIN$_2$ 1 UGULA 6 6 UGULA] 10.T⸢A.À⸣M; (13′) *ša* [11 *ša* 12 *ša*] 17 ERIN$_2$ "Total: 1 overseer of 6, 6 overseers of 10 each, one of 11, one of 12, one of 17 workers". If this is plausible, one may also read ⸢17⸣ in line 13′.

(14′) Lines 14′-16′ may have stated (14′) LÚ.MEŠ GN (15′) *ša aš-šum ma-*[*aṣ-ṣa-ar*] (16′) KÁ.GÁL ME[Š(?) *šūšubū*] "(being) men from GN who were set to guard the city gates of. . . .".

OBTIV 152

A7670

Unaddressed Letter Order

Obv. (1) 2(GUR) 1(PI) 4(BÁN) GUR ŠE
a-na Lu-mu-ur-ša-^{d}UTU
i-di-in-ma
pu-ḫi-šu
(5) [*a*]*-na Ḫa-aš-ḫu-ur*$^{[KI]}$
mu-ḫu-ur
Rev. [I]TU *A-bi-i*
UD.3.KAM
(8) MU É SÁ.GAR.NI É ^{d}EN.ZU

Seal Legend

I-⸢x⸣*-za* DUMU *A-bi-*⸢x⸣

NOTES

The term "letter order" was first put forward to describe certain Ur III letters, either addressed or unaddressed, which typically direct the recipient to hand over some commodity to (a) named person(s) or to carry out some transactions for their benefit. Cf. W. W. Hallo "The Neo-Sumerian Letter Orders" *BiOr* 26 (1969) 171-175. This term was later applied by J. J. Finkelstein, YOS 13 3-7, to certain texts of rounded shape—*ze'pum* (see most recently, M. Stol "Broodjes, Kleitabletten en Munten" *Akkadica* 9 (1978) 25-29, many of which are unaddressed letters or administrative accounts containing second person directions. In the texts from Ishchali, only OBTIV 217 fits securely into Finkelstein's proposed category; it is a small round tablet, an unaddressed letter, ordering the unnamed recipient to give lard to PN. OBTIV 152 fits into his category by its contents although not by its shape. OBTIV 152 is also unusual in having a full date; the inclusion of a date is a feature most commonly associated with administrative texts (cf. pp. 196ff. above.) and not at all with letters. It is thus a "hybrid" in character. OBTIV 217 also bears a seal; the presence of a sealing on an unaddressed letter could serve as a means of identifying the sender; but then, they are so much more often omitted. Sealings are an atypical, although by no means an unknown, feature of Finkelstein's *ze'pum* category. The use of a seal on (the envelope of) an addressed letter is seen in OBTIV 1; this is an equally rare phenomenon.

OBTIV 154

A21990

Unspecified Commodity; Memo of Amount and Person

Obv. (1) 14(GUR) 1(PI) GUR
A-ḫu-ni
DUMU ⸢*Ú*⸣*-mu-ta-mar*
Rev. – uninscribed –

NOTES

OBTIV 154-158, 161-162, 165, 171-175, 178, 183-186, 188, 190, 192, 194, 197, 199-213, UCP 10/1 101 comprise a group of texts dealing with unspecified or unknown commodities. There are no records in this group; the documents are all clearly ephemeral in nature. They are mostly lists and memos, including a number written on perforated tags which accompanied and identified containers or packages of goods.

The unspecified commodity is probably barley. For this reason, they were placed among the texts dealing with barley in OBTIV. Many of these texts closely resemble documents involving barley. In some instances, even the same persons are involved, e.g.: the overseer Meranum in OBTIV 194-195; the overseer Irra-gamil in OBTIV 184-188. Only one of these similar texts explicitly mentions barley and that is OBTIV 187. Additional linkages are seen in the overseer Sin-gamil in OBTIV 197-198 and Išbi-Irra in OBTIV 191-192. The omission of the commodity is probably related to the temporariness of the documents; we see this illustrated in OBTIV 196, where ŠE is omitted for the first entry and added—almost as an afterthought—for the second. In OBTIV the group of documents involving unspecified commodities were merged with those involving barley because of their close similarities.

(3) The PN is obscure. The first sign could be [LU] (!) but the second sign is not easily to be read as UŠ(!) for *Lu-uš-ta-mar*. For similar MU signs (without the unexplained vertical scratch/wedge) cf. OBTIV 161:2, 171:2 and 183:3. The second element in the PN would appear to be the verb *ammar*; but the first element is unclear.

OBTIV 163

A7733

Barley, Tally of Amounts and Persons

Obv. (1) ⸢2(PI) 5(BÁN)⸣ ŠE
^{1}*Be-el-šu-nu*
1(GUR) 2(PI) 2(BÁN) GUR ŠE
^{1}*Sa-li-ma-ti*
L.E. (5) 2 GUR *I-mi-ru*
^{1}*Ma-ti* LÚ(?).⸢TU⸣(?).TA
Rev. ŠU.NIGIN 4(GUR) 1(BÁN) ⸢GUR⸣ ŠE

NOTES

(5) In order for the total in line 7 to be correct, ll. 5-6 can only record one item, i.e., 2 GUR. According to the documentary pattern, l. 5 should contain the commodity and l. 6 (note DIŠ at the beginning) the PN. *I-mi-ru* should thus belong with the designation of the commodity rather than be a PN, Imiru/Immeru(?). *I-mi-ru* appears as a PN in OBTIV 167:5 and thus may also be read here. If so, this occurrence should be added to the Index of PNs in OBTIV p. 85.

(6) In OBTIV p. 95b LÚ.TU(?).TA is placed among the professions on a purely arbitrary basis.

OBTIV 164

A7641

Barley: Talley of Shares in Temple Fields

Obv. 15(GUR) 1(PI) GUR ŠE *zi-ti*(?) ⸢SANGA⸣
7(GUR) 3(BÁN) GUR *zi-ti*(!) *La-aḫ-bat*
15(GUR) 3(PI) GUR *zi-ti*(!) SANGA
7(GUR) 1(PI) 3(BÁN) GUR *zi-ti*(!)
ARAD-^{d}IŠ
13(GUR) 4(PI) GUR *zi-ti*(!) SANGA
L.E. 6(GUR) 2(PI) GUR *zi-ti*(!)
Ap-pa-an-DINGIR X
Rev. 5(GUR) 3(PI) GUR *zi-ti*(!) ⸢SANGA⸣
2(GUR) 4(PI) GUR *zi-ti*(!)
30-*i-din-nam*
ŠU.NIGIN$_2$ 50(GUR) 1(PI) GUR ŠE *zi-ti*(!) ⸢SANGA⸣
SU.NIGIN$_2$ 25(GUR) 3(PI) GUR *zi-ti*(!)
be-el šu-⸢*ku*⸣-*sa-tim*

NOTES

(1) "15.1 kors barley, share of the head priest." The ratio between what the SANGA gets and what the fiefholders get is in each case 2:1. The forms of the TI signs in ll. 1-10 are unusual but clear; there is no way to read TI without supplying missing elements in every case. Cf., however, the similarly defective forms of TI found in Fossey 4999, 5000 (CT 8 49a:3, VS 8 19:28). Another text recording distribution of shares is UCP 10/1 10.

(6) The reading *Ap-pa-an*-DINGIR rather than ^{d}X is based on similar names: Appan-ili or Ana-pani-ili (cf. Stamm, *Namengebung* 231 and UCP 10/1 60:5,7; 108:24). The genitive *ilim* would preclude reading the PN, *Ap-pa-an*-DINGIR-*um*.

(10) Literally, "the holder of fiefs" but no doubt plural "holders" is intended. For fem. pl. *šukusātum* cf. CT 45 117:4.

OBTIV 165

A21965A

Unspecified commodity; Tally of Amounts, Persons

Obv. [ ] [ ]]
[ ] ⸢x⸣ É *ṣa*-⸢*al*(?)⸣-*mi*
[ ] *Im-gur*-30
[ ] [x] *A-ša*(?)-<*si*>-*šu-um*-DINGIR

[ ]

[ ] *Lu-zu*(?)*-um*

[ŠU.NIGIN$_2$] 8 GUR

Rev. – uninscribed –

NOTES

This tablet is mysterious; it bears the museum number A21965 but it does not seem to be part of the other tablet that bears the same museum no. (i.e. A21965), which is OBTIV 156. There is no separate find spot data apart from what is known about OBTIV 156. We have therefore assigned it the number A21965A. Is it possible that this tablet was assigned to the Ishchali corpus in error? Cf. OBTIV 304, another "unlikely" tablet.

(2′) The signs as preserved can be read: É *ṣa-*⌜*al*⌝*-mi* "statue room" cf. CAD Ṣ 85b. This expression is, however, only attested from NA times. Note, also, the omission of mimation here and consider, too, the obscurity surrounding the origin of this tablet. Another possibility would be to take the É or *bītum* in a PN; but the rest of this putative PN remains uncertain.

(4′) *Ašassī-šum-ilim* is a conjecture to replace an even more uncertain reading, *A-ra*(?)*-šu-um*-DINGIR, as read previously in OBTIV p. 80b. For the RA(?) sign cf. OBTIV 158:6.

OBTIV 167

A22002

Barley; Tally of Outlays

Obv. 4(GUR) ⌜3(BÁN)⌝ GUR ŠE

⌜x x⌝ 16 ⌜IM x x x⌝

1(PI) 4(BÁN) *Ia-ta-ru-um*

2(PI) 4(BÁN) *Ša-ir-mu-uš-ši*

2(BÁN) *I-mi-ru* ŠA ⌜x x x⌝

3(BÁN) 6(!) SILA$_3$ *Ta-ri-*⌜x x⌝

1(BÁN) 2 SILA$_3$ I- ⌜x⌝ [ ]

ša UD.4.[KAM]

1(BÁN) 6(SILA$_3$) *A-bu-w*[*a-qar*] (?)

Rev. 5 SILA$_3$ [*ṣú*]*-ḫa-ru*

ša ⌜*a*⌝*-na* ÈŠ.[NUN.NA^{KI}]

1(BÁN) *I-ku-un*(?)*-pí-x*

3(BÁN) DUMU ⌜*Ak*(?)*-ša*⌝ [ ]

4(BÁN) DUMU *Pu-ḫa-*⌜*lum*⌝(?)

ú-tap-pu-[*šu-ú*]

ŠU.NIGIN$_2$ 6(GUR) 2(PI) 2(BÁN) 9 SILA$_3$ Š[E]

NOTES

(2) In view of the unreferred amount in line 1, one would expect some statement in line 2 like *š*[*a* U]D.16.KAM ⌈x x x⌉.

(6) It is possible to read 15 SILA$_3$ in line 6 but then it would be most unusual to find so large a number of SILA$_3$ standing unconverted to larger units. The U (or 10) could be a scratch and it is possible to read 6(!) in place of the 5 on the copy (collation).

(11) Alternatively: *ša* [IT]U *Na-ab*-[*ri-i*], "for the month of Nabru."

(15) Perhaps "they have been accounted for"; cf. CAD E 232b and AHw 227a (*epēšu*)D said of barley).

(16) The total given in line 16 does not tally with the figures listed in lines 1-15. Lines 3, 5, 7, 9, 10, 12, 13, 14 are clear and without question; their figures must therefore stand. The only "variables" are in lines 1, 4, 6. In line 1, only the second sign is uncertain; it would be a unit of 1-3 (BÁN) or 1(!)(PI). In line 6, a reading of 15 SILA$_3$ is possible but 6(!) will fit the total in line 16 better; this is an argument in addition to the considerations already mentioned above in the note to line 6 (see further presently). Line 4 is only partially uncertain; one could read as above but one may also consider 2(PI) 3(BÁN) ^{d}(!)UTU-*ir-mu-uš-ši* or even ^{d}(!) *Wi*(!)-*ir-mu-ša*(!)-*lim*. However, none of the figures in lines 1, 4, 6 can be sufficiently manipulated to arrive at the total in line 16. For if one adds up all of the figures in lines 3, 5, 7, 9, 10, 12, 13, 14 plus a safe "minimum" of 4(GUR) from line 1, 2(PI) from line 4, and 3(BÁN) from line 6, one is still left with 1.1.0; 6 kor "missing." The 6 SILA$_3$ could be supplied from line 6 as now emended and read; but there is simply no way to find another 1.1.0 kor in the above-mentioned lines, despite repeated collations. It is not possible to read 5(!) GUR in line 1; there are clearly only 1 horizontal wedges in the top part of the first sign. The lower line of horizontal wedges is not in sequence with the top two wedges. One could restore a third horizontal in the lower line but then this would be an abnormal way of writing 5–inverted, as it were, with two wedges in the top row and three in the bottom. The only "solution," assuming that the ancient scribe did not make any error, is to try and restore [1](GUR) [1](PI) in line 2; this is graphically possible but yields no clear reading with the 16 following.

OBTIV 168

A7814

Barley; List of Amounts and Persons

NOTES

(10) Alternatively, perhaps, AN.PA.DINGIR <.MEŠ> , *Anum-ḫat-ili*.

OBTIV 169

A21902

Barley; Tally of Outlays

. . .

Obv. (6) ⸢1(BÁN)⸣ MÁ.LAḪ$_4$ *ša* ŠE.GIŠ.Ì ⸢*x*⸣

⸢x⸣ BA KA ⸢x⸣

⸢1(BÁN) *Ka*⸣*-lu-mi-lí*

(9) 3(BÁN) ⸢ŠÀ⸣.GAL 3 UDU. ⸢GA⸣(?)

. . .

. . .

Rev. ⸢2⸣ [Š]UK AGA(?).UŠ *ša* GUD.ḪI.[A] ⸢*du nim*⸣

[ ] ⸢1(BÁN)⸣ ŠUK *mu-še-ni-iq-tum*

[ ] ⸢1(BÁN)⸣ SÀ.GAL GUD.ḪI.A *ša* UD.2.KA[M]

[ ] ⸢1(BÁN)⸣ NIG.⸢DU⸣ UD.2.KAM *i-na wa-*⸢*ṣi*⸣(?)[*-im*]

(10′) [ ] *Ib-ni-Ìr-ra*

. . .

NOTES

(6) Lines 6-7 seem to state: "0.0.1 kor (for) the boatman who . . . the sesame. . . ." In OBTIV p. 91a, the PN *Sú-qà-q*[*um*] was read in line 7; this is a conjecture at best.

(9) "0.0.3 kor fodder (for) three nursing ewes."

Rev.

(6′) The conjectured reading is a suggestion of M. Stol; "0.2.0 kor, ration for the soldier who . . . the cattle." Line 7′ speaks of the "ration of a wetnurse."

(9) Lines 9′-10′ perhaps state: ". . . 1 kor, a meal for the second day when Ibni-Irra departed."

OBTIV 174

A21986

Unspecified Commodity; Memo of Amounts, Persons, and Place

Obv. (1) 1(GUR) 1(PI) GUR ⸢*Bu*-x-x⸣

1(GUR) 3(PI) GUR *A-pil*-30

L.E. *ša Bu-ku-da-a*

Rev. – uninscribed –

NOTES

(1) *Bu*-⌈*ti*(?)-*ta*⌉ as read in OBTIV p. 81b, is only a conjecture. *Bu*-⌈*na*(?)-EŠ$_4$DAR⌉ is also worth considering, even though CAD B 317a records this PN only for MB texts.

OBTIV 176

A21877

Barley; Memo of Amount, Person, and Field

Obv. (1) 1(PI) 4(BÁN) ŠE
30-*ri-me-ni*
Rev. A.ŠÀ *šu*(?)-⌈*ku*⌉-*s*[*í*]

NOTES

(2) This line apparently reads "(for his) field of alimentation (cf. AHw 1266b *šukūšu*/*šukussu*). For another occurrence of this term at Ishchali and another case of a strangely written ŠU, see TIM 2 7:8 *i-na A-ga-ga*[KI] A.ŠÀ *šu*(?)-*ku-si*. Note also, the lack of mimation in both cases. In OBTIV 177, 178, 180, the fields mentioned are usually designated by *Flurnamen*; *šukūsu* is a general term. However, Edzard, *Tell-ed-Dēr* pp. 77f., considers the occurrence of *šu-ku-si-im* GAL in no. 34:1 to be the equivalent of a *Flurname* there; it is a context, similar to here, where a proper noun rather than a general term is expected.

OBTIV 177

A21895

Barley: Memo of Amount, Person, and Field

Obv. (1) 4(PI) ŠE *Qí-šu-ša*
Rev. (2) A.ŠÀ ⌈*Šu-x-x-num*⌉

NOTES

(2) The name of this field is uncertain; the last sign could also be read EŠ$_4$.DAR; cf. the OB *Flurname* *Ta-aš-ku-un*-ES$_4$.DAR in Edzard, *Tell-ed-Dēr* 32:2.

OBTIV 182

A21985

Barley; List of Outlays

Obv. (1) 1(BÁN) *a-na* É NAR(?)
2(BÁN) *i-na* É ^{d}UTU
GÌR *A-ḫu-wa-qar*
UD.2.KAM
Rev. (5) 3(BÁN) ŠE SIPA
1(BÁN) ^{d}*Ki-ti-tum-um-mi*
2(BÁN) ^{d}*La-qí-pu-um-ga-mi-il*
2(BÁN) MU
[UD] NE *šà* ⸢^{d}UTU⸣

NOTES

(9) These outlays were made in connection with the day(s) when the *kinūnu* ritual is performed; see CAD K 395a.

OBTIV 187

A21991

Barley; Memo of Amount, Person, and Overseer

Obv. (1) 3(PI) 3(BÁN) 6 $SILA_3$ ŠE
I-pí-iq-Nu-nu
L.E. UGULA *Ìr-ra-*<*ga*> *-mi-il*
Rev. (4) *šà* MAŠ.EN

OBTIV 189

A21971

Barley; Memo of Amount, Person, and Overseer

Obv. (1) 7(GUR) 1(PI) GUR ŠE
Iš-me-Ìr-ra ⸢x⸣
UGULA *Ìr-ra-ga*(!)-⸢*mi-il*⸣
L.E. *ù* 30-*ri-me-ni*
Rev. (5) *šà* MAŠ.KAK.EN

NOTES

(2) The sign in question can be read either as SANGA or IŠ. In the first case, see OBTIV 5f for a discussion of this office at Ishchali; in the second case, one may compare below UCLMA 9/2827 and CAD K 477f *sub kizû* "groom." This latter reading perhaps fits in better with the social level of the *muškēnu* (l. 5) which CAD K 272ff relates to "commoner" or "destitute" classes.

(3) For the GA sign compare OBTIV 195:2.

OBTIV 191

A21996

Barley; Memo of Amount, Person, and Overseer

Obv.	(1)	2(PI) 2(BÁN) 4 $SILA_3$ ŠE
		A-lí-PA.DINGIR
L.E.		*šà* MAŠ.EN
Rev.	(4)	UGULA *Iš-bi-Ir-ra*

NOTES

(3) MAŠ.EN is apparently an abbreviation for MAŠ.EN.KAK which appears once (OBTIV 16:3) in the collection alongside of more commonly attested MAŠ.KAK.EN. The abbreviated writing MAŠ.EN is repeatedly written and is not a scribal error (see p. 4 for discussion.)

(4) Line 3 apparently belongs to line 4 following and designates Išbi-Irra as an UGULA *šà* MAŠ.EN. This "inverted order," where the phrase *ša muškēnim* precedes rather than follows UGULA PN, is apparently only a variation of the more common pattern where the reverse is true, namely, UGULA PN *ša muškēnim*. The more common pattern is found in OBTIV 183:4-5, 185:3-4, 186:3-4, 187:3-4, 188:3-4, 189:3-5, 192:4-5, 193:4-5, 194:3-4, 195:4-5, 196:5-6. Išbi-Irra is a well-known UGULA of the *muškēnu* and appears as such in OBTIV 190 and 192. In addition to the "inversion" of the phrases *ša muškēnim* and UGULA PN, we also encounter a number of other variations. *Šà* is omitted in OBTIV 184:3 and 190:3-4; thus, UGULA PN MAŠ.KAK.EN. We encounter omission of *šà* together with "inversion" of phrases in OBTIV 197:3 [MAŠ.EN] 30-*ga-mi-il*. Sin-gamil, the UGULA, appears with *šà* MAŠ.EN in OBTIV 196:5-6 and as *šà* MAŠ.KAK.EN (without UGULA) in OBTIV 198:1-2. The phrase *ša muškēnim* apparently denotes a supervisory position over the *muškēnu* and is not simply a designation of membership in the class. We see this from its frequent juxtaposition with PNs who are also designated as UGULA (*waklum*) and by its juxtaposition with *šà* KÁ.GAL (*šà* KÁ.GAL *šà* MAŠ.KAK.EN) in OBTIV 199:2.

OBTIV 197

A21987

Unspecified Commodity; Memo of Amount, Person, and Overseer

Obv. (1) 3(PI) 3(BÁN) 6 $SILA_3$ 20(GÍN)
30-SIPA
⸢MAŠ.EN⸣ 30-*ga-mi-il*

Rev. – uninscribed –

NOTES

(1) "0.3.3; 6.20 kor"; GÍN is the unit after $SILA_3$ in decreasing size. This is a rare OB occurrence and should be added to the evidence in AHw 1248a.

OBTIV 205

A7898

Unspecified Commodity; Perforated Tag, With Seal, Bearing Memo of Amount and Person

Obv. (1) ⸢2(PI)⸣ *I-bi-*^{d}IM
ŠA.GI

Rev. – uninscribed –

Seal Legend [AN].KA[ ]
DUMU *A-mur-na-ar-b* [*i-šu*]
ARAD ^{d}*I-pí-iq-*^{d}I[M]

NOTES

Although there is a seal on this document, it is a memo not a record (cf. the discussion on pp. 196 ff.) This is not because the text is written on a tag; indeed, we have a number of records written on tags: e.g. OBTIV 118, 121, 125, 126, UCP 10/1 72. They are, however, more complete in contrast to the present text, with the names of the commodities being specified and the names of authorizing officials included. One may note, in this connection, the presence of seals on the tags OBTIV 244-245; there are no texts written on these tags; they can thus not be memos, let alone records!

(2) The meaning of ŠA.GI is uncertain. The ŠA is written more clearly in OBTIV 200, 201, 207, 208. The GI is most clear in the present example, less clear in other cases; but the reading seems to be correct. The title is perhaps to be associated with /sagi/ (perhaps rather /šagi/), the Sumerian value suggested for the reading $SILA_3$.ŠU.DU_8(A) = *šāqium*, "cupbearer" by Jacobson ZA 52 119[50].

OBTIV 218

A7783

Oil; Memo of Receipt

Obv. ⸢1 GUR⸣ Ì.⸢GIŠ x x⸣ [ ]
i-na É *Ḫa-ia-*[*ša*]-[*rum*]
i-na li-bi 5 GUR ŠE.⸢Ì⸣.[GIŠ] *iš-ša-ak-*[ ]
[*ù*] *ne-se-ep-ta-šu-nu*
10 GUR Ì.GIŠ *i-ma-*⸢x⸣
L.E. *ma-aḫ-ra-ak-ku*
Rev. 1(GUR) 1(PI) GUR Ì.GIŠ DINGIR-*šu-na-ṣir*
1(GUR) Ì.GIŠ *Im-gur*-30
1(GUR) Ì.GIŠ DINGIR-*šu-na-ṣir* DUMU 30-[*e*]-[ ]
⸢ŠÀ⸣ 10 GUR ŠE.Ì.GIŠ
[*m*]*a-aḫ-ra-ak-ku*

NOTES

(3) For *ina libbi*(m) and ŠÀ (line 10) cf. CAD L 174b; note the lack of mimation after *libbi*. If one will read *iš-ša-ak-*[*nu*] in this line, one may translate ll. 1-4: "1 kor sesame (or linseed?) oil . . . , in the house of Ḫaja-šarrum, out of the 5 kors of sesame (that) was set aside together with their containers".

(10) " . . . (oil) out of the 10 kors sesame I have received."

OBTIV 225

A21879

Oil; Record

Obv. 1(PI) 1(BÁN) Ì.GIŠ
1(PI) 1(BÁN) Ì.ŠAḪ
[1(PI) 1(BÁN)] Ì.ESIR$_x$(A.SUK)
L.E. – destroyed –
Rev. ⸢*I-bi*⸣-30
DUMU ⸢LÚ.UG$_x$(BAD)⸣-*mu-ba-lí-iṭ*
ITU ⸢*Ma*⸣-*aq-ra-tim*
U.E. ⸢MU É ^{d}EN⸣.LÍL(?)
⸢*in-ne-ep-šu*⸣

NOTES

The tablet is covered with impressions of a pictorial seal (not copied); there is no seal legend preserved.

Obv.

(1) For lines 1-3 cf. UCP 10/1 83.

(3) Cf. Thompson DAC 43, CAD I 312a *šaman ittê*; according to CAD I 310, *ittû* "crude bitumen" is usually written A.ÉSIR (LAGAB x NUMUN); yet variants do occur; CAD I 320a notes A.BUL (LAGAB x EŠ) and Goetze AASOR 31 CE § 1 (A 12,20), has Ì.ÍD (LAGAB x ḪAL)); The writing here, SUK (LAGAB x ⸢A⸣), represents yet another variant. Cf. further OBTIV 153:4, 232:1 and UCP 10/1 83:3, Ì.ESIR$_x$(SUK).RA. Note also the Ishchali writings of A.SUK for ÍD in UCP 10/1 22:26 and UCLMA 9/2827:32.

Rev.

(2) The PN is perhaps better taken as *Mītam-muballiṭ* rather than as *Awīlam-muballiṭ* as in OBTIV p. 80b. Note the extra "Winkelhacken" in the MU. For PNs of this type cf. CAD M/2 141b.

OBTIV 227

A21914

Flour; List of Amounts, Persons, and Dates

Obv.	(1)	⸢2(PI) 5(BÁN)⸣ ZÍD.ŠE	(1)	0.2.5. kor barley flour
		^{d}EN.ZU-*še-mi*		Sin-šemi
		1(PI) LÚ *A-wa-al*^{KI}		0.1 kor the man from Awal
		1(PI) LÚ *Ì-lí-ka-ab-ka-bu*		0.1 kor the man from Ili-kabkabu
	(5)	UD.⸢14⸣.KAM	(5)	the 14th day.
L.E.		3(PI) 5(BÁN) (1) ⸢ZÍD.ŠE⸣		0.3.5 kor barley flour
Rev.		[^{d}EN.ZU]-⸢*še-mi*⸣		Sin-šemi
		1(PI) LÚ *A-wa-al*^{KI}		0.1 kor the man from Awal
		[U]D.24.KAM		the 24th day.
	(10)	⸢3(PI) 5(BÁN)(!) ^{d}EN.ZU⸣-*še-mi*	(10)	0.3.5 kor Sin-šemi
		[ ]LÚ *A-wa-al* <KI>		. . . the man from Awal
U.E.		⸢LÚ x x DU⸣		the . . .
		2(BÁN) ZI.GA		0.0.2 kor (given out) as expenditure
Edge	(14)	UD.26.KAM	(14)	the 26th day.

NOTES

(4) Jacobsen OIP 43 125[34] understands LÚ *Ilī-kabkabu* to refer to an emissary sent by the father of Šamši-Adad, king of Assyria. This is possible but is by no means a certainty. In the Assyrian King List, that king's name is written ^{I}DINGIR-*kab-ka-bi* (Gelb, JNES 13 (1954) 212f); cf. also *I-la-kab-ka-bu-ú* at Mari (see Huffmon, *Amorite Personal Names in the Mari Texts*. The Johns Hopkins Press: 1965, p. 24). Jacobsen *loc. cit.* also states that "this tablet [i.e. OBTIV 227] was

found in the Kititum temple in the top stratum which dates from the reign of Ibalpiel II." According to Jacobsen's field notes, the top stratum also yielded tablets bearing year dates of Ḫadati, Ipiq-Adad, Sin-abušu, and Naram-Sin. This information appears in connection with tablets: Ish. 75-T.26, Ish. 34-T.90, Ish. 34-T.28, Ish. 34-T.112; the year dates are OBTIV pp. 29-34, year date formulas 34, 29, 59, 50. For Ibalpiel II see Ish. 34-T.23, Ish. 35-T.62 (OBTIV 56, year date formulas 46, 36). The top stratum at Ishchali thus cannot be solely associated with Ibalpiel II; Naram-Sin and Ipiq-Adad (II) do precede Ibalpiel II and so, too, does some 28 years of Šamši-Adad's reign (cf. OBTIV pp. 14ff.). If *Ilī-kabkabu* here does in fact refer to Šamši-Adad's father, then the evidence from the kings mentioned fits in well, since Naram-Sin and Ipiq-Adad precede Ipalpiel II. In OBTIV pp. 19-22, we assigned Ḫadati and Sin-abušu to the period before Ipiq-Adad II. The stratigraphic clustering of year dates in the top stratum would support this conclusion.

(5) The day is given but not the month; this document is thus not a record but more temporary.

(8) For Awal, see note to OBTIV 86:10 above.

(12) LÚ ⸢MÁ.LAḪ$_4$⸣ is also possible here.

OBTIV 228

A7629

Water and Vessels; Tally of Expenditure; With Dates

Obv.	(1)	3(GUR) 3(PI) 3(BÁN) GUR *mu-ú*	(1)	3.3.3 kors water
		6 *la-aḫ-ta-na-tum*		(and) 6 cooking vats
		4(PI) *mu-ú* ZI.GA		0.4 kor water, expenditure
		ŠU.NIGIN$_2$ 4(GUR) 2(PI) 3(BÁN) GUR ITU *Za-ḫa-ra-tum*		Total: 4.2.3 kors (in the) month of Zaḫaratum
	(5)	4(GUR) 1(PI) GUR *mu-ú a-na* É.GAL	(5)	4.1 kors water to the palace
		qa-du-um 3 *la-aḫ-ta-na-tum*		together with 3 cooking vats
		1(PI) 4(BÁN) ZI.GA		0.1.4 kor, expenditure
Rev.		ŠU.NIGÍN$_2$ 4(GUR) 2(PI) 4(BÁN) GUR ⸢*mu*⸣-*ú*		Total: 4.2.4 kors water
		ITU *Ki-nu-ni*		(in the) month of Kinunu

NOTES

(1) In OBTIV p. 43, we read *qú*(?)-*ú* in lines 1, 3, 5, 8—thus "peas and vessels." For *qû* "peas" see the suggestion of Levine and Hallo, HUCA 38 57 and AHw 925a; that translation is not certain. The sign, however, is clearly MU and, were it not for the measuring, would be read as such without hesitation. We are unable to explain how water came to be measured in such precise amounts. But cf. YOS 13 383:2 ŠÁM 4 GUR *me-e*.

OBTIV 247

A7707

Utensils and Objects; List of Deposited Items

Obv. 2 GIŠ SI MI ⸢x x⸣
1 *e-si-tum*
2 *na-am-zi-tum*
3 *la-aḫ-ta-nu-um*
2 GIŠ.IG.MEŠ
L.E. [*pi-qí*]-*tum*
⸢*an-ni-tum*⸣
Rev. ⸢*it-ti* ^{d}EN.ZU⸣
pa-aq-⸢*da*⸣*-at*

NOTES

(1) One seeks to read: 2 GIŠ *si-mi-*⸢*da*(?)*-tum*⸣ "2 (wooden) mills"; cf. AHw 1018a. But the DA is not sufficiently represented, especially if one compares the DA in line 9. The last 2 signs look like ⸢DI LUM⸣ or ⸢X TUM⸣.

(2) This reference may be added to the short list in CAD E 337a.

(3) Note the sg. in place of pl. in lines 3-4.

OBTIV 248

A21927

Harness and Wagon Gear; List of Items Given Out

Obv. 2 *ni*(?)*-ru-ù ra-bu*(!)*-tum*
2 *li-ù ra-bu-tu-um*
4 *ta-*[*a*]*m-ša-ra-*[*tu*]*m*
ša ma-a[*š-ki*]
3 *ki-ša-d*[*u*](?)
ša ma-aš-ki
Rev. [1]*Lu-ša-li-im*
2 *na-du-ur-r*[*u*](?)
A-na-ša-⸢*ru*⸣-^{d}I[M]
Wa-ki-il-ì-lí
ŠU.BA.AN.TI.ME

NOTES

(3) For *tamšaru* "whip" see note to OBTIV 123:2.

(5) "3 (wheel) rims of leather." Cf. *kišād magarri* cited by CAD M/1 32v *sub magarru* lex. sect. and Salonen, *Landfahrzeuge* 108.

(8) Cf. perhaps *na-tur-ru* cited in Hh VII B (MSL 6 p. 129) 182f for which AHw 766b conjectures "chisel."

(9) For ŠU.BA.AN.TI see the discussion in the note to OBTIV 94:28.

OBTIV 251

A21921

Implements; List of Items Loaned

Obv. 3 ⸢*ša*⸣-*šu*-⸢*gu*⸣
2 ⸢x⸣-*nu-ù*
2 ⸢*zi*⸣-*ru-ù*
2 *ri*-⸢*ti*⸣-*tu-um*
ša e-⸢*pí-ni*⸣-*im*
1 *na-al-ba-t*[*um*]
1 *ki*-⸢*iš-ki*⸣-[*rum*]
Rev. KI 30-*a-bu*(sic)-⸢x⸣
DUMU ARAD-30

NOTES

(1) "3 (pieces of) . . . wood"; for *šaššūgu* as a kind of wood, see AHw 1198 and OBTIV 266:10 below.

(2) Perhaps [*bi*]-*nu-ù* "2 (pieces) of tamarisk wood"; cf. CAD B 241b.

(3) Translation is uncertain.

(4) Lines 4-5 describe parts of a plow (*epinnum*); CAD E 237a lists *rittu* "handle." Our form here could be **rittētum*, a Babylonian pl. of *rittu*; for the shift to *-ētum* in place of *-ātum* cf. GAG § 10d. One may also consider a relationship of our form with *retû* "to fasten"; thus perhaps **retītum*. This form, however, would be not attested elsewhere.

(6) The sequence of *nalbattum*, *kiškirrum* is attested elsewhere in the Ishchali documents (cf. OBTIV 265, especially ll. 11-12) where we learn that it is part of a brick mold. Many of the Ishchali attestations are cited in CAD K 424a; the reference from this text should be added to the ones cited by CAD.

(8) Lines 8-9 state that the above objects "are in the possession of PN, son of PN_2"; for the expression of KI PN see the note to OBTIV 78:3.

OBTIV 253

A7654

Implements; Memo on Items Given Out

Obv.	(1)	10 *u_4-mi-im a-na* $^{d(!)}$*Šul-gi-*<*na*>*-an-na*$^{KI(!)}$	(1)	10 plow beams to Šulgi-nanna
	(2)	*a-na* 40 *sú-sú-li*		(in exchange ?) for 40 containers
	(3)	5 *u_4-mi-im a-na* DU_6.DUB^{KI}		5 plow beams to Tutub
Rev.		– uninscribed –		

NOTES

(1) For *ummu* "plow beam," see Salonen, *Agricultura Mesopotamica* 71f, 97.

The GN, Šulgi-nanna, is variously written: (1) ^{d}Šul-gi-^{d}ŠEŠ.KI$^{(KI)}$ as in the Harmal Geographical List, published by Levy, Sumer 3 (1947) 50-83 A iii 85 and B iii 12 (see now most recently MSL 11 p. 57); this same form also appears in the OB Forerunner AO 6447 obv. IV 46 (see now MSL 11 p. 132) and in TIM 3 36:16; see also the unpublished Ishchali references cited in OBTIV p. 34 no. 60 and Hh XXI 7:34, MSL 11 p. 17. (2) ^{d}*Šul-gi-na-na*^{KI}, which appears in TIM 3 125:20; Harris JCS 9 (1955) p. 120 no. 109:7; Ish 34-T.41 (as reported in OBTIV p. 74 no. 61); IM 63139 cited by F. Reschid, *Nuršamaš* 5 *sub* ac; and defectively, ^{d}*Šul-gi-na-*<*na*>^{KI}, in TIM 3 14:22 (3) ^{d}*Šul-gi-na-na-ru* in UCLMA 9/2864:20 (infra) (4) ^{d}*Šul-gi-na-an-ná*^{KI}, Chiera SLT 216 IV 6-7 as collated by Kramer Sumer 3 72 (see now MSL 11 p. 104 266); the variation in writing *ná* for *na* is seen again in that same list in MSL 11 p. 105 304 and note.

The form occurring here in the present text is defectively written; it may be restored as $^{d(!)}$*Šul-gi-*^{d}*Na-*<*na*>^{KI} as suggested in OBTIV p. 98b on the analogy of defective writings of no. 2 above or as $^{d(!)}$*Šul-gi-*<*na*>*-an-na*^{KI}, following no. 4. We have adapted the last reading here as slightly more likely in view of the lack of evidence for writing ^{d}*Na-na.*

(3) For DU_6.DUB^{KI} = *Tutub*, cf. Gelb OR NS 39 (1970) 539-40; see further, for examples, Harmal Geographical List A iv 124 and B v 1, Levy Sumer 3 (1947) 50-83 and MSL 11 p. 58 and Harris JCS 9 (1955) 31ff, nos. 12, 13, 14, 20, 23, 31, 41 and *passim.*

OBTIV 254

A21919

Implements; Memo on Items Returned and Outstanding

Obv.	(1)	16 *iš-il*(?)*-tu-um*	(1)	16 borrowed items (?)
		^{1}30*-ma-gi-ir*		Sin-magir
		ù ^{1}A*-pil-Ku-bi*		and Apil-Kubi
		ub-lu-ni-im		brought (hither)
	(5)	*uš-tu* A*-ga-ga-a*	(5)	from Agaga.
Rev.		*ṭú-bu-ù*		They have made good (these items)
		45 *i-mi-i*		(but) 45 plowshares (remain outstanding).

NOTES

(1) Our translation assumes the form here to be an *ipristu* of *ša'ālu* "to ask." Another proposal is to read *it*(!)-*ta*(!)-*tu-um* "seed plows" (cf. CAD I 312a) but the first signs need to be emended to read what they are not now on the tablet. *Da*(!)*il-tu-um* is also a possible reading but yields no ready interpretation.

(6) Admittedly a conjecture. Alternatively, (6) "(but) they were sunk (and lost) (7) 45 plowshares (remain outstanding)".

OBTIV 255

A21929

Implements; List of Items Returned

Obv. 8 ⌈*ma*⌉-*az-ru-ù*
2 *ma-aš-la-ḫu*
6 *ra-ap-šu*
8 *mu-ša-am-qí-ta-tum*
⌈$^{d(!)}$⌉ID_x(A.SUK)-*ma-ia-an*
L.E. [*iš*]-*tu Maš-kán*-⌈^{d}⌉
[*B*]*a-ar-mi*
Rev. ⌈*ub*⌉-*la-am*
7 *ma-aš-la-ḫu*
li-bu 22 *ma-aš-la-ḫi*
ša e-ri-qa-ti
U.E. $^{d}ID_x$(A.SUK)-*ma*(?)-*ia-an*
Edge [*ub*]-*la-am*

NOTES

(1) Lines 1-10 are translated in CAD M/1 379b; CAD M/1 439a posits a form *mazrû*, separate from *mazruttu*, *mazrūtu*—also a basket, and translates our form as "sowing basket." The latter term, *mazruttu*, is translated lexically as "gleaning basket" (cf. AHw 637b). CAD Z 71b posits the existence of 2 "homophonous" Akkadian roots ZR^{c}—one "to sow" and the other "to winnow." Von Soden, on the other hand (AHw 637b), combines "sowing" and "winnowing" in the single term *mazrūtu*; if he is correct, then *mazrû* here (and in OBTIV 261:2, pp. 70f.) may be construed as an older plural form alongside of later *mazrūtu*, with *mazruttu* being a late "back-formation" from the later plural. Note that CAD M/1 379b also translates *mazrû* as "winnowing baskets."

(2) AHw 628a and CAD M/1 325b recognize a possible relationship between /*maslaḫu*/ and /*mašlaḫu*/. The first form is only attested in the meaning of "sprinkling pot"; the latter—our term here, attested so far only at Ishchali—is obscure. A relationship to "sprinkling" is made questionable by ll. 8-12 below, which show a connection of *mašlaḫu* with wagons (*eriqqāti*).

(4) Cf. CAD M/2 258a *lex sect* sub. *mušamqit(t)u*, "fine sieve."

(5) This name is apparently to be read as *Id-majan*. For the writing A.SUK in place of A.ENGUR see note to OBTIV 225:3. For the reading Id for ^{d}ÍD see CAD I 8; according to the passages collected there relating to the role of the river in judgment and the MB PN *Ḫuršān-dajjān* (cited in CAD H 255a) strongly suggest that one should seek here also to read ^{d}*Id-da*(!)*-ia-an*; but this is impossible—both in lines 5 and 11. For *ma-ja-an* one may consider perhaps *meānu* (mānu) "crown" or even the element *mēnu* that is found in some OAkk PNs (see CAD M/2 19f).

OBTIV 257

A21934

Implements; List of Items Given Out

Obv. 5 *i-mu-ù*
1 *i-tu-um*
e-ši-tu-um
2 *ma-aš-qa-ra-tum*
1 *qú-pu-um*
1 *mu-ša-am-qí-tu-um*
1 *ma-*⸢*da*⸣(?)*-nu-um*
Rev. *a-na Maš-kán-*A*-bi*
ša 30*-mu-ba-li*⸢*-iṭ*⸣
^{1}A*-pil-Ku-*⸢*bi*⸣
ù ARAD.^{d}[UTU] [ ]

NOTES

(1) Lines 1-7 are translated in CAD M/2 258a *sub mušamqittu*.

(7) See CAD M/1 208b as the likeliest suggestion, in preference to reading *ma-da-nim* as a PN, which was done in CAD M/1 11a; see the note to UCP 10/1 3:7 for discussion.

(8) "To Maškan-Abi"; this is the destination of the items in lines 1-7.

(11) One expects lines 9-11 to say something like "which PN$_1$, PN$_2$, and PN$_3$ transported"; thus one might restore the verb [*ub-lu*] or [*il-qu-(ù)*] at the end of line 11.

OBTIV 259

A21936

Implements; Memo on Items Given Out

Obv. (1) 4 *ma-ru-ù*
ku-uš-ti-bu-um
Ṣí-il-Be-el-ga-še-⌜er⌝
a-na A-*ga-ga-a*
Rev. – uninscribed –

NOTES

(1) CAD K 601b reads 4 *ma-ru ù ku-uš-ti-bu-um*; this is unlikely for two reasons: first, the writing of *ù* on the previous line, and second, the well attested Ishchali custom of writing plurals in *ù*; cf. *i-mu-ù*, OBTIV 257:1; *pa-nu-ù*, *ma-az-ru-ù* OBTIV 261:1f; *zi-ru-ù* OBTIV 251:3, to cite a few examples. This memo thus describes "4 spades (plus) a dust shovel" which "Ṣil-Belgašer (took) to Agaga." Our translation "dust shovel" is based on the Sumerian lexical equivalent giš.mar.saḫar.ra (cited in CAD K 601b).

OBTIV 260

A21939

Implements; Memo on Items Given Out

Obv. (1) 1 *mar eḫ-zi-im*
1 *mar-ru-um* ⌜*iš-šu*(!)⌝*-um*
3 *ku-uš-ra-ḫu*
[1]ARAD(!)-EŠ$_4$.DAR
Rev. (5) *a-na pí pa-al-gi-im*

NOTES

(1) "1 thin (bladed) shovel"; cf. the note to OBTIV 265:27; our passage is cited by CAD M/1 287b.

(2) "1 new shovel."

(3) Cf. CAD K 600a for our passage.

(4) The items in lines 1-3 were given to "Warad-Ištar at (literally "unto") the inlet of the canal."

OBTIV 262

A21941

Implements; List of Items Given Out

Obv. ⸢6⸣ *ku-uš-r*[*a-ḫ*]*u*
^{1}*Si-bi-lu-um*
6 *ku-uš-ra-ḫu*
^{1}I-*lí-tu-ra-*⸢*am*⸣(?)
3 *ku-uš-ra-ḫu*
^{1}*Ra-šu-bi-tum*
Rev. 2 *ku-u*[*š-ra-ḫu*]
a-na *Tu-tu-*x x x
6 *ku-uš-ra-ḫu*
1-na É(?) ARAD.^{d}UTU
3 *ku-uš-ra-ḫu*
I-*pí-iq-Ìr-*⸢*ra*⸣

NOTES

(1) *Kušraḫḫu* is so far only attested at Ishchali; cf. CAD K 600a. It is not part of a wagon as suggested by CAD there; CAD M/1 382b offers a corrected reading of OBTIV 266:2, where we find 6 *kuš-ra-ḫu ša ma-aš-qà-ra-tim*. The meaning of *mašqartu*, as CAD M/1 382b notes, is however also obscure and is likewise attested so far only at Ishchali. CAD K 600a conjectures that *kušraḫḫu* may be a loan-word from Sumerian.

(2) Lines 2, 4, 6, 12 contain the names of persons who were apparently given the *kušraḫḫu*s enumerated in lines 1, 3, 5, 11.

(8) One would wish to read a PN in this line, following the pattern described above and also apparent in lines 9-10 (see presently). The first unread sign may be [*ub*] but the next two cannot be [*ma-gir*(!)] (it is the *gir* rather than the *ma* which is the problem). In OBTIV p. 98b we read *Tu-tu-*[*ub*]^{KI} using the first and third unread signs and assigned the second to line 7, reading *ku-u*[*š-ra-ḫu*]*-ù*(?). But there is no real reason to read *ù* in line 7 since it is not written elsewhere in connection with a plural of *kušraḫḫum*.

(9) Lines 9-10 state: "6 *kušraḫḫu* (implements) to the house of Warad-Šamaš."

OBTIV 263

A7693

Utensils and Implements; List of Items

Obv. ⸢x x⸣ [ ]
1 GIŠ ⸢x⸣ [ ]
1 *ḫa-ṣ*[*í-nu* X MA].NA ⸢KI.LAL.BI⸣

2 *ša-an-da-la-tum ša* 3 SILA$_3$
4 AN.ZA.AB ša ⸢1/2⸣ SILA$_3$
2 *ma-aš-ka-nu* 12 MA.NA KI.LAL.BI
1 *ne-em-si-tum*
1 *pa-šu-um* 1/2 MA.NA K[I.LA]L.BI
1 *ḫa-pu-tum* 1/2 MA.NA KI.LAL.BI
1 *ši-ik-rum ša ab-ni-im*
Rev. *it-qú-ra-tum* 2/3 MA.NA 4 GÍN KI.LAL.BI

OBTIV 265

A21924 + 21925

Implements; List of Items and Persons

Obv. 2 *ki-ir-gu*
ARAD-^{d}*Ma-mi*
a-na Ḫu(!)*-ri-ib-ši-im*
ŠU.BA.AN.TI
⸢4⸣ *na-al-ba-na-tum*
⸢*ša a-gu*⸣*-ri-im*
[*ki-iš-k*]*i-ru-um*
[ ] ⸢*ka-ra-*x⸣
[^{1}] ⸢30-*e-ri-ba-am*⸣
DUMU *Na-ra-am-ì-lí-*⸢*šu*⸣
1 *na-al-ba-tum*
1 *ki-iš-ki-ru-um*
L.E. *ša a-gu-ri-im*
Rev. ^{1}*Ri-im-*^{d}IM
DUMU *Ku-ri-ti-im*
1 *na-al-ba-*⸢*tum ša*(?) *ki*⸣*-li-im*
1 *ki-iš-ki-*[*ru-u*]*m*
[3]0-*din-*≪⸢x⸣≫*-nam*
[ ] ⸢x⸣*-zi-tú*
[30-*i-d*]*in-nam*
[DUMU A-*pi*]*l-ì-lí-šu*
[1 *na-a*]*l-ba-tum*
[1 *ki-i*]*š-ki-ru-um*
1 *ša-ḫa-ru-um*
1 *ma-ad-lu-um*
1 *tu-up-ši-ku*
2 *ma-ru-ù* ⸢*ša te*⸣*-li-*⸢x⸣
U.E. 1 *ma-ru-um ša* ⸢*eḫ-zi-im*⸣

Edge ¹*A-a*-⸢x⸣ [ ] ⸢x⸣-*ak*

NOTES

(1) Lines 1-4 state: "Warad-Mami took 2 . . . to Ḫuribšum."

(5) Lines 5-6 list: "4 molds for baked bricks"; cf. lines 12-13 below.

(9) Lines 5-10 apparently form a unit with verb omitted: "Sin-eribam son of Naram-ilišu (took/ borrowed) . . . (the items listed in lines 5-8)."

(11) Lines 11-15 form a unit: "Rim-Adad son of Kuritum (took) 1 brick mold, 1 board for (making) baked bricks." CAD K 424a translates lines 11-13.

(18) The grouping of lines 16-21 are uncertain; lines 20-21 seem to close a unit but the apparent repetition of the PN Sin-iddinam in line 18 raises questions: do lines 16-18 form one unit and line 19-21 another separate unit? Or, would one restore [*ù A-pi*]*l-ì-lí-šu* in line 21 and take lines 19-21 to be an item stored by Sin-iddinam and Apil-ilišu, with the items in lines 16-17 being held only by the former?

(27) Lines 27-28 are cited by CAD M/1 287b but no reading is suggested for the end of line 27. We translate them "2 shovels . . . 1 shovel with thin blade." For *eḫzu* cf. CAD A/1 217b (*sub aḫzu*, which is apparently more an adjective than a substantive).

(29) One expects a PN at the beginning of this line (so OBTIV p. 78a); the end of the line should contain a patronymic or a verb.

OBTIV 266

A21928

Implements; List of Items

Obv.

6 *ku-uš-ra-ḫu*
ša ma-aš-qà-ra-tim
5 [*k*]*u-uš-ra-ḫu*
4 *ma-za-ku*
⸢4⸣ *mi*-ḪI-tu_4
⸢2⸣ *ka-bil-lu*
ga(?)-*i-tu*
2 *mes*(?)-*rik*(?)-*ku*
4 *ḫa-aḫ-ḫa-ru*
3 *ša-šu-gu*
⸢x⸣-*bu-tum*
⸢x⸣-*nu-um*
⸢x⸣-*bu-tum*
[ ] ⸢x x⸣-*ru*

[ ] ⌈x x⌉ [ ] ⌈x⌉-*tim*

Rev. *ša* ⌈*a*⌉-*bu-tim*

ša ⌈*A*⌉-*ga-ša-a*

NOTES

(1) For lines 1-3 see note to OBTIV 262:1.

(6) Perhaps this form is to be related to *kabbillum*, which CAD K 20a takes to be part of a chariot frame. CAD M/1 103a supports this interpretation, saying that line 5 appears in a "list of parts of a wagon." *Ga*(?)-*i-tu* in line 7 appears to be an adjective in the plural.

(10) Line 10 reads "3 pieces of *šaššugu* wood"; cf. note to OBTIV 251:1; for the use of this wood in building wagons, see Salonen, *Landfahrzeuge* 143. It may be possible to read ⌈*ra*⌉-*bu*-tu_4 in line 11 and thus have 11. 10-11 contain "3 large pieces of š. wood."

(12) In OBTIV 251:2, pieces of *bīnu* wood (tamarisk) are listed after pieces of *šaššugu* wood. One may consider reading ⌈*bi*⌉$_4$-*nu-um* in line 12; but then how to fit this together with possible ⌈*ra*⌉-*bu-tum* in line 13? One would have expected *rabûm*, sg. or else a pl. form in line 12. One may also consider reading in 11. 11-12 ⌈*bu*⌉-*bu-tum* ⌈*im*⌉(!)-*nu-um* "a right side *bubūtum*"; cf. CAD B 302b and OBTIV 261:6 which shows the use of this term along with *kabbilum* (see line 6) at Ishchali.

(16) Apparently a PN, *Agašaja*. It is likewise possible, if there were some compelling reason, to consider reading *A-ga-ga*(!)-*a*, which is well-known GN in the Ishchali corpus.

OBTIV 281

A7630

School Tablet; List of Names

Obv. ^{1}*A-ia-e-ni-iš-ì-lí*

^{1}*Su-mu-bi-na-šu*

^{1}*Su-mu-ṭe-el-du-ri*

^{1}*Su-mu-a-bu-um*

^{1}*Ia-ap-ḫu-ur-li-im*

^{1}*Ia*-⌈*aḫ*⌉-*ni*-DINGIR

^{1}*Nu-nu*-APIN

^{1}⌈*Ia*⌉-*an-ti-na-ra-aḫ*

⌈^{Id}ŠEŠ.KI⌉-[ ]

^{Id}*Ḫa*-[ ]

Edge ^{d}ŠE.SUM.NI ZA.<SAL> (?)

NOTES

(11) If line 11 is correctly restored, then this tablet must be a scribal PN list similar to 280; Çiğ and Kizilyay AS 16 41f record the presence of the formula ᵈNidaba zag.sal on scribal PN lists from Nippur. Our tablet appears to be an excerpt from a list of Amorite PNs similar to the one commented on by Chiera PBS 11/12 111f. Cf. further TIM 2 17.

OBTIV 284

A21874

Exercise Tablet; Leather Items

Obv.	(1)	⌈dub x⌉	
		kuš	gud
		kuš	am
		⌈kuš⌉	⌈am.si⌉
	(5)	⌈kuš⌉	⌈am.si⌉.[kur.ra]
Rev.		– illegible –	

NOTES

This tablet appears to be an excerpt based on Hh XI 2-10 (MSL 7 123), specifically ll. 2,8,9.10. Our school text gives the proper sequence of lines in Hh XI, correctly omitting ll. 3-7 as we now also see from the correction in MSL IX 176. Cf. the OB forerunner to Hh XI (MSL 7 213f) ll. 14,20-22.

OBTIV 287

A7656

Exercise Tablet; Fish

Obv.	(1)	⌈ubi⌉ KU_6
		⌈ubi⌉.ab.ba KU_6
		izi KU_6
Rev.		– uninscribed –

NOTES

(1) Line 3 is the same as MSL 8/2 101 (Hh XVIII) 17 = *nu-ú-nu i-šá-ti* "the fire fish." Ll. 1-2 very much resemble Hh XVIII 11-12 (MSL 8/2 96-101) ubi KU_6 and ubi.a.ab.ba which equal *a-bu-tum* and MIN *tam-ti* respectively. The first sign in ll. 1-2 would thus appear to be ubi or SUḪUR(?) x ŠE, a graphic variant of ŠE+SUḪUR described by Landsberger on p. 100 in his note to Hh XVIII 11.

OBTIV 288

A21896

Exercise Tablet; Goats

Obv. (1) zeḫ(SAL.ÁŠ.GÀR)

zeḫ.ga

zeḫ.gì[š.zu].zu

Rev. – uninscribed –

NOTES

(1) Ll. 1-3 appear to be an excerpt from Hh XIII belonging to the section MSL 8/1 (Hh XIII) 276-277; zeḫ.ga apparently represents 1. 276a, sandwiched between zeḫ and zeḫ.gìš.zu on the analogy of sila$_4$.ga, Hh XIII 241, and of amar.ga which appears in Hh XIII 341 some eight lines before [amar.zu].zu in l. 350.

(3) On the reading of this line cf. the variant zeḫ.gìš.zu.zu in the Nippur forerunner cited by MSL 8/1 86 line 172, corresponding to Hh XIII 277 zeḫ.gìš.zu.

OBTIV 290

A21882

Exercise Tablet; Wagon Parts

Obv. (1) [g]iš (ERASURE) ⸢šudun⸣.mar.⸢gíd.da⸣

[g]iš.kak.⸢šudun⸣.mar.⸢gíd.da⸣

[g]iš.ŠID.bar.[ra]

Rev. – illegible –

NOTES

(1) Our text seems to be an excerpt from Hh V, however it reflects a *vorlage* not quite identical with MSL VI. Ll. 1-2 are not found in the extant edition of Hh V but closely parallel Hh V 49-50 (MSL VI 9) giš.šudul.gigir = *nīru*, giš.kak.šudul.gigir = *sikkat nīrim*. For šudun/šudul cf. Civil JAOS 88 (1968) 9f and AHw 793b. The erasure in line 1 is apparently for KAK which appears in 1.2.

(3) GIŠ.ŠID.bar.ra appears in V$_4$ 2, a forerunner to Hh V 68 giš.na$_4$.ŠID.bar.ra = *tak-da-*[x], cited in MSL VI 11. Cf. also giš.ŠID.umbin mar.gíd.da = *kanasarru*, (MSL VI) Hh V 99, which CAD K 143b explains as "part of the wagon wheel, probably the pole pin."

OBTIV 292

A21948

Table of Area Measures

Obv. col. i

			Sexagesimal Notation	Conventional Equivalent
[1/3	SAR		0;20]	20/60 (SAR)
[1/2	SAR		0;30]	30/60
⸢2/3⸣	SAR		0;40	40/60
[5/6]	SAR		0;50	50/60
[1]	SAR		1	1 (SAR)
⸢1 1/3⸣	SAR		1;20	1 + 20/60
⸢1 1/2⸣	SAR		1;30	1 + 30/60
⸢1 2/3⸣	SAR		1;40	1 + 40/60
⸢1 5/6⸣	SAR		1;50	1 + 50/60
[2]	SAR		2	2 etc.
⸢3⸣	SAR		3	
⸢4⸣	SAR		4	
⸢5⸣	SAR		5	
6	SAR		6	
7	SAR		7	
8	⸢SAR⸣		8	
9	⸢SAR⸣		9	
10	SAR		10	
11	SAR		11	
⸢12	SAR		12⸣	
⸢13	SAR		13⸣	
14	⸢SAR⸣		14	
⸢15	SAR⸣		15	
16	SAR		16	
17	SAR		17	
18	SAR		18	
19	SAR		19	
20	SAR		20	
SANTAK$_2$	GÁN		25	
30	SAR		30	
40	SAR		40	
SANTAK$_3$	GÁN		50	
SANTAK$_3$	GÁN	10 SAR	1,0	60 (SAR) i.e. 60[1]
SANTAK$_3$	GÁN	20 SAR	1,10	70
SANTAK$_3$	GÁN	30 SAR	1,20	80

Obv. col. ii

			Sexagesimal Notation	Conventional Equivalent
[			]	
[1	GÁN]	⸢40 SAR⸣	[2,20]	140
[SANTAK$_3$]	GÁN		2,30	150
2	GÁN		3,20	200
[3]	GÁN		5,0	300
5	GÁN		8,20	500
1 eše	GÁN		10,0	600
1 eše, 1	GÁN		11,40	700
1 eše, 2	GÁN		13,20	800
1 eše, 3	GÁN		15,0	900
1 eše, 4	GÁN		16,40	1000
1 eše, 5	GÁN		18,20	1100
2 eše	GÁN		20,0	1200
2 eše, 1	⸢GÁN		21,40⸣	1300
⸢2 eše, 2	GÁN⸣		23,20	1400
[2 eše, 3]	GÁN		25,0	1500
[2 eše], 4	GÁN		⸢26,40⸣	1600 (SAR)
[2 eš]e, 5	GÁN		28,20	1700
1 bùr	GÁN		30,0	1800
1 bùr, 1 eše	GÁN		40,0	2400
1 bùr, 2 eše	GÁN		50,0	3000
2 bùr,	GÁN		1,0,0	3600 i.e. 60^2
3 bùr	GÁN		1,30,0	5400
4 bùr	GÁN		2,0,0	7200
5 bùr	GÁN		2,30,0	9000
6 bùr	GÁN		3,0,0	10,800
7 bùr	GÁN		3,30,0	12,600
8 bùr	GÁN		⸢4,0,0⸣	14,400
9 bùr	G[ÁN		4,30,0]	16,200
1 bùr.u	GÁ[N		5,0,0]	18,000
1 bùr.u, 1 bùr	⸢GÁN		5⸣,[30,0]	19,800
1 bùr.u, 2 bùr	GÁN		[6,0],0	21,600
1 bùr.u, 3 bùr	GÁN		6,30,0	23,400
1 bùr.u, 4 bùr	GÁN		⸢7,0,0⸣	25,200

Rev. col. iii

		Sexagesimal Notation	Conventional Equivalent
1 bùr.u, ⸢5⸣ bùr	GÁN	7,30,0	27,000
1 bùr.u, ⸢6 bùr	GÁN⸣	8,0,0	28,800
1 bùr.u, ⸢7 bùr	GÁN	8,30,0	30,600
1 bùr.u, 8 bùr	GÁN	⸢9,0,0⸣	32,400
1 bùr.u, 9 bùr	⸢GÁN	9,30,0⸣	34,200
2 bùr.u	GÁN	10,0,0	36,000

Rev. col. iii

		Sexagesimal Notation	Conventional Notation
3 bùr.u	⸢GÁN⸣	15,0,0	54,000
⸢4 bùr.u⸣	GÁN⸣	20,0,0	72,000 (SAR)
5 bùr.u	⸢GÁN⸣	25,0,0	90,000
1 šár	⸢GÁN⸣	30,0,0	108,000
1 šár, 1 bùr.u	⸢GÁN⸣	35,0,0	126,000
1 šár, ⸢2 bùr.u	GÁN	40,0,0⸣	144,000
1 šár ⸢3 bùr.u	GÁN	45,0,0⸣	162,000
⸢1 šár, 4 bùr.u⸣	GÁN	⸢50,0,0⸣	180,000
[1 šár], ⸢5⸣ bùr.u	GÁN	55,0,0	198,000
⸢2 šár⸣	GÁN	1,0,0,0	216,000 i.e. 60^3
⸢3 šár⸣	GÁN	1,30,0,0	324,000
[4 šár]	⸢GÁN⸣	2,0,0,0	432,000
[5 šár]	⸢GÁN⸣	2,⸢30,0,0⸣	540,600
⸢6 šár	GÁN⸣	3,0,0,0	648,000
⸢7 šár	GÁN⸣	3,30,0,0	756,000
⸢8 šár⸣	GÁN	4,0,0,0	864,000
⸢9 šár	GÁN⸣	4,30,0,0	972,000
⸢1 šár.u	GÁN	5,0,0,0⸣	1,080,000
⸢1 šár.u, 1 šár	GÁN	5⸣,30,0,0	1,188,000
1 šár.u, ⸢2 šár	GÁN	6,0,0,0⸣	1,296,000
1 šár.u, ⸢3 šár	GÁN	6,30,0,0⸣	1,404,000
[1 šár.u, 4 šár]	GÁN	7,0,0,0	1,512,000
[1 šár.u], ⸢5⸣ šár	GÁN	7,⸢30⸣,0,0	1,620,000

Rev. col. iv

1 šár.u, 6 šár	GÁN	8,0,0,0	1,728,000
1 šár.u, 7 šár	GÁN	8,30,0,0	1,836,000
1 šár.u, 8 šár	GÁN	9,0,0,0	1,944,000 (SAR)
1 šár.u, 9 šár	GÁN	9,[30,0,0,]	2,052,000
1 šár.niš	GÁN	10,0,0,0	2,160,000
[1 šár.ušù]	GÁN	15,0,0,0	3,240,000
[1 šár.nimin]	GÁN	20,0,0,0	4,320,000
[1 šár.ninnu]	GÁN	25,0,0,0	5,400,000
1 ŠÁRxGÉŠ.GEL	GÁN	30,0,0,0	6,480,000
1 ŠÁRxGÉŠ.MIN.GAL	⸢GÁN⸣	1,0,0,0,0	12,960,000 i.e. 60^4

NOTES

Obv. (1′) 1/3 SAR equals in sexagesimal notation 0;20 or 20 GÍN; ll. 2-5 continue in increments of 10 GÍN until l. 5 which is 60 GÍN or 1 SAR. How many lines preceded this 1/3 SAR entry is uncertain; one might expect an entry for 1/6 SAR = 0;10, i.e. 10 GÍN, but one cannot be certain about how many additional lines may have preceded the entry for 10 GÍN. On this question of missing lines, see further the note for col. ii: 1′, where 4 additional lines are suggested.

(6′) 1 1/3 SAR = 1(SAR) + 20(GÍN), i.e. 1;20.

(20′) For SANTAK_2 and its varying degrees of "tilting" to represent 25 SAR, cf. Powell ZA 62 (1972) 194ff, 216, 218. According to Ea II 209 (cited by Powell, loc. cit.) ú-za-LAK = SANTAK_2 = 25 SAR. Powell, ZA 62 (1972) 203, maintains that GÁN is a semantic indicator for area and was not read as iku in Sumerian texts of the 3rd millennium, although this reading was introduced in the OB period. This text appears to purposefully alternate GÁN and SAR in 11. 29′-35′ as well as in ii: 2′. We will, however, leave the sign as GÁN and make no final judgment as to its reading here.

(32′) Powell ZA 62 (1972) loc. cit. describes SANTAK_2 tilted as here and cites Ea II 200 *ú-bu* = SANTAK_2 = *ú-bu-ú*.

Obv. ii (1′) Working back from 11. 2′-3′, one might reconstruct in 1. 1′ [1 GÁN 30 SAR = 2,10] and in the unestimated break seek; [1 GÁN 20 SAR = 1,50], [1 GÁN = 1,40], [SANTAK_3 GÁN 40 SAR = 1,30]. Col. i appears to have ended with 1. 35′ – SANTAK_3 GÁN 30 SAR = 1,20, and no more than at the most two lines can be interpolated between i:35′ and ii: 1′; the top of the tablet is clearly preserved and there is just no room for all of these intermediate values.

iii (24) 1 šár.u = 1 šár x 10, i.e. 108,000 x 10 = 1,080,000.

iv (5ff) 1 šár.niš = 1 šar x 20, i.e. 108,000 x 20 = 2,160,000.
1 šár.ušù = 1 šár x 30. 1 šár.ninnu = 1 šár x 50.

(9f) For the numbers šár.u through ŠÁRxGÉŠ.GAL cf. CT 12 24 Col. ii: 1-8. We can interpret ŠÁRxGÉŠ.GAL as 1 sár x 60, i.e. 108,000 x 60 = 6,480,000; 1 ŠÁR.GÉŠ.MIN.GAL is šár x 120 or 108,000 x 120 = 12,960,000. From the evidence of the tablet it appears that only ŠÁRxGÉŠ.MIN.GAL (or ŠÁR.GAL+GEŠ.MIN in CT 12 24 ii:8) is equal to 60^4; and that, in CT 12 24 ii:6-7, ŠAR.GEŠ and ŠAR.GAL+GÉŠ are but graphic variants of the same number–1 šár x 60 or 6,480,000. We would imagine that the term šár.gal šu.nu.tag, BE 10/1 29 obv. 4:9 (also cited by ŠL 408), should be reserved only for 60^4. These problems are more fully discussed by Powell in his dissertation (unpub.) *Sumerian Numeration and Metrology* (University of Minnesota, 1971), pp. 74ff.

OBTIV 302

A21959

Literary Text

NOTES

Rev. 4′ Perhaps [^{d}NIN].KAR.RA.AK; cf. the incantation mentioning divine dogs cited in CAD K 71a. Cf. further [*ka-al-bu-um ṣ*]*a-al-mu-um*, *ka-al-bu-um* ⌜SIG_7⌝, [*ka-al-bu*]*-um sa-mu-um* mentioned in lines obv. 1-3.

OBTIV 304

A22009

Apparent Forgery

NOTES

The text of this tablet is unintelligible; the wedges do not "hang" from the ruled lines in the normal way; the "text" of the reverse is written on an unexpected axis in relation to the axis of the obverse. For all of these reasons we would have dismissed this tablet as an outright forgery if it were not for the find spot data (cf. OBTIV p. 57); only because of this data has the tablet been retained in the corpus.

CHAPTER 3

ADDITIONS AND CORRECTIONS TO OLD BABYLONIAN TABLETS FROM ISHCHALI AND VICINITY (OBTIV)

p. 2[7] To the list of Oriental Institute Ishchali tablets published outside of OBTIV one should add A7895 A-B, MSL XI pp. 147, 160.

p. 3 In note 12, bottom three lines–"Index" not index".

p. 6 Add to list of persons who bear the title SANGA: *Awat-ilim* (INIM-DINGIR) 243:12.

p. 19 Išme-Bali is included among the rulers of Ishchali because of his year date formula MU *Iš-me-ba-li* LUGAL BÀD GAL *Ne-ri-ib-tum* BA.DÍM.MA, cited in the discussion of Harris, JCS 9 (1955) p. 47 no. 21.

p. 29 The translation of year date formula no. 26 should be translated "The year the golden plow (entered) the temple of Tišpak".

p. 29[35] The verb *iḫazu* has caused some discussion since the expected form of *aḫāzum* would be *iḫuzu*. This problem is excellently summarized by K. Deller Or. 35 (1966) 33-35 (reference courtesy of M. Stol). Deller in his discussion already noted the relationship between the various formula variants discussed under year date formula 25 but some of the readings he gives must be changed in view of our collations. Deller suggests that *i-ḫa-zu* represents *imḫaṣṣu* > *iḫḫaṣṣu* "he smote," which would fit well with the variants with BA.SÌG.

p. 44 The literary content of OBTIV 302 has now been confirmed by W. Farber, ZA 71 (1981) 57f; it is an incantation.

p. 75 Line 29) should read [*ṣi*]-*im-da-a*[*t*].

p. 78 To the list of conventions add *Warad* = ARAD.
Sub PN A . . . , ^{d}A . . . omit 1).
A-bi-sa-ma-SU not *su*.
In footnote, it should state: "The PNs listed in texts no. 280-282 have not been included in the index. . . ."
*Sub A-da-a-a, A-da-ia** read:
1) s. of ⌈*Tà*⌉-*ab-ṣil*-⌈*la-šu*⌉
5) f. of ^{d}*Sin-ba-ni*, 31:4.

p. 79 *Sub Aḫam-arši* (ŠEŠ.PA.TUK) read 241:15.

p. 80 Read *A-ša-<si>-šu-um-ilum* in place of *A-ra(?)-šu-um-ilum*, *Ar-wu-um* (*Arwum*) in place of *Ar-wi-im.*
Von Soden, ZA 71 (1981) 150 suggests possibly *A-ṣú*(?)*-tum*(!?) in place of *A-su-šum*(?)
For ⸢*Awīlam*⸣*(?)-mu-ba-lí-iṭ* read now ⸢*Mītam*⸣(LU.BAD)*-mu-ba-lí-iṭ*.

p. 81 Omit BARAG(?)⸢BIL(?)⸣ 120:6.
Read ⸢*Bu-ni-ṭà-a-bu-um*⸣.
*Sub Bu-ri-ia, Bur(?)-ri-ia** 1) s. of *Ip-qú-ša*
read 34:19 in place of 34:9.
Sub Bu-ur-Sin etc. read:
1) s. of ⸢*I*⸣*-bi-*^{d}*T*[*išpak*]
2) f. of AN-(*um*)-KA-^{d}*Šamaš*, 34:24.***
Read *Bu-*⸢x-x⸣ in place of *Bu-*[*ti*(?)*-ta*].
In place of ⸢*Da-qa-tum*⸣ read ⸢IŠ*-qa-tum*⸣.

p. 82 *Sub E-ri-ib-*^{d}*Sin* etc. 4) and 5) should be merged into a single entry.
Read . . . , *Ga-*⸢*mil*(?)*-lum*(?)⸣ (add missing half-bracket).

p. 83 *I-bi-*^{d}*Sin* 73:16(R) is out of alphabetic order and should be placed with *Ib-bi-Sin* etc. further down on the page.
Sub Ib-bi-Sin, etc. omit 2) f. of Bur-^{d}S[in], 29:29 (s) and see now *sub I-bi-*^{d}T[IŠPAK].
Insert entry for *I-bi-*^{d}T[ISPAK] f. of *Bur-*^{d}*Sin* following UCLMA 9/2827:4.

p. 84 Read *I-la-ma-*⸢x⸣ in place of *I-la-ma-*⸢*lik*⸣.
Ì-lí-iš-qú-tu-ul is out of alphabetic order, this entry belongs after *Ì-lí-šar-ra-*. . .

p. 85 Read *Im-gur-ru-um* in place of *Im-gu-ru-um*.
*Sub Im-gur-rum*** read 1) s. of *A-da-ia*, 79:19(w)** and f. of *Síl-lí-*^{d}*Ištar*, 47:20;** etc.
After *I-mi-ru* insert additional citation, 163:5.
Insert *Iš-qa-tum* after *Iš-me-kə(?)-ra-ab*.

p. 86 Read *Ka-ad-ri-ia* in place of *Ka-at-ri-ia*.
In 229:13 read *Ma-*KU*-ia-tum* rather than *Ma-ki-ia-tum*.

p. 87 Insert *Mītam*(LÚ.BAD)*-mu-ba-lí-iṭ* as read on p. 80 after *Mi-nu-na-tim*.
Sub Mu-na-wi-ru-um, etc. 2) s. of *Ì-lí-Ku-*⸢*bi*⸣ read 35:17 in place of 35:18.

p. 88 Read *Qí-*⸢*ip*⸣*ṭi-ba-al*⸢*ṭí*⸣ (*ṭí* in place of *ṭi*).
Von Soden ZA 71 (1981) 150 reads *Ra-ma-aš* "Liebte ihn" in place of *Ra-ma-rum*.

p. 89 Insert ^{d}*Sin*-x-x, after ^{d}*Sin-*. . . , followed by the entry 273:9. This is in place of ^{d}*Sin-dannum* (KALAG.GÁ) read below.

In place of ^{d}*Sin-dannum* (KALAG.GÁ) etc., read ^{d}*Sin*-x-x, *Sin*-x-x 273:9, 323:9; omit the reference to 319:9.

p. 91 *Su-qà-qù-um, Sú-qà-qu* [*m*]*
1) f. of *Me-ra-nu-um*, 193:3
2) 38: rev. 5′, 169:7.*
Ša-ka-ra(?)-*ḫu* 216:12.

p. 92 *Ši-ip-*⌈DINGIR(?)⌉-*šu*(?) 216:14.
Ta-pí-we-d[*i-m*]*a* (or -*we-d*[*e-k*]*u*) 123:2.
Add *Tu-tu*-x-x-x 262:8.

p. 94 *Za-bu-lum* f. of *Ka-ad-ri-ia* etc.

p. 96 *Sub* SANGA add 243:12.
At bottom of page, note should read: "The DNs in text no. 283, being part etc."

p. 98 *Sub* URU *Tu-tu-ub*^{KI} etc. remove reference to 262:8 (see p. 92).

p. 99 ITU ^{d}DUMU.ZI, ^{d} < DUMU > .ZI* 90:14; 117:4; 121:6;* 133:2.

plate XIV Remove line numbering 10 at L.E. of OBTIV 27 (that line is line 8′).

CHAPTER 4

LUTZ, *LEGAL AND ECONOMIC DOCUMENTS FROM ASHJÂLY* (UCP 10/1) TEXTS, COLLATIONS, AND CORRECTIONS

In the course of reviewing the 110 tablets in Lutz's volume we prepared transliterations for each document. But it would be repetitive to publish these in full inasmuch as Lutz himself supplied these for thirty-three texts[1] and Seif did the same for ten of the texts already treated by Lutz plus another twelve besides,[2] bringing the number of treated texts to forty-five out of the 110.

Moreover, many of the Lutz texts are similar in character. There are forty-two *ḫubuttātum* loans in all; and eleven of these are treated by Lutz and Seif, giving little reason to present all of the thirty-one other *ḫubuttātum* texts in full.[3] So we have seventy-six texts (i.e. forty-five treated plus thirty-one very similar) which are essentially masterable, using available resources. And if we add to these the seven additional Lutz tablets dealing with loans, of which four[4] are treated by either Lutz or Seif, we come to seventy-nine out of 110 texts.

In the above cases, we have usually confined our remarks to difficult or obscure lines in need of elucidation or confirmation and only in a few cases give a full transliteration; and these were, again, for texts that neither Lutz nor Seif had previously treated.[5]

For tablets which were not previously discussed and which are not loans, our presentation is much fuller. For these texts, we usually provide a full transliteration or a partial one that focuses on the difficult lines needing comment or clarification.[6]

We have for all texts included information on signs, words, or passages which, with collation, did not appear as Lutz had copied them. A number of texts are completely omitted in our presentation; but they are all cases where Lutz's copies are accurate and require no comment or correction.[7] Our collations and corrections, henceforth referred to as 'COPY', are found in Chapter 8.1.

[1] UCP 10/1 2, 3, 6, 8, 10-11, 18, 20, 22, 26, 27, 32-34, 36, 43, 48-49, 52, 55, 58, 61-62, 65, 68-69, 90-91, 97, 99, 102, 105, 109.

[2] Seif again treated UCP 10/1 3, 11, 26, 33, 36, 43, 61, 68, 91, 105; she also added to the texts already treated UCP 10/1 4, 9, 12, 23, 28, 46, 53, 58, 66, 75, 77, 94.

[3] The following are *ḫubuttātum* loans, treated by Lutz or Seif: UCP 10/1 2, 6, 8, 9, 18, 20, 23, 32, 34, 61, 69; the other *ḫubuttātum* loans are UCP 10/1 1, 5, 7, 13-17, 19, 21, 24-25, 28-29, 38-40, 42, 44-45, 50, 55, 59, 63, 74, 81, 85, 93, 95, 103-104.

[4] UCP 10/1 4, 46, 68, 77 are treated by either Lutz or Seif; UCP 10/1 51, 80, 82 are not treated but similar. We have in our presentation given full transliterations of UCP 10/1 51, 80; 82, as noted below is a redundant fragment requiring no comment or correction. We have also given a full transliteration of UCP 10/1 46.

[5] We have given full transliterations of UCP 10/1 38 and 74. There are a number of instances where we have felt the need to offer treatment of documents already discussed by Lutz or Seif; this has been the case for UCP 10/1 3, 10, 12, 22, 36, 43, 46, 48, 58, 65, 91, 94, 105.

[6] UCP 10/1 30-31, 35, 37, 41, 47, 54, 56-57, 60, 62, 64, 67, 70-72, 76, 78-80, 83-84, 86-89, 92, 95-96, 98, 100-101, 106-107, 108, 110.

[7] We have omitted UCP 10/1 26, 53 which are treated by Lutz or Seif; also omitted is 45 which is a *hubuttatum* loan; and, in addition, 73 and 82.

UCP 10/1 1

UCLMA 9/2326

Barley *ḫubuttātum* Loan

NOTES

(4) UCP 10/1 p. 63 and Seif 45 read *Ta-ku-ma-tum*; our reading is based on the similar forms of 2nd and 3rd signs (see COPY) and the clearly written *Du-ba-ba-tum* in UCP 10/1 87:3.

(5) "After the moratorium of Dur-Rimuš was established;" see OBTIV pp. 1[1], 6 . See COPY. Here, as in UCP 10/1 18:14, the scribe wrote *iš-ša-*<*ak*>*-nu*; Lutz's copies are inaccurate.

(16) LI is clear.

UCP 10/1 2, p. 21

UCLMA 9/2375

Silver *ḫubuttātum* Loan

. . .

Rev. (14) DUMU *Pa-ra-ri-im*

. . .

IGI *Pu-zú-ur-ša*

(20) DUMU *Qí-šu-šu*

MU ÍD 30-*a-bu-šu iḫ-ru-ú*

NOTES

(14) RA as Lutz.

(19) PN is written over erasure (see COPY).

(20) PN is written over erasure (see COPY).

(21) For *iḫ-* see COPY. For this year date formula see OBTIV p. 31, no. 38.

UCP 10/1 3, p. 29; Seif 33

UCLMA 9/2411

Barley; Talley of Expenditures

Obv. (1) 1(PI) ŠE *a-na Ne-ri-ib-tim*

GÌR ^{d}TIŠPAK-*a-si-i*

1(BÁN) 7 SILA$_3$ ŠÀ.GAL *bu-ra-tim*
i-nu-ma i-di-ša
2(BÁN) 3 SILA$_3$ *a-na na-pí-tim*
ù ma-ḫa-al-tim
2(BÁN) *a-na ma-da-nim*
1(PI) ŠE Á GUD.ḪI.A *ša pu-uḫ*
ar-ḫi-im ša E-ri-ib-^{d}EN.ZU
L.E. *i-li-ku*
1(PI) ŠÀ.GAL *ar-ḫi-im*
ša E-ri-ib-^{d}EN.ZU
Rev. *i-nu-ma ri-qa-at*
1(BÁN) *a-na mi-ir-ti*
1(BÁN) *ki-sa-at*
ANŠE *i-nu-ma*
par-si Im-gur-^{d}EN.LÍL
ù Ta-ri-ba-tim
ŠU.NIGIN$_2$ 4(PI) 3(BÁN) ŠE ZI.GA

NOTES

(3) For 11. 3f, see CAD B 334a and COPY; the *-tim* of line 3 is directly below the *-tim* of line 1.

(7) Lutz UCP 10/1 p. 29 and Seif 33 take *ma-da-nim* to be a PN; CAD M/1 11a does the same for OBTIV 257:7. Otherwise, both the CAD and AHw 571b know *Madānum* as a DN only; so it is not, by itself, a clear PN. More fitting to the Ishchali contexts is the suggestion that *madānum* is a tool or implement. This is indeed the thinking reflected in CAD M/1 208b, where *ma-da-nim* is put with *mandanu*, a kind of basket (cf. AHw 806a *sub nusḫu*). One should also ponder the possibility of relating this term to OB *maddānu*, CAD M/1 126.

(16) As Seif 33[130] observes, something comparable with what is added above in 11. 4 and 13 is expected here; but there is nothing more on the tablet. The total in line 19 does not include any items beyond line 15.

(17) The second sign is SI rather than 2/3; the last sign is LÍL (see COPY). The sense of 11. 15-18 might thus be: "... fodder for the donkey when (it threshed?) the separate land parcels (cf. *parsum*, AHw 835a) of PN$_1$ and PN$_2$." The missing verb should have appeared after line 18.

UCP 10/1 4; Seif 22

UCLMA 9/2328

Silver Loan with Interest (MÁŠ ^{d}UTU)

...

Obv. (3) KI DINGIR-*šu-na-ṣir*

(4) *ù* ᵈŠEŠ.KI.ARḪUŠ$^{\text{ḪU.UŠ}}$

. . .

Edge (21) MU *Qa-ba-ra*^{KI} ^{1}*I-ma-tum*

(22) *Da-du-ša iṣ-ba-tu* DUB.SA[R]

NOTES

(4) See COPY for PN. This PN is discussed in OBTIV p. 8. For additional examples, see COPY *sub* UCP 10/1 5:3, 6:4, 7:3, 8:5, 13:3, 14:4, 21:4, 28:6, 39:4, 40:4, 42:9, 44:4, 68:4, 69:7, 85:3, 93:2, 95:3.

(12) See COPY for ᵈGÌR.

(20) As Lutz's copy; there is room at the end of the line for no more than [*ni*] plus, at most, one other small sign.

(21) The form of the MA sign is "equivocal," allowing the possibility of BA as well (see COPY); but cf. also UCP 10/1 7:15 (COPY) and 108:33, which appears just as Lutz copied it.

(22) DA is as Lutz copied it; the last two signs are DUB.SA[R] (see COPY). The name of the scribe, Imatum, is written at the end of lines 21-22. For the year date formula "The year Daduša captured Qabara" see OBTIV p. 33, no. 52.

UCP 10/1 5
UCLMA 9/2339
Barley *ḫubuttātum* Loan

NOTES

(5) DUMU ARAD-ᵈTIŠPAK(!); see COPY.

(8) Lower edge, following line 8, is uninscribed except for erasure (see COPY).

UCP 10/1 6, p. 34
UCLMA 9/2327
Barley *ḫubuttātum* Loan

NOTES

(4) See COPY for lines 4-6.

UCP 10/7
UCLMA 9/2344
Barley *ḫubuttātum* Loan

. . .

Obv. (4) [1]EN.ZU-*i-din-nam* *Ia-ás*(!)-*kur*-DINGIR

. . .

Rev. (15) IGI *I-ma-tum* DUB.SAR

(16) DUMU *Ri-im*-^{d}IM

U.E. (17) MU *Ma-an*-[*ki-su*]^{KI}

(18) *Da-du-ša iṣ-ba-tu*

NOTES

(4) See COPY: this PN is found, identically written, in Huffmon, *Amorite*, p. 246.

(14) This PN (same individual) is written *Ia-ar-ši-nu-um* in UCP 10/1 13:3.

(15) See COPY and note to UCP 10/1 4:21.

(17) See COPY for 11.17-18. The year date is "The year Dadusa captured Mankisu"; it is OBTIV p. 32 no. 47.

Lutz, UCP 10/1 8, p. 28
UCLMA 9/2324
Barley *ḫubuttātum* Loan

. . .

Rev. (12) IGI ^{d}EN.[ZU] ⌜*ù*⌝(!) ^{d}UTU

[1]*A-bu-um*-DINGIR DUMU ^{d}EN.ZU-*eri*$_{4}$-*ba*

[1]*An-um*-KA-^{d}UTU *ù* *Ip-qú-ša*

(15) DUMU.MEŠ *Bur*-^{d}EN.ZU

ù *Mu-na-nu-um*

U.E. MU *Ra-pí-qum*^{KI} BA.GUL

NOTES

(12) The third sign from the end of the line must be [*ù*] despite the apparent traces (see COPY); *maḫar Sin ù Šamaš* also occurs in UCP 10/1 9:11 and in OBTIV 53:12. For divine witnesses,

see p. 196 below. Stamm, *Namengebung* 135c considered these to be PNs invoking two divinities.

(17) For the year date formula, cf. OBTIV p. 33 no. 53.

UCP 10/1 9; Seif 24
UCLMA 9/2355
Barley *ḫubuttātum* Loan

. . .

Obv. (6) *i-na Ša-du-tim*

(7) *a-na* Ì.DUB *il-qú*

L.E. (8) *še-a-am ú-ta-ar*

(ERASURE)

. . .

Rev. ^{1}*Iš-du-ki-nu-um*

DUMU *Na-ra-am-ì-lí-šu*

^{1}*Še-li-bu*

DUMU *Im-gur-*^{d}EN.ZU

Edge (20) MU SAḪAR *zi-ku-ra-*[*at*] ^{d}UTU<<DIŠ>>

NOTES

(7) See COPY.

(8) There is an erasure below line 8 (see COPY).

(14) See COPY.

(15) See COPY.

(20) See COPY. For the year date formula, see OBTIV p. 34 no. 55.

UCP 10/1 10, p. 21
UCLMA 9/2405
Flour and Barley; Tally of Shares

Obv. (1) 10 GUR ZÍD *zi-ti*

^{1}*Im-gur-*^{d}EN.LÍL

5 GUR ZÍD *zi-ti*

^{1d}EN.ZU-TAB.BA-*we-di*

2 GUR ZÍD *a-na ga-gi-im*
1 GUR ZÍD *mu-ṣí-e*
1 GUR *a-na im-ta-ti*(!)
4(BÁN) *mu(!)-ša-di-nu*
L.E. ⌜4⌝(BÁN) *a-na* KAŠ
SU.NIGIN$_2$ 19(GUR) 1(PI) 2(BÁN) GUR ZÍD
Rev. 9(GUR) 4(PI) 4(BÁN) GUR ŠE
zi-ti Im-gur-^{d}EN.LÍL
4(GUR) 4(PI) 5(BÁN) GUR ŠE *zi-ti*
^{Id}EN.ZU-TAB.BA-*we-di*
2(BÁN) *ki-sa-at* ANŠE.MEŠ
1(BÁN) *a-na* KAŠ
SU.NIGIN$_2$ 15 GUR ŠE.
Edge *na-aš-pa-ak Ḫa-aš-ḫu-ur*

NOTES

(1) CAD Z 142a read ZÍZ for ZÍD in lines 1ff. This is an attractive suggestion since the total for ZÍZ in 1. 10 would nicely "balance" the total for ŠE in 1. 17. Unfortunately, this reading is not really clearly supported by the signs on the tablet (see COPY); the horizontal wedges never really cross the vertical "in strength;" they appear, rather, as "trails" of wedges and not as "purpose-ful" strokes; in line 10, the horizontals do not cross at all and the sign can only be ZÍD. Contrast these "weak" signs with the "robust" ZÍZ in UCP 10/1 23:2. However, other "weak" ZÍZ/AŠ signs also occur in the corpus: UCP 10/1 7:4 (yet this sign has 4 horizontals) and the label *Ma-áš-qum* in UCP 10/1 22; this last sign does not actually appear as Lutz copied it but rather as three horizontals and no "trails" at all (collated but not recopied). But the evidence overall requires us to read ZÍD and not ZÍZ and so we have done. For another Ishchali text dealing with shares, cf. OBTIV 164.

(2) For EN.LÍL instead of EN.ZU in lines 2 and 12, see COPY.

(6) See COPY. For *muṣû*, "a type of garment," see AHw 679b and CAD M/2 245f. Our passage shows the occurrence of this term in OB contexts.

(7) See COPY. The IM has only one vertical but the same thing is true of the IM in line 12 (not as Lutz copied it). The vertical of the TI is not really visible as a wedge; it appears to have been "over-struck" and "obscured" by the *winkelhacken*; only a "depression" remains to suggest its presence. Perhaps we could read this line: *im-*<*mi*>*-ta-ti* (pl. of *imittu*), "taxes."

(8) See COPY; in the MU, the head of the horizontal wedge is very tall at the beginning; there is clear suggestion of a vertical below it (a "trail"); the head of the vertical is less certain. The entire vertical is apparently an erasure.

(9) For the 4(BÁN) see COPY; the total in 1. 10 is correct for the amounts listed in 11. 1-9.

(10) See COPY for line 1 above; the ZÍD sign in line 10 was omitted by Lutz.

(15) See COPY. CAD K 427b and AHw 487a list this passage, along with UCP 10/1 3:5, under the heading "chopped straw (as fodder . . .);" these listings are in error since both texts involve only grain.

(18) See COPY. Seif 47 suggests reading *Ḫa-aš-ḫ*[*u-u*]*r-ri*[*m*]; there is no room on the tablet for more signs. For *našpak Ḫašḫur*—similarly written, cf. OBTIV 137:12f, 229:20.

UCP 10/1 11, pp. 22-23; Seif 27

UCLMA 9/2323

Sale of House

Seal Legends

A *A-bu-um*-DINGIR
DUMU ^{d}EN.ZU-*e-ri-ba-am*
ARAD *ša* ^{d}IM

B *Mu-na-wi-rum*
DUMU *Gu-ul-lu-bi-ia*
ARAD *ša* ^{d}NIN.URTA

NOTES

Seal Legend A

As UCP 10/1 p. 67 states, the seal of Abum-ilum appears on the edge of the tablet; it is also impressed twice on the upper edge. In fact, the entire surface of the tablet is covered with rolled seal impressions.

Seal Legend B

Munanum, the scribe, here uses the seal of his brother Munawwirum; see discussion in OBTIV p. 3[12]. See COPY for Seal Legends A and B.

UCP 10/1 12; Seif 32f.

UCLMA 9/2332

Leather; Record of Sheep and Wolf Hides

Obv.	(1)	6 KUŠ UDU.NITA$_2$ *ša* MU.TÚM ŠÀ 1 KUŠ BAR.SÙ.A	(1)	6 hides (from) rams which were (originally taken in as) income (and) including 1 plucked hide
		7 KUŠ UDU.NITA$_2$		7 ram hides
		1 KUŠ UDU *ši-ni-a-nu*		1 hide of a 2 year old ram
	(5)	14 KUŠ UDU.NITA$_2$	(5)	(Total:) 14 ram hides
		12 KUŠ UR$_4$		12 hides (from) young sheep
		1 KUŠ *ši-ni-an-tum*		1 hide (from a) two year old female sheep
L.E.		1 KUŠ UR$_4$ BAR.SÙ.A		1 plucked hide (from a) young sheep

	Transliteration	Translation
	2 KUŠ *ši-ni-*⌈*na*⌉*-tum*	2 hides from two year old females
	3 KUŠ *bar-ba-ru-ú*	3 wolf skins
	17 KUŠ UR$_4$	(Total:) 17 hides (from) young sheep
	ŠU.NIGIN$_2$ 31 KUŠ UDU.ḪI.A	Total: 31 sheep hides
	NA.QÀD *Nu-ri-ia*	shepherd: Nurija
U.E.	ITU *E-lu-nu* UD.1.KAM	The month of Elunu, the first day
	MU SAḪAR *zi-ku-ra-tum* ^{d}UTU	The year the earth (for) the ziggurat of Šamaš

NOTES

(2) The reading of this line confirms Landsberger, MSL 8/1 14 (Hh XIII) 80; see COPY. ŠÀ "*libbu*," is translated as if written ŠÀ.BA.

(5) The number 14 is clear on the tablet.

(6) For UR$_4$ as an age category of sheep, see CAD B 322b (sub *buqāmu*), citing the discussion of Landsberger, MSL 8/1 pp. 36f.

(7) *Šiniānum* and *šiniāntum* are discussed in AHw 1242a; the related form in line 10 is unfortunately not fully preserved; from the traces (see COPY) one could read *ši-ni-*⌈*an*⌉*-tum*, with a sg. form being written for an expected pl. (as AHw 1242a); or one could, as we have done, consider a possible pl. form *šinînātum*—either contracted or defectively written for *šini'ānātum*. For the possibility of contraction cf. Lambert CRRA XV (1967) 31ff.

(10) See COPY and previous note.

(11) See COPY; note that the wolf hides are not figured into the totals, which are for sheep only. The reading *šu-lu-ú*, given in CAD M/2 3776, is not possible. For wolf hides cf. MSL 7 123 (Hh) 12.

(14) See COPY. The reading of this line was anticipated by CAD M/2 377b.

(16) TUM is clear. For this year date formula see OBTIV p. 34 no. 55.

UCP 10/1 14

UCLMA 9/2352

Barley *ḫubuttātum* Loan

. . .

Obv. (5) [1]*A-pil-Ku-bi* NAR

. . .

NOTES

(5) See COPY.

UCP 10/1 15

UCLMA 9/2343

Barley *ḫubuttātum* Loan

. . .

Obv. (3) 3(PI) 2(BÁN) (ERASURE)
Ma-na-ba-al-ṭe₄-el 2.KAM
. . .

NOTES

(3) See COPY.

UCP 10/1 16

UCLMA 9/2413

Barley *ḫubuttātum* Loan

. . .

Obv. (5) EGIR NÍG.SI.A(sic) BÀD-*Ri-muš*
iš-ša-ak-nu
. . .

NOTES

(5) NÍG.SI.A is wirtten with two verticals; so the sign could remain in question if it were not for UCP 10/1 20:4 and 55:5, where the A is clear; see COPY. NÍG.SI.A can thus not be "corrected" to NÍG.SI.ZA(!), taking ZA as a phonetic error for SÁ. The number of parallel passages where *mi-šar* is written (UCP 10/1 1:5, 9:10, 17:5, 18:3, 34:5, 104:6; Szlechter, *Tablettes* 32f., MAH 16.163A:8) demonstrates that the scribe intended to write NÍG.SI.A as the Sumerogram for *mīšarum*. Wc cannot explain how he came to do so.

UCP 10/1 17

UCLMA 9/2345

Barley *ḫubuttātum* Loan

Obv. (1) 2(GUR) 3(PI) 2(BÁN) GUR
ŠE *ḫu-bu-ta-tum*
. . .

Rev. (11) [IGI *Šu-mu*]-*li*-[*b-ši* GÌ]R.NITA$_2$

. . .

IGI *Ḫu-za-lum* DUMU ⸢*Ḫu-bu*⸣-[*šum*]

(15) IGI ⸢*Su*⸣-*mu*-DINGIR-LUGAL

NOTES

(1) For 3 in place of Lutz's 4, see COPY.

(11) For traces of this line, see COPY.

(14) This PN can be restored from UCP 10/1 34:12f.

(15) This is a most interesting PN, apparently incorporating the name of an archaic king; there is no possibility of this text being contemporary with Sumu-ilum (of Larsa) since the life and career of Ilšu-naṣir record year formulae of Dadusa and Ibalpiel II, who are contemporary with Šamši-Adad I of Assyria and Zimri-Lim of Mari. See Koschaker ZA 43 (1936) 211[4] and OBTIV pp. 15, 19. Cf. further the Ishchali PN, *Su-mu-le-el-du-ri*, OBTIV 281:3. Another possibility is to read ^{d}LUGAL; see Deimel, *Pantheon* 1853, and RLA 4 107f.

UPC 10/1 18; pp. 48ff.
UCLMA 9/2331
Barley *ḫubuttātum* Loans

Obv. (1) 4(PI) 2(BÁN) ŠE *ḫu-bu-ta-tum*

^{Id}EN.ZU-*ib-ni* DUMU GEMÉ-É.SIKIL.LA

1(GUR) 1(PI) 4(BÁN) GUR ŠE *ḫu-bu-ta-tum*

. . .

L.E. (11) [5(?)] *ḫu-bu-ta-t*[*um*]

Rev. [ŠU.NIGIN$_2$ 5(GUR) 3(PI) 4(BÁN)]

GUR ŠE *ḫu-bu-ta-tum*

(13) *wa-ar-ki mi-šar* BÀD-*Ri-muš*

iš-ša-< *ak* >-*nu*

. . .

U.E. (23) DUMU *Šu(!)-um-ru-uṣ*-30

IGI *Am-mu*-DINGIR DUMU ARAD-^{d}INNIN

Edge (25) MU GUD.APIN KÙ.GI

NOTES

(2) For these PNs see COPY.

(3) The tablet has 1(PI) instead of 2(PI); see COPY.

(11) See COPY. There are five *ḫubuttātum* loans recorded in 11.1-9. The form *ḫubuttātum* can here function as a true plural form as well as the more common *plurale tantum* form (see AHw 352b). The sg. *ḫubuttum* and the "new" *plurale tantum ḫubuttūtum* seem to come into use only later, in the late OB and MB periods. For late OB occurrences of *hubuttūtum*, cf. YOS 13 404:2, 6.

(14) See COPY; here as in UCP 10/1 1:5, the scribe wrote *iš-ša-*<*ak*>*-nu*; Lutz's copies are inaccurate.

(23) The ŠU is written like a SU (see COPY).

(24) See COPY.

UPC 10/1 19
UCLMA 9/2380
Barley *ḫubuttātum* Loan

. . .

[1]*Ì-lí-iḫ-nu-ú*

Obv. (5) DUMU ^{d}UTU-*gim-la-an-ni*

. . .

U.E. (13) ITU *Ki-in-kum*

MU GUD.APIN KÙ.GI

Seal Legends

A. *A-bu um* DINGIR

DUMU ^{d}EN.ZU-*e-ri-ba-am*

ARAD *ša* ^{d}IM

B. *Ì-lí-iḫ-nu-ú*

DUMU ^{d}UTU-⌜*gim-la-an-ni*⌝

ARAD ^{d}⌜*Ša-ḫa-an*⌝

Label KIŠIB ⌜SIG⌝-[*ši-na*]

NOTES

(4) See COPY.

(13) The KI is clear; see COPY.

(14) For this year date, see OBTIV p. 30 no. 33.

Seal Legend A

For this seal legend, see the COPY for UCP 10/1 11. It is impressed on the left edge of the tablet; cf. Lutz UCP 10/1 p. 68.

Seal Legend B

See COPY. This seal legend is impressed on the right edge of the tablet; cf. Lutz UCP 10/1 p. 68.

Label See COPY. This label identifies a pictorial seal on the left edge of the tablet.

UCP 10/1 20; p. 42.
UCLMA 9/2414
Barley *ḫubuttātum* Loan

. . .

Rev. (10) [ ]

[IGI E]-[*ri*]-⸢*ba-am*⸣-30

DUMU *Lum-ma*-AN

IGI *Mu-ḫa-ad-du*

. . .

NOTES

(10) It is very likely that there is no line 10 at all on the tablet; that is, nothing is written in that space.

(11) See COPY.

(12) See COPY. For PN cf. *Lum-ma-nu-um, Lum-ma-a-nu-um,* YOS 14 pp. 66f.

(13) See COPY.

UCP 10/1 21
UCLMA 9/2363
Barley *ḫubuttātum* Loan

Obv. (1) 13(GUR) 1(BÁN) GUR ŠE

. . .

(5) ᴵPUZUR$_4$-*Ìr-ra* NAGAR

ŠU.BA.AN.TI

(7) *a-na maš-kán-nim*

L.E. (7a) (PARTIAL ERASURE)

Rev. *še-a-am* Ì.ÁG.E

NOTES

(1) This line appears as Lutz copied it; 1(BÁN) is correct.

(5) The horizontal wedge following the vertical of NAGAR on Lutz's copy is an error; it is not a new wedge but the continuation of the "header" of line 10 on the reverse.

(7a) See COPY. Line 7a was commented upon by Lutz, UCP 19/1 p. 68. The U or 10 preceding the 9 is an erasure; the "30" following the 9 appears likewise to be the remnant of an erasure. But the 9, even if not erased by the scribe, is still not a sensible part of the text.

UCP 10/1 22, p. 24

UCLMA 9/2337

Sale of Slave

. . .

Rev.

NU.MU.UN.GI$_4$.GI$_4$.DAM
MU ^{d}TISPAK *ù I-ba-al-pi-el* LUGAL
IN.PÀD.DÈ.MEŠ
ba-qir i-ba-qa-ru 2 MA.NA KÙ.BABBAR Ì.LAL.E
ù li-ša-an-šu iš-ša-la-ap
IGI ^{d}EN.ZU-*mu-ba-lí-iṭ*
^{I}*Ig-mil*-^{d}EN.ZU DUMU *Ša-ma-ia*
^{I}ARAD-^{d}UTU DUMU *Ṣíl-li*-30
^{I}*Er-ṣi-tum*-GAL DUMU *Be-el-šu-nu*
^{Id}EN.ZU-*i-qí-ša-am* DUMU *I-pí-iq*-^{d}*Bu-ni-ni*
^{Id}*Še-rum-ì-lí* DUMU *Il-lu-rum*
^{I}*A-na*-DINGIR-*li-ṣí* DUMU ^{d}ID$_x$(A.SUK)-*da-lu-rum*
ù Mu-na-nu-um DUB.SAR

Seal Legends

A. ^{d}EN.ZU-*mu-ba-lí-iṭ*
DUMU *Da qa-ni-ia*

B. *Mu-na-wi-rum*
DUMU *Gu-ul-lu-bi-ia*
ARAD *ša* ^{d}NIN.URTA

Labels

A. KIŠIB ^{d}*Se-rum-ì-lí*
B. KIŠIB *Ma-áš-qum*
C. KIŠIB *Ig-mil*-30
D. KIŠIB KI-GAL

NOTES

(15) More of this line is now visible; see COPY.

(16) For TIŠPAK see COPY.

(21) In OBTIV 68:16 we have one Igmil-Sin s. *Ša-ma-ia-tum*; the context is a *ḫubuttātum* loan issued by Ilšu-naṣir and Nanna-arḫuš; the tablet is written by Munanum, the scribe. There is, however, no trace of a "missing" TUM in the Lutz text.

(24) This line appears exactly as Lutz copied it; for the occurrence of ^{d}*Bu-ni-ni* in OB PNs, see Deimel, *Pantheon* p. 60, no. 377.

(26) See COPY. Seif 43 wanted to read ^{d}ÍD(?)-*íl*(!)-*lu-rum* but this is not altogether possible; the DA is clear and the ID_x(A.SUK) is just about the same as the one in UCP 10/1 11:4. The writing of SUK i.e., LAGAB x A, in place of LAGAB x ḪAL is apparently a Diyala variant; cf. the similar variations that occur in the writing of *šaman ittê*, where Ì.ESIR_x(SUK) is written alongside of Ì.ÍD; see note to OBTIV 225:3.

Seal Legend A
See COPY. This seal is inscribed on the edge of the tablet and upon the face of the obverse.

Seal Legend B
This seal is rolled upon the face of the obverse. For COPY see UCP 10/1 11.

Labels Label A appears on the lower edge; B and D are on the left edge of the tablet; and C on the upper edge. These labels identify pictorial seals; A's seal, however, is not preserved. A comment on the writing of the ÁŠ sign in label B is incorporated in the note to UCP 10/1 10:1.

UCP 10/1 23; Seif 25

UCLMA 9/2376

Barley and Emmer *ḫubuttātum* Loan

. . .

Obv. (7) ^{1}*Su-mu*-^{d}*Be-el*-x-x(x)

. . .

Rev. (15) ^{1}*Ì-lí-um-ma-nu*

IGI *A-bu-um*-DINGIR DUMU 30-*e-ri-ba*

. . .

NOTES

(7) See COPY. The two unread signs are clearly preserved. Veenhof, *Symbolae Böhl* (1973) 378, wishes to read ^{d}*Be-el*-ŠINIG (the deity *Bēl-bīnim*). This is an attractive suggestion and, *a priori*, more likely than Landsberger's *be-el* É GEŠTIN, which is reported in CAD K 206b (references courtesy of M. Stol). We hesitate only because the signs do not really conform with GIŠ.GAD.NAGA/ŠÚ.NÁG, which are the expected configurations for ŠINIG given in CAD B

239a (*sub bīnu*), MSL 2 pp. x, 93, MSL 14 p. 303, and in the PN dLUGAL.GIŠ.ŠINIG-*a-bu* which Veenhof cites from CT 47 14:23′. The signs here look like GIŠ.PA(!).TUM. Consider perhaps *ḫaṭṭum*; but then why isn't this noun in the genitive case?

(11) The TE is as Lutz copied it.

(15) This line appears as Lutz copied it.

(16) There is no AM on the tablet after the BA as Lutz's copy has it.

(18) For the year date formula see COPY and OBTIV p. 28 no. 25.

UCP 10/1 24

UCLMA 9/2354

Barley *ḫubuttātum* Loan

Obv. (1) 1(GUR) 1(PI) 4(BÁN) GUR ŠE *Maš-qú*
2(PI) 2(BÁN) ŠE *Um(!)-mi-*d*Iš-ḫa-ra*
1(GUR) 3(PI) 2(BÁN) GUR ŠE
. . .
U.E. (13) IGI *A-bu-um*(!)-DINGIR
. . .

NOTES

(1) The numbers are as Lutz copied them. If there is an *-um* following *Maš-qú*, it is buried under a clay adhesion. For a defective writing of this PN, see UCP 10/1 23:17.

(2) See COPY for UM and compare with UM in line 13 (see COPY also). The sign, however, does look more like a RA.

(3) See COPY. The scribe made an error; the total should have been 1.4.0 GUR.

(13) See COPY.

UCP 10/1 25

UCLMA 9/2403

Barley *ḫubuttātum* Loan

. . .
Rev. (13) 1*Mu-na-wi-rum*
DUMU *Gu-ul-lu-bi-ia* DUB.SAR

U.E. (15) ⸢MU⸣ É EŠ$_4$.DAR
⸢*I-ba-al*⸣*-pi-el*
⸢*i*⸣*-pu-šu*

NOTES

(13) DUB.SAR here almost certainly identified Munawwirum rather than his father; Gullubija is never identified as a scribe in our corpus, while Munawwirum is the scribe in Szlechter, *Tablettes*, MAH 16163A:17. Elsewhere, his brother Munanum uses his seal regularly; cf. OBTIV p. 3[12].

(15) See COPY. For this year date formula, "The year Ibalpiel built the temple of Ištar," see OBTIV p. 26 no. 21.

UCP 10/1 27, p. 10

UCLMA 9/2412

Personnel; Tallies of Workers and Cattle Shares

Obv. (1) ^{I}*Ar-ma-da-al*(!)
. . .

NOTES

(1) There is no AŠ after the AL. What Lutz saw as a horizontal wedge is actually the head of a vertical one. Unfortunately, the portion of tablet with the head of the vertical in AL that Lutz "saw" and "copied" is now not preserved. And there is no way of knowing if the tablet was in a better state of preservation when Lutz copied it. Only the vertical "tail" of that wedge is now visible. It appears that there should have been only one vertical here and that the AŠ is the head of the "tail" which is still preserved. There is a slight "misalignment" between the AŠ and the preserved "tail"; Lutz may have interpreted this "misalignment" as two separate wedges and thus the AŠ. As now read, this PN may indeed be interpreted as a Ḫurrian name in *-atal* as suggested by Gordon, JCS 21 (1967) 84 (ref. courtesy of M. Stol).

UCP 10/1 28; Seif 24

UCLMA 9/2353

Barley *ḫubuttātum* Loan

Obv. (1) 2(GUR) 3(PI) 2(BÁN) GUR ŠE 3.KAM ⸢^{d}⸣[ ] ⸢x x x⸣
2(GUR) 3(PI) 2(BÁN) ^{d}EN.ZU-*mu-ša-lim* 2.KAM
1(PI) 4(BÁN) *Ip-qú*-x(x) 3.KAM
ŠU.NIGIN$_2$ 5(GUR) 3(PI) 2(BÁN) GUR ŠE *ḫu-bu-ta-tum*

. . .

a-na maš-kán-nim

Rev. KI LÚ.SILA.MA.DAM

(10) *ù* LÚ.GI.NA.DAM

ŠE ŠU.BA.AN.TI

. . .

(16) ^{1} ⸢x-*ša-num*⸣

. . .

NOTES

(1) See COPY.

(3) See COPY.

(6) See COPY for ARḪUŠ.

(10) See COPY. For the phrase in lines 9-11, cf. the note to UCP 10/1 46:10-14.

(11) ŠU.BA.AN.TI must here be written for expected present-future *ileqqí*; cf. for examples the CAD and AHw passages mentioned in the note to UCP 10/1 46:10-14; *ileqqí* in fact does occur in the passage there.

(16) ŠA is likely for the second sign, but TA is not excluded; see COPY.

UCP 10/1 29

UCLMA 9/2360

Barley *ḫubuttātum* Loan

. . .

Rev. (12) [UR]U.KI *Za-la-ḫu*(!)^{KI}

U.E. [M]U ⸢A.LAM$_{x}$(LUM) KÙ.GI⸣ É ^{d}EN.ZU

⸢*ù*⸣ [E ^{d}EN].LÍL BA.DÍM

NOTES

(11) There is a strong line separating 11.11 and 12; there is no line following line 12 (as on Lutz's copy).

(12) "The city of Zalaḫu(m)." The ḪU is apparently written over another sign which was not completely erased; see COPY. For this city, see OBTIV p. 28[34].

(13) See COPY. The year date is "The year he built the golden statue and the temples of Sin and Enlil"; See OBTIV p. 23 no. 3.

UCP 10/1 30
UCLMA 9/2371
Sesame; Record of Receipt

Obv. (1) 1 ŠU.ŠI 8(GUR) 1(PI) 1(BÁN) GUR ŠE.⌜GIŠ.Ì⌝
NÍG.ŠU I-*bi*-30
nam-ḫa-ar-ti
[l]*Mu-na-nu-um*
Rev. (5) URU.KI *Maš-kán*(?)-⌜x⌝[ ]
U.E. MU É EŠ$_4$.DAR BA.DÍM

NOTES

(1) See COPY.

(5) For this city, apparently a local site, see COPY and the discussion OBTIV p. 28[34].

UCP 10/1 31
UCLMA 9/2426
Barley; Record of Storage

Obv. (1-2) ŠÀ ⌜ŠU.ŠI⌝ [ ] ⌜GUR⌝ ŠE GIŠ PI
NÍG.ŠU *Mu-na-n*[*u-u*]*m*
ša a-na DINGIR-[*šu-na*]-*ṣir ú-ša-nu*
(5) 6(GUR) 1(PI) GUR *a-n*[*a*] ⌜x⌝ *i-ša-ar*
⌜*iš-ša-x*⌝ [ ] ⌜x⌝
Rev. 12(GUR) 1(PI) GUR ŠE
a-na É.DUB *ru-ug-bi*
NÍG.ŠU DINGIR-*šu-na-ṣir*
(10) *ša-pí-ik*

NOTES

(1) See COPY for ll. 1-6. Line 2 of Lutz's copy does not exist; the vertical wedge he copied is merely the continuation of the vertical (in ŠÀ) in line 1. Note also the absence of *-ak-* in line 4, which Lutz copied and the *-ša-* in place of Lutz's *-ta-* in line 5.

UCP 10/1 32, p. 20

UCLMA 9/2428

Silver *ḫubuttātum* Loan

. . .

Rev. (10) IGI ^{d}EN.ZU-*i-mì-ti*

DUMU BA-^{d}EN.LÍL

. . .

(15) DUMU *Ša-ma-ia-tum*

ù ARAD-^{d}TIŠPAK DUB.SAR

NOTES

(10) See COPY; the PN is Sin-imitti. The last signs were (inadvertently) partially erased by the scribe.

(11) See COPY FOR PN.

(15) The TUM is now missing from the tablet in its present state of preservation.

(16) The upper edge of the tablet immediately follows on line 16 but is broken away.

UCP 10/1 33, p. 41; Seif 34f.

UCLMA 9/2373

Barley; Record of Outlay for Cattle Feed and Workers

Obv. (1) 3(BÁN).DA.ÀM 3 GUD.ḪI.A

UD.20.KAM *i-ku-lu*

. . .

(5) 1(PI) NINDA(!) *A-na-*^{d}UTU-*ták-la-a-ku*

. . .

Rev. (10) 3(BÁN) *Ma-*⌈*ki*⌉*-ia-ma*

NOTES

(1) DA.ÀM is apparently written for TA.ÀM.

(2) As Koschaker, ZA 43 (1936) 221, observed, this entry must be understood to mean "20 days" and not simply "(on) the 20th day;" the same holds true for UD.10.KAM in line 3. Otherwise, the total in 1. 11 will not be correct. The entry in 11. 1-2 thus yields 2 GUR (i.e. 0.0.3 x 20 days); and the entry in 11. 3-4 yields 0.2.3 kor (i.e. 0.0.1; 5 x 10 days); their combined total is 2.2.3 kors. If this sum is added to the entries in 11. 5-10, then they correctly yield the total given in line 11. For other examples of UD.X.KAM being written for ordinal numbers, see UCP 10/1 94, 62, 41.

(5) See COPY; for the counting of bread in units of barley measure, cf. Seif 34f and CAD A/1 242b.

(10) See COPY. The PNs in lines 5-10 are identical to those of UCP 10/1 62:3-10 except for *Ma-ki-ia-tum* there and *Ma-ki-ia-ma* here. Perhaps it should here simply be read as *Makija*, leaving the *-ma* as an enclitic emphatic particle. But this usage is unexpected.

UCP 10/1 34; p. 37

UCLMA 9/2335

Barley *ḫubuttātum* Loan

. . .

Obv. (5) *wa-ar-ki mi-šar* BÀD-*Ri-muš iš-ša-ak-nu*

. . .

Rev. (12) IGI *Ḫu-za-lum*

. . .

(16) MU GUD.APIN KÙ.GI

U.E. URU *Ki-maš É-kal-la-tim*

NOTES

(5) WA was omitted by Lutz; see COPY.

(9) The scribe here lapsed into the more usual sg. form instead of the plural.

(12) The beginning of this line was under a clay adhesion (only now removed); Lutz's copy was based upon a conjectured reading. See COPY for covered signs.

(15) See COPY for BA.

(16) See COPY; this year date formula is OBTIV p. 31 no. 33, "The year the golden plow ox (and) the cities Kimaš and Ekallatum." Seif 47 wished to read the end of the formula as URU.KI *maš-kán-kal-la-tim*. This suggestion is discussed above in a note to UCP 10/1 30:5.

UCP 10/1 35

UCLMA 9/2407

Vessels, Utensils, Furnishings, Foodstuffs; List of Items

Obv. (1) 1 GI.PISAN *nu-nu-tu-ku*

2 GI.PISAN 3(BÁN) *kur-zi-za-ku*

1 GI.PISAN *ki-iṣ-ri-i*

1 GI.PISAN *kur-zi-za-ku ša* 1 GUR

2 *ḫi-id-la-tum*
3 *nu-us-ḫu*
1 *na-ap-ra-aḫ-tum*
1 GIŠ *za-ru-um*
1 GI.PISAN *ku-bu-si*
2 *qa-ab-la-tum ša i-ir-tim*
1 *ma-aḫ-ra-lum*
3 GIŠ.GU.ZA
2 NA$_4$ *i-ru-um*
ša zi-bi-i
Rev. 2 *na-ar-ka-bu*
3 *ma-a-*⸢*tum*⸣
4 *ma-aq-r*[*a-tu*]*m*
3 MA.NA *ši-*[ ]-[*x*]
2 NA$_4$ *i-ru*[ ] ⸢x⸣*-ba-rum*
3 GIŠ *e-er-ši-*[*im*]
1 TÚG NÍG.⸢Ú⸣
2(PI) ŠE.GIŠ.I
6 1/2 MA.NA SÍG
2(GUR) 3(PI) 3(BÁN) GUR ŠE *ḫu-ur-pu*
1(PI) 3(BÁN) ŠE *up-li-tum*

NOTES

(1) This line appears as Lutz copied it. The reading *mu-nu-tu-ku* given in CAD M/2 208b is incorrect.

(2) See COPY for ZI and cf. CAD K 583b for this basket.

(3) The last sign is a clear I as Lutz copied it; there is no graphic basis upon which to read TUR as was done in CAD K 442a. The reason for the long vowel is unclear; perhaps the term is plural.

(6) The last sign is really ḪU; see COPY. Lutz erred because of a "shadow" in the top wedge; but it is not enough of a mark to warrant reading RI. Besdies, the *nusḫum* basket is well attested; cf. AHw 806a (and CAD Ḫ 182b).

(16) The first signs (MA) in ll. 16 and 17 are identical; line 16 appears as Lutz copied it.

(17) See COPY. *Maqrattum* is also a month name at Ishchali, alongside of *Maqrānum* in UCP 10/1 99:10; see Index for occurrences.

(18) See COPY; Lutz saw more after ŠI than is now preserved; but, at the same time, he missed the broken sign at the end of the line. The traces would support the reading *ši-*[*im-tu*]*m*, "3 minas paint," as suggested by AHw 1238b.

(19) See COPY for the last signs; perhaps the line read 2 NA$_4$ *i-ru-*[*um*] [*a*]*t-ba-rum* "2 basalt millstones," with sg. being written in place of expected plural forms (as in line 13).

(20) This line appears as Lutz copied it. CAD E 315a was satisfied with *erši* but the placement of the ŠI seems to require another sign at the end of the line; thus our reading *erši*[*m*].

(21) See COPY.

(23) See COPY.

UCP 10/1 36, pp. 35f.; Seif 28f.

UCLMA 9/2395

Sale of Vacant Lot

Obv.	3 SAR KI.GÁL	3 sar vacant lot –
	ŠÁM.TIL.LA.NI.ŠÈ KÙ.BI Ì.LAL	for its complete price he paid silver (for it) –
	KI *Ḫa-an-ba-ti*	from Ḫanbati
	^{I}*Šu-ri-im-ku*	did Šurimku
	ù A-ta-na-aḫ-ì-lí ŠEŠ.A.NI	and Atanaḫ-ili, his brother,
	IN.ŠI.IN.ŠÁM	purchase.
	^{I}*Bi-tum*-ŠAG$_5$ KÙ.BI Ì.LAL	Bitum-damiq weighed the silver.
	IGI ARAD-^{d}EN.ZU DUMU *Ma-šum*	Witnessed by Warad-Sin son of Mašum
	^{I}*Bur-ia* DUMU *Sa-si-ia*	Burja son of Sasija
	^{I}*Ìr-ra-ba-ni* DUMU *Ši-ki-ti*	Irra-bani son of Šikitti
	^{I}*Me-ra-ni* DUMU *Ú-ba-lum*	Merani son of Ubalum
	^{I}*Pa-la-ru-um*	Palarum
	DUMU *Ì-lí-id-na-ni*	son of Ili-idnanni
Rev.	^{I}*Na-bi-tum* AD.KID	Nabitum, the reedworker,
	ÚS.SA KI.GÁL.LA	a neighbor to the vacant lot
	^{I}*I-pí-iq-Ìr-ra* SUKAL	Ipiq-Irra, the *sukkallum*
	ù BA.AN.GI.GI DUB.SAR	and Bangigi, the scribe
	SPACE OF 3 LINES (SEAL)	SPACE
	LÚ.INIM.MA.BI.ME	(These are) the witnesses
	IGI.NE.NE.ŠÈ	before whom
	MU LUGAL.LA.BI IN.PÀD	he swore (an oath) by the name of the king.
	^{I}*Na-bi*-EN.ZU KA.KI IN.GÍD	Nabi-Sin, the *kakikkum*, measured (the plot).
	MU *I-ba-al-pi-el*	The year Ibalpiel
	GU.ZA ZÚ.AM.SI KÙ.GI GAR.⌜RA⌝	23) fashioned the ivory throne inlaid with gold
	^{d}TIŠPAK.⌜KA⌝ BA.DÍM	24) for (lit. of) Tišpak
Seal Legend		
	I-ba-al-pi-el	Ibalpiel
	na-ar-am ^{d}TISPAK	beloved of Tišpak
	ENSÍ ÁŠ.NUN.NA^{KI}	ruler of Eshnunna
	Na-bi-^{d}EN.ZU	Nabi-Sin
	⌜KA⌝.KI	the *kakikkum*
	[DUMU] U UR.É.⌜NINNU⌝	son of Ur-Eninnu

NOTES

This tablet is written in an archaic script.

(5) See COPY for ŠEŠ.

(7) ŠAG$_5$ is as Lutz copied it.

(10) This line appears as Lutz copied it.

(11) This line appears as Lutz; BA is better than ZU (as read by Seif 28).

(14) See COPY for KID; for *atkuppum* cf. CAD A/2 494b.

(16) See COPY for SUKAL.

(17) See COPY for BA.

(21) See COPY for signs omitted by Lutz. For a recent discussion of this phrase see R. Whiting's comments in *Seals and Sealing in the Ancient Near East*, ed. M. Gibson and R. D. Biggs (*Bibliotheca Mesopotamica* VI); Malibu: 1977 #68.

(22) For this year date formula see OBTIV p. 31 no. 37.

(23) See COPY for RA.

(24) This line is as Lutz copied it; the third sign is KA and cannot be RA (as UCP 10/1 p. 36 might imply).

Seal Legend

There is only one seal on the tablet; it is impressed into the space between ll. 17-18 and over all the surfaces of the tablet. See COPY.

UCP 10/1 37
UCLMA 9/2419
Barley; List, with Receipt

Obv.
1(PI) 4(BÁN) ŠE ⸢Ì⸣ GIŠ ⸢ša x⸣
1(PI) ŠE ^{d}EN.ZU-*mu-ba-lì-*[*iṭ*]
1 GUR ŠE KÙ.BABBAR-^{d}EN.ZU
1(GUR) 4(BÁN) ŠE ⸢x x⸣ [ ]

Rev.
1(GUR) 4(PI) 2(BÁN) GUR ŠE [ ]
nam-ḫa-ar-t[*i*]
DINGIR-*šu-na-*[*ṣir*]
⸢x x⸣ [ ]

NOTES

(1) See COPY; as the text now stands, one should read it "0.1.4 kor barley, oil of . . . ;" this is not wholly satisfactory. Could ŠE Ì GIŠ be written in place of ŠE.GIŠ.Ì? Note the inclusion of ŠE in ll. 2ff.

(3) See COPY for lines 3 - 4.

(7) Lines 7-8 appear as Lutz copied them.

UCP 10/1 38

UCLMA 9/2389

Barley *ḫubuttātum* Loan

Obv. 3(GUR) 1(PI) GUR ŠE *ḫu-bu-ta-tum*
KI DINGIR-*šu-na-ṣir*
DUMU *Bur*-^{d}EN.ZU
^{Id}EN.ZU-*iš-me-a-an-ni*
DUMU ^{d}EN.ZU-*da-ia-an*
L.E. ŠU.BA.AN.TI
a-na maš-kán-nim
Rev. *še-a-am* Ì.ÁG.E
IGI *Ṣú-ḫu-tim*
DUMU *Bu-ri-ia*
MU KÁ.GAL
U.E. *Ki-ku-ri-im*

NOTES

(4) This line appears as Lutz copied it. For the use of a vowel sign to represent ʾ, cf. GAG § 23e, Hecker, AnOr, 44 95e.

(5) See COPY for AN.

(9) See COPY for ṢÚ.

(11) See COPY for *Ki-ku-*. For the year date formula, "the year the gate of the Chapel," see OBTIV p. 32 no. 46.

UCP 10/1 39

UCLMA 9/2359

Barley *ḫubuttātum* Loan

. . .

Obv. (5) [I]*Be-el-tum* NIN.DINGIR

. . .

NOTES

(5) NIN.DINGIR is written over erasure; see COPY.

UCP 10/1 40

UCLMA 9/2351

Barley *ḫubuttātum* Loan

NOTES

(8) Lines 8-10 are partly covered by a clay adhesion; there is no way at all that Lutz could have seen these lines! But he copied them as if he could. (There is, of course, no quarrel with the correctness of his reconstructions.)

UCP 10/1 41

UCLMA 9/2409

Barley; Tally of Outlays for Cattle and Workers

Obv. (1) 1(PI) ŠE Á GUD.ḪI.A
ù ṣú-ḫa-ri ša UD.3.KAM
2(BÁN) ŠÀ.GAL *ar-ḫi-im*
ša Gu-lu-bi-ia
Rev. (5) ŠU.NIGIN$_2$ 1(PI) 2(BÁN) ŠE
Á GUD.ḪI.A

NOTES

(3) See COPY for AR.

(4) See COPY for GU.

(5) This line appears as Lutz copied it.

UCP 10/1 42

UCLMA 9/2420

Barley *ḫubuttātum* Loan

. . .

Rev. ^{1}*Im-gur-*^{d}UTU
DUTU *Ib-ni-*^{d}EN.LÍL
[^{1}] ⸢*A*⸣*-bu-um-*⸢*wa*⸣*-*[*qar*]
[DUMU *E-r*]*i-*[*ba-num*]
[*ù* PN DUB.SAR]
[MU]
⸢*I*⸣*-ba-al-*⸢*pi-el*⸣

NOTES

(13) See COPY for ll. 13-15.

(16) Lines 16-17 are restored.

(18) See COPY; there is no room for LUGAL after the RN. For this year date formula, see OBTIV p. 35 no. 69a and note there.

UCP 10/1 43, p. 9; Seif 34

UCLMA 9/2393

Silver; Record of Payments of Service Obligations

Obv. 2 MA.NA 11 2/3 GÍN 10 ŠE KÙ.BABBAR
ma-za-aš-ti ÈŠ.NUN.NA^{KI}
5 MA.NA 2 5/6 GÍN KÙ.BABBAR
ma-za-aš-ti Ša-du-pu-um
2 2/3 MA.NA 6 1/2 GÍN 2 ŠE KÙ.BABBAR
Rev. *ma-za-aš-ti Ne-ri-ib-tim*
2 2/3 MA.NA 2 1/2 GÍN KÙ.BABBAR
NÍG.ŠU UGULA DAM.QAR
ŠU.NIGIN$_2$ 12 2/3 MA.NA 3 1/2 GÍN
12 ŠE
ši-ta-at ni-ka-⸢*si*⸣

NOTES

(2) Lines 2, 4, 6, 11 are cited in CAD M/1 229b. The "service of Eshnunna" being mentioned together with those of Šaduppum and Neribtum (lines 4, 6) is surprising. The last two cities are clearly in the vicinity of Ishchali: Neribtum may be Ishchali itself or close by (cf. ORTIV 1[1]) while Šaduppum is Tell Harmal, a site about 10 km. to the east (cf. R. Adams, *Land Behind Baghdad* (Chicago: University of Chicago Press, 1965) p. 152 and fig. 3). Eshnunna, however, lies over 20 km. away and was not always in the same sphere of political activity (cf. OBTIV p. 14).

(3) For 5/6 (in place of Lutz's 2/3) see COPY.

(4) The DU is clear; see COPY. The correct reading of this line was already surmised by Goetze, Sumer 14 (1958) 8.

(6) See COPY for IB.

(7) For the correct reading of line 7 see COPY.

(9) See COPY; the total is correct in terms of the amounts listed in ll. 1, 3, 5, 7. Lutz omitted KÙ.BABBAR in his copy.

(11) See COPY; for the phrase *šittāt nikkassī* "balance of accounts", see AHw 1252b. The situation is apparently an accounting on collections of *mazzaštu* payments. One would like to know more about the role of the UGULA DAM.QAR (line 8) in this business; did he function as the collector?

UCP 10/1 44

UCLMA 9/2329

Barley *ḫubuttātum* Loan

. . .

Obv. (6) DUMU *A-du(?)-an-ni-a-am*

. . .

U.E. (15) MU É ^{d}EN.LÍL

⌜*ù* A⌝.LAM$_{x}$(LUM) KÙ.GI

⌜*I*⌝-*ba-al-pí-*[*el* BA.DÍM]

NOTES

(6) See COPY for what is now preserved of line 6; the DU looks more like a TA, but cf. the PN *Ḫa-du-an-*[*ni*]*-a-am* in OBTIV 74:2.

(13) There is no *-am* written after the *-ba-* in ^{d}EN.ZU*-e-ri-ba*.

(15) See COPY for the year date formula: "The year Ibalpiel built the temple of Enlil and (fashioned) the golden statue." For this formula, see OBTIV p. 26 no. 19.

UCP 10/1 46, Seif 24

UCLMA 9/2421

Barley Loan with Interest

Obv.
19 GUR ŠE
1 <GUR>-*um* 1(PI) 4(BÁN).TA.À[M]
MÁŠ *ú-ṣa-ab*
KI DINGIR-*šu-na-ṣir*
ù ^{d}ŠEŠ.KI.ARḪUŠ(!)⌈ḪU⌉.[UŠ]
[1]^{d}EN.ZU-*we-de-ku*
ù Ri-iš-Ìr-ra
DUMU.MEŠ *Za-ri-i-im*
ŠU.BA.AN.TI.MEŠ
KI *ša-al-mi-šu-nu*
ù ki-ni-šu-nu
a-na maš-kán-nim
še-a-am ù MÁŠ.BI

Rev.
i-li-qí
IGI *Ip-qí*-EŠ$_4$.DAR
DUMU *Ì-lí-we-de-ku*
IGI AN-KA-*ša* DUMU *Im-gu-*⌈*ia*⌉
IGI ARAD-*Iš-* <*ḫa-*> *-ra* DUMU *Šum-*⌈*ma-nu-um*⌉
[IGI] ⌈*A-li*-⌉-*ba-nu-um*
[DUMU] ⌈*I*⌉-*bi*-⌈^{d}EN⌉.[ZU]
– remainder broken –

NOTES

(1) Line 1 begins with a slight, unexplained indention; the signs appear as Lutz copied them but the indention does not go as far to the right as Lutz's copy suggests; the U (i.e., the 10 sign) is actually over the UM of line 2.

(2) Ths line appears as Lutz copied it; the expected GUR is omitted.

(5) See COPY for lines 5-6; the vertical after the KU is part of the ⌈ḪU⌉ in the line above.

(8) See COPY for IM.

(10) The phrase in Ll. 10-14 implies joint responsibility for the entire loan by each and any one of the debtors; cf. CAD K 390f., AHw 1149b. It is not clear how (or whether) considerations of the physical health of the debtors affected the collectability of their debts. CAD B 68a suggests a situation of decease and survivorship. Cf. also UCP 10/1 28:9-11 and the similar idea in OBTIV 47:8-12.

(15) This PN was apparently pronounced /Ip^{e}q-Ištar/, to judge from the alternative writings Ipiq-Ištar for this same person; cf. UCP 10/1 109:21, UCLMA 9/2878:1, and TIM 3 127:12.

(16) See COPY for KU.

(17) See COPY for ŠA and ⸢IA⸣.

(18) See COPY for lines 18-20. Išḫara is written without DINGIR in OBTIV 147:1.

UCP 10/1 47

UCLMA 9/2349

Barley; Record of Receipt

. . .

Obv. (2) AŠ x x *ka-ta-mu*

. . .

NOTES

(2) See COPY for this line.

UCP 10/1 48, p. 27

UCLMA 9/2347

Barley; Storehouse Record

Obv. (1) 2 GUR ŠE
[1]*A-ḫu-ni*
na-aš-pa-ak
BÀD-*Ri-muš*[KI]

Rev. (5) [ ] ⸢x KI⸣
(6) MU KÁ.GAL ⸢*Ki-ku*⸣ *ri im*

NOTES

(4) See COPY for KI omitted by Lutz.

(5) See COPY for traces.

(6) See COPY for this line. A space of 2 (unruled) lines separates lines 5-6. For the year date formula, "The year the Gate of the Chapel," see OBTIV p. 32 no. 46.

UCP 10/1 49, p. 26

UCLMA 9/2374

Barley; Storehouse Record of Expenditures

. . .

Obv. (3) 3 (GUR) *Qur-ru-du-um*

. . .

U.E. (11) MU KÁ.GAL *Ki-kur-ri*

NOTES

(3) See COPY for QUR.

(11) See COPY for KI; there is no *-im* after the *-ri-*. For the year date formula "The year the gate of the chapel," see OBTIV p. 32 no. 46.

UCP 10/1 50

UCLMA 9/2367

Barley *ḫubuttātum* Loan

. . .

Obv. (4) [1]*Un-nu-bu-um*

. . .

Rev. (10) IGI *Ḫu-pu-du-*⸢*um*⸣
DUMU *A-ḫu-ši-na*
MU GIŠ.TUKUL ^{d}UTU
[1]*Da-du-ša*
ú-še-ri-bu

NOTES

(3) The ARHUŠ sign is present but badly preserved.

(4) See COPY for the NU omitted by Lutz.

(10) See COPY for *-du-um*.

(12) See COPY for DA: the last two lines of the text are not indented, as would normally be expected. The year date is "The year Daduša brought in the divine weapon of Šamaš"; it is OBTIV p. 30 no. 32.

UCP 10/1 51

UCLMA 9/2341

Barley *ḫubullu* Loan

Obv. (1) 5 GUR ŠE UR$_5$.RA

1 GUR-*um* 1(PI) 4(BÁN) ŠE

MÁŠ [*ú*]-*ṣa-ab*

KI [*Im-gu*] ⸢*r*-^{d}EN.LÍL

(5) [DUMU ^{d}EN.LI]L-*a-bu*-⸢*um*⸣

[ ] ⸢x ^{d}IM⸣

(7) [DUMU] ⸢NI⸣

(7a) [ŠU.BA.AN.T]I

Rev. *a-na maš-kán-nim*

še-am ù MÁŠ.BI

(10) Ì.ÁG.E

IGI ^{d}UTU.ZI.MU DUMU (ERASURE) AN-*i-lu*(!)-*um*

IGI AN-*um*-KA-^{d}UTU

DUMU *Bur*-^{d}EN.ZU

IGI *Ṣíl-lí*-^{d}INNIN DUMU *Im-gu-rum*

(15) IGI *A-pil-ì-lí-šu* DUB.SAR

U.E. MU GIŠ.GIGIR^{GÌR} ^{d}IM

NOTES

(2) See COPY for UM.

(4) See COPY for PN; Imgur-Enlil s. of Enlil-abum is the lender of barley in OBTIV 54:4 and 58:4f; he also appears as a witness in UCLMA 9/2878:3f.

(5) See COPY for ll. 5-7 as now preserved.. Line 7a was inadvertently omitted by Lutz, who apparently considered the AN in line 6 to be part of the expected ŠU.BA.AN.TI.

(11) See COPY; the LU(!) appears more as KU; there is, however, a faint trace of a second vertical, which would not be noticed if one were not specifically looking for it. For the PN, cf. UCP 10/1 92:3f.

(16) See COPY for GÌR. For the year date formula cf. OBTIV p. 29, no. 27.

UCP 10/1 52, pp. 12f.

UCLMA 9/2383

Sale of Garden

Obv. (1) 25 SAR GIŠ.SAR
ÚS.SA.DA GIŠ.SAR BA-^{d}EN.LÍL
ù ÚS.SA.DA GIŠ.SAR *ša* ^{d}EN.ZU
SAG.1.KAM A-⸢x⸣-^{d}IM
. . .

Rev. (15) ^{d}TIŠPAK *ù I-ba-al-pi-el* LUGAL
. . .
(20) ^{I}*Sa-at-lu-ma ù* BA-^{d}EN.LÍL(!)
. . .
(24) ^{I}*A-bu-um*-DINGIR DUMU ^{d}EN.ZU-*eri*$_4$(!)-*ba*
. . .

NOTES

(2) See COPY for ^{d}EN.LÍL.

(4) For the broken sign see COPY; the sign does not appear to be BIL. One could also consider reading A.Š[À]^{d}IM (suggestion of M. Stol).

(15) See COPY for TIŠPAK.

(20) BA-^{d}EN.LÍL here appears to be written more like ^{d}EN.ZU; but LÍL is correct and is supported by clearer writings in line 2, as well as in UCP 10/1 74:2, 107:24, and UCLMA 9/2826:11.

(24) See COPY for ^{d}EN.ZU-*eri*$_4$-*ba*. The scribe apparently first wrote *eri*$_4$ in a faulty fashion; he then erased it but left the final vertical somewhat obliterated, This person is well known in the corpus and also appears in one of the two Seal Legends appearing on this tablet. See COPY *sub* UCP 10/1 11.

UCP 10/1 54
UCLMA 9/2416
Implements; ŠU.TI.A

Obv. (1) 6 URUDU.KIN
. . .

NOTES

(1) "6 sickles" as read by CAD N/2 213a; cf. also OBTIV 252:1, 4.

UCP 10/1 55, p. 19
UCLMA 9/2358
Barley *ḫubuttātum* Loan

Obv. (1) 2(PI) 1(BÁN) 3 1/3(SILA$_3$) ŠE *E-ri-ib*-30
2(PI) 1(BÁN) 3 1/3(SILA$_3$) *E-ri-ba-am* LÚ X IM
ŠU.NIGIN$_2$ 4(PI) 3(BÁN) GUR ŠE *ḫu-bu-ta-tum*
. . .

NOTES

(1) See COPY for lines 1-2. There is a discrepancy between the amounts listed and the total given in 1.3; the total exceeds the amounts listed by 3 1/3 SILA$_3$. It would be "neat" to be able to read 6 2/3 (SILA$_3$) in line 1 (or 2); but the 2/3 copied by Lutz is not there; one cannot, likewise, read 6 in place of 3 in either lines 1 or 2.

(2) Seif's (p. 51) reading LÚ *ki-din-nu*(!) is not possible; Lutz's (UCP 10/1 p. 19) KI-*im* is likewise questionable.

UCP 10/1 56
UCLMA 9/2379
Barley; Storehouse Record

Obv. (1) 2(GUR) 2(PI) GUR ŠE *a-na* ⌈x⌉ [ ]
1 GUR GU NU(?) A Ḫ[I(?)]
1(GUR) ^{d}EN.ZU-*a-ḫi-i*-⌈x x⌉
1(GUR) GIŠ.TUKUL-*ú* KUR UM

3(PI) 2(BÁN) ^{d}UTU-*a-bu-um* KUR UM
3(PI) 2(BÁN) *A-pil-i-lí-šu* KUR UM
⸢1(!)⸣(GUR) ⸢x⸣ ^{d}UTU-*a-bu-*⸢*um*⸣
L.E. 2(GUR) *A-tam-ma-ri-lì*-30
1(PI) KUR KI ŠUM ⸢GI⸣
Rev. ⸢4⸣(PI) ⸢^{d}EN.ZU-*i*⸣-*din-*⸢*nam*⸣
ŠU.NIGIN$_{2}$ 10(GUR) 3(PI) 4(BÁN) GUR ŠE
na-aš-pa-ak
Na-ra-am-tim
UD.25.KAM
ITU *Na-ab-ri(!)-i*

NOTES

(1) See COPY for lines 1-11.

(2) The repetition of GUR in this unintelligible line is unexpected.

(3) The signs *i-*⸢x were read as ID by Lutz, UCP 10/1 p. 61 (and Seif 44); but this reading is unsatisfactory. One may consider *i-*⸢*qí*⸣*-š*[*am*], *i-na*(!)-⸢*x*⸣, or similar; *i-din-n*[*am*] is not possible.

(4) The KUR UM which appears at the end of ll. 4-6 is puzzling; instead of KUR one might also consider reading KUD. Kakku (GIŠ.TUKUL-ú) as a PN is also a bit uncertain; one could also read *is-qú-ú*.

(6) The amount in lines 5-6 are identical: 3(PI) 2(BÁN) in both cases; see COPY.

(7) One needs to read 1(GUR) here in order for the total in line 11 to be correct; our reading follows from the fact that the vertical element in the first sign seems to be an erasure (see COPY). The second sign, however, is a problem; Lutz UCP 10/1 p. 55 read *Gimil-*^{d}UTU *a-ḫi-šu*; and this was essentially followed by Seif 42, who read BA|(*Iqîš*)-*Šamaš*. However, *a-ḫi-šu* seems to be excluded by the traces (see COPY); hence, our own reading *Šamaš-abum*. But this still leaves the preceding sign uninterpreted; M. Stol suggests ⸢Á⸣ "wages (of PN)." The repetition of this PN (again in line 5) should also be noted.

(10) Lutz seems to have been able to make out a clearer ^{d}EN.ZU than is now preserved.

(13) "Storehouse of Naramtum." There is nothing more written after the PN; cf. Lutz UCP 10/1 110:iv 12 where LUKUR follows this PN.

(15) The ending of this line is now missing; our reading is based on parallels and the traces but requires one to assume (as did Seif 47) that Lutz's fourth sign was miscopied.

UCP 10/1 57

UCLMA 9/2418

Barley: Tally of Allotments

Obv. 2 GUR ŠE *ma-ša-ar-ti*
^{I}*Im-gur*-^{d}EN.LÍL UD.1.KAM
3 GUR *ma-ša-ar-ti*
^{I}*Im-gur*-^{d}EN.LÍL A.RÁ 2.KAM
2 GUR *ma-ša-ar-ti*
^{I}*A-li-wu-um* A.RÁ 3.KAM
L.E. (ERASURE)
(ERASURE)
Rev. [ ] GUR ŠE
[*ma-ša-ar*]-*ti*
[^{I}*Im-gur*]-⸢^{d}EN⸣.LÍL A.RÁ 4(!).KAM
[ ] ⸢GUR(?)⸣ *na-aš-pa-ak*
Sa-mu-la-ši-di
ma-ša-ar-ti
^{I}Im-gur-^{d}EN.LÍL A.RÁ 5 KAM
3(PI) ŠE *ša* ŠU.I
^{Id}IM-*ra-bi*
Edge 3(PI) 2(BÁN) ŠE EŠ
^{I}*I-nir-a-ia-bi-šu*
ŠU.NIGIN$_{2}$ 11(GUR) ⸢3⸣(PI) [ ]

NOTES

(1) In lines 1-15 allotments (*maššartu*) of barley are given out on five occasions: 4 times to Imgur-Enlil (lines 2, 4, 11, 15) and once to Aliwum (line 6). The disbursements in lines 16 and 18 are not labelled as *maššartu*.

(2) For ^{d}EN.LÍL in lines 2, 4, see COPY.

(7) Lines 7-8 on the lower edge contain erasures only; see COPY for l. 9.

(11) See COPY for this line; 4 is unquestionably correct in view of line 15.

(12) This line appears as Lutz copied it.

(13) See COPY for this line; Seif 47 wanted to read URU *Mu-la-lim*^{KI} but this is not possible; the first sign is not URU and the last sign is not KI, without emendation. Lines 12-15 thus state: ". . . kors (out of) the granary of Samulašidi." We, provisionally, take this form to be a PN.

(15) See COPY for the end of this line–not copied by Lutz.

(16) See COPY for this line. Lines 16-17 state: "0.3.0 kor for the barber (given to) Adad-rabi."

(18) This line appears as Lutz copied it except that the surface is badly battered between the ŠE and the EŠ; something could have been written there—but no more than 2 wedges, e.g. a ME sign.

(19) See COPY for lines 19-20.

UCP 10/1 58, pp. 15f.; Seif 30
UCLMA 9/2370
Hire of Shepherd

Obv.	ITU *A-bi-i*	(In) the month of Abu
	^{1}*Pa-ki-ku-um*	Pakikum
	DUMU *I-si-da-na*	son of Issi-danna
	^{1}DINGIR-*šu-sa-ṣir* DUMU *Bur*-30	Ilšu-naṣir son of Bur-Sin
	a-na MU.1.KAM *a-na* UDU.ḪI.A *re-im*	for one year to herd sheep
	i-gu-ur-šu	hired him.
	5 GUR ŠE *i-du-šu* 2(GUR) 2(PI) GUR ŠE.BA	5 kors barley are his wages; 2.2.0 kors his alimentation;
	1 GÍN KÙ.BABBAR SÍG.BA	1 shekel silver is his clothing allowance.
L.E.	*i-na* UDU.ḪI.A *ša i-ṣa-ba-*tu_4	Out of the sheep which he will hold,
	i-na 1 *me-at* ZI(!) ŠU.ŠI	for every one hundred living (lambs), sixty
	i-na-ad-di-in ù a-na	he will give; and in addition
Rev.	*ḫa-li-iq-tim i-za-az*	be responsible for any lost animal.
	i-na-ad-di-ma i-na i(?)-di-šu	Should he be negligent, his wages
	i-te-el-li	he will forfeit.
	IGI ^{d}UTU-*na-ṣir* DUMU *I-bi-*^{d}EN.ZU	Witnessed by Šamaš-naṣir son of Ibbi-Sin,
	^{1}*A-lí-am-mu-ú* ⌈DUMU⌉-*šu* ≪NI≫	Ali-ammu, his son,
	^{1d}EN.ZU-*ga-mil* DUMU *A-ḫi-um-mi-šu*	Sin-gamil son of Aḫi-ummišu,
	^{1}*A-bu-um-*DINGIR	Abum-ilum,
	ù Mu-na-nu-um DUB.SAR	and Munanum the scribe.
U.E.	MU ERIN$_2$ *ma-at Šu-bar-tim*	The year Ibalpiel captured the
	^{1}*I-ba-al-pi-el i-ḫa-zu*	army of Subartum
Seal Legend		
	*A-bu-um-*DINGIR	Abum-ilum
	DUMU ^{d}EN.ZU-*e-ri-ba-am*	son of Sin-eribam
	ARAD *ša* ^{d}IM	servant of Adad

NOTES

(3) J. J. Finkelstein, JAOS 88 (1968) 33[13], read this PN as *I-si-da-na* but adduced no philological evidence for this PN. This is critical because the sign he read as DA (see COPY) can in fact also be safely read as ID; cf. for examples (see COPY): the DA in UCP 10/1 7:18, 109:16,

UCLMA 9/2827:22; and compare these with the ID in UCP 10/1 110.iii 5, 11 and OBTIV 58:11a. The ID is in fact most often not written as elaborately as Lutz invariably "copied it," although more elaborate forms do at times occur: e.g., UCLMA 9/2831:11 and OBTIV 17:10, 136:4. We have tentatively derived this PN from **Issī-(id)danna* "she cried out in difficulty," a form reminiscent of later PNs like *Ina-dannati-alsī(š)*; cf. Stamm, *Namengebung* 200.

(5) See COPY. The correct reading of this line was already suggested by Seif 30 and supported by Finkelstein, *loc. cit.*

(7) Seif's translation of lines 7-8, as our own, follows Lautner, *Personenmiete* 108[352].

(9) See COPY. Seif 30 correctly anticipated the missing *-tu*$_4$, which is in fact present below, at line 10; it is the sign which Lutz copied as I. The use of TUM for /*tu*/ is attested elsewhere at Ishchali; see the discussion above on p. 3. Finkelstein's attempt to relate this verb to *waṣābum* (JAOS 53 [1968] 33 and note 14 there–essentially following Lautner, *Personenmiete* 91[305]) can thus be set aside.

(10) See COPY. ZI is defectively written; but it seems preferable to the earlier reading of MÁŠ suggested by Landsberger and Koschaker *apud* Lautner, *Personenmiete* 91[305] (and taken up by Seif 30). Finkelstein's reading (*loc. cit.*) 1 *me-at* 60+20 *šu-ši* has many problems (see his note 15 there and the question raised by Postgate JCS 20 [1975] 5[2]), not the least of which is that it requires one to ignore (in the ZI sign) the horizontal wedge and also one of the verticals. As Driver and Miles, *Bab. Laws* I 457, and Finkelstein (*op. cit.* pp. 33ff) note, a yield of 60% (i.e., 60 out of 100 new-born lambs) was considered reasonable at other times in Babylonia.

(13) See COPY for this line. MA in place of Lutz's ŠU was already noted by Finkelstein (*loc. cit.*) through his collation.

(15) See COPY for lines 15-16.

(21) For the verb *i-ḫa-zu* see above p. 93.

UCP 10/1 59

UCLMA 9/2368

Barley *ḫubuttātum* Loan

Obv. (1) ⌈2⌉(PI) 4(BÁN) ŠE *Na-ra-am-tum*
DUMU.SAL *Ḫa-ma-nim*
1(PI) 2(BÁN) *Be-el-ta-ni* DAM
Mu-na-wi-rum
⌈3⌉(PI) 2(BÁN) ^{d}EN.ZU-*i-din-n*[*am*]
⌈ḪA.LI⌉
⌈2⌉(PI) 2(BÁN) DUMU *Iš-ku-un-*[30]
. . .

Rev. (11) IGI ARAD-^{d}UTU
^{I}*Ig-mil*-30
^{I}*Ra-šum*-É
ù Mu-na-nu-um DUB.SAR

⸢MU A.LAM$_{x}$(LUM) KÙ.GI⸣

NOTES

(1) See COPY for lines 1-4. If Lutz was able to read more at the beginning of line 1 than is now visible, then one should read ⸢4⸣(PI) instead of ⸢2⸣(PI). Lutz's reading of 2(PI) at the beginning of line 2 is clearly an error.

(3) There is no room for the DUMU which Lutz "copied"; our own reading is further supported by UCP 10/1 108:35.

(4) See COPY for UN. This PN is also attested in UCLMA 9/2889a:i 4, ii 2.

(11) The four PNs in lines 11-14 here also appear in OBTIV 70:10-13.

(13) See COPY for É. For this PN cf. OBTIV 70:10, 262:6, and YOS 14 158:25. This name—preceded by DINGIR—also appears as the name of a minor deity, "a lion and envoy" of the goddess (Ištar); cf. R. Kutscher and C. Wilcke ZA 68 (1978) 115f ll. 42, 92 and CAD N/2 77a.

(15) See COPY for this line. The year date formula is OBTIV p. 23 no. 1.

UCP 10/1 60

UCLMA 9/2432

Sale of Vacant Lot

Obv.
12 SAR KI.ŠUB.BA
ḪÉ.DIRIG ḪA.BA.LA
DA É ^{d}EN.ZU-*e-ri-ib*
SAG.BI SILA
É *A-pa-an*-DINGIR
ù Gi-mil-lum DUMU.MEŠ ^{d}⸢x⸣ [ ]
KI *A-pa-an*-DINGIR
ù Gi-mil-lum DUMU.MEŠ ^{d}⸢x⸣ [ ]
^{Id}EN.ZU-*e-ri-ib* DUMU ^{d}EN.ZU[ ]
IN.ŠI.ŠÁM
ŠÁM.TIL.LA.BI.ŠÈ
1 GÍN KÙ.BABBAR

Rev.
[ ]
[ ]⸢GÁL⸣
[ ]
[ ] ⸢x⸣

U.E.
[ ] ⸢x⸣

Seal Legends

A ⌜x⌝ AN ⌜x⌝ [ ]
[DUMU] dEN.ZU-*e-r*[*i*]

B ⌜dEN.ZU⌝-*mu*-[

NOTES

(2) In Akkadian: *lītir limṭī*; cf. CAD A/2 488b, AHw 636a. ḪA.BA.LA is here written phonetically for more usual ḪA(ḪÉ).BA.LÁ. See COPY for ḪÉ.

(3) See COPY for IB sign in lines 3 and 9.

(5) See COPY for erasure following DINGIR.

(7) See COPY; this line was written over three erasures.

(8) See COPY for ⌜x⌝.

Rev. (2′)
There does not appear to have been any writing on the now only partly preserved lower edge. Rev. (2′) is either the first or second line on the reverse. For GÁL see COPY.

Rev. (4′)
See COPY for traces of lines 4′-5′.

Seal Legends
See COPY for Seal Legends A and B.

UCP 10/1 61, p. 30; Seif 22
UCLMA 9/2369
Silver *ḫubuttātum* Loan

Obv. (1) 4 MA.NA KÙ.BABBAR

. . .

(5) DUMU *Bur-Nu-nu*

Rev. ITU *Níg-gal*(!)-*lim*

. . .

Envelope Variants

(1) KIŠIB 4 MA.NA KÙ.BABBAR

(6) ITU *Níg-gal-lim* KÙ.BABBAR

Seal Legend

A-wi-⌜*il*⌝-DINGIR
DUMU *Bur-Nu-nu*

NOTES

(1) See COPY for envelope variants.

(4) There are no more signs after the DINGIR; cf. the almost similar PN LÚ-^{d}NIN.URTA DUMU *Bur-Nu-nu* in UCLMA 9/2864:16.

(6) For GAL and envelope variant see COPY.

(9) There are no witnesses to this loan, although the borrower has affixed his seal. Witnesses are also missing in the *ḫubuttātum* loan UCP 10/1 29. For other examples of loans without witnesses see Koschaker HG V1 155, Edzard, *Tell ed Dēr* nos. 11, 15-16, 27.

Seal Legend
See COPY.

UCP 10/1 62

UCLMA 9/2410

Barley; Record of Outlay for Cattle Feed and Workers

Obv. (1) 1(BÁN) 5 SILA$_3$.TA.AM
3 GUD.ḪI.A UD.27.KAM *i-ku-lu*
5(BÁN) 4 SILA$_3$ *A-na-*^{d}UTU-*ták-la-a-ku*
5(BÁN) 4 SILA$_3$ ^{d}UTU-*tap-pé-e*
(5) 5(BÁN) 4 SILA$_3$ *Šar-rum-*^{d}IM
L.E. 1(BÁN) 4 SILA$_3$ *A-di-du-um*
ša 7 *u*$_4$*-mi* ŠU.ḪA
Rev. 4(BÁN) *Ki-na-nu-um*
(9-10) 2(BÁN) 7 SILA$_3$ *Ma-ki-ia-tum*
ŠU.NIGIN$_2$ 2(GUR) 4(BÁN) GUR 8 SILA$_3$
ŠÀ.GAL GUD.ḪI.A
(13-14) *ù ṣú-ḫa-re-e*
(15) *ša* ITU *Ki-is-ki-súm*

NOTES

(2) For UD.27.KAM meaning "27 days" instead of "27th day" see note to UCP 10/1 33:2. On the need to correct Lutz's 28 to 27, see COPY and note to line 11 below. Lines 1-2 thus state: "0.0.1; 5 kor per day, 3 cattle ate (for) 27 days".

(3) See COPY for KU.

(7) See COPY; the LU sign which Lutz saw between the ŠU and the ḪA is not really there; it is "formed" by the intersection of the *-um* of line 6 and one wedge of the *-um* in line 8.

(9) The *-tum* of Makijatum does not really occupy a separate line; it is just "squeezed in." For the PNs in lines 3-10 see the note to UCP 10/1 33:10.

(11) The total in line 11 will be correct only if the 28 which Lutz read in line 2 is corrected to 27. Lines 3-10 yield a sub-total of 0.4.0; 3 kor; if 0.0.1; 5 kor of line 1 is multiplied by 27, it yields 1.1.4; 5 kors; these two amounts added together give 2.0.4; 8 kors, which is the total in line 11. Note that the entry in ll. 1-2 must be understood as above and not as "so much kor per animal per day" (i.e. 0.0.1; 5 kor x 3 x 27); this would yield too large a figure. Cf. further the same situation in UCP 10/1 33:1-4. Lines 11-15 state: "Total: 2.0.4; 8 kors feed for cattle and the young men for the month of Kiskissum."

(15) The last vertical in Lutz's copy of the *-súm* sign is an error (see COPY); it is the extension of the second horizontal in DINGIR in line 1 on the obverse!

UCP 10/1 63

UCLMA 9/2362

Barley *ḫubuttātum* Loan

Obv. (1) 1(GUR) 1(PI) 4(BÁN) ⸢GUR⸣
[ŠE] ⸢*ḫu-bu*⸣-[*ta-tum*]
^{I}⸢*A*⸣ [ ] ⸢x *-na*⸣
2(PI) 1(BÁN) 3 1/3 SILA$_3$
Na-ru-⸢x⸣ [ ]
ŠU.NIGIN$_2$ 1(GUR) 3(PI) 5(BÁN)
3 1/3 SILA$_3$ [*ḫu-bu-ta-t*]*um*
. . .

Rev. (11) IGI ^{d}ŠARA.MA.AN.SUM
DUMU DINGIR-*pí-laḫ*(!)
IGI [*I-p*]*í-iq-ì-li-šu*
DUMU [*Ad-ma-t*]*i-ì-li*
(15) IGI [ ] ⸢x⸣-*ni*-DINGIR
DUMU *Im-gu-rum*

U.E. MU GIŠ.MAR.GÍD.DA KÙ.GI KÙ.BABBAR

NOTES

(1) See COPY for ll. 1-4.

(4) Note the traces of -⸢*tum*⸣ at the end of line 4; these traces appear on the right edge of the tablet; see further note to line 15.

(11) See COPY for ^{d}ŠARA; for the sign cf. further UCLMA 9/2860:9f. For reading, cf. ŠL 344, 15.

(12) Line 12 appears as Lutz's copy.

(14) This line appears as Lutz copied it; there is enough space for [*Ad-ma-t*]*i*-.

(15) There is no TUM at the end of this line (see COPY); the wedges so interpreted by Lutz belong to line 4.

(17) "The year the gold and silver wagon"; for this year date formula, see OBTIV p. 30 no. 30.

UCP 10/1 64
UCLMA 9/2417
Barley; Record

Obv. (1) 1(GUR) 2(PI) 3(BÁN) GUR ŠE
Na-ap-sa-nu-um
1(GUR) 2(PI) 4(BÁN) *I-din-bi-nu-um*
2.KAM
ŠU.NIGIN$_2$ 3(GUR) 1(BÁN) GUR
⌈x⌉ BI ⌈x⌉
2.KAM
. . .

NOTES

(1) See COPY for PN in present state of preservation.

(2) See COPY for PN and 2.KAM between ll. 2-3.

(3) See COPY for this line; it is difficult to read; what may be a ŠE sign after the GUR is only partly preserved. The line seems to be written over erasures; the last vertical, which Lutz incorporated into his LA, is an erasure. It would be possible to read in line 3: [I]-[*din*]-*bi-nu*(!) but then how to explain the 2.KAM and how to account for only one PN with the total?

UCP 10/1 65, p. 14
UCLMA 9/2372
Silver; Record of Obligation

Obv. (1) ŠÀ.BI 10 ŠE KÙ.BABBAR
ša LÚ-MAR.TU *im-ḫu-ru*
1 ŠE IGI.6.GÁL KÙ.BABBAR
KI LÚ-MAR.TU
(5) *i-ba-aš-ši*
Rev. ITU *Níg-gal-lim* UD.22.KAM
MU KÁ.GAL *Ki(!)-kur-ri*

NOTES

(1) See COPY for 10 ŠE.

(3) See COPY for IGI.6.GÁL.

(5) For the expression KI TN *bašû* as an indication of an outstanding debt, cf. the note to OBTIV 78:3.

(7) See COPY for *Ki(!)-kur-ri*.

UCP 10/1 66; Seif 34

UCLMA 9/2429

Barley; Storehouse Record

. . .

Obv. (3) 1(GUR) *Ṣīl-li-*^{d}TIŠPAK

ša ⌈UR$_5$.RA⌉

Rev. (5) É.DUB É.DINGIR

. . .

U.E. (8) MU É EŠ$_4$.DAR BA.DÍM

NOTES

(3) For 1(GUR) see COPY; the PN is as Lutz copied it. Mašqum is connected with the purchase of an ox and slave in UCP 10/1 89:1, 6.

(4) See COPY for this line.

(5) The last sign on the line is DINGIR; see COPY.

(8) See COPY for this line. For the year date formula see OBTIV p. 26 no. 21.

UCP 10/1 67

UCLMA 9/2377

Barley; Record of Receipts

Obv. (1) 254 GUR ŠE ⌈BA.RÍ(?)⌉.GA

nam-ḫa-ra-tum ša Ú-za-ar-nim

ša a-⌈*na* SAL.⌉LA *šu-un-nu*

Rev. (4) MU É EŠ$_4$.DAR BA.DÍM

NOTES

(1) See COPY. If our reading is correct, then one may translate "barley (strictly measured) according to the *parsiktu* measure." Cf. ŠE.BA.RÍ.GA = *še-ʾi par-sik-ti*, Hh II 117 (MSL 5 p. 60 as corrected by MSL 6 102) and CAD M/2 38f in numerous OB passages cited there sub *mešēqu*.

(2) For this GN, see UCLMA 9/2826:7a, UCLMA 9/2957:1, and the Harmal Geographical List, MSL XI p. 59 line 189. This place must be located in the vicinity of Ishchali.

(3) See COPY for this line. M. Stol suggests taking this line to say: *ša ana raqqim šunnū*, "which have been converted to 'light' measure." For *raqqu* in this sense cf. CAD M/2 38a and AHw 958a.

(4) See COPY for this line. For the year date formula see OBTIV. p. 26 no. 21.

UCP 10/1 68, p. 32; Seif 23

UCLMA 9/2333

Barley *ḫubullu* Loan

Obv. (1) 44 GUR ŠE UR_5[.RA]

. . .

Rev. (18) MU *Ra-pí-qum* (ERASURE)

⌈É ^{d}⌉NIN.A.ZU BA.AN.DAB_5

NOTES

(1) The RA is presumably present, hidden under a clay adhesion which is part of the envelope (now missing); cf. Lutz's comments, UCP 10/1 p. 32, note 1.

(2) See COPY for 4 (not 3) (BÁN).

(18) There is an erasure after QUM; see COPY.

(19) See COPY for this line. For this year date formula see OBTIV p. 33, no. 53.

UCP 10/1 69; p. 33

UCLMA 9/2366

Barley *ḫubuttātum* Loan

. . .

Obv. (2) 3(PI) 2(BÁN) ^{d}EN.ZU-*eri*$_4$-*ba* ⌈SIPA⌉ (ERASURE)

3(PI) 2(BÁN) AN-KA-*ša* ⌈x⌉ (ERASURE)

DUMU *Na-ra-am*-^{d}IM

. . .

NOTES

(2) See COPY for this line. What Lutz saw as 2.KAM is definitely an erasure; the LU of PA.LU (SIPA) is partially erased at the beginning of its left side, but cannot have been meant to be erased since the ⌈PA⌉ is written on the surface of the clay covering LU. The PA itself is obscured by an adhering piece of envelope. Lutz UCP 10/1 p. 71 notes the erasures in 11.2-3.

(3) There is a sign following ŠA which is partly covered by a clay adhesion. The clay in which this sign is impressed appears in turn to be a clay erasure, i.e., a layer of clay laid down anciently over the face of the tablet. That layer partially covers the 2 of 2.KAM following; the 2.KAM is further obscured by additional clay filling and the KAM is also "smeared over." Thus, everything after the *ša* ⌈*x*⌉ is an erasure.

UCP 10/1 70

UCLMA 9/2402

Implements; List of Items

Obv. 1 KUŠ.GUD(!)
5 GIŠ *ka-na-zi-ra-*tu_4
1 GIŠ *qa-qa-ad* GIŠ.APIN
1 GIŠ *ḫi-ir-ṣum ša* GIŠ.BAN
5 GIŠ *li-ú* GIŠ.MAR
2 *li-ú ša* GIŠ.APIN
1 GIŠ *su-su-lu*
1 GIŠ *um-mu ša* GIŠ.APIN
1 GIŠ *li-ú we-de-nu*
14 *tu-up-ši-ka-tu*
3 GIŠ *li-ú ša up-li-tim*
6 *da-da-*tu_4 *ša i-mi*
1 *i-mu-um e-šu-um*
5 *ma-al-qa-*tu_4
L.E. 1 *um-mu ša ma-aš-ka-ka-*[*tim*]
Rev. 3 *a-ḫu-ú*
4 *ra-ap-šu*
10 *gi-sa-pu*
15 *pa-ri-sa-*tu_4
1 GIŠ *i-tu-um*
2 *šu-ši mi-ir-tu*
3 *šu-ši ši-na-*tu_4 *ša ma-às-sú-tim*
1 GIŠ.BAN
8 DUG *ri-qí-*tu_4
1 GIŠ.APIN *ša ḫu-ur-pí*
1 *ni-ru ḫu-ur-pí*
2 *a-su-ú ša ba-ba-ti*

11 MA-*nu-ut* KI-*e*

U.E. 2(PI) 5 SILA$_5$ *ši-qú-um*

2 GIŠ.MAR.GÍD.DA 5 *ma-ga-ru*

NOTES

(1) This line appears as Lutz copied it; cf. further CAD M/2 377b.

(2) See COPY; for *kanazir(r)ātum*, "a kind of agricultural implement (pl.)" cf. CAD K 143b, AHw 435b.

(3) See COPY for GIŠ.APIN; this term was read *qaqqad epinnim* in AHw 900a and is apparently identical with GIŠ.SAG.APIN discussed by Salonen, *Agricultura* 91.

(6) See COPY for GIŠ.APIN; for translation see Salonen, *Agricultura* 85.

(7) See COPY for this line; see further AHw 1063b.

(8) Salonen, *Agricultura* 71f, 94, 97.

(11) This line appears as Lutz copied it; for *uplītum* see AHw 1423b.

(12) See COPY; this line was collated by J. J. Finkelstein and read by him as *id-da-tum* (cf. CAD I 8f); Lutz, however, perceived these signs as DA-DA (by his copy; otherwise, he would have drawn them as ID; cf. note to UCP 10/1 58:3. In this he was followed by AHw 149a. The "simple" sign forms which appear here in line 12 are in fact most often DA; cf. UCLMA 9/2827:28; 2889a: ii 7, iii 9; UCP 10/1 109:16. On occasion, however, ID is written in simpler form like DA: e.g. OBTIV 55:15, 57:13, 91:2. But, as the signs now stand, one must continue to read *da-da-tu*$_4$, unless for etymological reasons, ID is preferable. This step is not yet clearly indicated, to judge from the slender evidence available so far.

(13) See COPY; for *imûm*, "plowshare," see Salonen, *Agricultura* 77f (sub *emû*).

(14) AHw 596b.

(15) See COPY for this line; the TIM is partly visible, apparently written on an angle below the second KA. It comes at the end of line 15, on the corner of the tablet—now broken away. The traces of the horizontal that Lutz copied after the 2nd KA is not a sign but a crack in the clay. Since the first sign is UM and not I, the reference in CAD E 156b (sub *emû*) must be corrected; Salonen's (*Agricultura* 78) doubts about this reading must then be upheld. *Ummu* must here refer to the main beam of the harrow (*maškakum*); this is its meaning in connection with the better attested *epinnum* (plow); see Salonen, *Agricultura* 71, 97.

(16) Salonen, *Agricultura* 74.

(17) See COPY for numeral; only 4 wedges are visible. For *rapšum*, cf. AHw 957a.

(18) See COPY for 10 in place of Lutz's 11.

(21) This line is as Lutz copied it; for *mirtûm*, consider *martû*, *mertû*, AHw 614f, 646b—apparently from *retû* "to fasten" (AHw 976).

(22) See COPY for this line; Lutz omitted the second ŠI. ZU is likely but LU is not excluded. CAD M/1 368b read 3 *šušši* <*ši*>*-na-tum ša ma-aš-ka-*<*ka*>*-tim* "66 teeth for a harrow." This reading is most attractive but unfortunately does not correspond to what actually appears on the tablet. AHw 628a *mašlûtum* is likewise unsatisfactory for the meaning of this line.

(24) This line appears as Lutz copied it. The reading with DUG follows CAD K 220a.

(26) See COPY for this line; for *ḫurpu* see CAD H 252a.

(27) See COPY for *ba-ba-ti* (2nd BA could be a MA). CAD A/2 347b reports a collation of SU for the first BA—very attractive but unfortunately not present, unless one assumes a scribal error and reads *ṣu*(!)-. This passage, incidentally, has been collated by the writer on three separate occasions. Perhaps one can interpret this entry as "2 *asû* (type) doors for doorways;" cf. CAD A/2 347b *asû* C—apparently a type of door and not just part of one, to judge from the Sumerian equivalent.

(28) See COPY. The reading of this line is uncertain; the first signs 11 + MA could be joined to read *ù*(!); the MA could be BA or ŠU(!). AHw 925b read *unūt qê*, following the original (incorrect) reading of Lutz (*ú-nu-ut*) and MSL 6 53 (Hh VI) 33 where we find [giš].a.kar.túk.ba = *unūt qí-e*. It is possible to "merge" the 11 plus the MA to read *ù* (!)*-nu-ut qí-e* in line 28 but then where is the expected numeral?

(29) This line appears as Lutz copied it. The intrusion of foodstuffs into this list of objects is surprising; AHw 1248a tentatively takes it to be a seasoned sauce. Perhaps it could also have been used as an industrial lubricant or grease coating for tools and implements.

(30) See COPY.

UCP 10/1 71

UCLMA 9/2396

Barley; Tally of Outlays

Obv. (1) 1 GUR ŠE *Sa-ni-pu-um*

. . .

L.E. (5) 1(PI) 4(BÁN) *Še-li-bu-um*

Rev. (6-7) 2(PI) ⸢2(BÁN)⸣ *Mu-na-nu-*<*um*> *ba-a-*⸢*ru*⸣

. . .

(10) ŠÀ *ša* ŠE.BAL(?)

NOTES

(1) For SA see COPY.

(5) The vertical following the 4(BÁN) in Lutz's copy is an error.

(6) See COPY for this line; note that the total in line 8 agrees with the sums of lines 1-6.

(10) See COPY for this line; the first sign is acceptable as ŠÀ (and so read) but could be a MA, since it is written on the corner of the tablet. For ŠE.BAL see note to UCP 10/1 75:6.

UCP 10/1 72

UCLMA 9/2385

Barley; Perforated Tag Bearing Storehouse Record

Obv. 5 GUR ŠE
ZÍZ *Ta-ri-im-tum*
1(GUR) *Sa-at-lu-ma*
4 GUR ŠE
^{ld}*Wi-ir-i-din-nam*
É.DUB É *Še-li-bu-um*
NÍG.ŠU KI-^{d}UTU-*ba-la-ṭú*
ù LÚ-MAR.TU

NOTES

(2) This line appears as Lutz copied it; it is possible to read the first sign as 3(BÁN) (!) but this would interrupt any continuity between lines 1-2. Note that the entries in ll. 1, 3, 4 are also for full kor amounts. ZÍZ is not precluded since there is no unifying total; the text is a label identifying a shipment of grain. For the PN, Tarimtum, cf. YOS 14 331:11.

(3) See COPY for 1(GUR); Lutz's 1 (PI) is incorrect.

(6) See COPY for the end of this line; there is no trace of the KI as Lutz copied it in; nor could it ever have been there at all since the UM "backs on" to the perforated hole of the bulla.

(7) See COPY for BA.

UCP 10/1 74

UCLMA 9/2342

Silver *ḫubuttātum* Loan

Obv. ⸢2 1/3 GÍN⸣ 12 ŠE ⸢KÙ.BABBAR⸣
ḫu-bu-ta-tum
KI DINGIR-*šu-na-ṣir*
^{ld}EN.ZU-*na-da*
ù Ib-na-tum
DUMU.MEŠ *E-ri-ib*-30
L.E. ŠU.BA.AN.TI.MEŠ
Rev. *a-na maš-kán-nim*
še-a-am Ì.ÁG.E
IGI *A-lí-ba-ni-šu* GÌR.NITÁ
^{l}*Sa-at-lu-ma*

ù BA-^{d}EN.LIL

DUMU.MEŠ ^{d}E[N.ZU-*i-qí-ša-am*]

ù [DUB.SAR]

U.E. (15) MU ⸢^{d}UTU-*ši*-^{d}IM BA⸣.[UG$_{x}$(TIL)]

NOTES

(1) See COPY for this line.

(4) See COPY for DA.

(9) Note that barley is to be repaid in place of silver. For recent discussions of this type of "mixed loans" see D. O. Edzard, *Tell ed Dēr* 30-34; N. Yoffee, *The Economic Role of the Crown in the Old Babylonian Period*, Bibliotheca Mesopotamica 5 (Undena Publications: Malibu 1977) 14.

(12) See COPY for PN.

(13) See COPY for ^{d}E[N. The PN is restored on the basis of parallels in UCP 10/1 52:20f and 107:24-25.

(15) See COPY for this line. For the year date formula, cf. OBTIV p. 34, no. 59.

UCP 10/1 75; Seif 35

UCLMA 9/2325

Barley; Record of Outlay for Cattle Feed

. . .

Obv. (6) 3(GUR) ŠE.BAL *i-na li-bu še-e-im*

ša i-ti Tu-tu-ub-ma-gir ni-im<-*ḫu*>-*ru*

3(GUR) 3(PI) 2(BÁN) ^{d}EN.ZU-*i-din-nam ša-gu-um*

1(GUR) 1(PI) GUR *a-na šu-pí-ul-tim*

L.E. (10-11) *nam-ḫa-ar-ti Im-gur*-^{d}EN.LÍL

Rev. 2(PI) 4(BÁN) *A-bu-wa-qar*

ŠU.NIGIN$_{2}$ 17(GUR) 4(PI) 2(BÁN) GUR ŠE

ša-ap-ti Šar-rum-^{d}IM

(15) *a-na* ŠÀ.GAL GUD.ḪI.A

NOTES

(6) For ŠE.BAL cf. the note to OBTIV 113:1 above; the ŠE.BAL in our text was destined for feeding cattle. It is not possible *a priori* to distinguish ŠE.BAL in this meaning from ŠE.BAL = *šupi''ultu, qīptu* (see ŠL 367, 40a-b); line 9 below does speak of *šupi''ultum*. Grain is probably also indicated in the passage *ù* ŠE.BAL-*šu lu al-qí-it*, Harris JCS 9 (1955) pp. 101, 117 no. 98: rev. 3′ (reference courtesy of M. Stol) as well as in MSL 11 83 (Hh XXIV) 155.

(7) The reading *ni-im*<*-ḫu*>*-ru* follows Seif 35; see also COPY. For translation, one must assume a "confusion" between *itti* and *ištu*. Accordingly lines 6-7 should state: "3.0.0 kors exchange, part of the barley which we received from Tutub-magir."

(8) For 3 GUR instead of Lutz's 2 GUR, see COPY. The addition of this kor balances the total in line 13.

(9) For the form *šupe''ultum* cf. GAG § 57d; see also UCP 10/1 79:8. Lines 9-11 state: "1.1.0 kors for exchange, received by Imgur-Enlil."

(10) For PN see COPY.

(14) This line appears as Lutz copied it. Lines 13-15 state: "Total 17.4.2 kors barley (at the) command of Šarrum-Adad, (given out) for cattle feed." For *šaptum* "command", cf. AHw 1176b.

UCP 10/1 76

UCLMA 9/2394

Sheep; Record of Shorn Animals

Obv.	(1)	35 UDU.NITA$_2$ MU.DU#SUMUN
		šà 4-*šu* ÚS.SA
		33 UDU.NITA$_2$
		1 UR$_4$ MU.DU GIBIL
	(5)	ŠU.NIGIN$_2$ 1 *šu-ši* 9 UDU.ḪI.A
		ša MU.DU
		34 UDU.NITA$_2$
		40 UR$_4$
L.E.		ŠU.NIGIN$_2$ 74 UDU.ḪI.A
Rev.	(10)	NA(!).QÀD *Nu-ri-ia*
		ŠU.NIGIN$_2$ 1 ME 43 UDU.NITA$_2$
		ša a-na É *bu-qú-mi i-ru-bu*
		ITU *E-lu-nu* UD.3.KAM
	(14)	MU SAḪAR *zi-ku-ra-at* ^{d}UTU

NOTES

(1) Cf. UDU.MU.UN.DU = *immer šūrubti*, MSL 8/1 22 (Hh XIII) 164. According to AHw 1287b, *šūrubtum* can refer either to the harvest crop or to a harvest tax. Our text deals with the delivery of sheep at shearing time, some of which came into the owner's hands (the temple?) through taxes and other sheep which were in the keeping of the shepherd, Nurija.

(2) See COPY for this line which appears to refer to sheep "which are being driven through (the shearing house) for the fourth time" (*ša erbēšu irdū*/*irredū*). For ÚS.SA = *redûm*, said of livestock, see AHw 965b(4d), 968a.

(4) UR_4 appears as Lutz copied it. UR_4 = *buqāmum* according to Landsberger, MSL 8/1 36f, note to Hh XIII 256; and 31, note to lines 217-224. SUMUN and GIBIL (see COPY) in the present context apparently contrast sheep which have been shorn before with younger (and newly acquired) animals being shorn for the first time.

(10) See COPY for NA.QÀD. The DIŠ is partially erased.

(11) See COPY for UDU.NITA$_2$.

(12) Cf. CAD B 326a for this line.

(14) For this year date formula, see OBTIV p. 34 no. 55.

UCP 10/1 77; Seif 23

UCLMA 9/2357

Mixed Loan: Barley, Emmer with Interest, Silver with Interest (MÁŠ ^{d}UTU)

. . .

Obv. (3) ⸢x⸣ MA.NA KÙ.BABBAR MÁŠ ^{d}UTU

. . .

(6) ⸢DUMU⸣ ^{d}UTU-*mu-uš-te-še-er*

⸢^{I}⸣PUZUR$_4$-EŠ$_4$.DAR

[DUM]U *Bur*(!)-^{d}EN.ZU

[ŠU].BA.AN.TI

– remainder destroyed except for a few signs on the reverse –

NOTES

(3) See COPY for traces of the missing number.

(6) See COPY for traces of DUMU.

(7) See COPY for ⸢^{I}⸣ at the beginning of the line.

(8) See COPY. NÍG is written for BUR; this same defective writing occurs again on OBTIV 55:4, 73:4; ŠUR is written for BUR in OBTIV 34:24 and 56:5.

Rev. (5′)

See COPY for traces of ll. 5′-9′.

UCP 10/1 78

UCLMA 9/2401

Barley; Memo

Obv. (1) 78 ⸢GUR ŠE x x x⸣
É.DUB É ^{d}*I-šar-ki-di-s*[*u*]
85 (GUR) 4 (PI) GUR ŠE *qa-du-u*[*m*]
ZI.GA *a-na ḫar-ra-na-at* ⸢x⸣
(5) *ṭup-pa-tim* DINGIR-*šu-na-ṣir*
L.E. *ma-aḫ-ru*
– remainder destroyed –

NOTES

(1) See COPY for this line; the traces correspond closely to Lutz's copy and reflect the same state of preservation. The traces could support reading ⸢SAG.GAR.RA(!)⸣ "capital (for use)" (the last oblique wedge is not clear).

(2) See COPY for DN.

(3) See COPY for UM; the phrase in ll. 3-4 seem to state "together with the expenses for the journeys of . . ."

(4) Lutz copied the ZI sign with only one vertical wedge; there are actually two; see COPY for ZI.GA. The last fragmentary sign, copied by Lutz, is no longer preserved.

(5) See COPY for DUB. Line 5 apparently begins a new statement which can be interpreted: "the tablets PN received . . . ," with this phrase serving as the object of a verb lost on the reverse now destroyed. Alternatively, "they received the tablets (from) PN."

UCP 10/1 79

UCLMA 9/2340

Barley; List of Amounts and Persons

. . .
Obv. (4) 1(GUR) 1(PI) 4(BÁN) GUR *A-ḫu-ni* (ERASURE)
(5) 1(GUR) 2(PI) 2(BÁN) GUR ^{d}EN.ZU-*e-ri-ba-am*
3 GUR *ša na-aš-pa-ak* É ^{d}[EN]
3(GUR) 4(PI) GUR ^{d}EN.ZU-*i-din-nam ša-gu*[*-um*]
1(GUR) 1(PI) GUR *ša šu-pí-ul-tim*
. . .

NOTES

(4) For ERASURE see COPY; UCP 10/1 75:4 adds his father's name.

(6) See COPY for this line.

(7) Restored from UCP 10/1 75:8.

(8) ŠA is written over an erasure; see COPY; the wedge following TIM may belong to a line written on the reverse—now all is missing. For *šupi"ultum* see note to UCP 10/1 75:6.

(11) Line 11 contains only an erasure; see COPY.

UCP 10/1 80

UCLMA 9/2404

Silver Loan with Interest (MÁŠ ^{d}UTU)

Obv. (1) 1 1/2 MA.NA KÙ.BABBAR
MÁŠ ^{d}UTU *ú-ṣa-ab*
KI *Bur-*^{d}EN.ZU
[ ] ⌈x⌉ [ ] ⌈UD⌉
bottom half missing

Rev. (1′) [MU] [ ]
(2′) ⌉30-*a-*⌈*bu*⌉-[*šu*]

NOTES

UCP 10/1 80 and 82 could very well be fragments of the same tablet; they are alike in color, shape, and writing; but there is not enough tablet remaining to corroborate the join beyond question.

(4) See COPY for traces.

Rev. (1′)
This restoration is conjectural; if acceptable, it could relate to OBTIV p. 34, year date formula no. 60.

UCP 10/1 81

UCLMA 9/2350

Barley *ḫubuttātum* Loan

(5) DUMU ⌜*Bu*⌝-[ ] **NOTES**

. . .

NOTES

(4) See COPY for lines 4-5, which are probably in the same state of preservation as when Lutz saw them, to judge from his difficulty in making out line 5. I am uncertain as to how to read the PN in line 4; ZU(!)-LU-⌜x⌝ is also possible.

UCP 10/1 83

UCLMA 9/2415

Oil; Record of Receipt

Obv. (1) 2(PI) Ì.GIŠ

1(PI) 5(BÁN) Ì.ŠAḪ

1(PI) 2(BÁN) Ì.ESIR$_x$(SUK).R[A]

nam-ḫa-ar-ti

Rev. (5) [l]*I-bi*-[d]EN.ZU

NOTES

(2) See COPY for ŠAḪ.

(3) See COPY. For the writing of ESIR$_x$ as SUK (LAGAB x A) at Ishchali, cf. note to OBTIV 225:3.

(5) See COPY for this PN; the BI is strangely written but seems to be correctly read.

UCP 10/1 84

UCLMA 9/2382

Record of Outlay

Obv. (1) 5(GUR) 3(PI) 2(BÁN) 5 SILA$_3$ *Ri-iš*-30

. . .

(5) 2(GUR) ⌜*Ki*⌝-*ma-nu-um*

. . .

Rev. (2′) MU KÁ.GAL *Ki-kur-ri-im*

[l]*I-ba-al-pí-el*

NOTES

Less than one third of the original tablet is preserved.

(1) On the tablet, there is no DIŠ between the $SILA_3$ and RI.

(5) ⸢KI⸣ is a valid reading; but ⸢MI⸣ is not excluded.

Rev. (2′)
See COPY for KI. For this year formula "The year the Gate of the Chapel, Ibalpiel" see OBTIV p. 32 no. 46.

UCP 10/1 85

UCLMA 9/2398

Barley *ḫubuttātum* Loan

		. . .
Rev.	(10)	IGI ^{d}UTU-[*i-q*]*í-šam*
		. . .

NOTES

(10) See COPY for this PN.

(12) See COPY for this line.

UCP 10/1 86

UCLMA 9/2391

Barley; List of Amounts and Persons

Obv.	(1)	[ ]	*A-ḫa-am-ni-šu*
		1(GUR)	*I-di-na-tum*
		. . .	
		⸢1(GUR)⸣	*Za-*⸢*ru*⸣*-um*
	(10)	⸢1(GUR)⸣	^{d}EN.ZU-*iš-me-an-ni*
		[ ]	⸢*A* x x x⸣-*bi*
		– break in text –	
Rev.	(13)	⸢1(GUR)⸣	*A-bi-ia-tum*
		[ ]	^{d}EN.ZU-*mu-ba-lí-iṭ*
	(15)	[ ] ⸢1(BÁN)⸣	*Za-ku-re-e-el*
		[ ]	*E-ri-ib*-30

NOTES

The text is written on the upper portion of a rather flat tablet of unknown length. We have retained Lutz's line numbering, counting the first line on the reverse as line 13; but this is in fact an error. There is no way to estimate the missing number of lines. It would have been more accurate simply to begin a new count on the reverse.

(1) For NI see COPY; there is no reason to read IR as Lutz's copy suggests.

(2) The PN begins with I (see COPY) and not DUMU as Lutz's copy; this PN was correctly read in Seif 41.

(8) The reading, 1(GUR), is strengthened by the thickness of the horizontal wedge.

(9) See COPY for PN.

(11) See COPY for traces of this line.

(13) See COPY for ⸢1(GUR)⸣.

(15) See COPY. The horizontal line is best read as 1 (BÁN). The vertical line before the ZA is not a wedge but appears to be the edge of a clay lump into which the ZA is impressed. Perhaps it is an erasure. The signs following ZA appear essentially as Lutz copied them.

UCP 10/1 87

UCLMA 9/2346

Barley; Record of Withdrawal

Obv. (1) 3 GUR ŠE *A-bu-um*-DINGIR
2(GUR) 3(PI) 2(BÁN) ARAD-^{d}NIN.ŠUBUR
ù Du-ba-ba-tum
3(PI) 4(BAN) ^{d}EN.LÍL-*a-bu-um*
(5) 1(PI) 4(BAN) *Ib-ni*-^{d}MAR.TU
DUMU *A-ḫi-ša-gi-iš*
6(GUR) 3(PI) 4(BÁN) GUR ŠE UR$_5$.RA
– break in text at lower edge –
Rev. (8) [AR]AD-*ì*-⸢*lí*⸣
[ ] *Mu(?)-ti-Ar-ra-ap*-⸢*ḫe*⸣
(10) [ ] *a-na* ⸢SIG$_4$⸣.ÍL
1 (PI) *Mu-sa-li-lum* LÚ[ ]
1 (PI) *Ḫa-zi-qa-ia*
a-na ZÍD.DA *a-na bu-qú-mi-im*
1(GUR) 3(PI) 4(BÁN) GUR ŠE ZI.DIDLI
(15) ŠU.NIGIN$_2$ 8(GUR) 2(PI) 2(BÁN) GUR ŠE *ni-iš-rum*
É.DUB *aš-lu-ka-tim*
U.E. NÍG.ŠU ^{d}UTU-LUGAL

ITU.DIRIG *Ki-in-k*[*i-im*]
(19) MU GUD.APIN KÙ.GI

NOTES

(4) See COPY for ^{d}EN.LÍL.

(7) The amount in Line 7 is the sum of the amounts in lines 1-5. This grain was apparently lent out in *ḫubullu* (UR$_5$.RA) loans.

(8) See COPY for lines 8-9, which are omitted by Lutz. Line 8 probably does not follow directly upon line 7; there is room for at least one line on the lower edge. Line 7 is written at the lower edge.

(9) The mention of Arrapḫa is unusual but not unknown in OB texts; cf. Rép. géog. 3 21f., which also cites the PN *Mu-tu-Ar-ra-ap-ḫi-im* in AOAT 3/1 34:3.

(10) See COPY; the reading SIG$_4$.ÍL = *zābil libittim* follows a suggestion of M. Stol; cf. CAD Z 8f.

(11) See COPY; there is room in the break for another sign after LÚ.

(13) "For flour at (sheep) shearing (i.e. plucking) time." See COPY for ZÍD.DA and for the "missing" *-im*, which CAD B 325b expected and restored after the *-mi-*.

(14) This line is as Lutz copied it. Perhaps one can read ZI.< GA>.DIDLI "various expenses."

(15) Lines 15-17 state: "Grand Total. 8.2.2 kors barley, withdrawal (out of) the long storehouse, (under) the control of Šamaš-šarrum."

(17) See COPY for this line; there is nothing now preserved after LUGAL. It seems that the ⌜KI⌝ in Lutz's copy is misplaced from line 18, due to the similarity of the LUGAL and IN signs. Lutz inserted the ⌜KI⌝ into line 17 instead of into line 18, where it belongs.

(18) See COPY.

UCP 10/1 88

UCLMA 9/2334

Barley; Tally of Collections

Obv. (1) 7 GUR ŠE *E-ri-ib-*^{d}EN.ZU
5 GUR *Ì-lí-ki-ma-a-bi-ia*
7(GUR) 1(PI) 4(BÁN) ^{d}EN.ZU-*ma-gir*
4(PI) 3(BÁN) *I-di-šum*
(5) 3(PI) 2(BÁN) DAM(?) *Na-ra-*< *am-*> ^{d}IM
(6) 3(PI) 2(BÁN) *Ša-bu-lum* DUMU 30-*eri*$_4$*-ba*
(7) 1(GUR) ^{d}UTU-*nu-ri*

(7a) 2(PI) 3(BÁN) *Sa-ri-qum*
(8) 2(PI) 3(BÁN) *Sú-du-rum*
(9) 1(GUR) ^{d}UTU-*ú-ṣa-am*
L.E. (10) [ ]-⸢*li-sú*⸣-*nu*
[ ]-⸢*na*⸣-*an-ni*
Rev. [-*ṣi*] *r*
[ ]
[N]*I-šu*
(15) [ ] ⸢x⸣
[ ]
[ ]
[ ]-*ri*
[ ] ⸢x⸣-*si-ia*
(20) [ ]-*ia*
(21-22) [ŠU.NIGIN$_2$] ⸢10+⸣ 9(GUR) 1(PI) 1(BÁN) GUR ŠE
U.E. (23) *ša uš-ta-di-nu*

NOTES

(4) See COPY for ŠUM.

(5) See COPY for DAM and RA.

(6) Lutz's drawing is "shakey" for -*eri*$_4$-*ba* but essentially correct. Our reading of the PN follows UCP 10/1 p. 61 and Seif 44.

(7a) Lutz omitted this line by error; see COPY.

(8) See COPY for SÚ.

(10) See COPY for ⸢sú⸣, which is better preserved on Lutz's copy; one may perhaps restore the PN [*Be*]-⸢*li-sú*⸣-*nu*.

(11) See COPY for traces of lines 11-12 (no trace of 13), 14-15.

(19) See COPY. There is room for three intervening lines between lines 14 and 18. In Lutz's hand copy, his designation of lines 20 hovers between lines 20 and 21; but its placement is with line 20 as read here; cf. the fragmentary PNs of lines 18-19 in UCP 10/1 p. 65.

(21) Lines 21-23 state: "Total: . . . 9.1.1 kors barley which were collected."

UCP 10/1 89

UCLMA 9/2336

Barley; Storehouse Record of Expenditures

. . .

Obv. (4) 2 GUR ŠE KÙ.BABBAR 5 GUR ŠE KÙ.BABBAR TAB(!).BA

(5) ^{I}KI-*ra-bi-at*

. . .

(10) 1(GUR) *I-gu-us*$_{x}$(AZ)-*su-um*

1(GUR) ^{d}EN.ZU-*mu-ba-lí-iṭ*

3(GUR) 2(PI) *E-ri-iš-tum*

. . .

(18) 1(GUR) *Na-sú-la-tum*

. . .

L.E. (21) ⌜1(GUR)⌝ *I-din*-^{d}⌜Mi⌝-[*šar*]

⌜1(GUR)⌝ *A-ḫu-ki-n*[*u-um*]

1(GUR) *I-túr-A*[*š-du-um*]

. . .

Rev. ⌜2(BÁN)⌝ *Ib-ni*-^{d}MAR.TU

(30) ⌜3(BÁN)⌝ *A-ḫa-su-nu*

. . .

(35) [ ] 3(BÁN) ⌜*Šu-ma*⌝-[ ]

1(PI) 1(BÁN) [ ]

1(PI) *Še*-[ ] ⌜x⌝

2(GUR) ⌜x⌝ [ ] ⌜x⌝

2(BÁN) [ ] ⌜x⌝-*ti*-DINGIR

(40) ŠU.NIGIN$_2$ ⌜1 *šu-ši*⌝ 3 GUR ŠE ZI.GA

É.DUB É ^{d}⌜*Mi-šar*⌝ *ša* BÀD-*Ri-muš*

U.E. NÍG.ŠU DINGIR-*šu-na-ṣir*

(43) MU É EŠ$_4$.DAR BA.DIM

NOTES

(2) Lines 2-5 state: "6.0.0 kors barley, (for) silver, (given to Erṣitum-rabi'at; 2.0.0 kors barley, (for) silver on a second occasion, (by the) authority of Ipquša, (given to) Erṣitum-rabi'at; 2.0.0 kors barley, (for) silver; 5.0.0 kors barley, (as) partnership money (i.e. risk capital), (given to) Erṣitum-rabi'at." KÙ.BABBAR is clear in lines 2-4. Our translation assumes that barley was being spent in order to purchase silver; cf. UET 5 73:25, cited by CAD K 245b.

(4) See COPY for TAB(!).BA.

(7) See COPY for ^{d}TIŠPAK in Ṣilli-Tišpak.

(10) See COPY and line 25 for this PN. The US_x value is already anticipated in the OB usage of UZ/Ṣ_4; see von Soden Syllabar 18 and the discussion above on Syllabary, p. 3.

(12) See COPY for ⸢IŠ⸣; Lutz's copy is inaccurate. Cf. further the PN in line 19.

(15) See COPY for 3(BÁN) in place of 4.

(18) See COPY for ZU.

(21) See COPY for ⸢^{d}*Mi*⸣.

(22) See COPY for this line.

(23) This line appears as Lutz copied it.

(24) See COPY for ⸢IA⸣ in Ummijatum.

(25) See COPY and note to line 10 for this PN.

(29) See COPY for ⸢2 (BÁN)⸣.

(30) See COPY for this line.

(32) There is nothing following the NU. Perhaps it is an abbreviation for NU.GIŠ.SAR.

(33) See COPY for this PN.

(34) See COPY for this PN; perhaps one could restore *Ib-ni-*⸢^{d}EN.ZU⸣.

(35) See COPY for this PN.

(37) There is a slight space between the 1(PI) and the ŠE: we take it to be the beginning of a PN.

(38) See COPY for traces.

(39) See COPY for traces.

(40) Lines 40-42 state: "Total: 63.0.0 kors barley, expenditure, storehouse of the temple of Mišar in Dur-Rimuš: (under the) control of Ilšu-naṣir." See COPY for ⸢1 *šu-ši*⸣.

(41) See COPY for ^{d}⸢*Mi-šar*⸣.

UPC 10/1 90, pp. 39f.

UCLMA 9/2422

Sale of Slave

. . .

Rev. (20) [^{Id}UTU]*-na-ṣir* DUMU ^{d}EN.ZU*-i-qí-šam*
[^{I}*I*]*m-*[*g*]*ur-*^{d}UTU DUMU *Ib-ni-*^{d}EN.LÍL
[^{I}*Ma-n*]*a-ba-al-ṭe*$_4$*-*⸢*el*⸣

[ ] ⸢x⸣ [ ]

– remainder destroyed except for fragments –

NOTES

(3) See COPY for ll. 3-5. One could restore in line 3: ARAD/GEME$_2$ *ša* PN; the PNs in ll. 3-4 both end in *-tum*.

(4) The ⸢KI⸣ is difficult to make out; Lutz's copy for the beginning of lines 4-5 is suspect (see note to line 5) and is not good evidence for the reading of these signs. Perhaps one should restore: . . . (3) [KI ^{f}P]N$_1$ (4) ⸢*ù*⸣ [^{f}P]N$_2$ (5) NIN.A.NI.IR, with NIN.A.NI, sg., being written for an expected plural form NIN.A.NE.NE.

(5) See COPY for NIN; Lutz's LUGAL is incorrect.

(13) See COPY for BAL.

(14) See COPY for MU.UN.

(21) See COPY for traces of [*I*]*m*-[*g*]*ur*.

(22) See COPY for this line and a trace of line 23.

There are three small fragments: A-C (see COPY), difficult to place because of their small size and the lack of certain fit with the tablet in its present state; they perhaps come from lines 1-3. Fragment A, for example, could belong in the space above the vertical tail in the middle of the break in line 3.

UCP 10/1 91, pp. 43f.; Seif 37f.

UCLMA 9/2431

Court Record: Theft and Penalty Service

Obv.	(1)	^{ld}EN.ZU-*a-bu-um* NA.B[É.A]	(1)	Sin-abum—(the following) is what he said:
		1 SAG ARAD ^{ld}UTU-*ma-gir*		"the slave Šamaš-magir
		KI ^{d}ŠEŠ.KI.MA.AN.SUM DAM.QAR		from Nanna.mansum, the merchant
		a-ša-am-šu a-na ši-mi-šu ga-am-[*ri-im*]		I bought; for his complete price
	(5)	KÙ.BABBAR *aš-qú-ul i-tu-úr-ma*	(5)	I paid silver." He went back
		^{ld}UTU-*ma-gir i-na* É *I-pí-iq-* [EŠ$_4$.DAR]		–Šamaš-magir (did)–and in the house of Ipiq-Ištar
		i-na šu-ur-qí-im ^{ld}UTU-*ma-gir*	7)	they caught Šamaš-magir
		*iṣ-ṣa-ab-tu-šu a-na I-pí-iq-*EŠ$_4$.DAR	8)	with stolen property. Unto Ipiq-Ištar
		be-el šu-ur-qí-šu DI.KU$_5$ *Ne-ri-ib-tim*^{KI}		the owner of the stolen property the judge of Neribtum
	(10)	*ik-šu-šu-ma a-na* ÈŠ.NUN.NA^{KI}	10)	bound him over in penalty service; but
		^{ld}UTU-*ma-gir il-li-kam-ma*	11)	Šamaš-magir came to Ešnunna and

	um-ma šu-ma DAM.QAR *a-li-ia-ma*	thus he (declared): "the merchant of my city
	i-bé-el-la-an-ni KA.KI *ù* DI.KU$_5$.MEŠ	owns me." The *kakikkum* and the judges
	^{Id}UTU-*ma-gir i-ša-lu-ma*	interrogated Šamaš-magir; and
	ki-ma šu-ur-qá-am i-na Ne-ri-ib-tim^{KI}	that he had committed a theft
	iš-ri-qú-ma ik-šu-⸢šu⸣-šu	in Neribtum and (that) they had bound him over for penalty service
	IGI KA.KI *ù* DI.KU$_5$.MEŠ	before the *kakikkum* and the judges
Rev.	^{Id}UTU-*ma-gir* INIM-*šu ú-ki-in*	Šamaš-magir confirmed his word(s).
	^{I}EŠ.DAR-*šar-ra-at ù* ^{d}UTU-*ma-gir*	(Thereupon) Ištar-šarrat and Šamaš-magir
	a-na ^{d}EN.ZU-*a-bu-um ki-a-am iq-bu-ú*	spoke to Sin-abum
	um-ma šu-nu-ma ki-ma ša-nu-um	—thus they said: "since a second party
	i-BI-⸢x *qá-a*⸣-*ti at-ta-a-ma*	. . . my hand, will you
	[ ] ⸢x⸣-*ni ki-a-am*	. . . me?"
	[ ]*ma* ^{d}EN.ZU-*a-bu-um*	. . . Sin-abum
	[ ] ⸢KÙ⸣.BABBAR ^{Id}UTU-*ma-gir*	. . . the money for Šamaš-magir
	[ ] ⸢x⸣ *um-ma-šu*	. . . his mother
	[*it*-] *ta-la-ku*	. . . (and) went off.
	[ ] ⸢^{d}⸣UTU-*ma-gir*	. . . Šamaš-magir
	[ ] ⸢x⸣-SI(?)	. . .
	[ ] ⸢x⸣	. . .
	^{I}[ ]	. . .
	^{I}⸢x⸣ [ ]	. . .
	^{I}[ ]	. . .
	[ ]	. . .
U.E.	[MU] ⸢x LUGAL⸣	The year . . . the king
	É AD.⸢DA⸣.NI <.ŠÈ> BA.AN.KU$_4$	entered his father's house (as king)

Seal Legends

A	^{d}EN.ZU-*mu-ba-li-iṭ*	A	Sin-muballiṭ
	DUMU *Ki-ir-ki-ru-um*		son of Kirkirum
	ARAD *Da-du-ša*		servant of Daduša
B	*An-um-pí-ša*	B	Anum-piša
	DUMU ^{d}EN.ZU-*i*-⸢*qí*⸣-*ša-am*		son of Sin-iqišam
	ARAD *Da-du-ša*		servant of Daduša
C	*A-bu-wa-qar*	C	Abum-waqar
	DUMU ^{d}EN.ZU-*še-mi*		son of Sin-šemi
	ARAD *Da-du-ša*		servant of Daduša
D	*Za-ab*-[ ]	D	Zab . . .
	DUMU *I*-⸢x⸣-*ru*-⸢x⸣		son of I . . . ru . . .
	ARAD *Da-du-š*[*a*]		servant of Daduša

NOTES

Significant excerpts from this text are made in CAD K 44a (ll. 12-18) and 286b (ll. 8-16).

(1) See COPY for the end of this line; for NA.BÉ.A cf. ŠL 70.80 and Sollberger TCS 1 192 no. 830.

(3) See COPY for DAM.QAR.

(6) See COPY for PN.

(9) See COPY for DI.KU_5, which probably should be emended to DI.KU_5.<MEŚ> in order to conform with the pl. verbal form *ikšušūma* in l. 10.

(13) The purpose of this remark is obscure; CAD B 201a suggests that it implies: "I have no possessions." Another possibility is that it says: "Don't leave me here in penalty service; my master will take responsibility and arrange for my release." It seems that *tamkār ālija* may refer to Sin-abum rather than to Nanna.mansum, since the latter is not involved at all; and line 18 implies that Šamaš-magir had convinced the judges of the truth of his remarks. Then, Sin-abum is addressed in ll. 19f.

(16) See COPY for *ik-šu-*⌈*šu*⌉*-šu*.

(19) The identity of Ištar-šarrat is uncertain; perhaps she is the mother of Šamaš-magir. Cf. *um-ma-šu* in line 26 and the note to line 24.

(21) See COPY for *ša-nu-um*. There is no question about NU; the extra wedge above the sign in Lutz's copy belongs to the KI at the end of line 15, which was written onto the reverse.

(22) See COPY for the beginning of this line and for the traces of lines 23-26. The third and fourth signs are partly broken; *qá* seems possible for the fourth sign but the reading of the third is uncertain. ⌈LA⌉ is possible and perhaps ⌈LÍ⌉. One could get sense here from a verb like *bêlu*, i.e., "another has power over my hand;" but the final vowel resulting from LA/LÍ would be difficult to explain, unless one has recourse to GAG § 82e. Another possibility is to read *i-bi-*⌈il_5*(!)-ni(!)-a*⌉*-ti* "has power over us."

(23) At present, the sign copied by Lutz as DI is not fully preserved (see copy). If, as it appears, the tablet is in the same state of preservation as when Lutz saw it, the sign could also be read as [Š]A, [T]A, [N]A.

(24) Perhaps [*iq-bu*]*-ma*, repeating the statement earlier made in line 20. Following this, one might consider restoring: (25) [*im-gur-ma*] ⌈KÙ⌉.BABBAR [1d]UTU*-ma-gir* (26) [KI EŠ.DAR*-šar-ra-a*]*t um-ma-šu* (27) [*il-qí-ma it*]*-ta-la-ku*, "Sin-abum agreed and took the price of Šamaš-magir from Ištar-šarrat his mother and left." Lines 29-30 might then contain the satisfaction of the penalty imposed by the judges in favor of Ipiq-Ištar. Lines 31-34 would contain the list of judges.

(27) Lines 27-28 appear as Lutz copied them.

(29) For lines 29-33, see COPY.

(34) There is room for another line (and perhaps even more); note that the obverse has 17 lines; the reverse should contain about the same number. See COPY for ll. 35f.

Seal Legends:

See COPY for seals. Seals A and B are inscribed on the left edge; seals C and D are on the lower edge. Perhaps the PN *I-*[*k*]*a-ru-u*[*um*] could be restored in seal D.

UCP 10/1 92
UCLMA 9/2425
Unknown Commodity; Memo on Interest

. . .

L.E. (7) ^{1}⸢*El*⸣ [ ]

⸢DUMU ^{d}EN⸣ [ ]

– Reverse completely gone –

U.E. (13) *aš(!)šum* ⸢x⸣ [ ]

i-ba-la-k[*a-tu*]

Edge MÁŠ *ú-ṣa-ab*

(16) *iq-bu-ú*

NOTES

(7) See COPY for lines 7-8. These lines both are on the lower edge; the reverse is completely gone and was estimated by Lutz to contain about six lines, like the obverse. He thus numbered the first lines visible on the upper edge as 13ff. We have retained Lutz's numbering. However, since lines 7-8 are now to be added on the lower edge, and if there were some 6 lines on the reverse, then the lines on the upper edge might better have been numbered as 15ff.

(13) See COPY for this line.

(14) This line appears as Lutz copied it; the MA could also be BA.

(16) See COPY for this line. We may tentatively see ll. 1-8 as listing the names of persons who made the statement in ll. 13-16. That statement may perhaps have said: "Because . . . they transgressed, they said 'I will pay interest.'"

UCP 10/1 93
UCLMA 9/2365
Barley *ḫubuttātum* Loan

NOTES

(13) See COPY for lines 13-17.

(15) The visible sign looks more like KA(!) than AB as Lutz copied it; but then there is no clear trace of a second vertical.

(16) See COPY. The year date formula is OBTIV p. 23 no. 3.

UCP 10/1 94; Seif 35f

UCLMA 9/2381

Cattle; Tallies of Work Use

. . .

Obv. UD.10 *ša-ra-*⌈*nu*⌉*-um*

UD.2 *a-na ṣí-im-di-im*

UD.2 *a-na pa-nu a-bi-im su-mu-na-tum*
i-li-ka

ŠU.NIGIN$_2$ 1 ITU *ù* UD.12.KAM *ni-*[*nu*] *ni-ir-di*

1 ITU *ù* UD.11.KAM *a-na* LÚ.^{d}IŠKUR.RA

UD.1.KAM *a-na ša* É.GAL*-lim*

. . .

NOTES

While most of the lines in this text are "hung" from ruled lines, some of the lines are heavier and more distinctly drawn, indicating the scribe's intention to divide the text into sections. Heavy lines appear below lines 7, 10, 20. Distinct but not heavy lines appear below lines 14 and 25.

(4) See COPY for ⌈NU⌉; this reading is almost a certainty. Seif 35 restored ⌈MU⌉ and von Soden, AHw 1184b, accepted this reading as given (without brackets for MU), i.e., *šarāmum* "weeding." But there is no way to read MU in this spot, although the meaning given by *šarāmum* fits the context nicely. Perhaps we might consider a *nebenform*, *šarānum*, much in the same way as other *tertia* m roots exhibit "free variation" between /m/ and /n/. Cf *baqāmu/baqānu* and *pasāmu/pasānu* (AHw 840a, 856b has *paṣānu, pesēnu*) cited by E. Reiner, *A Linguistic Analysis of Akkadian* Studia Memoriae Nicolai van Wijk Dedicatae, Series Practica XXI (The Hague: Mouton and Co., 1966) 116. Cf. also *šakānu/šakāmu*, AHw 1134b. See further the unexplained changes of m>n in Old Assyrian listed by Hecker, AnOr 44 54.

(6) See COPY for this line. For *abum*, cf. Salonen, *Agricultura* 73f; for *summunātum* (sg. *summuntum*), cf. AHw 1058b. Line 6 may be translated: "(For) six days the eight-spanned plows went in front of the seeder."

(8) In Lutz's copy, the horizontal line after the first NI appears to be a scratch.

(9) See COPY for lines 9-10.

(16) See COPY for the end of this line–no change from Lutz. Ajaja is an official in OBTIV 103:11.

(17) GU appears as in Lutz's copy.

(20) The NI and IR are clear; for *erbenītum*, cf. CAD E 255b (and correct reference to line 22 from *i-li-ku* to *i-li-ka*).

(21) The total in line 21 is the sum of lines 15 and 18; the amount in line 20 is re-capitulated in line 22. See COPY for [ŠU.NIG]IN$_2$.

(23) The number 8 is clear. The total in line 23 is the sum of lines 15 and 22; the amount in line 15 is added twice.

(25) See COPY for *ip-ṭú-ru*.

UCP 10/1 95

UCLMA 9/2428

Barley *ḫubuttātum* Loan

NOTES

(1) The top of the tablet is missing, but the text seems to begin with line 1.

(3) See COPY for ARḪUŠ$^{\text{ḪU.UŠ}}$.

(5) See COPY for LUM.

(10) See COPY for *A*-⸢*pil*⸣-[ ].

(16) See COPY for [DUMU]-⸢*ì-lí-šu*⸣.

UCP 10/1 96

UCLMA 9/2392

Barley; Record of Outlays

Obv. (1) 2 GUR ŠE ^{d}*Še-rum-ì*(!)-*li*(!)
2(GUR) *E-ri-*<*iš-*> *ti-*^{d}UTU
1(GUR) 1(PI) 4(BÁN) *A-ḫa-ta-tum* NIN[.DINGIR]
2(PI) 3(BÁN) *Uš-ta-aš-ni-*DINGIR
(5) 1(GUR) *E-ri-iš-ti-*^{d}U[TU]
DUMU.SAL ^{d}EN.ZU-*i-din-n*[*am*]
. . .

NOTES

(1) See COPY for *ì-lí*; the signs must be so read.

(2) This line appears as Lutz copied it; reading follows UCP 10/1 p. 55.

(3) The NIN appears as Lutz copied it.

(6) See COPY for N[AM].

(7) See COPY for traces of line 7.

(13) See COPY for lines 13-15. For the city Zalaḫum, see OBTIV p. 28[34]. Line 15 is written on the edge of the tablet.

UCP 10/1 97, p. 47

UCLMA 9/2390

Barley; Record of Storage

NOTES

(12) See COPY for lines 12-13. For the year date formula see OBTIV p. 35 no. 68.

UCP 10/1 98

UCLMA 9/2424

Silver; Tally of Receipts for Diviners' Services

Obv. (1) 1 GÍN KÙ.BABBAR *Ṣíl-lí*-^{d}TIŠPAK DUMU 30-*a-ša-ri-id*
. . .
(7) 1 GÍN *Síl-lí*-^{d}KA.DI DUMU *Šu*-30-*i-qi-ša*
. . .
Rev. 1/2 GÍN A-⌈*pil-i-li-šu*⌉ [ ]
1 GÍN DINGIR-*šu-ba-ni* [ ]
(15) 1 GÍN ^{d}*Še-rum*-DINGIR [ ]
1/2 <GÍN> *Ni-iš*$_6$-30 DUM[U]
1/2 GÍN *Šu-um*-[ ] DUMU ⌈I⌉ [ ]
1/2 GÍN GÌR-EŠ$_4$.DAR DUMU *Ri*-⌈*mu*⌉ [ ]
1/2 GÍN ^{d}ŠEŠ.KI.MA.AN.SUM DUMU *Si-ia-tum*
(20) 1/2 GÍN *A-ḫu-ši-na* DUMU *Nu-úr-ì-lí-šu*
1/3 GÍN BA-^{d}TIŠPAK DUMU *Na-ga-ri*
. . .

NOTES

(1) See COPY for PNs.

(7) See COPY for PN.

(13) See COPY for lines 13-18.

(16) One may perhaps also consider reading *Ni-is-Sin*, reflecting a possible spoken pronunciation with šš > ss. M. Stol suggests that we read 1(BÁN) I.GIŠ 30-*i*-[ ] in this line. This is graphically possible but the total in line 23 gives only silver. It is true that this total of 18 GÍN does not conform with the entries listed. But replacing 1/2 <GÍN> in line 16 with the cash value of 1(BÁN) Ì.GIŠ (approximately 5/6 GÍN according to Goetze LE §1) will still not yield a correct result.

(21) See COPY for GA.

(22) See COPY for TIŠPAK.

(23) CAD K 612a reads *Ku-tu-um*, PN; but this is not decisive. The sign can be read either as KU or MA; see COPY.

(24) Lines 24-25 appear as Lutz copied them. They should be translated: "(Total: 18 shekels silver) which were brought for the hire of diviners' services (Á *barūtim*)." CAD I 295a (followed by AHw 403b) take the form to be *itbārūtim*, an otherwise unattested word meaning "partnership money." The usual term for "partnership fund" in Ishchali is *tappūtum* (cf. UCLMA 9/2864:2 and UCP 10/1 89:4). It is difficult to conceive of a partnership involving only 18 shekels and some 23 partners! In our view, these small amounts represent fees collected by the temple for divination services. *Bārûs* are known to have worked at Ishchali; cf. UCP 10/1 71:6f, 75:3; UCLMA 9/2878 seal; OBTIV 85:22; and cf. VAS 16 22:27f, cited by CAD B 121b.

UCP 10/1 99, p. 46

UCLMA 9/2361

Barley; Record of Receipt

. . .

Obv. (2) É DUB *ru-ug-bi-im*

ša ⌈x⌉-*ḫa-nu*

. . .

NOTES

(3) See COPY for this line; the last sign is NU not NA.

UCP 10/1 100

UCLMA 9/2399

Personnel; Tally of Workers

Obv. (1) [ ]⸢x⸣
[^{1d}UT] U.TAB.BA-*e*
. . .
L.E. [^{1}]*Ab-nu-tum*
(9) [ ] ⸢x⸣-*a-su*
(9a) [ ] ⸢x⸣ [ ]
Rev. (10) [ ] ⸢x⸣-*la*-⸢*ni*⸣ [ ]
. . .
(16) ŠU.NIGIN$_2$ 14 GURUŠ.SAL.MEŠ
A-⸢x⸣ [ ] ⸢x⸣
Edge ⸢x x x⸣

NOTES

(1) See COPY for lines 1-2.

(7) See COPY for ID; this PN is read *Ì-lí-ṣi-id-qum* by H. Huffmon, *Amorite Personal Names in the Mari Texts* (Baltimore: Johns Hopkins Press, 1969) p. 257.

(8) The second sign is NU; see COPY.

(9) See COPY for lines 9-9a; there is still room for another line after 9a on the lower edge; but no traces survive.

(10) This line appears as Lutz copied it.

(16) "Total: 14 young men, women." See COPY for MEŠ omitted by Lutz. There are 14 persons listed in lines 3-15 (counting 9a); if there are other persons in ll. 1-2, then the first sign in line 17 should be read as 2 and not A.

(17) See COPY for traces of lines 17-18. There could have been a line intervening between lines 17 and 18.

UCP 10/1 101

UCLMA 9/2400

Unspecified Commodity: List of Amounts and Persons

Obv. (1) 9(GUR) 3(PI) ⸢2(BÁN)⸣ [ ] ⸢*a*⸣-*nu*
3(GUR) *Ib-na-tum*
4(GUR) *Uš-taš-ni*-DINGIR

⸢5(GUR)⸣ 3(PI) 2(BÁN) *Ig-mil-*⸢dEN.ZU⸣
(5) [ ] ⸢x x⸣ [ ] ⸢x⸣
– remainder destroyed –

NOTES

(1) See COPY for this line; there must have been a PN or a common noun in this line, indicating the use or origin of the grain. There is not a great deal of room here. The sign which is read as ⸢2(BÁN)⸣ makes it unlikely that GUR was written in this line; there is room for no more than three signs following, including the NU at the end (there is nothing written after the NU). In considering short names, Manum comes to mind; perhaps one could read *Ma*(!)-*nu* following the ⸢2(BÁN)⸣. The lack of mimation is a problem but not an insuperable one; one can compare the non-occurrence of mimation in the PN Masqum in UCP 10/1 23:17, 24:1, and UCLMA 9/2858:17.

(4) Line 4 is now lost after the IG.

(5) See COPY for traces of this line.

UCP 10/1 102, p. 45
UCLMA 9/2430
Wood; List of Objects

Obv. (1) 12 GIŠ *gu-šu-ru* GAL
ša iš-tu Ú-pí-i ú-⸢*bi-lu*(?)*-ni*⸣
. . .
(8) 1 IG ù [ ]
. . .

NOTES

(2) See COPY for the end of this line, omitted by Lutz in his copy.

(8) See COPY for the third sign; one must assume that IG is written for GIŠ.IG.

(9) Lines 9-10 appear as Lutz copied them.

UCP 10/1 103

UCLMA 9/2384

Barley *ḫubuttātum* Loan

Obv. (1) [ ] ⸢*tum*⸣
[ ]
[NU.] ⸢GIŠ.SAR⸣
[ ] ⸢x⸣ [NU.] ⸢GIŠ.SAR⸣
. . .

Rev. [IG]I *A-bu-um*-DINGIR
[DU]MU 30-*eri*$_4$-*ba-am*
(15) [I]GI [BA]-^{d}EN.LÍL
. . .

NOTES

(1) See COPY for lines 1, 3-4. This loan transaction involved several borrowers, as can be seen from line 12. Line 6 probably contained a total as in UCP 10/1 18:11, 28:4, 63:4, 69:5, and 104:4. Lines 1-5, then, would have contained the amounts borrowed, followed by the names of the borrowers. The ends of lines 3-4 apparently record the professions of two of the borrowers. According to present traces, [NU].⸢GIŠ.SAR⸣ seems more likely in both cases than does DUB.SAR as Lutz has it in line 3. The tablet is in very poor condition and I question how much Lutz actually was able to read; he was on occasion accustomed to copy a bit more than he could actually see, when he believed something to be present in the text. Cf., for example, his correctly expecting ^{d}EN.ZU-*e-ri-ba-am* in line 14, but 30-*eri*$_4$-*ba-am* is what is actually there. He completely "misread" line 15, which is still covered by a clay adhesion, as is part of line 16 (see note).

(5) Lines 5-12 appear as Lutz copied them.

(13) See COPY for lines 13-15 and note to line 1 above.

(16) The traces support the copy of Lutz; but the QÍ is covered by a clay adhesion; its presence can safely be assumed.

UCP 10/1 104

UCLMA 9/2348

Barley *ḫubuttātum* Loan

Obv. (1) 1(GUR) 1(PI) 4(BÁN) GUR ŠE ⸢*Wa(?)*⸣-*qar-a(?)-bu(!)-šu*
. . .

Rev. (7) BÀD-*Ri-muš iš-ša-ak-nu(!)*
. . .

	IGI *Ḫu-za-lum* DUMU *Ḫu-bu-šum*
	IGI ⸢30-*iš-me-an-ni* DUMU DINGIR-*šu*⸣-GAL
U.E.	MU GUD.APIN KÙ.GI
	URU *Ki-maš* [*É-kál-l*]*a-tim*

NOTES

(1) This PN is not so clear as Lutz's copy suggests; the WA lacks oblique direction; the first vertical of the A is faint; the right lower vertical is not deeply impressed; the QAR+A could easily be read as ÍD; the horizontal of BU is faint. See COPY.

(3) See COPY for IṬ and for the erased line (3a).

(7) See COPY for the final three signs in this line.

(13) See COPY; the PN also appears in UCP 10/1 34:12f. Lutz erroneously incorporated part of the IṬ in line 3 into the NUM of his copy.

(14) See COPY for this line. For the PN, cf. UCP 10/1 16:12f.

(16) See COPY for the trace of LA. For the year date formula, see OBTIV p. 31 no. 33.

UCP 10/1 105, pp. 7f.; Seif 29

UCLMA 9/2388

Maintenance Agreement

Obv.	1 GEME$_2$ *Ku-te-e* MU.NI.IM	1 female slave, Kute by name,
	^{1}*Nu-ṭú-up-tum*	Nuṭṭuptum
	a-na Tu-li-iš AMA.A.NI	unto Tuliš her mother
	i-di-in-ši-ma	gave; and
	a-di ba-al-ṭà-at	as long as she (Tuliš) lives,
	i-ta-na-ši-iš-ši-ma	she (Kute) will on a continuing basis support her.
	u$_4$-um ši-ma-tu-ša	On the day her fates
	i-ta-ar-ra-ši	lead her away (to die)–
	^{1}*Tu-li-iš* AMA.A.NI	i.e., Tuliš, her mother–
	a-na Nu-ṭú-up-tum DUMU.MUNUS	she (Kute) will (again) belong to Nuṭṭuptum, the daughter.
	ma-la i-šu-ú	Whatever she (Tuliš) has
	ù i-ra-šu-ú	and will acquire
L.E.	(ERASURE) *Nu-ṭú-up-tum*	Nuṭṭuptum
	i-le-qé-e	will take (as her possession).
Rev.	[ ] ⸢x *ta-pi-e*⸣ [DUMU] ⸢*A*⸣-[*ḫu*]-*ši-na*	Witnessed by . . . - tappi son of Aḫušina

	[ ]		. . .
	[ ] ⸢x⸣*na-ši*		. . . -naši
(17a)	[ ] ⸢x⸣	(17a)	. . .
	[ ] ⸢*um*⸣		. . . um
	[ ] ⸢*ba*⸣-*am*		. . . bam
	[ ] ⸢x x x⸣ [ ]-*um*		. . . um
	[ ] ⸢*x*⸣-*ri-me-ni*		. . . -rimenni
	[ ] ⸢x⸣-*za*		. . . za
	[^{I}*N*]*a-ra-am*-^{d}EN.ZU		Naram-Sin
	[DUMU] ⸢x⸣ -*úr-ku-su*-[*um*]		son of . . . urkusum
	^{I}ARAD-^{d}TIŠPAK		Warad-Tišpak
	DUMU *Aš-qú-du-um*		son of Ašqudum
	^{I}*Na-ra-am*-^{d}EN.LÍL		Naram-Enlil
	DUMU *Ip-qú-ša*		son of Ipquša
	^{I}*Sa-ri-qum* DUMU ARAD-DINGIR		Sarriqum son of Warad-Ilim
	^{I}*Ip-qú-ša* DUMU ^{d}UTU-TAB.BA-⸢*e*⸣		Ipquša son of Šamaš-tappi
Edge	⸢x x(x) ḪA A⸣ *da-a*		. . . da
Seal Legend			
	Na-ra-am-^{d}EN.Z[U]		Naram-Sin
	[DUMU] ⸢x⸣-*úr-ku*-[*su-um*]		son of . . . urkusum

NOTES

(3) See COPY for PN and AMA.A.NI in lines 3, 9. The extra wedges that Lutz copied into the AMA in line 3 belong to the overlaid pictorial seal impression.

(10) There is nothing written after the MUNUS, which is already on the reverse.

(13) See COPY for erasure.

(15) See COPY for lines 15, 17-20.

(21) Lines 21-22 appear as Lutz copied them; the broken sign in line 21 is not ḪA.

(23) See COPY for lines 23-24, 27, 30-31.

Seal Legend

There is clear evidence of at least one seal—that of Naram-Sin (line 23). There are also traces of a pictorial seal impression (see note to line 3); but the evidence is insufficient to connect it either with Naram-Sin or any other person. The copy of Naram-Sin's seal is a composite; and there is a question of how to align line 2, which contains his father's name, with line 1. The second seal copy, if it belongs to Naram-Sin, may provide the clue. See copy for these seal legend traces.

UCP 10/1 106

UCLMA 9/2423

Silver; Record of Payment of Service Obligations

		. . .
Obv.		[ ] ⌜*An*⌝-*um*-KA-*ša*
	(5)	[ ] ⌜*I*⌝-*din*-^{d}UTU
		. . .
		[*R*]*i-im*-^{d}IM
	(10)	[ ] ⌜*Ra*⌝-*bu-ut*-^{d}EN.ZU
		. . .
	(12)	12(GÍN) ^{d}EN.ZU-*ma-gir*
		. . .
	(15)	10(GÍN) GÌ[R]-^{d}EN.ZU
L.E.		15(GÍN) DINGIR-*ni*
		[ ] *I-din*-DINGIR
		[*N*]*a-bi*-^{d}UTU
Rev.		[ ] ⌜x⌝-*ki-nu-um*
	(20)	1/3(GÍN) *Ri-iš*-^{d}IM
		⌜2⌝(GÍN) *Im-gur*-⌜^{d}IM⌝
		[ ] *Ib-ni*-^{d}NI[N]
		[ ] *Ḫa-li-wu-um*
		⌜x⌝(GÍN) *U-bar*-^{d}UTU
	(25)	[ ] *A-pil-ì-lí-šu*
		[ ] ARAD-ì-lí-šu
		[ ] ^{d}ŠEŠ.KI.DI.KU$_5$
		[ ] *Še-li-bu-um*
	(30)	[ŠU.NIGIN$_2$]8 5/6 MA.NA 1 1/3 GÍN
		(ERASURE)
		⌜*ma-za-áš*⌝-*ti Ne-ri-ib-tim*^{KI}
		NÍG.ŠU *Še-li-bu-um*
		(ERASURE)
U.E.	(33)	MU.ÚS MU GIŠ.MAR.GÍD.DA KÙ.GI

NOTES

(4) See COPY for lines 4-5.

(9) See COPY for lines 9-10, 12.

(13) Lines 13-14 are now missing; UCP 10/1 89:12, which Lutz read as *E-ri-sú-ma-tum*, upon collation, turned out to be *E-ri-iš-tum* (see note there).

(15) See COPY for lines 15-18.

(19) Perhaps one might here restore [*A-ḫ*]*u-ki-nu-um* or [*Iš-d*]*u-ki-nu-um*; the line appears as Lutz copied it.

(20) See COPY for 1/3(GÍN); the rest of line 20 appears as Lutz copied it.

(21) See COPY; the tablet is broken at IM.

(22) See COPY for the end of this line.

(24) See COPY for traces of the number at the beginning of this line; it appears to have been a fraction.

(30) See COPY for lines 30-32; the erasure below line 32 is due to the fact that the scribe started to write the year date on the bottom of the reverse before writing it again on the upper edge. It is almost certain that the total in line 30 is silver, to judge from UCP 10/1 43.

(33) See COPY for KÙ.GI. Lines 30-33 read: "(30) Total: . . . 8 5/6 minas, 1 1/3 shekels (31) (for) the service of Neribtum. (32) (Under the) control of Šelibum. (33) The year following the year the golden wagon." For the year date formula, see OBTIV p. 30 no. 31.

UCP 10/1 107; Finkelstein ANET^{3} 545b

UCLMA 9/2338

Court Record: Theft and Penalty Service

Obv.	(1)	^{1}DINGIR-*šu-na-ṣir*	(1)	Ilšu-naṣir
		ù Be-el-šu-n[*u*]		and Belšunu (appeared in court)
		aš-šum Ta-ri-bu-um		on account of Taribum
		ša a-na É DINGIR-*šu-*[*na-ṣir*]	(4)	who broke into the house
	(5)	⸢*ib-ba-al*⸣-[*ki*]-⸢*tu*⸣-[*ma*]	5)	of Ilšu-naṣir (and)
		iṣ-ba-tu-š[*u*]		whom they had caught (doing so).
		^{1}*Ta-ri-bu-um* DUM[U.NI]		Taribum—his son—
		IGI URU.KI *ù ši-bu-tim*		before the city (assembly) and the elders
		ša-ra-qa-ku iq-bi		said: "I am a thief."
	(10)	*aš-šum aš-ri-i*[*q*] *i*[*q-bu*]	(10)	Inasmuch as he said "I have stolen"
		ù šu-ur-⸢*qú-um*⸣ *i-na* ⸢*qa-ti-šu*⸣ *iṣ-ṣa-ab-tu*		and the stolen object was seized in his hand,
		URU.KI *ù ši-bu-tum i-na pa-aš-tim ša* ^{d}EN.ZU		the city (assembly) and the elders by the axe of Sin
		ù GIŠ.TUKUL ⸢*ša*⸣ *I-šar-ki-*[*di*]*-su*		and the weapon of Išarkidisu
		a-na ki-ša-tim ⸢*a-na*⸣ DINGIR-*šu-na-ṣir*	14)	gave him over into penalty service
	(15)	*i-di-nu-šu*	15)	unto Ilšu-naṣir.
Rev.		IGI *A-lí-ba-ni-šu* GÌR.NITA$_{2}$		Witnessed by Ali-banišu, the governor
		^{1}*Ig-mil-*^{d}EN.ZU DUMU DINGIR-*šu-a-bu-šu*		Igmil-Sin son of Ilšu-abušu

^{I}*Ma-ti-ia-tu-ú* DUMU ^{d}UTU-*za-aq-tum*	Matijatu son of Šamaš-zaqtum
^{I}*A-bu-um*-DINGIR DUMU ^{d}EN.ZU-*eri$_4$-ba*	Abum-ilum son of Sin-eriba
^{I}*Im-gur*-^{d}UTU DUMU *Ib-ni*-^{d}EN.LÍL	Imgur-Šamaš son of Ibni-Enlil
^{Id}EN.ZU-*ga-mil* DUMU *A-ḫi-um-mi-šu*	Sin-gamil son of Aḫi-ummišu
^{I}*Ri-iš*-^{d}UTU *ù* ^{d}EN.ZU-*i-qí-ša-am*	Riš-Šamaš and Sin-iqišam
DUMU.MEŠ ARAD-^{d}EN.ZU	sons of Warad-Sin
^{I}*Sa-at-lu-ma* BA-^{d}EN.LÍL	Satluma, Iqiš-Enlil
ù ^{d}UTU-*na-ṣir* DUMU.MEŠ ^{d}EN.ZU-*i-qí-šam*	and Šamaš-naṣir sons of Sin-iqišam
^{I}*Ma-na-ba-al-ṭe$_4$-el*	Mana-balṭi-᾿El
ù A-ḫu-ni-ia DUMU.MEŠ *Na*-⸢*ra*⸣-[*am*]	and Aḫunija sons of Naram-. . .
[^{I}] [ ]	. . .
^{Id}EN.Z[U]	Sin-. . .
^{I}*Ḫa-ia-ša-rum* D[UMU]	Ḫaja-šarrum son of . . .
ù Mu-na-nu-um DUB.SA[R]	and Munanum, the scribe.

Seal Legends

A	*A-li-ba-ni-šu*	A	Ali-banišu
	DUMU BA-^{d}EN.ZU		son of Iqiš-Sin
	ARAD *I-ba-al-pi-el*		servant of Ibalpiel
B	*A-bu-um*-DINGIR	B	Abum-ilum
	DUMU ^{d}EN.ZU-*e-ri-ba-am*		son of Sin-eribam
	ARAD *ša* ^{d}IM		servant of Adad
C	^{d}EN.ZU-*ga-mi*-x	C	Sin-gamil
	DUMU *A-ḫi-um-mi-šu*		son of Aḫi-ummišu
	ARAD [*Da*]-*du-ša*		servant of Daduša
D	*Mu-na-wi-rum*	D	Munawwirum
	DUMU *Gu-ul-lu-bi-ia*		son of Gullubija
	ARAD *ša* ^{d}NIN.URTA		servant of Ninurta

NOTES

(5) See COPY for lines 5-6.

(7) This line appears as Lutz copied it; perhaps one could restore: DUM[U *Be-el-šu-nu*].

(10) See COPY for lines 10-12.

(13) This line appears as Lutz copied it. The divine emblems typically played a part in oath-taking; no oath-taking is mentioned here; perhaps this use of the emblems relates to Taribum's testimony in lines 9f.

(14) See COPY for this line. The reading *kiššātim* was anticipated by R. Westbrook and C. Wilcke in AfO 25 (1974) 115. For *kiššātum* see Finet Akkadica 8 (1978) 12-18 and Kienast, *Kisurra* I 67ff (references courtesy of M. Stol).

(18) See COPY for this line.

(20) See COPY for ^{d}EN.LÍL.

(24) See COPY for BA-^{d}EN.LÍL.

(27) See COPY for lines 27-29; line 30 appears as Lutz copied it.

Seal Legends

Seals B and D are discussed in connection with UCP 10/1 11; see COPY for Seals A and C. There is an interesting feature in Seal Legend C: the seal-cutter apparently did not have enough room to execute the IL in Sin-gamil and so simply inserted a "token" sign—a square to fill up the line.

UCP 10/1 108
UCLMA 9/2387
Personnel; List

. . .

Obv. (11) [^{I}] ⸢x (x)⸣ [ ] ⸢x x x⸣
⸢^{I}*Bu*⸣-[ ] ⸢*um*⸣
⸢^{I}⸣ [ ] ⸢*šu* x⸣
⸢^{I} x⸣ [ ]

L.E. (15) ^{Id}ŠEŠ.K[I]
^{I}*An-um*-K[A-^{d}UTU]

. . .

Rev. (28) ^{I}⸢^{d}EN.ZU⸣-*pu-uṭ-r*[*a-am*]

. . .

Edge (36) ^{Id}EN.ZU-*i-qí*(?)-*š*[*a-am*]
⸢^{I}⸣ [ ]
[ ] ⸢x x⸣
^{I}DUMU.KI LÚ UŠ(?).BAR
(40) ^{I}30-⸢*i*-x⸣ [ ]
[ ] ⸢*ru*(?)⸣
^{I}*Ib*(?)-*ni*-^{d}IM
^{I}A-*bi-ki* ⸢x x⸣
⸢ x x *na-da*⸣

NOTES

(7) Lines 7-8 appear as Lutz copied them.

(9) See COPY for this line.

(11) See COPY for this line. The first sign, i.e. x (x), could be ZAG as Lutz interpreted it. After the break, Lutz's TI is unlikely; the last two signs could be ⸢MI-ÍL⸣.

(12) See COPY for traces of ⸢UM⸣; perhaps the PN is *Bu*-[*ra-nu-u*]*m*.

(13) See COPY for the end of line 13; the beginning, copied by Lutz, is now gone.

(14) Line 14 appears as Lutz copied it.

(15) Lutz "saw" more than is now preserved.

(16) See COPY for K[A].

(26) The broken sign appears as Lutz copied it.

(28) See COPY for this line.

(33) Lines 33-35 appear as Lutz copied them.

(36) Lutz numbered these lines 36-38, which are on the edge of the tablet. There are actually 3 columns of 3 rows each; see COPY; we have read and numbered them horizontally as 36-44.

(39) One cannot read LÚ.MAŠ.MAŠ here without emendation; there are clearly 2 horizontals after the LÚ.

UCP 10/1 109, pp. 17f.

UCLMA 9/2427

Sale of Field

NOTES

(1) See COPY for *Ḫa-aš-ḫ*[*u-ur*].

(6) The end of this line appears as Lutz copied it. M. Stol suggests reading DINGIR.AP[IN] or *Ilam-eriš*. This is very acceptable since this PN is attested in OB sources and in the Diyala; cf. e.g. YOS 14 1:15, YOS 12 p. 77. However, note also *Ilum-e-ri-is-sà*, YOS 13 95: rev. 7.

(8) This line is now preserved only up to *Na-b*[*i*-^{d}EN.LÍL].

(16) See COPY for DA and [LUGAL]; DA has an erasure in it.

(18) *I-za-a-az* is clear.

(19) See COPY for lines 19-21. In line 19, [*i*]-[*m*]*i*-[*t*]*i* is possible after *Ìr-ra*; but the last two signs: x MIN, yield no ready solution. In line 20, following *Iš-me*, and after the clay adhesion, the visible signs look like Ú x.

(21) Cf. for this PN, OBTIV 34:15, TIM 3 127:12, and note to UCP 10/1 46:15.

(22) The broken sign appears as Lutz copied it.

(24) This PN can be restored from the traces and TIM 3 127:10.

(25) Lines 25-26 appear as Lutz copied them; the missing portions of text in lines 25-29 are obscured by a clay adhesion.

(28) See COPY for lines 28-29. In line 28, ^{d}ŠEŠ of Lutz is unsupported since the clay adhesion still covers this part of the tablet.

(31) See COPY for lines 31-33. In line 31, Lutz's reading of ^{d}UTU is not excluded by the visible traces but there is no way for Lutz to have read it with certainty since a clay adhesion still covers this part of the tablet.

(33) For this year date formula see OBTIV 24 no. 8.

Seal Legend

See COPY for traces, which can come from one or possibly two seals. The ⸢ARAD⸣ could be the third line of a seal legend—ARAD DN/RN; or else it may belong to one of the other two line traces.

UCP 10/1 110

UCLMA 9/2406

Barley; Tally of Outlays

NOTES

On this tablet, cols. i-ii as labelled by Lutz are actually cols. iii-iv of the original tablet, of which only the reverse side is preserved.

(3) See COPY for 1 (PI) in place of Lutz's 2 (PI).

(5) See COPY for this line.

(11) See COPY for ID.

(12) See COPY for LUKUR; a similar sign is found in UCLMA 9/2826:5.

(15) See COPY for LAM.

(19) This line appears as Lutz copied it. The signs appear to read *Ni-ḫa-az* but one may consider reading *Ni-ḫa-tum*(!) in view of UCLMA 7/2889a col. i 18 (which has *Ni-ḫa-tum*) and the observations made above in the Introduction (p. 2[7]) pointing out a number of PNs appearing in both texts.

(20) This line appears as Lutz copied it except for the NI; there are no vertical wedges—only a horizontal line bisecting the triangle.

(21) See COPY for traces of the PN.

(23) See COPY for 2(PI) in place of Lutz's 1(PI).

(24) See COPY for ⸢^{d}TIŠPAK⸣.

(25) See COPY for *Ú-bar.*

(26) See COPY for this line.

(29) The mention of interest in lines 29 and 32 raise the interesting question as to whether interest payments are being collected or paid out. If the former, then it is possible that the entire tablet is a record of income.

(31) See COPY for PN.

(34) The sign is not the best SAL; it could also be NU. For ŠE.SAL, see CAD D 142b, *dillatu*, a kind of grain.

(41) ⌜ITU d(!)⌝ seems to be more accurately a reflection of what is preserved; see COPY.

CHAPTER 5

NEW ISHCHALI TABLETS IN THE COLLECTION OF THE LOWIE MUSEUM OF ANTHROPOLOGY UNIVERSITY OF CALIFORNIA, BERKELEY

In presenting the new Ishchali tablets from the collection of the Lowie Museum of Anthropology, University of California, Berkeley, we follow our earlier practice in not presenting each text in full. As before, we do this in order to create a smaller, more manageable manuscript; to avoid repetition of things already published; and in recognition of the fact that many passages, given transliteration, are readily masterable with the help of dictionaries and indexes.

There are six *ḫubuttātum* loans, very similar to those already known. We have given one of these in full and the balance in transliteration; and any salient differences among the other five are taken up in the notes.[1] In this same fashion we treat only one of the two *tappūtum* documents and the solitary sale.[2]

The balance of texts are given solely in transliteration, with discussion of noteworthy lines and references to similar or related documents in the Ishchali corpus being supplied in notes. No transliteration is given for one document, which is a long list of names; the readings of these are contained in the Indexes.[3] In two instances, only date formulae are presented; the rest of the tablet was not included because while these documents come from the Diyala region, there is no certainty that they are from Ishchali proper.[4] Our Autograph Copies of the New Ishchali Tablets, henceforth referred to as 'COPY', appear in Chapter 8.2.

LIST OF UCLMA TEXTS

9/2826	9/2862 (T)	9/2906 (T)
9/2827 (T)	9/2864	9/2942 (T)
9/2828 (T, P)	9/2866 (T)	9/2943 (T)
9/2831 (T)	9/2878 (T)	9/2957 (T)
9/2858 + 2863 (T)	9/2889 a-c (N)	9/2958 (T)
9/2859 (T, P)	9/2892 (T)	9/3019
9/2860 (T)	9/2895 (T)	9/3030 (T)

[1] The *ḫubuttātum* loans are: UCLMA 9/2826, 2853 + 2863, 2860, 2862, 2866, 2895.

[2] The *tappūtum* documents are: UCLMA 9/2864, 2906; the sale is 3019.

[3] UCLMA 9/2889 a-c is a long list of names.

[4] The date formulae are UCLMA 9/2828 and 2859. The Lutz-Kohlberg Collection contains tablets from sites other than Ishchali, including other Diyala locations: e.g., Khafaje, Abū Jāwan (probably the same as Adams, *Land Behind Baghdad* (University of Chicago Press: 1965) p. 160, No. 685), and Abū Ḫalāwa (cf. Adams, *op. cit.*, p. 141, Nos. 136-137).

UCLMA 9/2826

Barley *ḫubuttātum* Loan

Obv.	(1)	2(GUR) 3(PI) 2(BÁN) GUR ŠE	(1)	2.3.2 kors barley
		ḫu-bu-ta-tum		(as) a *ḫubuttātum* (loan)
		KI DINGIR-*šu*-<*na*>-⸢*ṣir*⸣		from Ilšu-naṣir
		ù ^{d}ŠEŠ.KI.ARḪUŠ		and Nanna.arhuš
	(5)	^{1}*E-ri-iš-ti*-^{d}UTU ·	(5)	did Erišti-Šamaš, the *nadītum*
		DUMU.SAL *I-pí-iq-ši-na*		daughter of Ipiqšina
L.E.		ŠU.BA.AN.TI	(7)	borrow.
			(7a)	In the city of Uzarnum,
Rev.		*a-na maš-kán-nim*		at threshing time,
		še-a-am Ì.ÁG.E		she will repay the barley.
	(10)	IGI *A-bu-*⸢*um*⸣-DINGIR	(10)	Witnessed by Abum-ilum son of Sin-eribam,
		^{1}BA-⸢^{d}EN.LÍL⸣		Iqiš-Enlil
		ù ^{d}UTU-*na-ṣir*		and Šamaš-naṣir sons of Sin-iqišam
		ù Mu-na-nu-um DUB.SAR		and Munanum, the scribe.
U.E.		MU É EŠ$_4$.DAR BA.DÍM		The year he built the temple of Ištar.

Envelope Variants

(1) KIŠIB (at beginning of line)
(5) adds LUKUR
(6) omits SAL
(7a) adds URU.KI *Ú-za-ar-num*
(10) adds [DUMU ^{d}]EN.ZU-*e-ri-ba-am*
(11) clear ^{d}EN.LÍL
(12) adds DUMU.MEŠ ^{d}EN.ZU-*i-qí-ša-am*

Seal Legends

A.	*A-bu-um*-DINGIR	A.	Abum-ilum
	DUMU ^{d}EN.ZU-*e-ri-ba-am*		son of Sin-eribam
	ARAD *ša* ^{d}IM		servant of Adad
B.	[Mu]-na-wi-[ru-um]	B.	Munawwirum
	[DUMU G]u-ul-lu-bi-ia		Son of Gullubija
	ARAD ša ^{d}NIN.URTA		servant of Ninurta

NOTES

(5) For a similar LUKUR sign, cf. UCP 10/1 110:12.

(7a) On the envelope, lines 1-7 are on the obverse; 7a is alone on the lower edge. For Uzarnum, see note to UCP 10/1 67:2.

Seal Legends

For copies of seals A and B, see UCP 10/1 11. Seal A is impressed twice on the obverse of the envelope. Seal B appears twice on the upper edge of the envelope. There are only the two seals.

UCLMA 9/2827

Silver Loan with Interest (MÁŠ ^{d}UTU)

Obv. 2/3 MA.NA K[Ù.BABBAR]
MÁŠ ^{d}UTU *ú-ṣa-ab*
KI *Bur*-^{d}EN.ZU
DUMU *I-bi*-^{d}TIŠPAK
^{Id}ŠEŠ.KI.MA.AN.SUM
DUMU *Šu*-^{d}NIN.KAR.RA.AK
LÚ.UD.KIB.NUN.NA^{KI}
ŠU.BA.AN.TI
a-na maš-kán-nim
KÙ.BABBAR *ù* MÁŠ.BI
Ì.LAL.E

Rev. IGI ^{d}EN.ZU-*ú-še-pí*
DUMU *Na-bi*-^{d}EN.ZU IŠ
IGI ^{d}UTU-*mu-uš-te-pí-iš*
DUMU *Ú-še-pí*
IGI 30-*a-bu-šu*
DUMU LÚ.SIG$_5$
IGI *Ga-mi*-DINGIR
DUMU ARAD-*ì-lí-šu*
IGI *Im-gu-rum*
DUMU *Na-ra-am-ì-lí-šu*
MU ÍD.DA *li-bi* URU.KI *ip-pí-tu*[-*ú*]

Envelope Variants

(1) KISIB 2/3 MA.NA K[Ù.BABBAR]
(22) *ip-pí-*≪*pí*≫*-tu-ú*

NOTES

(13) For IŠ see CAD K 477f, *kizû*.

(22) For ÍD written A.SUK cf. UCP 10/1 2:21 and see note to OBTIV 225:3. For this year date formula see OBTIV p. 31, no. 39 and note 49.

This tablet bears impressions of at least two elaborate pictorial seals (not copied).

UCLMA 9/2828
Date Formula

(24) MU UGNIM *Ra-pí-qú*^{KI}(?) É.GAL
(25) ^{d}*Da-du-ša* LUGAL *im-ḫa-áṣ-ṣú* (?)

Env. variant:

(24) MU UGNIM(!) (KI.< SU >.LU.KU.< GAR >)
Ki(?)-*su*(?)-*ra* É. GAL
(25) ^{d}*Da-du-ša* LUGAL

NOTES

This year date formula is noted in OBTIV p. 28[34]. One may venture a translation: "The year Daduša the king smote the army of Rapiqum (and) Ekallatum." The envelope appears to contain a variant: "The year Daduša the king (smote) the army (!) of Kisurra (and) Ekallatum." It is not clear whether or not this tablet comes from Ishchali; the year date formula is nevertheless included here because of its importance to the kings of Eshnunna and the Diyala region.

UCLMA 9/2831
Silver Loan with Interest (MÁŠ ^{d}UTU)

Obv. 11 GÍN KÙ.BABBAR
MÁŠ ^{d}UTU *ú-ṣa-ab*
KI *Bur-*^{d}EN.ZU
^{I}*Bur*-EN.ZU DUMU *Im-gur-*^{d}EN.ZU
ŠU.BA.AN.TI
a-na ITU *Ki-ri-ti*
KÙ.BABBAR *ù* MÁŠ.BI
L.E. Ì.LAL.E
Rev. IGI *Im-gu-rum*
DUMU *Na-ra-am-ì-*⸢*li*⸣*-šu*
IGI 30-*mu-ba-lí-iṭ*
DUMU *Šu-m*[*u-a-ḫi*]-*ia*
IGI *A-b*[*u-um*(?)-*d*]*a-lum*
DUMU ^{d}UTU-*ba-ni*
MU BÀD *Bi-is-ki-la*
U.E. ^{I}30-*a-bu-šu i-pu-šu*

Envelope Variants

(1) KIŠIB 11 GÍN KÙ.BABBAR
3a) DUMU *I-bi-*^{d}TIŠPAK
8) Ì.LAL

12) DUMU *Šu-mu-a-ḫi-ia*
13) IGI *A-bu-um*(?)*-da-lum*
15) MU BÀD *Bi-is-ki-la*^{KI}
16) ^{I}⸢^{d}EN.ZU⸣*-a-bu-šu i-pu-šu*

NOTES

The envelope bears the impressions of two or more pictorial seals.

(9) On the envelope, ll. 9-10 appear after ll. 11-12; i.e., the order of witnesses is reversed for these two entries.

13) For the DA sign cf. UCLMA 9/2906:5; this PN is obscure.

15) For this year date formula, see OBTIV p. 25, no. 13.

UCLMA 9/2858 + 2863
Barley *ḫubuttātum* Loan

Obv. 12(GUR) 3(PI) GUR ŠE
ḫu-bu-ta-tum ⸢*ša*⸣
KI DINGIR-*šu-na-ṣir*
DUMU *Bur*-^{d}EN.ZU
^{I}ARAD-^{d}UTU
DUMU *Ṣíl-lí*-^{d}EN.ZU
ŠU.BA.AN.TI
[*a-n*]*a maš-kán-*[*ni*]*m*
L.E. *še-a-am* Ì.ÁG.E
[*ù-še-te-e*]*q-ma* MÁŠ *ú-ṣa-*[*ab*]
Rev. I[GI] *Za-ru-u*[*m*]
DUMU 30*-šc mi*
^{I}*A-bu-um*-DINGIR
DUMU 30*-e-ri-ba*
^{Id}UTU*-na-ṣir*
DUMU 30*-i-qí-ša-a*[*m*]
ù Ma-áš-qú DUB.SAR
MU ERÍN <SU>.BIR$_4$ BA RA GIŠ KU BAR

Envelope Variants:

(10) *ù-še-te-e*[*q-ma*] MÁŠ *ú-ṣ*[*a-ab*]
(18) [MU ERIN$_2$ SU.BI]R$_4$ BA RA GIŠ KU BAR(?)
(18a) [ ] URU *Ki-maš É-kál-l*[*a-tim*]

Seal Legends:

A *A-bu-um*-DINGIR
DUMU ^{d}EN.ZU-*e-ri-ba-am*
ARAD *ša* ^{d}IM

B *A*(sic)-*ru-ú*
DUMU ^{d}EN.ZU-*še-mi*
ARAD *ša* ^{d}MAR.TU

NOTES

Translation follows UCLMA 9/2826 except where noted. The *ša* in line 2 is otiose. See COPY for the text, envelope, and Seal Legend B; for Seal Legend A see Seal A *sub* UCP 10/1 11.

(10) "If he lets it lapse, he will add interest."

(17) This scribe's name is usually written *Mašqum*. However, cf. also *Ma-aš-qú* DUB.SAR in UCP 10/1 23:17 and *Maš-qú* in UCP 10/1 24:1. For lack of mimation, cf. also the many writings of ^{d}EN.ZU-*e-ri-ba* for Sin-eribam, or in line 14, here. See Index for further examples of this PN.

(18) "The year . . . the army of Subartu"; for discussion of this year date formula, see OBTIV p. 28 no. 25 and notes 33-34.

Seal Legend B
The scribe evidently miscopied the A for ZA.

UCLMA 9/2859
Date Formula

[MU *I-b*]*i*-30 LUGAL
[*a-na* É *a-b*]*i-šu*
[*i-ru*]-*bu*

NOTES

This formula has been commented upon in OBTIV p. 32[51] and appears to be identical with Ishchali year date formula no. 41 cited there: "The year Ibbi-Sin entered his father's palace (as king)." It is not clear whether or not this tablet belongs to the Ishchali archive.

UCLMA 9/2860

Barley *ḫubuttātum* Loan

Obv. 3(PI) 2(BÁN) GUR ŠE *ḫu-bu-ta-tum*
KI DINGIR-*šu-na-ṣir*
^{1}*Ḫu-za-la-tum*
ŠU.BA.AN.TI
a-na maš-kán-nim
L.E. *še-am* Ì.ÁG.E
ú-še-te-eq-ma
MÁŠ *ú-ṣa-ab*
Rev. IGI ^{d}ŠARA.MA.AN.SUM
DUMU *I-bi-*^{d}EN.Z[U]
[IGI] *I-pí-iq-ì-lí-*⸢*šu*⸣
D[UMU] *Ad-ma-ti-ì-lí*
IG[I] *A-ḫu-ši-na*
DUMU ⸢*I-di*⸣*-šum*
U.E. ⸢x⸣ [ ] BU IŠ
⸢1/3 x⸣ ŠE KÙ.BABBAR
2(PI) 1(BÁN) 3 1/3 SILA$_3$ GEME$_2$-É<.SIKIL>.LA

Envelope

KIŠIB 3(PI) 2(BÁN) GUR [ ]
^{1}*Ḫu-za-l*[*a-tum*]
2(PI) 1(BÁN) 3 1/3 SILA$_3$ ŠE [ ]
^{1}GEME$_2$-É.S[IKIL.LA]
[ŠU].⸢NIGIN$_2$ 1 GUR 3(PI)⸣ [3 1/3 SILA$_3$ ŠE
ḫu-bu-ta-tum]
– remainder missing –

Seal Legend

^{d}⸢ŠARA⸣.MA.AN.SUM
– nothing more preserved –

NOTES

Translation follows UCLMA 9/2826.

(15) The three lines on the Upper Edge are problematic. Line 17 appears to have been an "afterthought" to judge from lines 3-4 on the Envelope. The tablet seems originally to have recorded only the loan to Ḫuzalatum; the second loan to Amat-Esikila seems to have been added at the "last moment" to the tablet, being written in at the point where the planes of the Obverse and Upper Edge meet. Line 17 is actually written on a surface that sits at 45° to both the Upper Edge and the Obverse; but this surface must be considered as part of the Upper Edge and apparently was not initially intended to bear the first line of the text. The secondary addition of the loan to Amat-Esikila seems to be borne out by the sequence of loans on the Envelope.

Lines 15-16, however, remain unclear. They are not reflected in the Envelope. These lines are covered by a clay adhesion; yet when one removes the edge of this clay adhesion, one finds no text underneath but only a smooth clay surface. It is possible that the scribe intended to erase both lines 15 and 16; there are ancient thumb prints smeared across the surface above BU and to the right of the IŠ and KÙ.BABBAR in lines 15-16. One could take line 16 as an error for line 17: [3(PI) 1(BÁN) 3] ⌜1/3⌝ SI[LA$_3$] ŠE; the KÙ.BABBAR could be the error that required the scribe to erase and re-write that line into line 17. But the intended content of line 15 remains an unsolved problem. One might consider trying to read in that line (and perhaps also line 16) a year date or maybe even the name of the scribe.

UCLMA 9/2862

Barley *ḫubuttātum* Loan

Obv. 1(GUR) 3(PI) 2(BÁN) GUR ŠE
ḫu-bu-ta-tum
KI DINGIR-*šu-na-ṣir*
ù ^{d}ŠEŠ.KI.ARḪUŠ
^{1}*Ga-mi*-DINGIR *ša* É
ŠU.BA.AN.TI
a-na maš-kán-[*im*]
Rev. [*še-a-am* Ì.ÁG.E]
IGI *A-lí-ba-*⌜*ni-šu* GÌR.NITÁ⌝
[I]GI *A-bu-um*-DINGIR
DUMU ^{d}EN.ZU-*e-ri-ba-am*
IGI [ ]
DU[MU]
[ ]
U.E. [M]U É EŠ$_4$.DAR BA.DÍM

NOTES

Translation follows UCLMA 9/2826 except where noted.

(5) "Gamilum, the palace steward."

(9) Line 7 is the last line that is written fully on the obverse; the lower edge is destroyed, and the first line on the reverse is likewise missing. Ali-banišu, the governor, is always the first witness when he appears; since there is no more than one line of text missing, it seems that (his name) must have been written on the first line of the reverse side, with the lower-edge left blank. Accordingly, the first line of the reverse has been numbered as line 8.

UCLMA 9/2864

Partnership (*tappūtum*) Agreement

Obv.	1 MA.NA KÙ.BABBAR	1 mina partnership
	TAB.BA *a-na ba-ab* KASKAL	money, (to be loaned) at the beginning of the trading journey,
	KI *Bur-*^{d}EN.ZU	from Bur-Sin
	^{1}*Na-ra-am-ì-lí-šu*	did Naram-ilišu
	DUMU ^{d}EN.ZU-*ba-ni*	son of Sin-bani
	ŠU.BA.AN.TI	borrow.
	i-la-ak i-tu-ra-am-ma	He will go; he will return and
	ṭe$_{4}$*-em-šu ma-ḫa-ar* UM.MI.A *i-ša*(!)*-kán*	present his report to (his) principal.
	i-qí-pa-am i-zi-ba-am-ma	(If) he has entrusted (goods to another or if) he has left them behind,
	i-na ki-si-šu-ma	out of his own capital
L.E.	*ú-ma-la*	he must pay it back;
Rev.	*qí-ip-ta-am*	(any merchandise) entrusted
	ba-ab-ta-am UM.MI.A	(or) debts outstanding the principal
	ú-ul i-la-ma-ad	will not acknowledge.
	IGI LÚ-^{d}NIN.URTA	Witnessed by Awil-Ninurta
	DUMU *Bur-Nu-nu*	Son of Bur-Nunu
	IGI 30-TAB.BA-*we-di-im*	Witnessed by Sin-tappi-wedim
	DUMU 30-*e-ri-ba-am*	Son of Sin-eribam
	IGI ARAD-^{d}ŠEŠ.KI DUMU 30-*ki-ma-ì-lí-*<*ia*>	Witnessed by Warad-Nanna son of Sin-kima-ilija
	(space)	(space)
	MU ÚS.SA ^{d}[*Šul*]*-gi-na-na-ru*	The year following (the year) Šulgi-nannaru
U.E.	*in-na-aq-ru-ú*	was destroyed

Envelope Variants

(1) KIŠIB 1 MA.NA KÙ.BABBAR

(8) *i-ša-ka-an*

Seal Legend

ARAD-^{d}ŠEŠ.KI
DUMU ^{d}EN.ZU-*ki-ma-ì-lí-*⌈*ia*⌉
ARAD ^{d}EN.ZU-*a-bu-šu*

NOTES

(2) The occurrance of the phrase *ana bāb ḫarrānim* here and in UCLMA 9/2906:2 may be an "Assyrianism"; CAD B 26a reports only examples from OA texts.

(8) The UM.MI.A or "principal" is the lender Bur-Sin. He may be the same person who is an UGULA DAM.QAR in OBTIV 29:9(s).

(12) For this phrase and its implications cf. Veenhof Old Assyrian Trade 419-422.

(20) For this year date formula see OBTIV p. 35 no. 61.

UCLMA 9/2866
Barley *ḫubuttātum* Loan

Obv. [ ] 2(BÁN) GUR [ ]
[*ḫu-b*]*u-t*[*a-tum*]
[KI] D[INGIR-*šu-na-ṣi*]*r*
⸢*ù* ^{d}⸣ [ŠEŠ.KI.ARḪUŠ]
[^{I}] ⸢^{d}⸣ [UTU-*na-*]
[DUM]U *Ia-*[*ar-*]⸢x⸣
ŠU.BA.AN.[TI]

L.E. (ERASURE)
a-na maš-kán-nim

Rev. *še-a-am* Ì.ÁG.E
IGI *A-bu-um-*DINGIR DUMU ^{d}EN.ZU-*eri*$_4$*-ba*
^{Id}UTU-*na-ṣir*
DUMU ^{d}EN.ZU-*i-qí-ša-am*
^{I}*Na-ra-am-ì-lí-šu*
DUMU ⸢x⸣ [ ] ⸢x⸣-*tu-ú*
[DUB.SA]R

U.E. [MU] BA.DÍM

Envelope
ù ⸢^{d}⸣ [ ]
^{Id}UTU-*n*[*a*]
DUMU *Ia-ar-*[ ]
– remainder destroyed –

NOTES

(8) The erased line after line 7 appears to have said: UD.⸢2⸣ KAM ; this line has no relationship to the content of lines 9-10; the text, moreover, appears not to have been dated.

(17) For this fragmentary year date formula, see OBTIV p. 35 no. 69.

UCLMA 9/2878

Envelope Fragment and Seal

Rev.(?) ⌈^{1}⌉*I-pí-i*[*q-*]
DUMU *Ì-lí-we-d*[*e-ku*]
^{1}*Im-gur*-^{d}EN.LÍL
DUMU ^{d}EN.LÍL-*a-bu-um*
^{1}*I-pí-iq-ši-na*
DUMU DINGIR-*a-bu-um*
^{1}*Si-pí-pu-um*
DUMU *Im-gur-r*[*um*]

Seal Legend

I-*pí-iq*-⌈*ši-na*⌉
MÁŠ.ŠU.GÍD.GÍD
DUMU DINGIR-⌈*a-bu-um*⌉

UCLMA 9/2889a-b-c

Barley; List of Amounts and Persons

NOTES

UCLMA 9/2889a-c appear to be part of a single large tablet. 9/2889a preserves three columns of the obverse and a small portion of the reverse; there is enough remaining to suggest that the original tablet contained three columns on the obverse (i.e. cols. i, ii, iii) and two or three columns on the reverse (i.e. cols. iv, v, and possibly vi). Fragment 9/2889b is part of the obverse; it is either the bottom of cols. i and ii or the top portion of cols. iii and iv; these cols. are labelled A and B. The repeated entries for DUMU *Iš-ku-un*-30 are instructive in revealing the order of fragments. This entry appeared for the first time in 9/2889a Obv. col. i 4; it appears for the second and third times in 9/2889b Obv. col. A 10′, 14′. Fragment 9/2889c belongs to the reverse; it could either have preceded the little that was preserved on the reverse of 9/2889a or it could come after it; it either contains part of cols. iv and v as 9/2889a or part of cols. v and vi. There was room for a sixth column on the original tablet but there is no evidence that it was used and inscribed.

UCLMA 9/2892

Goats; Record

Obv. 1 ÙZ *ša si-im*-[*tim*]
1 MÁŠ.GUB
ša la si-im-tim
a-na Ne-ri-ib-t[*im*]

Rev. *a-na* ⌈x⌉[ ]

(Erasure)
ITU ⸢A⸣-[bi-i]
MU É EŠ₄.DAR B[A.DÍM]

NOTES

(1) For *simtu* "fit" said of livestock cf. AHw 1046a (*simat ekallim*) and 1046b (*simat ekurri*).

(2) For MÁŠ.GUB = *lillidu* cf. CAD L 188ff, M/1 364b.

(4) This passage should be added to the comments about *ana Nēribtim* in OBTIV 1[1]. It should be noted, however, that there is no absolute certainty that this text indeed did come from Ishchali; its origin in the Diyala region is however clearly supported by the year date formula, which is OBTIV p. 26 no. 21. Cf. also the livestock documents OBTIV 112-122, UCP 10/1 12, 76, 94.

(5) It would be tempting to restore: *a-na* É(!) [DN], "to the temple of a deity"; cf. the usage of *simat ekurri* mentioned above in the note to line 1.

UCLMA 9/2895
Barley *ḫubuttātum* Loan

Obv. 61(GUR) 2(PI) GUR ŠE
ḫu-bu-ta-tu[*m*]
⸢KI DINGIR-*šu-na-ṣir*⸣
DUMU Bur-⸢{d}EN.ZU⸣
{1}*Mu-na-wi-*[*rum*]
ù Iš-⸢x⸣[ ]
[Š]U.BA.⸢AN.TI.⸣[MEŠ]
L.E. *a-na* ITU [ ]
[*še*]-⸢*am*⸣ [Ì.ÁG.E]
Rev. [ ]
⸢IGI⸣ [ ]⸢x⸣]
DUMU ⸢x x⸣[ ]
[IG]I ⸢{d}⸣UTU-*n*[*a-ṣir*]
[DU]MU ⸢{d}EN.ZU-*i-qi-*⸣-*š*[*a-am*]
[I]GI {d}E[N-Z]U-⸢*i-di*⸣-[*n*]*am*
U.E. [D]UMU ⸢{d}EN.ZU-*ta*-x⸣[ ]
[M]U É ⸢EŠ₄.DAR BA.DÍM⸣

NOTES

(6) One may perhaps restore the missing name as *Iš-m*[*e*-^{d}EN.ZU] ; he appears as a joint-debtor along with the sons of Munawwirum in UCP 10/1 68:5.

(10) This line probably contained: [*ú-še-te-qú-ma* MÁŠ Ì.ÁG.E] "if they let it lapse, then they will add interest."

UCLMA 9/2906

Partnership (*tappūtum*) Agreement

Obv. [M]A.NA [KÙ].B[ABBAR TAB.BA]
[*a-n*]*a ba-ab* KASKAL
[K]I ^{1}*Bur*-^{d}EN.ZU
^{1}*A-pil*-^{d}EN.ZU
DUMU *Wa-ar-da-nim*
ù *Bur*-^{d}EN.ZU DUMU *Im-gur*-^{d}EN.ZU
ŠU.BA.AN.TI.MEŠ
⸢*i-la*⸣-*ku-ú*
⸢*i-tu*⸣-*ru-ni-ma*
⸢*ṭe*$_4$⸣-*em-šu-nu ma*-⸢*ḫa-ar*⸣
L.E. *um-mi-a-nim*
i-ša-⸢*ka*⸣-*nu*
Rev. ⸢*i*⸣-*q*[*í-pu-nim*]
i[ ]
[ ]
[ ]
[ ]⸢x⸣BA.NI-*šu-nu*
[ ]
[ ] ⸢x⸣
[ ]
[ ]-⸢*i-lí*⸣-*šu*
[ ]-⸢*ri-im*⸣
]⸢BI-MA⸣
]⸢KI⸣
U.E. [ ]⸢x x⸣ [ ]
[30-*a*]-⸢*bu-šu* LUGAL⸣(?)[ ]

NOTES

(1) This document is similar to UCLMA 9/2864; the latter text serves as a basis for restoration. UCLMA 9/2864:1f has 1 MA.NA KÙ.BABBAR TAB.BA written in place of an "expected" form:

1 MA.NA KÙ.BABBAR KÙ.BABBAR NAM.TAB.BA; cf. AHw 1322b and Leemans, *The Old Babylonian Merchant*, SD III (1950), 30ff. There is no room for TAB.BA in line 2 of our text; it must therefore be present in line 1, which has been restored on the basis of UCLMA 9/2864.

(2) See note to UCLMA 9/2864.

(14) Cf. UCLMA 9/2864:9ff for possible restorations of lines 13ff.

(25) If the RN can be read in line 26, then this fragmentary year date formula should be added to the list in OBTIV pp. 23-35. UCLMA 9/2864, which records a similar *tappūtu* loan from Bur-Sin, is also dated to a year date of Sin-abušu. For the known year dates of this king see OBTIV p. 21[104] and Reschid, *Nuršamaš* 2-6. A certain restoration of ll. 25f is not forthcoming; but one may perhaps consider: [MU *a-k*]*i-t*[*a-m* [30-*a-b*]*u-šu* LU[GAL *iš-ku-nu*], following TIM 3 34:17-19 (where LUGAL is omitted and *akītam* is written *a-ki-tam*).

UCLMA 9/2942

Silver Loan with Interest (MÁŠ ^{d}UTU)

Obv. (1) 1/2 MA.NA KÙ.BABBAR
MÁŠ ^{d}UTU *ú-ṣa-ab*
KI *Bur*-^{d}EN.ZU
⸢1⸣ [ ] ⸢x⸣ [ ] ⸢x⸣

Remainder of Obv. and beginning of Rev. missing

Rev. (1′) [ ] ⸢x⸣ [ ]
MU *Šul-g*[*i-na-na*^{KI}]
^{l}30-*a-bu-šu* ⸢*iq-qí-ru*⸣

UCLMA 9/2943

Barley; Storage Record

Obv. (1) [ ] ⸢x⸣ KI ⸢x⸣ [ ]
[ ] ⸢x⸣ MA AD ⸢x⸣ [ ]
[ ] ⸢4⸣ GUR ŠE É.DUB BÀD-⸢*Ri-muš*⸣
[ ] ⸢x⸣-*ra-bi-at*

Rev. (5) MU ALAM KÙ.GI

NOTES

(1) The traces at the beginning of lines 1-2 could be read as [GU]R followed by PNs. The PN in line 2 could be *Ma-ad*-⸢x⸣ [ ]; cf. CAD M/1 25a.

(3) Line 3 may contain the total of lines 1-2, particularly if reconstructed as above: "[Total:] 4.0.0 kors barley, storehouse of Dur-Rimuš."

(4) If lines 1-3 are reconstructed as above, line 4 could very well contain [NÍG.ŠU] plus a PN like [ÉS$_4$.DA]R-*ra-bi-at.*

UCLMA 9/2957

Envelope Fragment and Seal Legend

URU.KI *Ú-za-ar-num*

. . .

Seal Legend

DINGIR-*šu-na-ṣir*

[DUMU] *Bur*-^{d}EN.ZU

[ARAD] ^{d}GÌR.UNUG.GAL

NOTES

For this tablet and its seal legend see OBTIV pp. 6f.

UCLMA 9/2958

Barley; ŠU.TI.A

Obv. (1) 7 GUR ŠE

É.DUB *Maš-kán-* x x ⌜x⌝

NÍG.ŠU *Mu-na-nu-um*

ŠU.TI.A DINGIR-*šu-na-ṣi*[*r*]

L.E. [*nam*]-*ḫa-ar-ti*

[ ] ⌜x x x⌝

– Rev. destroyed –

NOTES

For other documents of this type, dealing with barley, cf. OBTIV 94:28 (note), 128-132, UCP 10/1 53, UCLMA 9/3030.

UCLMA 9/3019
Sale of Property

Obv.	(1)	82 SAR ⸢x⸣ [ ]	(1)	82 sar . . .
		UŠ.BI PA$_5$ URU[ ]		alongside the canal of the city. . . ,
		SAG.BI A.ŠÀ DINGIR ⸢x x (x)⸣-*nu*		facing the field of. . . . ,
		ù DA *E-te-el-lum*		and (also) next to (the property of) Etellum,
	(5)	KI *Ma-ku-ú-um*	(5)	from Makum
		LUGAL.A.NI.IR		its owner
		^{1}DINGIR-*šu-na-ṣir*		did Ilšu-naṣir
		IN.ŠI.IN.ŠÁM		purchase.
		ŠÁM.TIL.LA.BI.ŠÈ		For its complete purchase price
	(10)	KÙ.BABBAR IN.NA.LAL	(10)	he paid silver
		ŠÀ.GA.NI Ì.DÙG		(and) satisfied him.
L.E.		INIM.BI AL.TIL		The transaction is concluded;
		GIŠ.GAN.NA IB.TA.BAL		they passed the pestle.
		NU.MU.UN.GI$_4$.GI$_4$.DAM	14)	He swore (by) the name of the king
Rev.	(15)	MU.LUGAL.BI IN.PÀD	15)	not to contest.
		ba-qir i-ba-qa-ru		Any party who raises a claim
		1 MA.NA KÙ.BABBAR Ì.LAL.E		will pay one mina silver.
		IGI ⸢d⸣ [ŠEŠ].KI.MA.AN.SUM		Witnessed by Nanna.mansum
		IGI [DINGIR-*šu*]-*i-bi-šu*		Witnessed by Ilšu-ibbišu
	(20)	DUMU *Be-el-šu-nu*	(20)	son of Belšunu
		^{1}*Qù-ru-du-um*		Qurrudum
		DUMU *Ì-lí-iš-me-*<*an*>-*ni*		son of Ili-išme'anni
		^{1}*Ri-iš*-^{d}UTU		Riš-Šamaš
		DUMU DINGIR-*šu-a-bu-šu*		son of Ilšu-abušu

Envelope Variants

(1)	⸢KIŠIB⸣ [82 SAR]	(1)	Tablet of 82 sar . . .
(5)	KI *Ma-ku-um* ù ⸢x⸣ [ ]	(5)	From Makum and . . .
(18)	[IGI ^{d}ŠEŠ.KI].MA.A[N.SUM	(18)	Witnessed by Nanna.mansum
(18a)	[ ] [x]-*nu-u*[*m*]	(18a)	. . . num
(19)	IGI DINGIR-*š*]*u-i-bi-šu*	(19)	Witnessed by Ilšu-ibbišu
(22)	DUMU *Ì-lí-i*]*š-me-an-ni*	(22)	son of Ili-išme'anni

Label

KIŠIB *Ri-iš*-^{d}UTU

NOTES

(18a) This line could record either the father of Nanna.mansum or perhaps even his title- [*ra-bi*]-⸢*a*(!)⸣-*nu-u*[*m*].

Label

This label appears on the envelope, where part of a pictorial seal impression is also visible.

UCLMA 9/3030
Barley; ŠU.TI.A

Obv. 1(GUR) 3(BÁN) GUR *ša iš-<tu> A-ḫi-ša-gi-iš*
2(BÁN) ŠE *a-na* LÚ.DIRI.GA
3(BÁN) *Qa-i-la-tum*
3(PI) ŠE ŠUG *Qa-i-la-tum*
ša ITU.3.KAM *iš-tu* ITU ^{d}Ù(!).GUL.LÁ UD.1.KAM
a-di ITU *Tam-ḫi-ru* UD.30.KAM
1(BÁN) *a-na* É ^{d}MAR.TU
5 SILA$_3$ *I-din-*^{d}MAR.TU *a-na* PA(?)*-tim*
1(BÁN) 3 SILA$_3$ *a-na* 1/3 SILA$_3$ Ì.ŠAḪ
ša LÚ.TÚG
L.E. ŠU.NIGIN$_2$ 1(GUR) 4(PI) 5(BÁN) 8 SILA$_3$
Rev. 2(PI) 2(BÁN) ŠE *Ma-sú-ú*
2(PI) 3(BÁN) *A-ḫi-ša-gi-iš*
1 GUR ŠE *La-bi-ir-tum*
ŠU.TI.A *ša* Ì.GIŠ *ù* Ì.ŠAḪ
ŠU.NIGIN$_2$ 1(GUR) 4(PI) 5(BÁN) ŠE
ŠU.TI.A *A-ḫi-ša-gi-iš*
– blank line –
ŠU.NIGIN 3(GUR) 4(PI) 4(BÁN) 8 SILA$_3$ ŠE
ŠU.TI.A *A-ḫi-ša-gi-iš*
KI DINGIR*-šu-na-ṣir*
U.E. ITU *Tam-ḫi-ru* UD.30.KAM

NOTES

(2) LÚ.DIRIG.GA, whether (*w*)*atru* (CAD A/2 500a) or (*w*)*attaru* (CAD A/2 510b), is an "extra" or "replacement."

(3) The occurrence of Qa'ilatum in this text should dispel the doubt of von Soden, AHw 839a, as to whether it is a PN.

(5) The month of ^{d}Ù.GUL.LÁ also occurs at Tell Harmal; cf. YOS 14 64:12. Our reading Ù(!) here follows what is apparently a more certain reading there.

(8) If one will read *pa-tim* here, then one may consider *pattû*, "a container" or *pātu*, an unknown object; cf. AHw 849a.

(11) For *massû*, as an element of PNs, cf. CAD M/1 328b.

(14) For ŠU.TI.A see note to UCLMA 9/2958 above.

CHAPTER 6

EXCURSUS*

6.1 MÁŠ ᵈUTU

Ṣibat Šamaš (MÁŠ ᵈUTU) "the interest of Šamaš" is normally found in connection with loans of silver; cf. Leemans RIDA 5 (1950) 15-19. The amount of interest to be collected is not expressly stated but Leemans assumes it to be 20 per cent for the following reasons: (1) CH § L (PBS 5 93 i 9-12) and CE § 18A set the interest rate for barley loans at 33 1/3% while the rate for silver loans is set at 20%; (2) in a number of OB documents, silver and barley are lent together; the barley is given as a *ḫubullu* loan at 33 1/3% while the silver is lent at "the interest of Šamaš." According to Leemans, one can assume first, that the "interest of Šamaš" would be less than the 33 1/3% for barley and, secondly, that it would not be more than the 20% "standard" interest for silver allowed by the Codes. The estimated rate of 20% for the "interest of Šamaš" thus appears to be a reasonable calculation.[1] The occurrence of the 20 per cent rate in both the Codes of Eshnunna and Hammurapi points to a uniform practice, followed both in Babylonia and in the Diyala and allows us to consider their sources as a unified evidence pool. Silver, to be sure, was on occasion lent at higher rates of interest; OB texts from Mari, Babylonia, and Susa yield examples of 25%, 30%, 33 1/3%, 40%, and even 50%;[2] and texts from the Diyala attest to a rate of 33 1/3%,[3] suggesting that other rates of interest were possible there as well. In the light of the higher rates of interest, the 20% rate emerges both as a concession to the borrower which sovereigns would underwrite in their law codes and as a model of fairness which could be attributed to Šamaš, the god of justice and righteousness.

The specific factors governing the selection of interest rates are not revealed: i.e., the texts do not tell us why some borrowers were favored by a 20 per cent rate and others were not. The silver loans at Ishchali are generally for large amounts:[4] here, the favor of *ṣibat Šamaš* cannot represent an extension of benefits to a poor, underprivileged debtor class. Leemans is of the opinion that the 20% rate represents the standard OB interest rate for silver and that higher rates are the exception rather than the rule; he equates *ṣibat Šamaš* with *ṣibat Šamaš kittu* (MÁŠ ᵈUTU GI.NA) and with *ṣibtu kittu* (MÁŠ GI.NA) and

*Excursus 6.1 relates back to p. 31; Excursus 6.2 relates to p. 40.

[1] Specific Diyala examples of OB loans involving both silver and barley are Simmons YOS 14, nos. 11, 15, 18, 20, 37, BIN 7 74, 76-78, 80-81, 84, 86, 88 (=Simmons JCS 13 [1959] pp. 109ff. nos. 14, 17, 25, 28, 30, 32, 37, 42, 43), TIM 2 12-20, 108. The lone example from Ishchali is UCP 10/1 77. For other parts of Babylonia, cf. Leemans RIDA 5 (1950) 16, 20[51]; additional OB examples are VS 8 128, CT 33 49a, CT 47 2, CT 48 71, PBS 8/2 190, Edzard, *Tell ed-Dēr* 19.

[2] For references cf. Leemans op. cit. 21[52], 24-25; G. Boyer ARM 8 203-206, and CAD Ṣ 160a.

[3] Simmons YOS 14 no. 72 and Harris JCS 9 (1955) 61 no. 6 (copy on p. 71).

[4] Out of fifteen Ishchali examples, six are for one mina or more; five are for ten shekels or more; and the least is for three shekels. The fifteen texts are OBTIV 43-51; UCP 10/1 77, 80, 82; UCLMA 9/2827, 2831, 2942, omitting UCP 10/1 82, which is fragmentary.

takes all of these terms to represent the same rate.[5] If he is correct, then there is no point in searching for a rationale to explain the application or use of *ṣibat Šamaš*; it is merely a label to designate a known and standard rate of interest.

There is, moreover, no correlation between the use of *ṣibat Šamaš* and the phenomenon of "temple loans:" i.e., loans in which the creditor is a god or else a god who acts with a human agent as co-creditor.[6] These loans sporadically mention *ṣibat Šamaš* but it is by no means a regular feature of these transactions.[7] The Ishchali texts do not offer sufficient examples to test this distribution. There are five "temple loans"[8] but only one for silver; the other four are for barley. The silver loan (p. 31) does mention *ṣibat Šamaš*: but as noted above, *ṣibat Šamaš* is mentioned only when silver is lent and never occurs in barley loans. The interest rate for "temple loans" is not always 20%; Leemans states that for barley loans, 20% is charged only when a god alone is lender; when a god plus a human agent are the creditors, the interest rate is 33 1/3%.[9] But the interest rate for silver is also subject to variations. At Mari, for example, the "joint loans," i.e., loans involving a god plus a human creditor, are uniformly for 30%.[10] At the same time, however, the interest rates for "temple loans" were often lower than 20%; the Ishchali "temple loans" for barley do not mention any interest at all, and the same is true for a large number of silver and barley "temple loans" elsewhere.[11]

[5] Leemans RIDA 5 (1950) 9-11, 15, 18. For additional references, cf. also CAD Ṣ 160a and TIM 3 139; BIN 7 203; BIN 2 84; Edzard, *Tell ed-Dēr* 15.

[6] "Temple loans" have most recently been studied by R. Harris, "Old Babylonian Temple Loans" JCS (1960) 126-137. Our discussion is based on her list of texts (pp. 126-127), to which one can add: UET 5 421; TCL 1 113, TIM 3 123, 130, 131; and IM 51177 and 51178 cited by Simmons JCS 14 (1960) 50. Harris's list includes loans of barley as well as of silver.

[7] *Ṣibat Šamaš* occurs only in a few cases out of the texts included in the previous note; we consider, of course, only the silver loans out of the larger barley and silver loan collection, since *ṣibat Šamaš* only occurs with silver loans. We find it mentioned in instances where a deity alone is lender in VS 8 128; CT 33 49 a; VS 13 59; TIM 3 130; Edzard, *Tell ed-Dēr* 16. In instances where DN and PN act together, we have: BIN 7 76, 79-81, 84, 88, 89, VS 9 83. By contrast, silver loans not mentioning *ṣibat Šamaš* are: (1) in cases where DN alone is lender: ARM 8 48; VS 9 29, 134, 187; CT 6 40c; TCL 1 107, 188; JCS 11 (1957) 18 CUA 75; JCS 5 (1951) 91 MAH 16354, 16361; ARN 124; BE 6/1 67; BE 6/2 20; Simmons YOS 14 nos. 64, 67, 68, 70; MDP 22 22, 119, 124; BIN 2 85; Boyer, *Contribution* 138; RA 12 71; (2) in cases where DN acts with PN: ARM 8 22-36, 45; VS 8 125, 183; MDP 23 271, 273.

[8] OBTIV 47, 72, 78, 79, and 80. Harris JCS 14 (1960) 127 cites under Neribtum four additional excavated tablets; these, however, are not among the Oriental Institute holdings but in Baghdad and were not available for study; we are thus unable to offer any further comment on their contents except for a note to OBTIV 80:8 relating to Ish. 34-T.144 (see above).

[9] W. F. Leemans RIDA 5 (1950) 12[24], 14[29]; cf. also TIM 3 123; Simmons YOS 14 no. 45; UCLMA 9/1876–said to come from Khafaje, a loan of barley at 33 1/3% from Šamaš and PN. There are, however, exceptions as Harris, JCS 14 (1960) 132, points out: e.g., Gautier Dilbat 58–DN alone at 33 1/3%. See also the texts cited in note 11 below.

[10] G. Boyer ARM 8 204, commenting on ARM 8 22-29, 32-36, 45. Simmons YOS 14 no. 19, which projects a rate of 40 per cent, may be an error; perhaps one should restore in line 2: MÁŠ 1 GUR <1 (PI)> ŠE *ú-sa-ab*. Cf. BIN 7 75:2 (=no. 29 in Simmons JCS 13 [1959] 114), where 1(PI) is clearly omitted; another possibility is to pattern no. 27 after Simmons YOS 14 no. 45, where interest is simply 1 PI or just 20 per cent.

[11] UET 5 325 is a silver loan with an interest rate of 10% (MÁŠ.BI 1 MA.NA.E 6 GÍN.TA.ÀM). More common are loans recording no interest at all. For silver loans cf. Simmons YOS 14 nos. 64, 67, 68, 70; VS 9 134, 183; CT 6 40c; TCL 1 107, 188; PBS 8/2 215; UET 5 284, 304, 310, 312, 318, 322, 324, 421. Barley loans without interest are OBTIV 72, 78, 79, and 80.

A number of "temple loans" list deities among the witnesses;[12] deities also appear as witnesses in non-"temple" silver loans where *ṣibat Šamaš* is charged.[13] Yet, here again, there is no clear pattern; for deities also occur as witnesses in loans given by private individuals and in situations where conventional interest is charged.[14] The above observations hold true both for Ishchali as well as for other OB texts. We can find no basis for positing any relationship between the occurrence of divine witnesses, the use of *ṣibat Šamaš*, or "temple loans."[15]

6.2 Administrative Documents[16]

There is a need to determine the boundary between private and administrative archives. Our first consideration is whether the ancient record relates to an individual or to a group or corporation.[17] One generally assumes that private documents reflect the affairs of individuals rather than of institutions or corporations. They are mainly what we call "legal records," e.g.: sales of real estate, slaves, adoptions, loans, marriage, divorce, etc. They are the types of documents scholars appeal to when they want to establish the roles of individual citizens apart from the affairs of the large corporations like the temple or palace.

By contrast, administrative records are seen to be the products of large households and relate to the organizing and recording of the activities of personnel, agriculture, industry, and government. Despite the large number of written records from ancient Mesopotamia, one has the definite impression that access to scribes and to their services was not uniformly available to all groups within the population. Only the larger households and institutions could employ and maintain scribes, and only in the greatest of these corporations do we find a group of scribes together, sufficient in number to form a school or library.

A second factor is the permanence of the record. Administrative bureaucracies, having the use of a staff of scribes, are able to generate all kinds of memos, notes—what may be

[12] For barley loans cf. OBTIV 80; Gautier Dilbat 58; MDP 23 179, 180, 182; MDP 28 428. For silver loans cf. BE 6/2 20; TCL 1 113, 188; BIN 2 85; UET 5 304, 310, 318. Cf. also OBTIV 86 in which deities appear as witnesses to a guaranty of a "temple loan" and OBTIV 77 a silver loan, where deities are included among the witnesses. For the possibility of an oath being sworn, see note there.

[13] No. 69; Edzard, *Tell ed-Dēr* 9.

[14] OBTIV 53; UCP 10/1 8, 9; VS 7 81; BIN 2 84; Riftin 7; Edzard, *Tell ed-Dēr* 12.

[15] Doubtlessly some reasons must underly these phenomena; for an attempt to explain why "temple loans" were granted, see Harris JCS 14 (1960) 131-137.

[16] The following comments contain many points that were made, in a more cursory fashion, in an unnumbered footnote appearing in OBTIV pp. 38-39. The comments given here are based on a paper, "Towards a Typology of Documents Produced by Bureaucratic Archives in the Old Babylonian Period," delivered by the writer at the Mid-West Regional Meeting of the American Oriental Society, The University of Indiana, Bloomington, February 27, 1978.

[17] The distinction made here between "individual and corporation" is derivative of but not identical with the distinction earlier made by Koschaker and Ungnad, *Hammurabi's Gesetz* VI (1923), pp. 155f, between *Privatrecht* and *öffentliches Recht*. We here do not wish to emphasize a distinction in law but rather a distinction based on the use of the documents. Indeed, in our analysis, the typical document kept in private hands is "public" in the sense that it may ultimately find itself being used in litigation to prove certain facts or to bolster the rights of the individual holding the document. The administrative document, on the other hand, is "private" in the sense that it is not intended to be read by other persons outside of the office of the scribe who wrote it.

termed "temporary or intermediate records" as opposed to documents that are "final or official" in character. "Final or official records" are documents like deeds of sale, loans, manumissions, lawsuit proceedings, adoptions, and similar documents. These final or permanent records were written to be kept for long periods of time and are generally pretty complete and fall into self-revealing categories. By contrast, many temporary records are non-descript and hard to classify precisely because they are ephemeral or "intermediate" records. They represent memos, notes, tags, and the like that were meant to be kept only for a while and destined eventually to be discarded or else absorbed or replaced by more "final" or "official" records. Temporariness is an important characteristic of archives in general and can be seen in archives from the Greco-Roman period as well as from Oriental antiquity.[18]

Almost all of the documents kept in the archives of private individuals are of the "final" or "official" variety, i.e., they are valuable proofs that certain transactions have taken place and their existence safeguards the continuing rights of the private individual or his family to enjoy what they possess or are entitled to possess in the future. Because of their typically evidentiary quality, the documents in private archives are almost invariably witnessed. The recording of witnesses is the thing that gives these documents their legal character. Most legal documents have witnesses because witnesses are the primary means of establishing the truth of a right or claim in ancient Mesopotamia. Documents in themselves have value, but they are, ultimately, essentially aids to memory; when there is a dispute, the courts did not simply rely on the written document but read the document and called the witnesses whose names were recorded therein to testify.[19]

It is precisely for this same reason that documents which come out of administrative archives are typically not witnessed. There is really no need for witnesses in the conduct of an office or bureau. So many of the administrative documents are of "temporary or intermediate" character; they are either the internal means of communication between one set of records and another or else a series of notes destined to be replaced or absorbed by a subsequent record. When authority is needed in bureaucratic circles or when final or official records are being prepared, the scribal administrators do not, typically, appeal to witnesses but to the hierarchical chain of authority within the corporation—the chain of command. We thus find the use of authorizations in expressions like GÌR PN, "under the foot or authority of so-and-so," NÍG.ŠU PN, "under the hand or control of so-and-so."[20] The use of dates, especially months and days of the month, is typical of administrative archives, where there are so many transactions and persons to keep track of. Notations of location or destination are likewise not uncommon. Private records, on the other hand,

[18] This important insight is made and developed in great detail by Ernst Posner, *Archives in the Ancient World*. Harvard University Press, Cambridge (1972).

[19] For a discussion of the evidentiary character of Mesopotamian legal documents, at least in the OB period, see the writer's comments in JAOS 83 (1969), pp. 513, 516-520. For a more recent re-statement of these same facts, see J. Renger, "Legal Aspects of Sealing in Ancient Mesopotamia," in M. Gibson and R. D. Biggs (eds.), *Seals and Sealing in the Ancient Near East*, Bibliotheca Mesopotamica 6. Undena Publications, Malibu (1977), p. 76 and note there.

[20] For the continuing discussion of the exact administrative role of the PN described in the expression GÌR PN, see P. Steinkeller, "Seal Practice in the Ur III Period," in Gibson and Biggs, *Seals and Sealing*, p. 42.

seldom include more than the year date if at all; at Ishchali, sale documents for land and slaves omit even the year date.[21]

The distinction between legal and administrative texts, based on the presence or absence of witnesses, is widely accepted because it appears essentially to be valid. However, there are exceptions; and these are numerous enough to warrant comment. Koschaker (*Hammurabi's Gesetz* VI [1923], pp. 155f) noted that there were legal documents that appeared to be similar to others of this category except for the omission of witnesses, e.g.: HG III 179, 183, 205; IV 865, 906. Such documents are also present at Ishchali; cf. OBTIV 27; UCP 10/1 61, 29. There were other texts (e.g. HG III 114, 116, 763-770) that were administrative in character, dealing mainly with what Koschaker termed "the business of the Palace"; some of these were witnessed, but others were not. Koschaker saw these as an intermediate group between the categories of "legal" and "administrative." OBTIV 127 and 235 are witnessed administrative texts but betray no traces of being "palace business." OBTIV 88, 89, 142, 144 are administrative documents that could easily be considered as "legal" if the names of witnesses were attached. The same is true of OBTIV 87, which we have taken to be a legal record, despite the absence of witnesses. It possesses a seal and envelope and seems to project a note of finality in what is stated therein.

On the basis of the exceptions noted, it clearly emerges that the use of witnesses was available to corporations as well as to individuals for the conduct of their legal affairs and business.[22]

Administrative documents are, typically, concerned with income or outlay of resources. This is the foundation of all bookkeeping; and administrative records emerge out of the ongoing bookkeeping activities which are a characteristic feature of the large economic units which employ scribes. It is possible to classify a good number of the Ishchali administrative tablets on the basis of the transaction—either income, outlay, or their associated terminology. We are talking here about terms like MU.TÚM, ZI.GA, *namḫartum, nišrum*, and forms of the verb *šuddunum*, etc.

When the specific transaction is unclear, the commodities involved offer a second line of classification. At Ishchali, when they are gold, jewelry, garments, we are probably dealing with income more than with outlay, but the latter is possible in the case of unworked precious metals. Other commodities are silver, livestock, fowl, grain, beans, oil, flour, bread, pitch, wood; there are also goods like tools, utensils, bricks, and harness fittings. Sometimes the commodity is not identified; the texts simply state amount, person and, occasionally, a total. Some of these texts appear to deal with grain.

[21] Seals are used both in legal and administrative documents at Ishchali; this observation should be noted after considering the cautionary note of Renger, "Legal Aspects of Sealing in Ancient Mesopotamia," in Gibson and Biggs, *Seals and Sealing*, p. 81 note 3.

[22] For the fuller consideration of this problem, i.e. the interpretation of the place of witnesses in administrative documents (the reverse situation does not seem to have generated the same degree of reaction), see Szlechter, TJG 146ff, who, in connection with MAH 16.426, sees the presence of witnesses as reflecting the activities of a tax-collector who acts as a private citizen, not being an official of the palace. N. Yoffee, *The Economic Role of the Crown in the Old Babylonian Period*, Bibliotheca Mesopotamica 5, Undena Publications, Malibu (1977) pp. 5-9 argues that scholars should not categorize documents as administrative solely on the basis of their lacking witnesses; he says that the private character of OB economy is exaggerated and that the palace influences are far more widespread than suspected. Renger, "Legal Aspects of Sealing in Ancient Mesopotamia," in Gibson and Biggs, *Seals and Sealing*, 8 of note 2 makes the same point as Yoffee.

These documents seem to be "temporary or intermediate" in character, as described above. The term "record" is much overworked in the classification of administrative documents. In one sense, of course, it is true that every administrative document is a record; but if we term every text a record, we lose the opportunity for meaningful distinctions. We reserve the term "record" for administrative documents that appear to be of a "final or official" character; the records are documents that were intended to be kept on file for a relatively long period of time. These documents gain their status as records by the fact that they contain seals, dates, and the names of authorizing officials. Records are full documents and must always identify the transaction, and often supply additional, explanatory terms or remarks.

But for the "temporary or intermediate" documents, i.e., documents lacking designation of the transaction, lacking date, the name of any authorizing official, a seal, or even the name of the commodity involved, we propose to use terms like "memo, list, and tally" to describe these documents. We use the term "memo" to describe a brief text of no more than two entries; these texts typically state amount, person, and generally omit any other information. Sometimes, no names are given and one wonders how the scribe was able to recall the transaction. Perhaps a system similar to the one attested in the Ur III period was employed. Among the Ur III texts we find perforated clay labels bearing personal names; these labels were attached to baskets containing tablets relating to the affairs of specific individuals.[23] We have found no personal tablet labels at Ishchali but we could imagine a system like the Ur III one being used to keep track of these otherwise anonymous and easily forgotten memos. We use the term "list" to describe a larger memo of three or more entries and the term "tally" for a list accompanied by a total.

[23] Cf., for examples, S. T. Kang, *Sumerian Economic Texts from the Drehem Archive*, Sumerian and Akkadian Cuneiform Texts in the Collection of the World Heritage Museum of the University of Illinois I. University of Illinois Press, Urbana (1972), nos. 191-192 and pp. 245f. A reference to a tablet filed in a basket occurs in S. T. Kang, *Sumerian Economic Texts from the Umma Archive*, Sumerian and Akkadian Texts, University of Illinois II (1973), no. 288. See further, Mogens Weitemeyer, "Archive and Library Technique in Ancient Mesopotamia," Libri 6/3 (1956), pp. 221-224.

CHAPTER 7

INDEXES TO LUTZ, *LEGAL AND ECONOMIC DOCUMENTS FROM ASHJÂLY* (UCP 10/1) AND TO NEW ISHCHALI TABLETS IN THE COLLECTION OF THE LOWIE MUSEUM OF ANTHROPOLOGY UNIVERSITY OF CALIFORNIA, BERKELEY (UCLMA)

7.1 Personal Names

In order to render the Akkadian names in a more familiar fashion, the following conventions have been used: ^{d}Adad = ^{d}IM, $^{(d)}$*Amurrum* = $^{(d)}$MAR.TU, *Akšak* = ÚḪ^{KI}, *Awīl* = LÚ, ^{d}*Enlil* = ^{d}EN.LÍL, ^{d}*Ilaprat* = ^{d}NIN.ŠUBUR, *Ilum, Il* = DINGIR, ^{d}*Ištar* = ^{d}INNIN, *Ištar* = ES$_4$.DAR, *mār* = DUMU, *mārtum* = DUMU. SAL, ^{d}*Nanna*, ^{d}NANNA = ^{d}ŠEŠ.KI, *Puzur* = PUZUR$_4$, ^{d}*Sin* = ^{d}EN.ZU, *Sin* = 30, ^{d}*Šamaš* = ^{d}UTU, ^{d}*Tišpak* = ^{d}TIŠPAK, *Warad* = ARAD. In addition, the following symbols are employed: s. = son, d. = daughter, f. = father, w. = wife, h. = husband, b. = brother, (w) = witness, (R) = royal name, (Y) = year date formulas, (s) = seal.

A . . . UCP 10/1 96:7

A . . . ^{d}*Adad* UCP 10/1 52:4

A-ba-ba-nu-um f. of *A-bu-um-ḫa-lum* UCP 10/1 109:5

Ab-di-e-ra-aḫ s. of *Warad-*^{d}*Tišpak* UCP 10/1 5:4

A . . . bi UCP 10/1 86:11

A-bi-ia-tum UCP 10/1 86:13

A-bi-ki . . . UCP 10/1 108:43

Ab-nu-tum UCP 10/1 100:8

A-⌜*bu*⌝*-um*(?)-⌜*da*⌝*-lum* s. of ^{d}*Šamaš-ba-ni* UCLMA 9/2831:13 (w)

A-bu-um-ḫa-lum s. of *A-ba-ba-nu-um* UCP 10/1 109:4

A-bu-um-ilum
1) s. of ^{d}*Sin-e-ri-ba-am, Sin-e-ri-ba-am**, *Sin-eri*$_4$*-ba-am***, ^{d}*Sin-eri*$_4$*-ba****, ^{d}*Sin-e-ri-ba*****, *Sin-e-ri-ba******, UCP 10/1 1:11 (w)**, 8:13 (w)***; 11:22 (w)(s); 13:10 (w)**; 14:9 (w); 15:11 (w)***; 19:9 (w)(s); 21:9 (w)***; 23:16 (w)*****; 24:13 (w)*; 25:11 (w)*; 28:12 (w); 39:10 (w); 42:10 (w); 44:12 (w)****; 45:11 (w)**; 52:24 (w***)(s); 58 (s); 68:13 (w); 90:19 (w)***; 95:11 (w); 103:13 (w)**; 107:19 (w***)(s); UCLMA 9/2826:10 (w)(s); 9/2858 + 2863:13 (w*****) (s); 9/2862:10 (w); 9/2866:11 (w)***
2) UCP 10/1 40:11 (w); 58:18 (w); 69:11 (w); 81:9 (w); 87:1

*A-bu-um-wa-qar, A-bu-wa-qar**
1) s. of *E-ri-ba-nim* UCP 10/1 7:11 (w)*; 11:24 (w)*; 42:14 (w); 95:13 (w)
2) s. of ^{d}*Sin-še-mi* UCP 10/1 91 (s)*
3) f. of *Mār-Ištar* UCP 10/1 93:5*
4) UCP 10/1 75:12*; 79:10*; 100:4*

^{d}*Adad-nu-ri* UCP 10/1 86:7

^{d}*Adad-ra-bi* UCP 10/1 57:17

A-di-du-um UCP 10/1 33:8; 62:6

Ad-ma-ti-ì-lí f. of *I-pí-iq-ì-lí-šu* UCP 10/1 63:14; UCLMA 9/2860:12

A-ḫa . . . UCLMA 9/2889a obv. col. iii 17

A-ḫa-am-ni-šu UCP 10/1 86:1

A-ḫa-su-nu UCP 10/1 89:30

A-ḫa-ta-tum UCP 10/1 96:3

*A-ḫi-*KU-ZU . . . s. of ⌜*Ba*⌝. . . UCP 10/1 81:4

A-ḫi-mar-ši s. of *Pa-ra-ri-im* UCP 10/1 2:13 (w)

A-ḫi-ša-gi-iš
1) f. of *Ib-ni-*^{d}*Amurrum* UCP 10/1 87:6
2) UCLMA 9/3030:1, 12, 16, 19

A-ḫi-um-mi-šu f. of ^{d}*Sin-ga-mil* UCP 10/1 58:17; 107:21 (s)

A-ḫu-ki-n[*u-um*] UCP 10/1 89:22

A-ḫu-ni
1) s. of *Ša-sa-am-tim* UCP 10/1 75:4
2) f. of [*Im*]-⌜*gur*⌝-^{d}*Adad* UCP 10/1 11:25
3) f. of *Šu-*^{d}*Amurrim* UCP 10/1 4:20
4) UCP 10/1 48:2; 79:4

4) f. of ⌜*Ìl-šu*⌝-*i-bi-šu* UCLMA 9/3019:20
5) f. of *Ta-ri-bu-um* UCP 10/1 107:2, 7
6) UCP 10/1 89:14; 106:8; 108:19; UCLMA 9/2889c rev. col. B 6′
Be-el-ta-ni
1) w. of *Mu-na-wi-rum* UCP 10/1 59:2
2) w. of ᵈ*Sin-mu-ba-lí-iṭ* UCP 10/1 17:3
3) UCP 10/1 89:17
Be-el-tum UCP 10/1 39:5
Be-lí-i f. of *Mār-*ᵈ*Šamaš* UCP 10/1 98:6
Bi-tum-damiq(ŠAG₅) UCP 10/1 36:7
⌜*Bu*⌝ . . . f. of *A-ḫi*-KU-ZU . . . UCP 10/1 81:5
⌜*Bu*⌝ . . . *um* UCP 10/1 108:12
*Bur-*ᵈ*Adad* UCP 10/1 69:1
Bu-ra-nu-um s. of *Sin-e-ri-ba-am* UCP 10/1 2:17 (w)
*Bu-ri-ia, Bur-ia**
1) s. of *Sa-si-ia* UCP 10/1 36:9 (w)*
2) f. of *Ṣu-ḫu-tum* UCP 10/1 38:10
3) UCP 10/1 106:6
Bur-nu-nu
1) f. of *A-wi-il-ilim* UCP 10/1 61:5 (s)
2) f. of *Awīl-*ᵈNIN.URTA UCLMA 9/2864:16
*Bur-*ᵈ*Sin, Bur-Sin**
1) s. of *I-bi-*ᵈ*Tišpak* UCLMA 9/2827:3; 9/2831:3
2) s. of *Im-gur-*ᵈ*Sin* UCLMA 9/2831:4; 9/2906:6
3) f. of *An-um-pî*(KA)-ᵈ*Šamaš* UCP 10/1 4:19*; 8:15; 51:13; 108:18
4) f. of *Ìl-šu-na-ṣir* UCP 10/1 9:2; 11:8; 19:3; 22:8; 23:6*; 24:6; 29:4; 38:3; 52:8*; 58:4*; 90:7; UCLMA 9/2858:4; 9/2895:4; 9/2957 (s)
5) f. of *Ip-qú-ša* UCP 10/1 4:19*; 8:15; 108:18
6) f. of *Puzur-Ištar* UCP 10/1 77:8
7) UCP 10/1 2:3; 11:3; 61:3; 80:3; UCLMA 9/2864:3; 9/2906:3; 9/2942:3

Da-du-ša UCP 10/1 4:22 (R)(Y); 7:18 (R)(Y); 50:13 (R)(Y); 91 (R)(s); 107 (R)(s); 109:16 (R); UCLMA 9/2828:25 (R)(Y); 9/2889a obv. col. ii 6; iii 9; 9/2889b obv. col. A 7′
Da-qa-ni-ia f. of ᵈ*Sin-mu-ba-lí-iṭ* UCP 10/1 22(s)
Du-ba-ba-tum w. of *Warad-*ᵈ*Ilaprat* UCP 10/1 1:4; 87:3

⌜*El*⌝ . . . s. of ⌜ᵈEN⌝ . . . UCP 10/1 92:7
⌜ᵈEN⌝ . . . f. of ⌜*El*⌝ . . . UCP 10/1 92:8
ᵈ*Enlil-a-bu-um*
1) s. of *Na-bi-*ᵈ*Enlil* UCP 10/1 109:8
2) f. of *Im-gur-*ᵈ*Enlil* UCP 10/1 51:5; UCLMA 9/2878:4′

3) UCP 10/1 87:4
E-ri-ba-am
1) f. of ᵈ*Sin-ma-gir* UCP 10/1 109:23
2) UCP 10/1 55:2
E-ri-ba-am-Sin s. of *Lum-ma-Anum*(AN) UCP 10/1 20:11 (w); 55:14 (w)
E-ri-ba-num f. of *A-bu-um-wa-qar, A-bu-wa-qar** UCP 10/1 7:12*; 11:24*; 42:15; 95:14
*E-ri-ib-*ᵈ*Sin, E-ri-ib-Sin**
1) s. of *Anum*(AN) . . . UCP 10/1 109:6, 18
2) s. of ᵈ*Sin-i-din-nam* UCP 10/1 25:4
3) f. of *Ib-na-tum*, ᵈ*Sin-na-da* UCP 10/1 74:6*
4) UCP 10/1 3:9, 12; 49:5*; 53:4; 55:1*; 79:9; 86:16*; 88:1
*E-ri-iš-ti-*ᵈ*Šamaš*
1) d. of *I-pí-iq-ši-na* UCLMA 9/2826:5
2) d. of ᵈ*Sin-i-din-*⌜*nam*⌝ UCP 10/1 96:5
3) UCP 10/1 96:2
E-ri-iš-tum UCP 10/1 89:12, 19
E-ri-súm-ma-tum UCP 10/1 106:13
Er-ṣi-tum-ra-bi-at, Er-ṣi-tum-rabi'at(GAL)*, *Er-ṣitum*(KI)-*ra-bi-at***, *Erṣitum*(KI)-*rabi'at*(GAL)***
1) s. of *Be-el-šu-nu* UCP 10/1 9:14; 22:23* (s***)
2) UCP 10/1 89:2, 3, 5, 32**; 110:34**
*E-te-el-lum, E-te-lu-um**
1) s. of ᵈNANNA.MA.AN.SUM UCP 10/1 4:13 (w)*
2) UCLMA 9/3019:4

Ga-ga-tum UCLMA 9/2889c rev. col. B 3′
Ga-mil . . . UCLMA 9/2889c rev. col. A 7′
Ga-mi-ilum
1) s. of *Warad-ì-lí-šu* UCLMA 9/2827:18 (w)
2) UCLMA 9/2862:5
Gi-mil-lum s. of AN . . . , b. of *A-pa-an-ilim* UCP 10/1 60:6, 8
*Gu-ul-lu-bi-ia, Gu-lu-bi-ia**
1) f. of *Mu-na-nu-um* UCP 10/1 42:6
2) f. of *Mu-na-wi-rum* UCP 10/1 11 (s); 22 (s); 25:14*; 52 (s); 107 (s); UCLMA 9/2826 (s)
3) UCP 10/1 41:4*
Gu-ru-ru-um UCP 10/1 27:3

Ḫa . . . UCP 10/1 98:12
Ḫa-ia-ab-ni-ilum UCP 10/1 110:10
Ḫa-ia-ša-rum
1) s. of PN (missing) UCP 10/1 107:30 (w)
2) UCP 10/1 15:1, 13 (w); 45:3
Ḫa-li-wu-um UCP 10/1 106:23

Ì-lí-iš-me-an-ni f. of *Qù-ru-du-um* UCLMA 9/3019:22
Ì-lí-ki-ma-a-bi-ia UCP 10/1 88:2
Ì-lí-ma-a-ḫi UCP 10/1 110:14
Ì-lí-ṣi-id-qum UCP 10/1 100:7
Ì-lí-tu-kúl-ti UCP 10/1 22:2
Ì-lí-um-ma-nu UCP 10/1 23:15
Ì-lí-we-de-ku f. of *I-pí-iq-Ištar, Ip-qí-Ištar** UCP 10/1 46:16*; 109:21; UCLMA 9/2878:2
Il-lu-rum f. of ^{d}*Še-rum-ì-lí* UCP 10/1 22:25
Ìl-šu . . . UCP 10/1 110:4
Ìl-šu-a-bu-šu
1) f. of *Ig-mil-Sin* UCP 10/1 52:19; 107:17
2) f. of *Ri-iš-*^{d}*Šamaš* UCLMA 9/3019:24
Ìl-šu-ba-ni
1) f. of ^{d}*Sin-iš-me-an-ni* UCP 10/1 34:15
2) UCP 10/1 98:14
⌈*Ìl-šu*⌉*-i-bi-šu* s. of *Be-el-šu-nu* UCLMA 9/3019:19 (w)
Ìl-šu-illassu(ILLAT-*su*) UCP 10/1 75:2, 79:2
Ìl-šu-na-ṣir
1) s. of *Bur-*^{d}*Sin, Bur-Sin** UCP 10/1 9:2; 11:8; 19:2; 22:7; 23:6*; 24:5; 29:3; 38:2; 52:8*; 58:4*; 90:6; UCLMA 9/2858 + 2863:3; 9/2895:3; 9/2957(s)
2) UCP 10/1 1:2; 4:3; 5:2; 6:3; 7:2; 8:4; 13:2; 14:3; 15:5; 16:2; 17:2; 18:15; 20:2; 21:3; 25:3; 28:5; 31:4, 9; 34:4; 37:7; 39:3; 40:3; 42:3; 44:3; 45:2; 46:4; 50:2; 55:4; 59:6; 63:5; 68:3; 69:6; 74:3; 78:5; 81:2; 85:2; 89:42; 93:2; 95:2; 103:7; 104:5; 106:11; 107:1, 4, 14; UCLMA 9/2826:3; 9/2860:2; 9/2862:3; 9/2866:3; 9/2958:4; 9/3019:7; 9/3030:20
Ìl-šu-rabi(GAL) f. of *Sin-iš-me-an-ni* UCP 10/1 16:13; 104:14
Ilum-a-bu-um f. of *I-pí-iq-ši-na* UCP 10/1 19:12; UCLMA 9/2878:6(s)
Ilu$_3$*-ni* UCP 10/1 106:16
Im . . . UCP 10/1 110:2
I-ma-tum
1) s. *of Ri-im-*^{d}*Adad* UCP 10/1 7:15 (w)
2) UCP 10/1 4:21; 108:33
Im-di-Ištar f. of *I-pí-iq-*^{d}*Sin* UCP 10/1 98:8
Im-gu-ia
1) s. of ⌈*Nu*⌉*-ri-ia* UCP 10/1 109:24 (w)
2) f. of *Anum*(AN)*-pí*(KA)*-ša* UCP 10/1 46:17
Im-gur . . . UCP 10/1 92:6; 98:11; 108:27
Im-gur-^{d}*Adad*
1) s. of *A-ḫu-ni* UCP 10/1 11:25 (w)
2) UCP 10/1 68:17 (w); 103:5; 106:21
Im-gur-Akšak s. of *Ia-ar-ši-Anum*(AN), *Ia-ar-ši-nu-um** UCP 10/1 7:13 (w); 13:12 (w)*; 52:25 (w)
Im-gur-^{d}EN . . . UCP 10/1 108:20
Im-gur-^{d}*Enlil*
1) s. of ^{d}*Enlil-a-bu-um* UCP 10/1 51:4; UCLMA 9/2878:3 (w)
2) UCP 10/1 3:17; 10:2, 12; 57:2, 4, 11, 15; 75:10
Im-gur-^{d}*Sin, Im-gur-Sin**
1) f. of *Bur-*^{d}*Sin* UCLMA 9/2831:4; 9/2906:6
2) f. of *Še-li-bu* UCP 10/1 9:19
3) UCP 10/1 89:31; 106:2; UCLMA 9/2889a obv. col. i 16*
Im-gur-^{d}*Šamaš*
1) s. of *Ib-ni-*^{d}*Enlil* UCP 10/1 42:12 (w); 52:22 (w); 90:21 (w); 107:20 (w)
2) b. of *A-lí-am-mu* UCP 10/1 52:22 (w)
*Im-gu-rum, Im-gur-rum**
1) s. of *Na-ra-am-ì-lí-šu* UCLMA 9/2827:20 (w); 9/2831:9 (w)
2) f. of *Si-pí-pu-um* UCLMA 9/2878:7*
3) f. of *Ṣil-lí-*^{d}*Ištar* UCP 10/1 51:14
4) f. of . . . *ni-ilum* UCP 10/1 63:16
5) h. of *Wa-qar-tum* UCLMA 9/2889a obv. col. ii 17
⌈*Im . . . ilum*⌉ . . . f. of . . . *ta-tum* UCP 10/1 109:29
In-bu-ša s. of *Šu-um-ru-uṣ-Sin* UCP 10/1 18:22 (w)
I-nir-a-ia-bi-šu UCP 10/1 57:19
Ip . . . f. of *Sa-kum* UCP 10/1 108:9
I-pí-iq-^{d}*Amurrim* UCP 10/1 110:37
I-pí-iq-^{d}*Bu-ni-ni* f. of ^{d}*Sin-i-qí-ša-am* UCP 10/1 22:24
I-pí-iq-ì-lí-šu s. of *Ad-ma-ti-ì-lí* UCP 10/1 63:13 (w); UCLMA 9/2860:11 (w)
I-pí-iq-Ìr-ra UCP 10/1 36:16 (w)
*I-pí-iq-Ištar, Ip-qí-Ištar**
1) s. of *A-ta-an-ni-am* UCP 10/1 44:5
2) s. of *Ì-lí-we-de-ku* UCP 10/1 46:15 (w)*; 109:21 (w); UCLMA 9/2878:1
3) UCP 10/1 91:6, 8
I-pí-iq-^{d}*Sin* s. of *Im-di-Ištar* UCP 10/1 98:8
I-pí-iq-ši-na, ⌈*Ipīq*(SIG)⌉-[*ši-na*]*
1) s. of *Ilum-a-bu-um* UCP 10/1 19:11 (s)*; UCLMA 9/2878:5 (w)(s)
2) f. of *E-ri-iš-ti-*^{d}*Šamaš* UCLMA 9/2826:6
I-pí-qum s. of *Nu-úr-ì-lí* UCP 10/1 2:6
*Ip-qú-*x(x) UCP 10/1 28:3
Ip-qú-ša
1) s. of *Bur-*^{d}*Sin, Bur-Sin**, b. of *An-um-pî* (KA)-^{d}*Šamaš* UCP 10/1 4:18(w)*; 8:14(w); 108:17
2) s. of ^{d}*Šamaš-tappī*(TAB.BA-⌈*e*⌉) UCP 10/1 105:30 (w)
3) s. of *Ú-bar-*^{d}*Šamaš* UCP 10/1 110:25
4) f. of *Na-ra-am-*^{d}*Enlil* UCP 10/1 105:28
5) UCP 10/1 18:8; 89:3

Mu-na-wi-rum
1) s. of _Gu-ul-lu-bi-ia, Gu-lu-bi-ia_* UCP 10/1 11 (s); 22 (s); 25:13*; 52:26 (w) (s); 107 (s); UCLMA 9/2826 (s)
2) f. of _Mār-Ìl-tum_ UCLMA 9/2889a obv. col. i 15
3) h. of _Be-el-ta-ni_ UCP 10/1 59:2
4) UCP 10/1 68:6; 89:20; UCLMA 9/2895:5

Mu-sa-li-lum UCP 10/1 87:11
_Mu-ta_ . . . UCP 10/1 110:3
_Mu-ta-nu-um_ UCLMA 9/2889a obv. col. i 19
_Mu-ti-Ar-ra-ap-ḫé_ UCP 10/1 87:9

_Na-bi-_^{d}_Enlil_ f. of ^{d}_Enlil-a-bu-um_ UCP 10/1 109:8
_Na-bi-ì-lí-šu_ f. of _I-bi-Sin_ UCP 10/1 4:16
_Na-bi-_^{d}_Ištar_ f. of ^{d}_Sin-i-din-nam_ UCLMA 9/2889a obv. col. ii 15
Na-bi-tum UCP 10/1 36:14 (w)
_Na-bi-_^{d}_Sin_
1) s. of _Ur-Eninnu_ (É.⌜NINNU⌝) UCP 10/1 36:21 (s)
2) f. of ^{d}_Sin-ú-še-pí_ UCLMA 9/2827:13

⌜_Na_⌝_-bi-_^{d}_Šamaš_ UCP 10/1 106:18
_Na-ga-ri_ f. of _Iqīš_(BA)-^{d}_Tišpak_ UCP 10/1 98:21
_Na-ap-sa-nu-um_ UCP 10/1 64:1
_Na-ap-še-ri-im-be-el-ti_ UCP 10/1 27:4
^{d}_Nanna_ . . .
1) s. of ^{d}_Sin_ . . . , b. of _A-pa-_[_an_ . . .] UCP 10/1 108:23
2) UCP 10/1 108:15

^{d}NANNA.ARḪUŠ, ^{d}NANNA.ARḪUŠ$^{\text{HU.UŠ}}$*
1) s. of ^{d}_Šamaš-mu-uš-te-še-er_ UCP 10/1 77:5
2) UCP 10/1 4:4*; 5:3; 6:4; 7:3*; 8:5; 13:3; 14:4; 15:6; 21:4; 28:6; 39:4; 40:4; 42:4*; 44:4; 46:5*; 50:3*; 68:4; 69:7; 81:3; 85:3; 93:3; 95:3; UCLMA 9/2826:4; 9/2862:4; 9/2863:4; 9/2866:4

^{d}NANNA.DI.KU_5 UCP 10/1 106:28
^{d}NANNA.MA.AN.SUM
1) s. of _Si-ia-tum_ UCP 10/1 98:19
2) s. of _Šu-_^{d}NIN.KAR.RA.AK UCLMA 9/2827:5
3) [s. of] . . . _nu-um_ UCLMA 9/3019:18 (w)
4) f. of _E-te-lum_ UCP 10/1 4:14
5) UCP 10/1 91:3

^{d}NANNA.MÉ.DÍM s. of _Nu-úr-ì-lí-šu_ UCP 10/1 2:4
^{d}_Nanna-tum, Na-na-tum_*
1) s. of ^{d}_Sin-mu-ba-lí-iṭ_ UCP 10/1 104:2*
2) UCP 10/1 110:9

_Na-_⌜_ra_⌝-[_am_ . . .] f. of _Ma-na-ba-al-_$ṭe_4$_-el_ and _A-ḫu-ni-ia_ UCP 10/1 107:27
_Na-ra-am-_^{d}_Adad_
1) f. of _Anum_(AN)-_pî_(KA)-_ša_ UCP 10/1 69:4
2) w. of PN (not given) UCP 10/1 88:5

_Na-ra-am-_^{d}_Enlil_ s. of _Ip-qú-ša_ UCP 10/1 105:27 (w)
_Na-ra-am-ì-lí-šu, Na-ra-am-ili-šu_*
1) s. of _Ma-ti-ia-li_ UCP 10/1 1:15 (w)*
2) s. of ^{d}_Sin-ba-ni_ UCLMA 9/2864:4
3) s. of . . . _tu-ú_ UCLMA 9/2866:14 (w)
4) f. of _Im-gu-rum_ UCLMA 9/2827:21; 9/2831:10
5) f. of _Iš-du-ki-nu-um_ UCP 10/1 9:17
6) UCP 10/1 21:12 (w); 40:12 (w); 71:4; UCLMA 9/2889a obv. col. iii 13

_Na-ra-am-_^{d}_Sin_
1) s. of . . . _úr-ku-su-_⌜_um_⌝ UCP 10/1 105:23 (s)
2) UCP 10/1 89:8

Na-ra-am-tum
1) d. of _Ḫa-ma-num_ UCP 10/1 59:1
2) UCP 10/1 56:13; 110:12; UCLMA 9/2889b obv. col. A 9′

_Na-ru_ . . . UCP 10/1 63:3
_Na-su-la-tum, Na-sú-la-tum_* UCP 10/1 89:18*; UCLMA 9/2889a obv. col. iii 8
_Na_ . . . _tum_ UCLMA 9/2889a obv. col. i 2
Ni-ḫa-tum UCLMA 9/2889a obv. col. i 18
_Ni-ḫa-az_ UCP 10/1 110:19
_Ni-id-nu-ša_ UCP 10/1 106:27; 110:11; UCLMA 9/2889a obv. col. i 14
_Ni-_$iš_6$_-Sin_ f. of PN (not given) UCP 10/1 98:16
NU-_a-ḫi_ UCP 10/1 56:2
Nu-ra-tum s. of _Akšak-še-mi_ UCP 10/1 9:12 (w)
_Nu-ri-ia_
1) f. of _Im-gu-ia_ UCP 10/1 109:24
2) UCP 10/1 12:14; 76:10

_Nu-úr-ì-lí_ f. of _I-pí-qum_ UCP 10/1 2:7
_Nu-úr-ì-lí-šu_
1) f. of _A-ḫu-ši-na_ UCP 10/1 98:20
2) f. of ^{d}NANNA.MÉ.DIM UCP 10/1 2:5

_Nu-úr-_^{d}_Iš-ḫa-ra_ UCP 10/1 86:8
_Nu-úr-_^{d}_Šamaš_ f. of _Ri-iš-_^{d}_Šamaš_ UCP 10/1 17:13
Nu-ṭú-up-tum
1) d. of _Tu-li-iš_ UCP 10/1 105:2, 10, 13

1) f. of *A-bu-um-ilum* UCP 10/1 1:12**; 8:13***; 11:22 (s); 13:11**; 14:10; 15:12***; 19:10 (s); 21:10***; 23:16*****; 24:14*; 25:12*; 28:13; 39:11; 42:11; 44:13****; 45:12**; 52:24*** (s); 58 (s); 68:14; 90:19***; 95:12; 103:14**; 107:19*** (s); UCLMA 9/2826:10 (w) (s); 9/2858 + 2863:14*****; 9/2862:11; 9/2866:11***
2) f. of *Bu-ra-nu-um* UCP 10/1 2:18*
3) f. of *Sin-tappā*(TAB.BA)*-we-di-im* UCLMA 9/2864:18*
4) f. of *Ša-bu-lum* UCP 10/1 88:6***
5) UCP 10/1 49:2; 69:2***; 75:3, 5; 79:3, 5; 89:26

^{d}*Sin-e-ri-ib*
1) s. of ^{d}*Sin* . . . UCP 10/1 60:9
2) UCP 10/1 60:3

^{d}*Sin-ga-mil*
1) s. of *A-ḫi-um-mi-šu* UCP 10/1 58:17 (w); 107:21 (w) (s)
2) UCP 10/1 68:16 (w); 86:5

^{d}*Sin-i* . . . , *Sin-i* . . . * UCP 10/1 108:26, 40*

^{d}*Sin-ib-ni* s. of *Amat-Esikila*(GEMÉ.É.SIKIL.LA) UCP 10/1 18:2

^{d}*Sin-i-din-nam*, *Sin-i-din-nam**, ^{d}⸢*Sin-i-di-nam*⸣**
1) s. of *Ib-ni-*^{d}*Adad*, b. of *Ia-ás*(!)*-kur-Ilum* UCP 10/1 7:4
2) s. of *Lum-ma-Anum*(AN) UCP 10/1 73:2, 95:4
3) s. of *Na-bi-*^{d}*Ištar* UCLMA 9/2889a obv. col. ii 15
4) s. of ⸢^{d}*Sin-ta*⸣. . . UCLMA 9/2895:15 (w)**
5) s. of *Sin-a-bu-um* UCP 10/1 98:4*
6) f. of *E-ri-ib-*^{d}*Sin* UCP 10/1 25:5
7) f. of *E-ri-iš-ti-*⸢^{d}*Šamaš*⸣ UCP 10/1 96:6
8) UCP 10/1 53:7; 56:10; 59:3; 75:8; 79:7; 94:19; 108:35*; UCLMA 9/2889a obv. col. ii 2*, 8

^{d}*Sin-i-me-ti* s. of *Iqīš*(BA)*-*^{d}*Enlil* UCP 10/1 32:10 (w)

^{d}*Sin-i-qí-ša-am*, ^{d}*Sin-i-qí-šam**, *Sin-i-qí-ša-am***, *Sin-i-qí-šam****
1) s. of *Ib-ni-Ìr-ra* UCP 10/1 9:3
2) s. of *I-pí-iq-*^{d}*Bu-ni-ni* UCP 10/1 22:24(w)
3) s. of *Warad-*^{d}*Sin*, b. of *Ri-iš-*^{d}*Šamaš* UCP 10/1 107:22 (w)
4) f. of *An-um-pí-ša* UCP 10/1 91 (s)
5) f. of *Iqīš*(BA)*-*^{d}*Enlil* UCP 10/1 52:21; 74:13; 103:16***; 107:25*; UCLMA 9/2826:12
6) f. of *Sa-at-lu-ma* UCP 10/1 52:21; 74:13; 107:25*
7) f. of ^{d}*Šamaš-na-ṣir* UCP 10/1 5:11; 6:13; 7:10**; 8:7; 11:23; 13:9***; 14:12; 24:12 (*-ša-*<*am*>)**; 28:15; 39:13; 44:11; 45:10* 68:12; 69:13; 90:20*; 107:25*; UCLMA 9/2826:12; 9/2858:16**; 9/2866:13; 9/2895:14
8) f. of *Warad-ì-lí-šu* UCP 10/1 11:28*
9) UCP 10/1 108:36; UCLMA 9/2889a obv. col. ii 9*; col. iii 7*; 9/2889b obv. col. A 4′*

^{d}*Sin-iš-me-an-ni*, ^{d}*Sin-iš-me-a-an-ni**, *Sin-iš-me-an-ni***
1) s. of *Ìl-šu-ba-ni* UCP 10/1 34:14 (w)
2) s. of *Ìl-šu-rabi*(GAL) UCP 10/1 16:12 (w)**; 104:14 (w)**
3) s. of ^{d}*Sin-da-ia-an* UCP 10/1 38:4*, UCP 10/1 108:30 (^{d}*Sin*-DI.KU$_{5}$)
4) b. of *Mu-na-nu-um* UCP 10/1 108:32
5) UCP 10/1 86:10 110:18

^{d}*Sin-ki-ma-ì-lí-*⸢*ia*⸣, *Sin-ki-ma-ì-lí-*<*ia*>* f. of *Warad-*^{d}*Nanna* UCLMA 9/2864:19* (s)

^{d}*Sin-ma-gir*, *Sin-ma-gir**
1) s. of *E-ri-ba-am* UCP 10/1 109:23
2) s. of ^{d} . . . SIPA UCP 10/1 109:30 (w)
3) f. of *A-pil-ì-lí-šu* UCP 10/1 98:2*
4) UCP 10/1 88:3; 106:12; 108:3

⸢^{d}*Sin*⸣*-mu* . . . UCP 10/1 60 (s)

^{d}*Sin-mu-ba-lí-iṭ*, *Sin-mu-ba-lí-iṭ**
1) s. of *Da-qa-ni-ia* UCP 10/1 22:20 (w)(s)
2) s. of *Ki-ir-ki-ru-um* UCP 10/1 91 (s)
3) s. of *Šu-mu-a-ḫi-ia* UCLMA 9/2831:11 (w)*
4) f. of *Na-na-tum* UCP 10/1 104:3
5) h. of *Be-el-ta-ni* UCP 10/1 17:4
6) UCP 10/1 37:2; 86:14; 89:11; 110:5; UCLMA 9/2889a obv. col. ii 10

^{d}*Sin-mu-ša-lim* UCP 10/1 28:2

^{d}*Sin-na-da* s. of *E-ri-ib-Sin*, b. of *Ib-na-tum* UCP 10/1 74:4

⸢^{d}*Sin*⸣*-pu-uṭ-*⸢*ra*⸣*-*[*am*] UCP 10/1 108:28

^{d}*Sin-ri-me-ni*, *Sin-ri-me-ni**
1) s. of *Ṣíl-lí-Sin* UCP 10/1 16:3
2) s. of ^{d}*Šamaš-ma-gir* UCP 10/1 98:5*

^{d}*Sin-še-mi*, *Sin-še-mi**
1) f. of *A-bu-wa-qar* UCP 10/1 91 (s)
2) f. of *Za-ru-*⸢*um*⸣ UCLMA 9/2858 + 2863:12* (s)

⸢^{d}*Sin-ta*⸣ . . . f. of ⸢^{d}*Sin-i-di-nam*⸣ UCLMA 9/2895:16

^{d}*Šamaš-za-aq-tum* f. of *Ma-ti-ia-tu-ú* UCP 10/1 107:18
Ša-am-sa-'tim f. of *A-ḫu-ni* UCP 10/1 75:4
^{d}*Šamši*(^{d}UTU-*ši*)-^{d}*Adad* UCP 10/1 5:15 (R) (Y); 6:14 (R) (Y); 74:15 (R) (Y)
^{d}ŠARA.MA.AN.SUM
1) s. of *I-bi-*^{d}*Sin* UCLMA 9/2860:9 (w) (s)
2) s. of *Ilam-pi-laḫ* UCP 10/1 63:11 (w)
Šar-rum-^{d}*Adad* UCP 10/1 33:7; 53:3, 6; 62:5; 75:14
Šarrum(LUGAL)-*Sin*; UCLMA 9/2889a obv. col. iii 15; 9/2889b obv. col. A 5′
Ša-sa-am-tim f. of *A-ḫu-ni* UCP 10/1 75:4
Še . . . UCP 10/1 89:37
*Še-li-bu-um, Še-li-bu**
1) s. of *Im-gur-*^{d}*Sin* UCP 10/1 9:18 (w)*
2) UCP 10/1 71:5; 72:6; 106:29, 32
Šēp(GÌR)-*Ištar* s. of *Ri-*⌜*mu*⌝. . . UCP 10/1 98:18
⌜*Šēp*(GÌR)⌝-^{d}*Sin* UCP 10/1 106:15
^{d}*Še-rum-ì-lí, Še-rum-ì-lí**
1) s. of *Il-lu-rum* UCP 10/1 22:25 (w)
2) UCP 10/1 96:1*
^{d}*Še-rum-ilum* UCP 10/1 98:15
Ši-ki-ti f. of *Ìr-ra-ba-ni* UCP 10/1 36:10
Ši-ta-ni UCP 10/1 110:20; UCLMA 9/2889a obv. col. i 13
⌜*Šu*⌝ . . . UCLMA 9/2889a rev. col. iv 4
Šu-^{d}*Amurrim*
1) s. of *A-ḫu-ni* UCP 10/1 4:20 (w)
2) s. of *Ṣí-lí-ia* UCP 10/1 2:15 (w)
Šu-kál-lim f. of *I-bi-*^{d}*Sin* UCP 10/1 29:6
⌜*Šu-ma*⌝ . . . UCP 10/1 89:35
Šum-ma-nu-um
1) s. of *Ma-la-ka . . .* UCP 10/1 92:13
2) f. of *Warad-Iš-*<*ḫa*>*-ra* UCP 10/1 46:18
3) UCP 10/1 32:4
Šu-mu-a-ḫi-ia f. of *Sin-mu-ba-lí-iṭ* UCLMA 9/2831:12
Šu-mu-li-ib-ši, MU-Ì-GÁL* UCP 10/1 16:14 (w)*; 17:11 (w); 20:3; 34:11 (w); 104:12 (w); UCLMA 9/2889a obv. col. iii 11
Šu-um-ru-uṣ-a-li UCP 10/1 100:12
Šu-um-ru-uṣ-Sin f. of *In-bu-ša* UCP 10/1 18:23
Šu-^{d}NIN.KAR.RA.AK f. of ^{d}NANNA.MA.AN.SUM UCLMA 9/2827:6
Šu-pí-ša UCP 10/1 11:2
Šu-ri-im-ku b. of *A-ta-na-aḫ-ì-lí* UCP 10/1 36:4
Šu-Sin-i-qí-ša f. of *Ṣil-lí-*^{d}*Sataran*(^{d}KA.DI) UCP 10/1 98:7

Ta-ku-la-tum UCLMA 9/2889a obv. col. i 10
Ta-ra-am-^{d} . . . UCP 10/1 18:10
Ta-ri-ba-tum UCP 10/1 3:18; 100:6
Ta-ri-bu-um s. of *Be-el-šu-nu* UCP 10/1 107:3, 7
Ta-ri-bu-ša UCP 10/1 110:31
Ta-ri-im-tum UCP 10/1 72:2
^{d}*Tišpak-a-si-i* UCP 10/1 3:2
Tu-li-iš mother of *Nu-ṭu-up-tum* UCP 10/1 105:3, 9
Tu-tu-ub . . . UCLMA 9/2889a obv. col. iii 16
Tu-tu-ub-ma-gir UCP 10/1 75:7
Tu-tu-ub-še-mi UCP 10/1 86:3; UCLMA 9/2889b obv. col. A 11′

Ṭà-ab-ṣil-lum UCLMA 9/2889a obv. col. i 11
Ṭà-bi-ia f. of *Ap-ka-tum* UCP 10/1 4:6

Ú-ba-lum f. of *Me-ra-ni* UCP 10/1 36:11
U-bar-rum
1) s. of *Ša-ma-ia-tum* UCP 10/1 32:14 (w)
2) f. of *Ma-áš-qum* UCP 10/1 22:4f.
3) UCP 10/1 89:16
U-bar-^{d}*Šamaš*
1) f. of *Ip-qú-ša* UCP 10/1 110:25
2) UCP 10/1 106:24
Um-mi-⌜*ia*⌝*-tum* UCP 10/1 89:24
Um (?)*-mi-*^{d}*Iš-ḫa-ra* UCP 10/1 24:2
Un-nu-bu-um UCP 10/1 50:4
Ur-Eninnu(UR.É.⌜NINNU⌝) f. of *Na-bi-*^{d}*Sin* UCP 10/1 36 (s)
Ú-še-pí f. of ^{d}*Šamaš-mu-uš-te-pí-iš* UCLMA 9/2827:15
*Uš-ta-aš-ni-ilum, Uš-taš-ni-ilum** UCP 10/1 96:4; 101:3*
^{d}UTU.ZI.MU
1) s. of *An-um-ilum*(DINGIR-⌜*um*⌝), *Anum* (AN)*-i-lu*(!)*-um** UCP 10/1 51:11 (w)*; 92:3
2) UCP 10/1 106:14

Wa-qar-a-bu-šu UCP 10/1 104:1
Wa-qar-tum w. of *Im-gu-rum* UCLMA 9/2889a obv. col. ii 17
Warad . . . f. of *I . . .* UCP 10/1 93:14
Warad-^{d} . . . UCP 10/1 85:11 (w)
⌜*Warad*⌝*-ì-*[*lí . . .*] UCP 10/1 87:8
Warad-^{d}*Ilaprat* h. of *Du-ba-ba-tum* UCP 10/1 1:3; 87:2

7.2 Titles and Professions

AD.KID UCP 10/1 36:14 (w)
*ba-a-ru, ba-ru**, MÁŠ.ŠU.GÍD.GÍD** UCP 10/1 71:6f.; 75:3*; UCLMA 9/2878 (s)**
DAM.QAR UCP 10/1 91:3, 12; see also UGULA DAM.QAR
DI.KU$_5$ UCP 10/1 91:9, 13
DUB.SAR UCP 10/1 4:22 (w); 5:14 (w); 7:15 (w); 11:29 (w); 14:14 (w); 15:14 (w); 21:13 (w); 22:27 (w); 23:17 (w); 25:14 (w); 28:17 (w); 32:16 (w); 36:17 (w); 39:14 (w); 40:13 (w); 44:14 (w); 51:15 (w); 52:26 (w); 58:19 (w); 59:14 (w); 68:15 (w); 69:16 (w); 81:12 (w); 107:31 (w); 108:10; UCLMA 9/2826: 13 (w); 9/2858 + 2863:17 (w); 9/2866:16 (w)
ENSÍ UCP 10/1 36 (s)
GÌR.NITÁ UCP 10/1 5:9 (w); 6:10 (w); 8:6; 11:21 (w); 13:8 (w); 15:10 (w); 16:14 (w); 17:11; 22:20 (w); 34:11 (w); 39:9 (w); 40:10 (w); 74:10 (w); 104:12 (w); 107:16 (w); 110:9; UCLMA 9/2826:9 (w)
ḪA.LI UCP 10/1 59:3; 108:25
IŠ UCLMA 9/2827:13
KA.KI UCP 10/1 36:21 (s); 91:13, 17
LÚ . . . UCP 10/1 87:11; 110:iii 5
LÚ.A.BA . . . UCLMA 9/2889c rev. col. B 7′-8′
LÚ . . . IM UCP 10/1 55:2
LÚ.DIRI.GA UCLMA 9/3030:2
LUGAL UCP 10/1 11:16; 22:16; 36:20; 52:15; 61:10 (Y); 90:15; 91:33 (Y); 109:16; UCLMA 9/2828:25 (Y); 9/2859 (Y); 9/2906:25 (Y)(?)
LUKUR UCP 10/1 110:12; UCLMA 9/2826:5; 9/2889a obv. col. ii 16; 9/2889b col. A 9′
LÚ UŠ (?).BAR UCP 10/1 108:39
LÚ.TÚG UCP 10/1 75:5; UCLMA 9/2889a obv. col. ii 10, 13; 9/3030:9
MÁŠ.ŠU.GÍD.GÍD see *ba-a-ru*
MU UCP 10/1 110:14; UCLMA 9/2889a obv. col. i 7
mu(!)*-ša-di-nu* UCP 10/1 10:8
na-di-tim UCP 10/1 71:3
NAGAR UCP 10/1 6:11 (w); 11:27 (w); 21:5; UCLMA 9/2889a obv. col. i 17
NA.QÀD UCP 10/1 12:14
NAR UCP 10/1 14:5
NIN.DINGIR UCP 10/1 39:5; 96:3(?)
NU UCP 10/1 89:32
NU.BANDA$_3$ UCP 10/1 110:7
NU.GIŠ.SAR UCP 10/1 69:1; 103:3, 4
[*ra*]*-bi-a-nu-um, ra-bi-nu-um** UCP 10/1 108:1*; 109:25; UCLMA 9/3019:18a(?)
sa-bu-um UCP 10/1 18:21 (w)
SIPA UCP 10/1 49:4; 69:2; UCLMA 9/2889a obv. col. i 16
SUKKAL UCP 10/1 36:16 (w)
⌜*ša* É⌝ UCLMA 9/2862:5
ša É.GAL*-lim* UCP 10/1 94:10
šà ERÍN UCP 10/1 108:33
ša-gu-um UCP 10/1 75:8; 79:7
ŠU . . . UCLMA 9/2889a obv. col. ii 3
ŠU.ḪA UCP 10/1 62:7
ŠU.I UCP 10/1 57:16
TUR UCP 10/1 27:3
UGULA DAM.QAR UCP 10/1 43:8; 108:3

7.3 Divine Names

^{d}*Adad* UCP 10/1 11 (s); 19 (s); 51:16 (Y); 52 (s); 58 (s); 107 (s); UCLMA 9/2826 (s)
^{d}*Amurrum* UCLMA 9/3030:7
^{d}É*-a* UCP 10/1 93:17 (Y)
^{d}*Enlil* UCP 10/1 13:14 (Y); 29:13 (Y); 44:15 (Y); 85:12 (Y); 93:16 (Y)
^{d}*I-šar-ki-di-su* UCP 10/1 47:5; 78:2; 107:13
Ištar UCP 10/1 14:15 (Y): 15:15 (Y); 21:14 (Y); 25:15 (Y); 26:7 (Y); 28:18 (Y); 30:6 (Y); 39:15 (Y); 40:14 (Y); 66:8 (Y); 67:4 (Y); 69:17 (Y); 81:13 (Y); 89:43 (Y)
^{d}*Nergal* (^{d}GÌR.UNUG.GAL) UCLMA 9/2857 (s)
^{d}NIN.URTA UCP 10/1 11 (s); 22 (s); 52 (s); 107 (s); UCLMA 9/2826 (s)
^{d}*Sin* UCP 10/1 8:12 (w); 9:11 (w); 24:15 (Y); 29:13 (Y); 52:3, 5; 85:12 (Y); 107:12
^{d}⌜*Ša-ḫa-an*⌝ UCP 10/1 19 (s)
^{d}*Šamaš* UCP 10/1 4:2; 8:12 (w); 9:11 (w), 20 (Y); 12:16 (Y); 50:12 (Y); 76:14 (Y); 77:3; UCLMA 9/2827:2; 9/2831:2; 9/2942:2
^{d}*Tišpak* UCP 10/1 11:16; 22:16; 36:24 (Y)(s); 52:15; 90:15; 109:16

7.4 Place Names

7.5 Month Names

ITU . . . UCLMA 9/2895:8
ITU *A-bi-i* UCP 10/1 47:6; 58:1; 64:5; 96:15
ITU DIRI *Ki-in-k[i-im]* UCP 10/1 87:18
ITU ^{d}DUMU.ZI UCP 10/1 66:7; 110:41
ITU *E-lu-nu* UCP 10/1 12:15; 54:4; 76:13
ITU *Ki-in-kum* UCP 10/1 19:13; 49:9
ITU *Ki-is-ki-súm* UCP 10/1 62:15; 109:32
ITU *Ki-ri-ti* UCLMA 9/2831:6
ITU *Ma-aq-ra-nu* UCP 10/1 99:10
ITU *Na-ab-ri-im, Na-ab-ri-i*, Na-ab-ri*** UCP 10/1 2:9; 56:15*; 84:rev. 1′*; 97:10**
ITU *Níg-gal-lim* UCP 10/1 61:6; 65:6
ITU *Ša-du-tim, Ša-ad-du-tim** UCP 10/1 4:8; 9:6; 32:6; 68:8*
ITU *Tam-ḫi-ru, Tám-ḫi-ri** UCP 10/1 33:14*; UCLMA 9/3030:6, 21
ITU ^{d}Ù(!).GUL.LÁ UCLMA 9/3030:5

8. COPIES

Copies are reproduced at approximately 1.5 x life size.

8.1
Copies, Collations, and Corrections to Lutz, *Legal and Economic Documents from Ashjâly* (UCP 10/1)

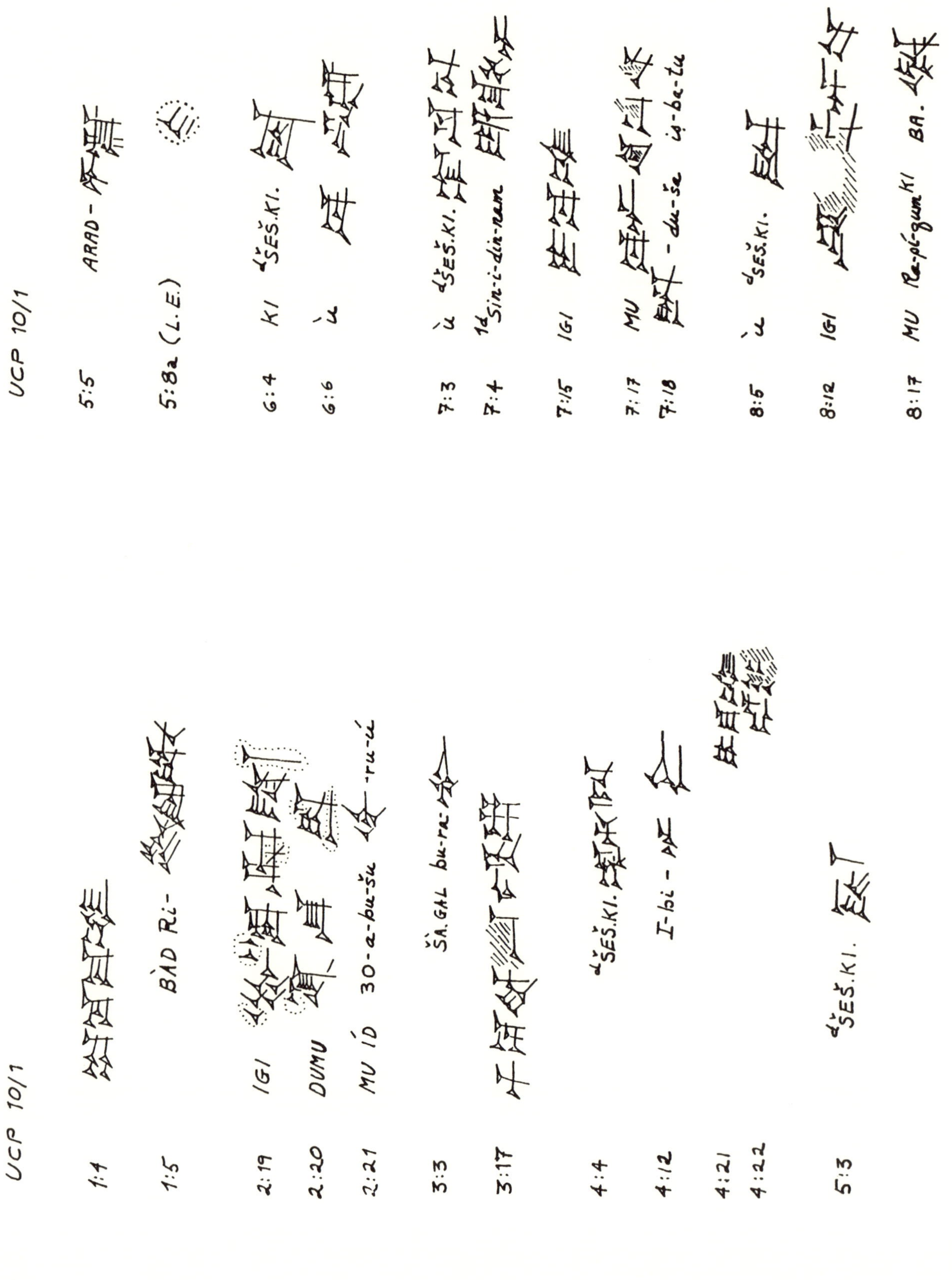

9:7 a-na 

9:8a (below l.8) 

9:14 [1]Er-ṣi-tum-ra-bi- 

9:15 DUMU  -šu-nu

9:20 MU zi-ku-ra- 

10:1,3,5,6,10 

10:2,12 

10:6 1 GUR ZÍD 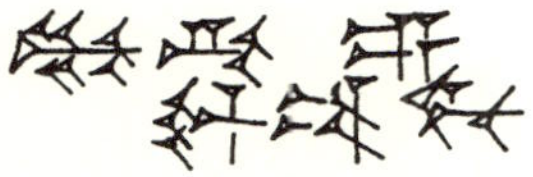

10:7 1 GUR a-na

10:8 4(BÁN)  -ša-di-nu

10:9  a-na KAŠ

10:16 2(BÁN) ki-sa-at  .MEŠ

10:18 na-aš-pa-ak Ha-aš- 

11

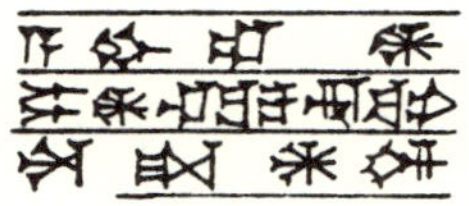

Seal Legend A
(composite of 11, 19, 52, 58, 107, UCLMA 9/2826)

Seal Legend B
(composite of 11, 22, 52, 107)

12:2,8  BAR. 

12:10 2 KUŠ ši- 

12:11 3 KUŠ 

12:14  Nu-ri-ia

13:3 ù ^{d}ŠEŠ.KI. 

14:4 ù ^{d}ŠEŠ.KI. 

14:5 [1]A-pil-Ku-bi 

15:3  -ba-al-ṭe$_4$-el

UCP 10/1

16:5 — 20:4 — 55:5

17:1

17:11 [IGI Šu-mu]- [ši]

17:14 IGI Ḫu-za-lum DUMU [šum]

17:15 IGI

18:2 [1d]Sin-ib-ni

18:3 ŠE ḫu-bu-ta-tum

18:11 ḫu-bu-ta-tum

18:14

18:23 DUMU -um-ru-uṣ-30

18:24 IGI PN_1 DUMU ARAD-

UCP 10/1

19:4 Ì-li- -nu-ú

19:13 ITU -in-kum

19 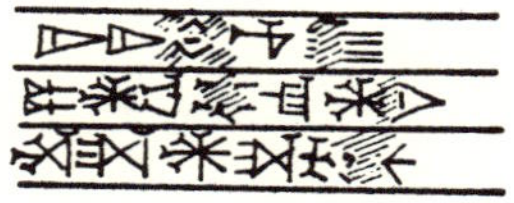 Label

Seal Legend B

20:11

20:12 DUMU Lum- -AN

20:13 IGI Mu-ḫa- -du

21:4 dŠEŠ.KI.

21:7a

22:15 $gi_4.gi_4$.dam

22:16 MU d etc.

22:26 [1] PN_1 DUMU d

UCP 10/1	
22	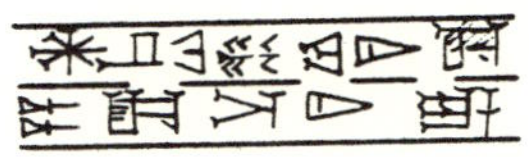
	Seal Legend A
23:7	¹Su-mu-ᵈBe-el- …
23:18	MU ERÍN SU.BIR₄ …
24:2	2(PI) 2(BÁN) ŠE … -mi-ᵈIš-ḫa-ra
24:3	… GUR ŠE
24:13	IGI A-bu- … -DINGIR
25:15 25:16 25:17	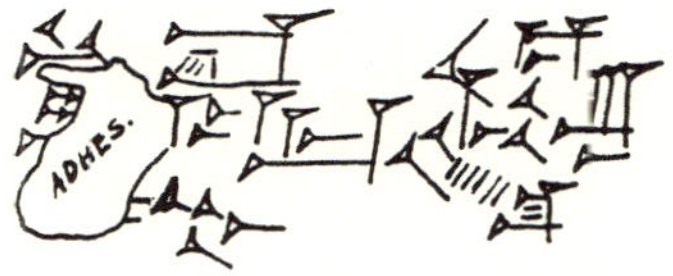
28:1	2(GUR) 3(PI) 2(BÁN) GUR ŠE 3.KAM …
28:3	1(PI) 4(BÁN) Ip-gú- …
28:6	ù ᵈŠEŠ.KI. …

UCP 10/1	
28:10	ù LÚ. … .NA.DAM
28:16	
29:12 29:13 29:14	
30:1	1 šuši 8(GUR) 1(PI) 1(BÁN) GUR …
30:5	URU.KI …
31:1-2 31:3 31:4 31:5 31:6	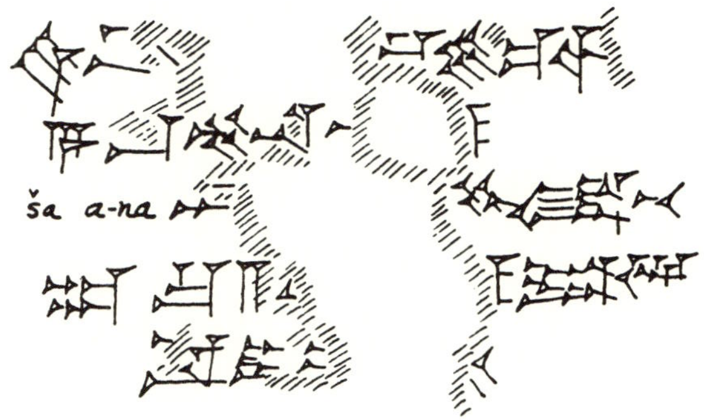 31:4 ša a-na …

UCP 10/1

32:10 IGI

32:11 DUMU

32:16 ù ARAD[d] DUB.SAR

33:5 PN

33:10 3(BÁN) Ma- -ia-ma

34:5 -ar-ki mi-šar etc.

34:12 IGI -lum

34:15 DUMU DINGIR-šu- -ni

34:16 URU Ki-maš

35:2 2 GI.PISAN 3(BÁN) kur- -za-ku

35:6 3 nu-ús-

UCP 10/1

35:17 4 ma-ag-

35:18 3 MA.NA

35:19 2 NA_4 i-ru[

35:21 1 TÚG NÍG.

35:23

36:5 ù PN .A.NI

36:14 PN AD.

36:16 PN

36:17 ù .AN.GI.GI DUB.SAR

36:21 PN

36:23 GU.ZA ZÚ.AM.SI KÙ.GI GAR.

36  Seal Legend

37:1 1(PI) 4(BÁN)

37:3
37:4
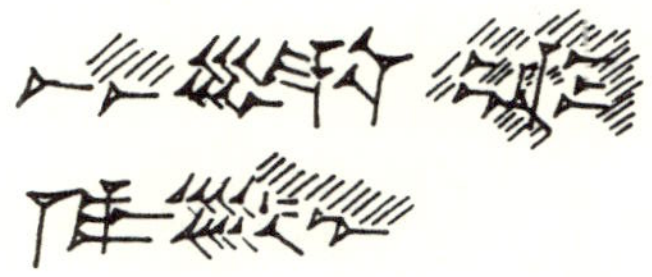

38:5 [1d]EN.ZU-da-ia-

38:9 IGI -hu-tum

38:11 -ri-im

39:4 ù [d]ŠEŠ.KI.

39:5 [1]Be-el-tum

UCP 10/1

40:4 ù [d]ŠEŠ.KI.

41:3 ŠÀ.GAL -hi-im

41:4 ša -lu-bi-ia

42:4 ù [d]ŠEŠ.KI. HU.UŠ

42:13 DUMU Ib-ni-

42:14
42:15

42:18 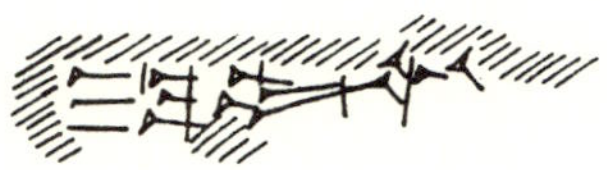

43:3 5 MA.NA GÍN etc.

43:4 ma-za-aš-ti ša- -pu-um

43:6 ma-za-aš-ti Ne-ri- -tim

43:7 2 2/3 MA.NA 2 1/2

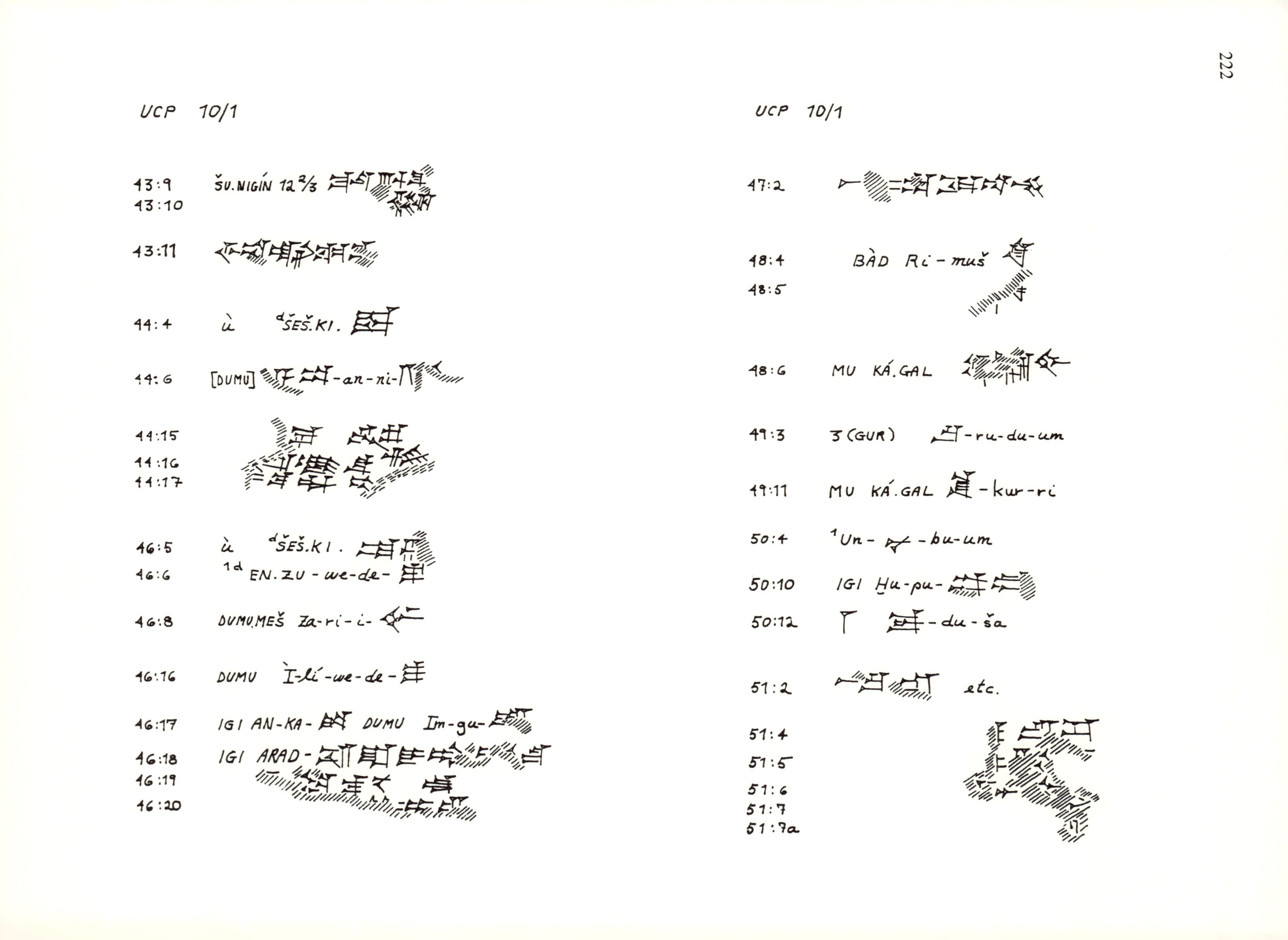

UCP 10/1

43:9 ŠU.NIGÍN 12 2/3
43:10

43:11

44:4 ù [d]ŠEŠ.KI.

44:6 [DUMU] -an-ni-

44:15
44:16
44:17

46:5 ù [d]ŠEŠ.KI.
46:6 [1d]EN.ZU-we-de-

46:8 DUMU.MEŠ Za-ri-i-

46:16 DUMU Ì-lí-we-de-

46:17 IGI AN-KA- DUMU Im-gu-
46:18 IGI ARAD-
46:19
46:20

UCP 10/1

47:2

48:4 BÀD Ri-muš
48:5

48:6 MU KÁ.GAL

49:3 3 (GUR) -ru-du-um

49:11 MU KÁ.GAL -kur-ri

50:4 [1]Un- -bu-um

50:10 IGI Ḫu-pu-

50:12 -du-ša

51:2 etc.

51:4
51:5
51:6
51:7
51:7a

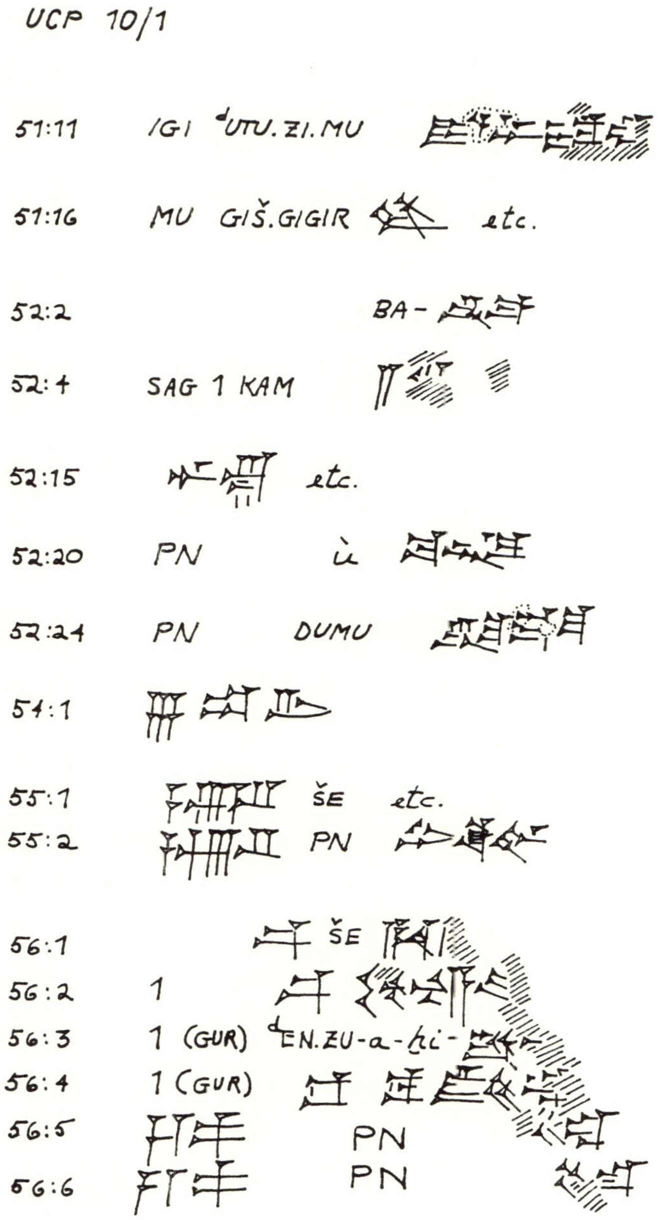
UCP 10/1
51:11 IGI ᵈUTU.ZI.MU
51:16 MU GIŠ.GIGIR etc.
52:2 BA-
52:4 SAG 1 KAM
52:15 etc.
52:20 PN ù
52:24 PN DUMU
54:1
55:1 ŠE etc.
55:2 PN
56:1 ŠE
56:2 1
56:3 1 (GUR) ᵈEN.ZU-a-ḫi-
56:4 1 (GUR)
56:5 PN
56:6 PN

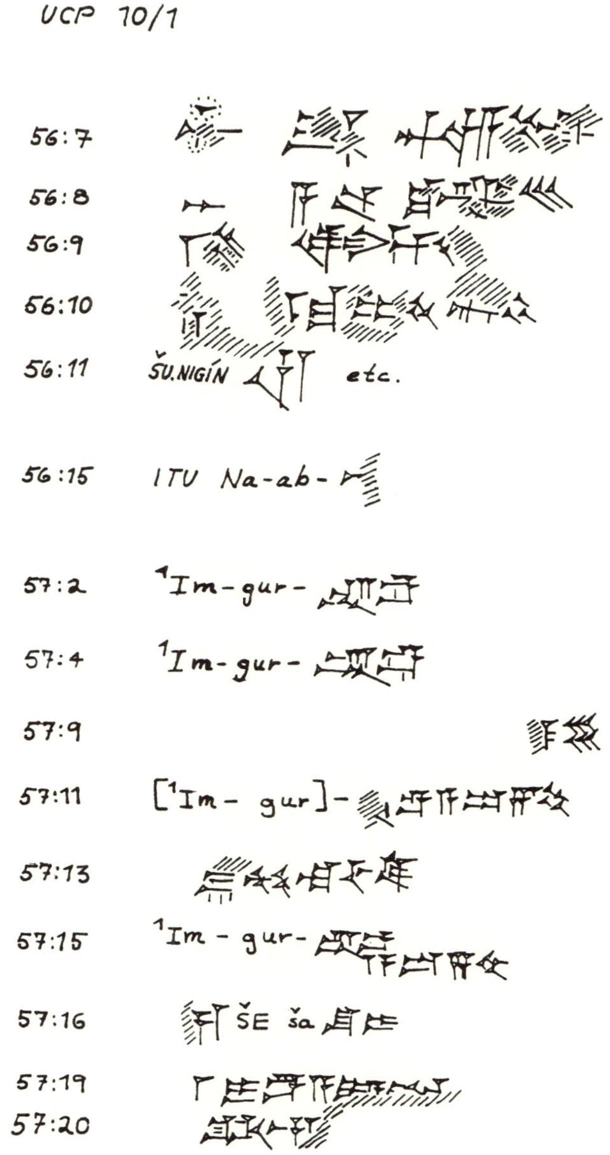
UCP 10/1
56:7
56:8
56:9
56:10
56:11 ŠU.NIGÍN etc.
56:15 ITU Na-ab-
57:2 ¹Im-gur-
57:4 ¹Im-gur-
57:9
57:11 [¹Im-gur]-
57:13
57:15 ¹Im-gur-
57:16 ŠE ša
57:19
57:20

UCP 10/1

58:2 DUMU I-si-

58:5 a-na MU.1.KAM re-im

58:9

58:10 i-na 1 me-at ŠU.ŠI

58:11 i-na-ad- -in

58:13 i-na-ad-di-

58:15 IGI PN DUMU

58:16 [1]A-lí-am-mu-

59:1 ŠE Na-ra-am-

59:2 2(BÁN) etc.

59:3 2(BÁN) dSin-i-

59:4 2(BÁN) DUMU Iš-ku-

59:13 [1]Ra-šum-

59:15

60:2 .DIRIG etc.

UCP 10/1

60:3 DA É dSin-e-ri-

60:5 É A-pa-an-

60:7

60:8 DUMU.MEŠ

60:9 [1d]Sin-e-ri- etc.

60:Rev. 2'

60:Rev. 4'

60:Rev. 5'

60 Seal Legend A

60 Seal Legend B

61:1 Env.

61:6 ITU Níg- -lim

61:6 Env. Níg-gal-lim

UCP 10/1

61 Seal Legend

62:2 3 GUD.HI.A UD. . KAM etc.

62:3 A-na-^{d}UTU-ták-la-a-

62:7 ša 7 u_4-mi A-di- Ki-na-nu-

62:15 ša ITU Ki-is-ki-

63:1

63:2

63:3 2(PI) 1(BÁN) 3 1/3(SILA$_3$) Na-

63:4 5 (BÁN)

63:11 IGI . MA.AN.SUM

63:15 IGI

UCP 10/1

64:1 Na-

64:2 1(GUR) 2 (PI) 4 (BÁN) I-din-

64:3 ŠU.NIGÍN

64:4

65:1 ŠÀ.BI KÙ.BABBAR

65:3 1 ŠE . GÁL KÙ.BABBAR

65:7 MU KÁ.GAL

65:3 Ṣíl-lí-^{d}TIŠPAK

66:4

66:5 É.DUB É

66:8

67:1 25+ GUR

UCP 10/1

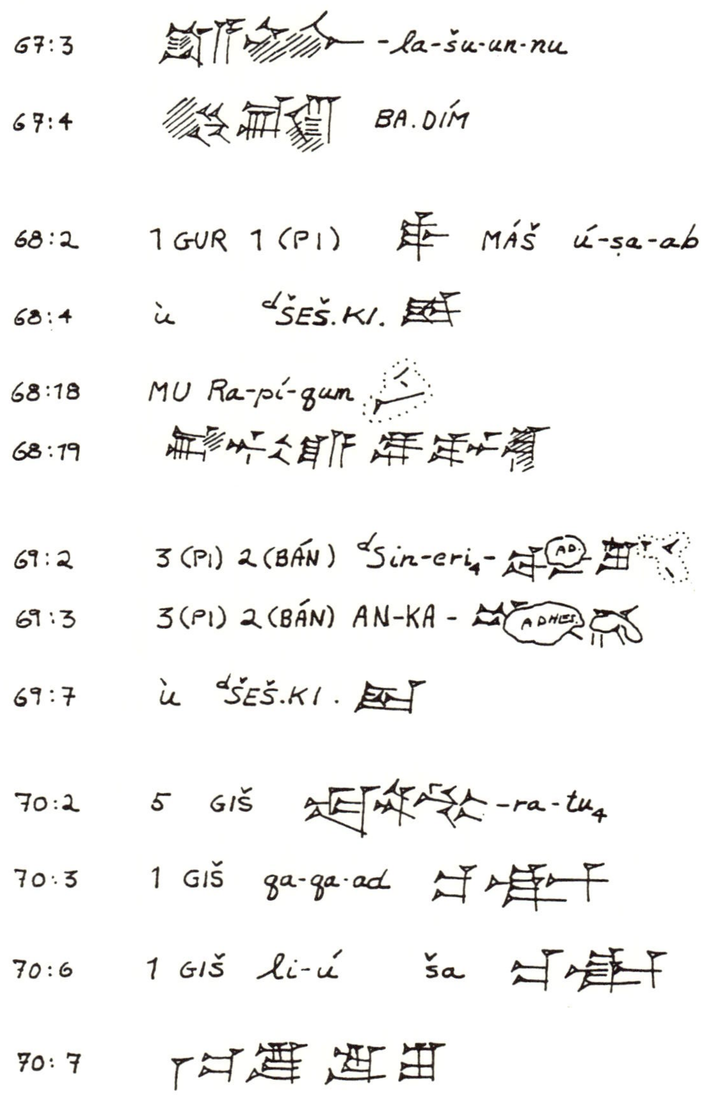

UCP 10/1

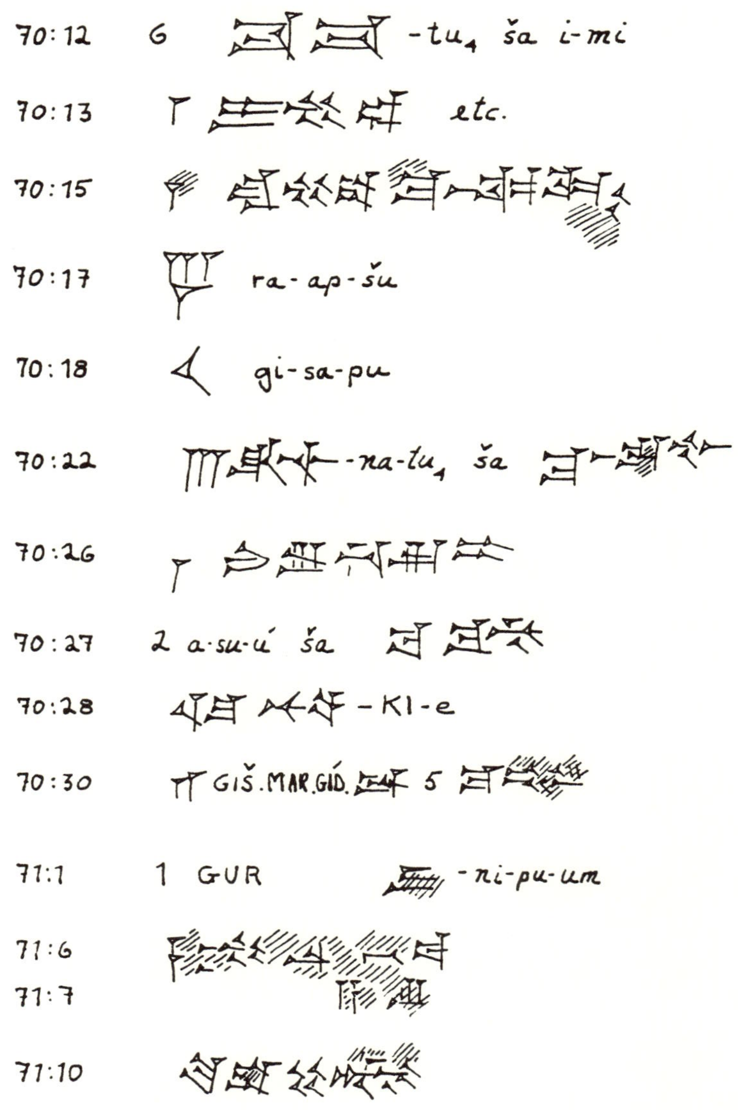

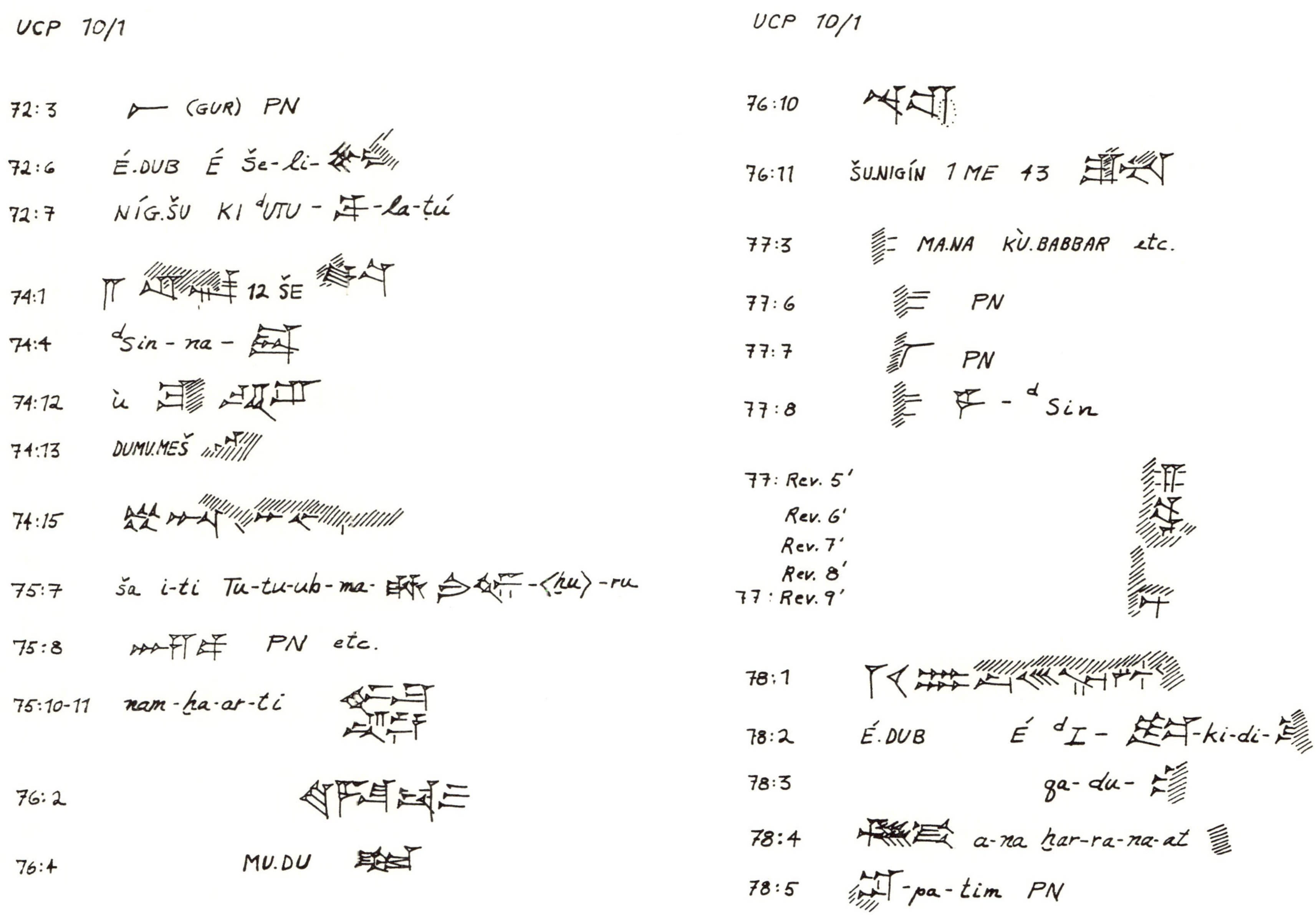
UCP 10/1
72:3 (GUR) PN
72:6 É.DUB É Še-li-
72:7 NÍG.ŠU KI dUTU - -la-ṭú
74:1 12 ŠE
74:4 dSin - na -
74:12 ù
74:13 DUMU.MEŠ
74:15
75:7 ša i-ti Tu-tu-ub-ma- -⟨hu⟩-ru
75:8 PN etc.
75:10-11 nam-ha-ar-ti
76:2
76:4 MU.DU
UCP 10/1
76:10
76:11 ŠU.NIGÍN 1 ME 43
77:3 MA.NA KÙ.BABBAR etc.
77:6 PN
77:7 PN
77:8 - dSin
77: Rev. 5'
Rev. 6'
Rev. 7'
Rev. 8'
77: Rev. 9'
78:1
78:2 É.DUB É dI- -ki-di-
78:3 ga-du-
78:4 a-na har-ra-na-at
78:5 -pa-tim PN

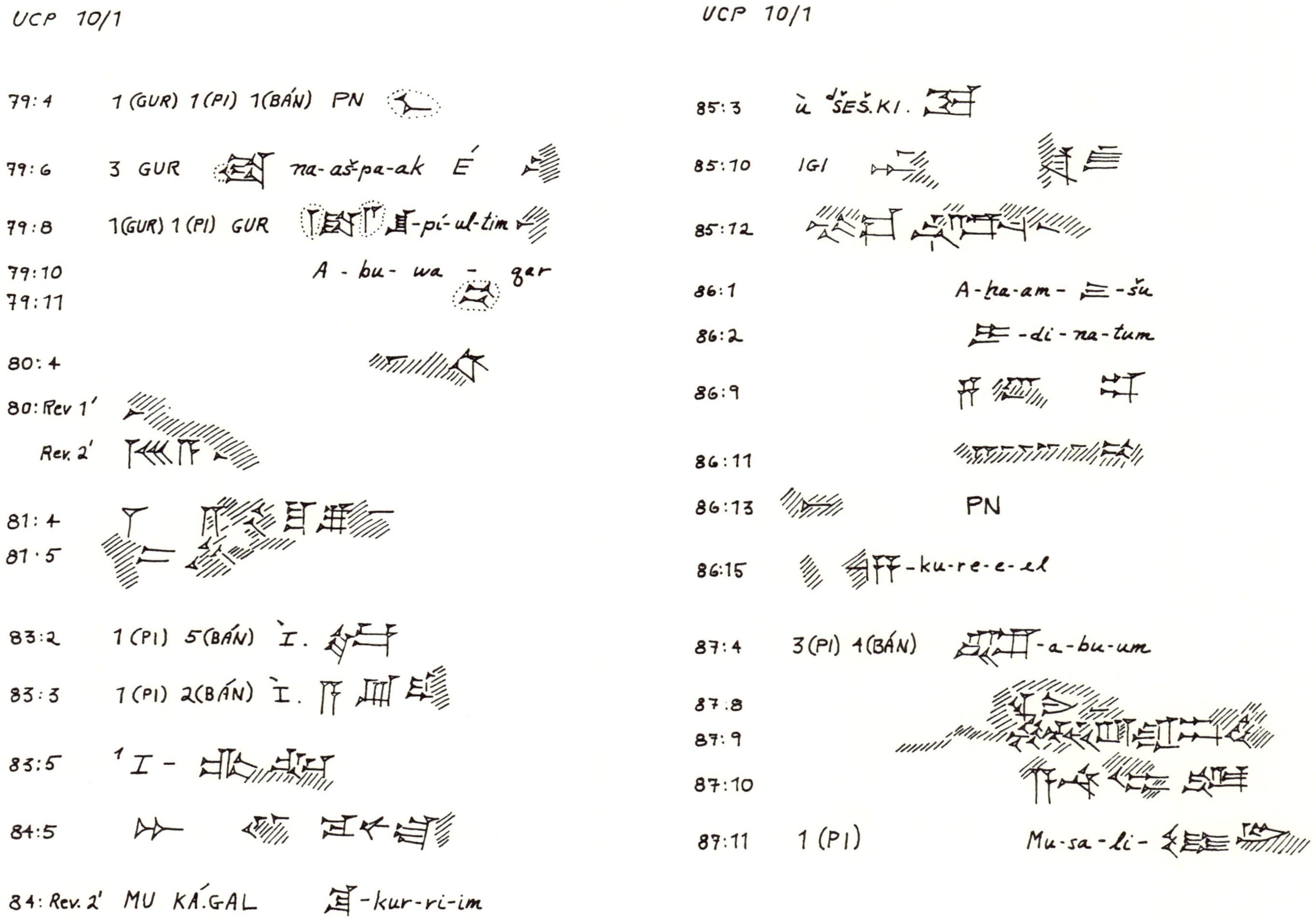
UCP 10/1
79:4 1 (GUR) 1 (PI) 1 (BÁN) PN
79:6 3 GUR na-aš-pa-ak É
79:8 1 (GUR) 1 (PI) GUR -pi-ul-tim
79:10 A-bu-wa-qar
79:11
80:4
80: Rev 1'
Rev. 2'
81:4
81:5
83:2 1 (PI) 5 (BÁN) Ì.
83:3 1 (PI) 2 (BÁN) Ì.
83:5 I-
84:5
84: Rev. 2' MU KÁ.GAL -kur-ri-im
UCP 10/1
85:3 ù ŠEŠ.KI.
85:10 IGI
85:12
86:1 A-ḫa-am- -šu
86:2 -di-na-tum
86:9
86:11
86:13 PN
86:15 -ku-re-e-el
87:4 3 (PI) 4 (BÁN) -a-bu-um
87:8
87:9
87:10
87:11 1 (PI) Mu-sa-li-

UCP 10/1

87:13 a-na a-na bu-gú-

87:17 NÍG.ŠU ᵈ

87:18

88:4 I-di-

88:5 Na- -⟨am⟩-ᵈIM

88:7a

88:8 -du-rum

88:10 [ ]-⌜li⌝-

88:11

88:12

88:14

88:15

88:19 -ia

88:21-22 [ŠU.NIGÍN] GUR ŠE

UCP 10/1

89:4 2 GUR ŠE KÙ.BABBAR 5 GUR ŠE KÙ.BABBAR

89:7 1 (GUR) Ṣíl-lí-

89:10 1 (GUR)

89:12 3(GUR) 2(PI) E-ri- -tum

89:15 1(GUR) PN

89:18 1 (GUR) Na- -la-tum

89:21 I-din-

89:22 A-ḫu-

89:24 1 (GUR) Um-mi- -tum

89:25 1 (GUR) I-gu- -um

89:29 PN

89:30

89:33 La-

89:34 Ib-ni-

89:35

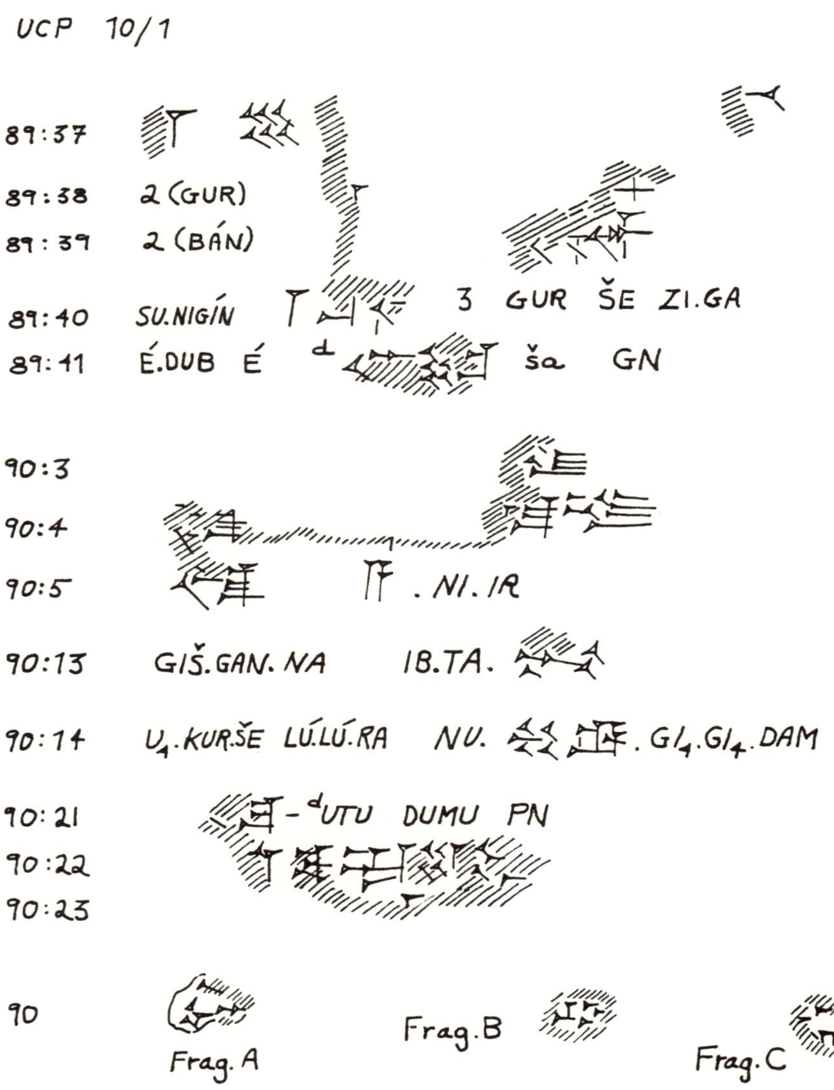
UCP 10/1
89:37
89:38 2 (GUR)
89:39 2 (BÁN)
89:40 SU.NIGÍN 3 GUR ŠE ZI.GA
89:41 É.DUB É d ša GN
90:3
90:4
90:5 .NI.IR
90:13 GIŠ.GAN.NA IB.TA.
90:14 U4.KUR.ŠE LÚ.LÚ.RA NU. . GI4.GI4.DAM
90:21 -dUTU DUMU PN
90:22
90:23
90
Frag. A
Frag. B
Frag. C

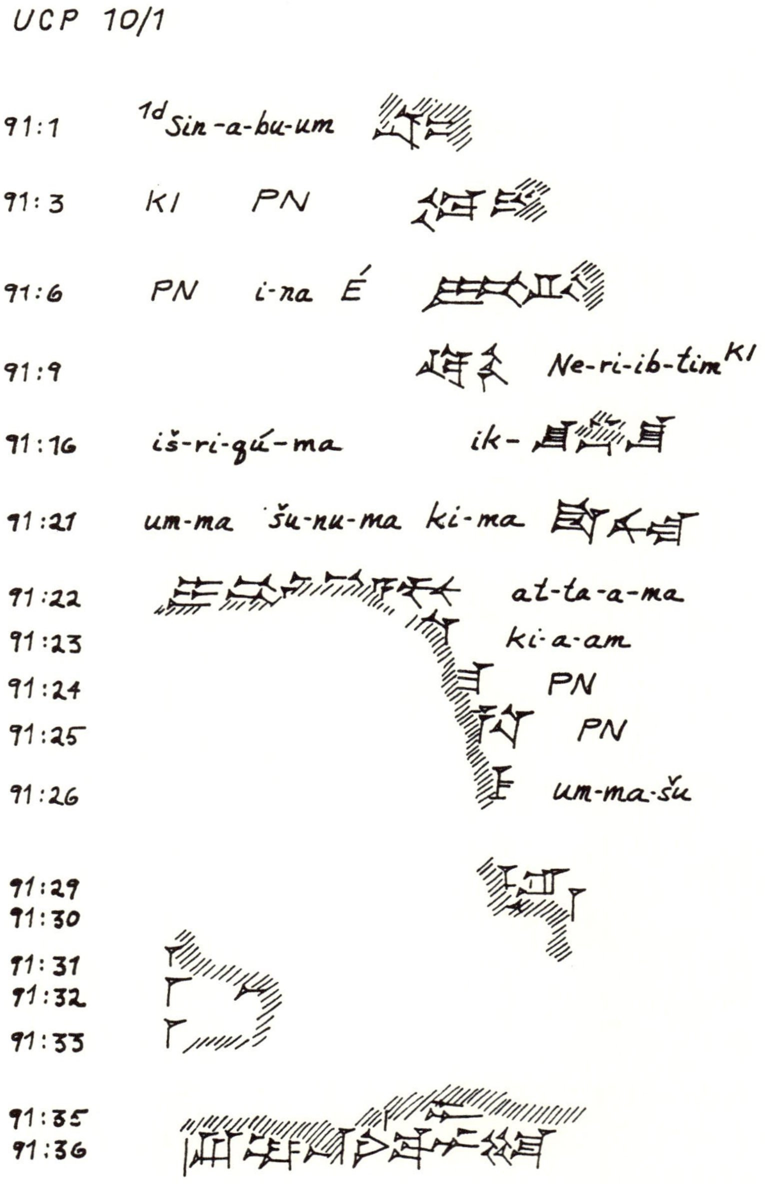
UCP 10/1
91:1 1dSin-a-bu-um
91:3 KI PN
91:6 PN i-na É
91:9 Ne-ri-ib-timKI
91:16 iš-ri-qú-ma ik-
91:21 um-ma šu-nu-ma ki-ma
91:22 at-ta-a-ma
91:23 ki-a-am
91:24 PN
91:25 PN
91:26 um-ma-šu
91:29
91:30
91:31
91:32
91:33
91:35
91:36

UCP 10/1

91 Seal Legends

A 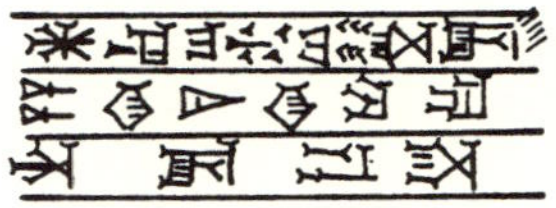

B 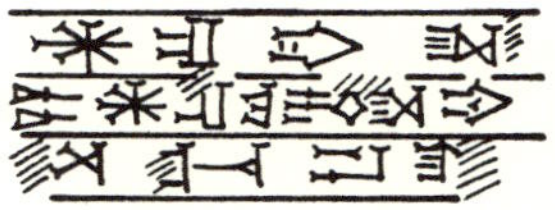

C 

D 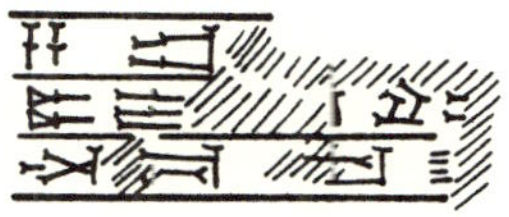

92:7 

92:8 

92:13 

92:16 

93:2 KI ^{d}ŠEŠ.KI. 

93:13
93:14
93:15 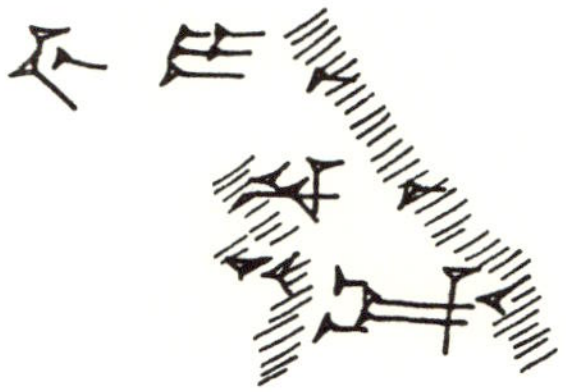

93:16 

UCP 10/1

94:4 UD.10 ša- 

94:6 a-na pa-nu a-bi-im 

94:7  . ^{d}IŠKUR.RA

94:10 a-na ša  -lim

94:16 iš-tu GUD.HI.A 

94:21  UD.7.KAM etc.

94:25 

95:3 ù ^{d}ŠEŠ.KI. 

95:5 DUMU  -ma-AN

95:10 PN DUMU 

95:16 

96:1 2 GUR ŠE ^{d}Še-rum- 

96:6 DUMU.SAL ^{d}Sin-i- 

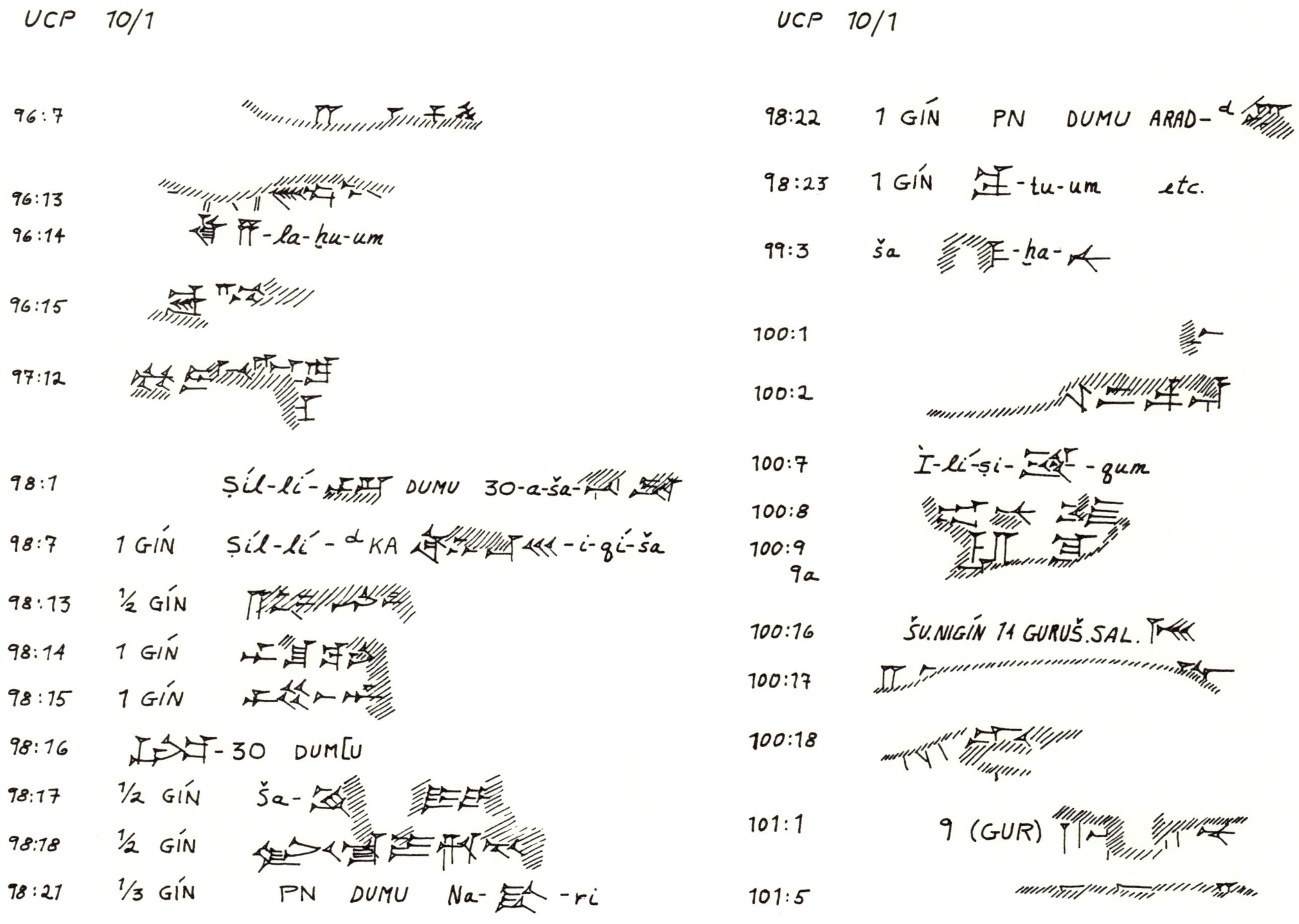
UCP 10/1
96:7
96:13
96:14 -la-hu-um
96:15
97:12
98:1 ṣíl-lí- DUMU 30-a-ša-
98:7 1 GÍN ṣíl-lí-ᵈKA -i-gi-ša
98:13 ½ GÍN
98:14 1 GÍN
98:15 1 GÍN
98:16 -30 DUMU[U
98:17 ½ GÍN ša-
98:18 ½ GÍN
98:21 ⅓ GÍN PN DUMU Na- -ri
UCP 10/1
98:22 1 GÍN PN DUMU ARAD-ᵈ
98:23 1 GÍN -tu-um etc.
99:3 ša -ha-
100:1
100:2
100:7 Ì-lí-ṣi- -qum
100:8
100:9
9a
100:16 ŠU.NIGÍN 14 GURUŠ.SAL.
100:17
100:18
101:1 9 (GUR)
101:5

UCP 10/1

102:2 ša iš-tu Ú-pí- 

102:8 1 IG 

103:1
103:3
103:4

103:13
103:14
103:15

104:1 1(GUR) 1(PI) 4(BÁN) GUR 

104:3 DUMU ᵈSin-mu-ba-li- 

104:3a 

104:7 BÀD-Ri-muš iš- 

104:13
104:14
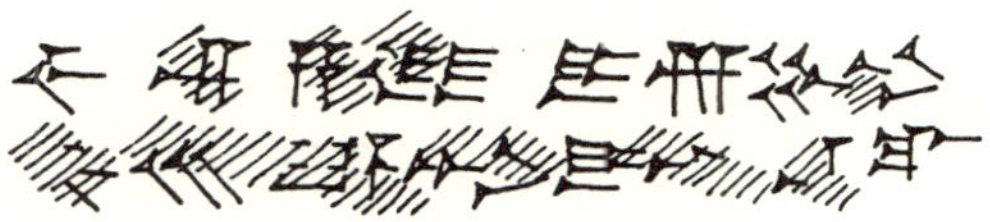

104:16 URU Ki-maš [É-kál]- 

UCP 10/1

105:3 a-na Tu-li- 

105:9 ¹Tu-li- 

105:13  -ṭú-up-tum

105:15 

105:17
105:17a
105:18
105:19
105:20
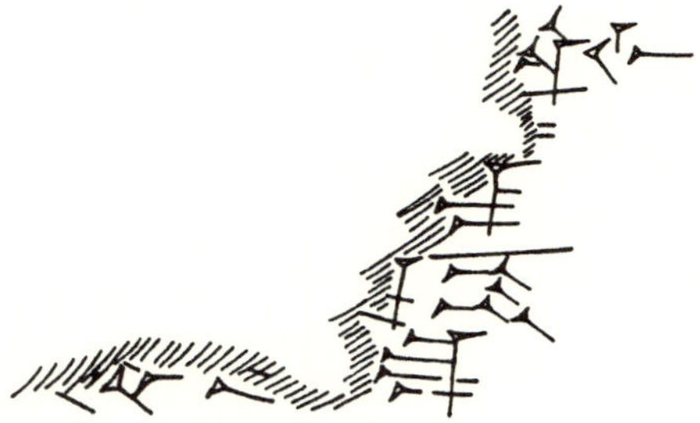

105:23
105:24
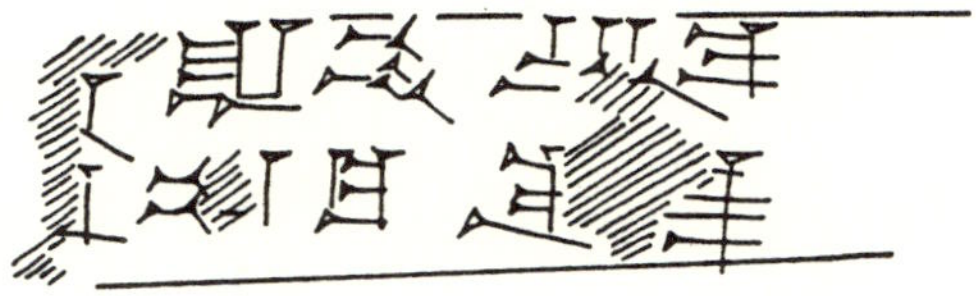

105:27 ¹Na-ra-am- 

105:30 PN DUMU ᵈUTU-TAB. 

105:31 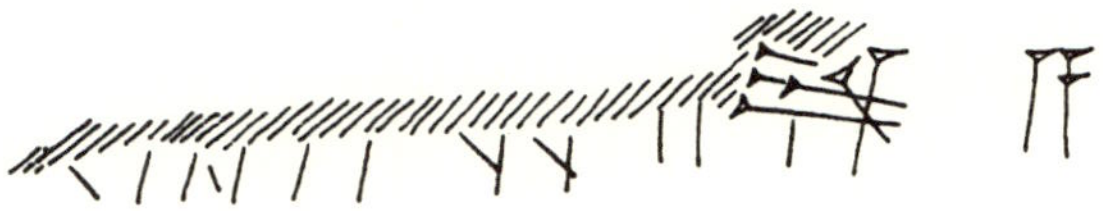

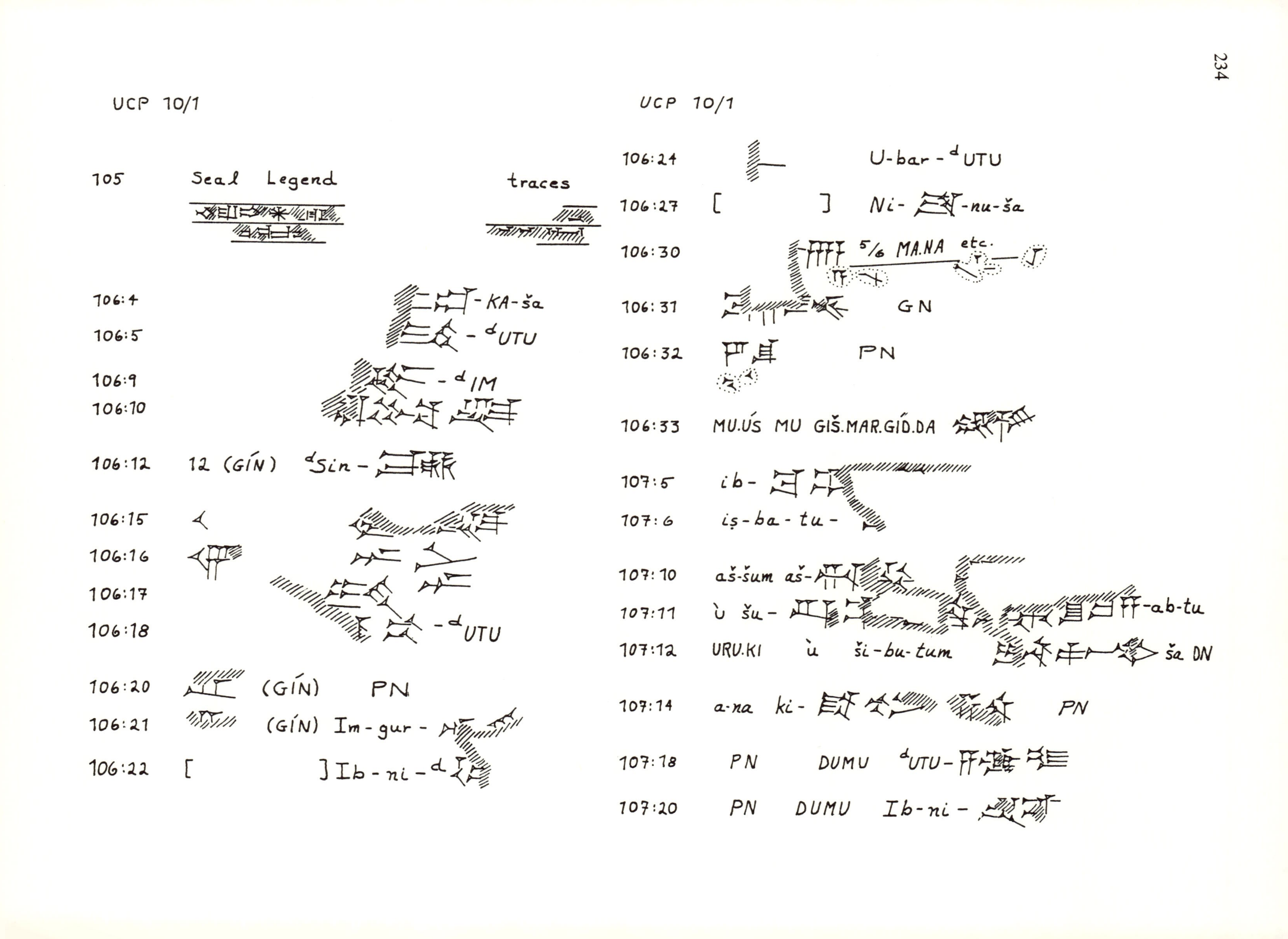

UCP 10/1

105 Seal Legend traces

106:4 -KA-ša

106:5 - ^{d}UTU

106:9 - ^{d}IM

106:10

106:12 12 (GÍN) ^{d}Sin -

106:15

106:16

106:17

106:18 - ^{d}UTU

106:20 (GÍN) PN

106:21 (GÍN) Im-gur -

106:22 [ ] Ib-ni- ^{d}

UCP 10/1

106:24 U-bar- ^{d}UTU

106:27 [ ] Ni- -nu-ša

106:30 5/6 MA.NA etc.

106:31 GN

106:32 PN

106:33 MU.ÚS MU GIŠ.MAR.GÍD.DA

107:5 ib-

107:6 iṣ-ba-tu-

107:10 aš-šum aš-

107:11 ù šu- -ab-tu

107:12 URU.KI ù ši-bu-tum ša DN

107:14 a-na ki- PN

107:18 PN DUMU ^{d}UTU-

107:20 PN DUMU Ib-ni-

107:24 ¹Sa-at-lu-ma

107:27 ù PN DUMU.MEŠ

107:28 [ ]

107:29

107 Seal Legends

A 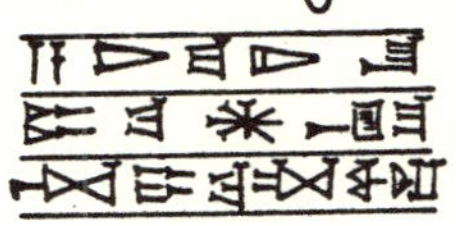

C 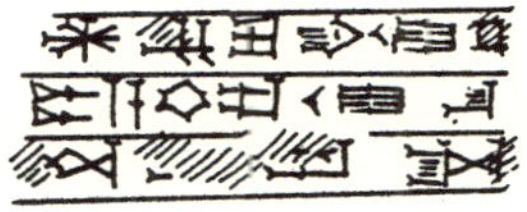

108:9 ¹Sa-kum

108:11

108:12 ⌜1⌝ Bu-⌝

108:13 ⌜1⌝ [ ]

108:16 ¹AN-um-

108:28 -pu-uṭ-

108:36ff.

108:39ff.

108:42ff.

UCP 10/1

109:1 2 EŠE GÁN A.ŠÀ i-na ṭì-a- CLAY ADHESION

109:16 MU DN ù -du-ša

109:19 IGI Ìr-ra- CLAY ADHESION

109:20 DUMU Iš-me-

109:21 IGI PN DUMU Ì-lí-

109:28 CLAY ADHESION CLAY ADHESION

109:29 DUMU CLAY ADHES. CLAY ADHES.

109:31 DUMU CLAY ADH.

109:32

109:33

109 Seal Legend traces

110 iii 3 P[N]

110 iii 5 2(PI) 2(BÁN) ᵈSin-mu-

110 iii 11 1(PI) 2(BÁN) Ni- -nu-ša 2.KAM

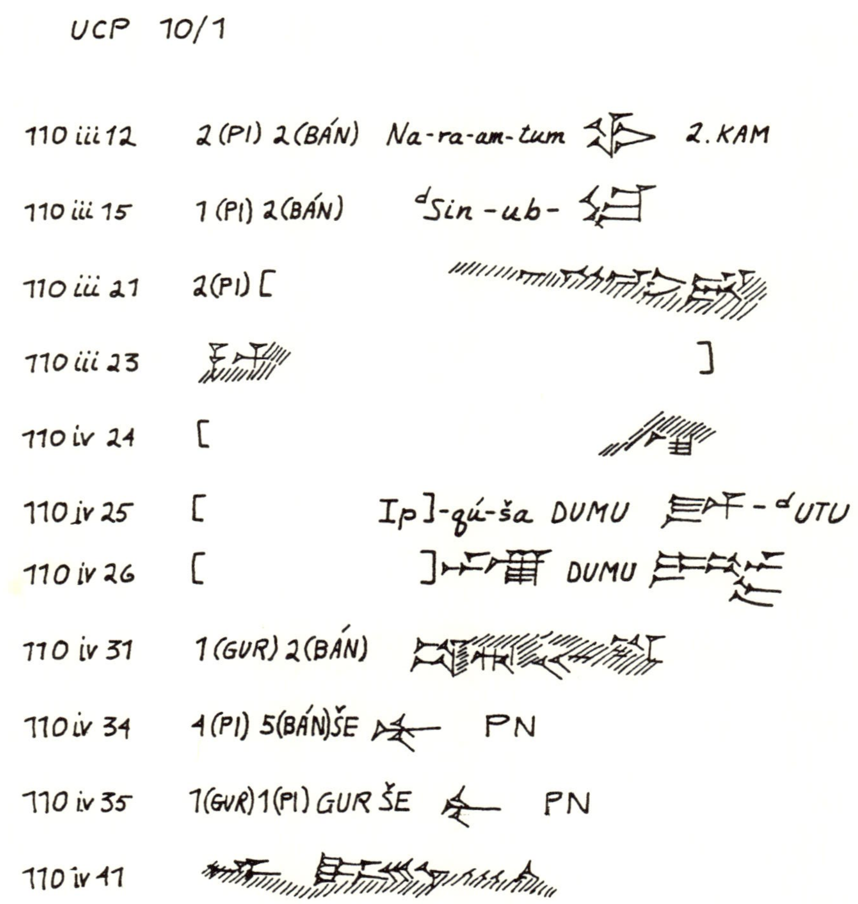
UCP 10/1
110 iii 12 2(PI) 2(BÁN) Na-ra-am-tum 2.KAM
110 iii 15 1(PI) 2(BÁN) dSin-ub-
110 iii 21 2(PI) [
110 iii 23]
110 iv 24 [
110 iv 25 [Ip]-qú-ša DUMU -dUTU
110 iv 26 [ ] DUMU
110 iv 31 1(GUR) 2(BÁN)
110 iv 34 4(PI) 5(BÁN) ŠE PN
110 iv 35 1(GUR) 1(PI) GUR ŠE PN
110 iv 41

UCLMA 9/2826
46 x 12 x 26 mm.

Obv.
1
5

L.E.

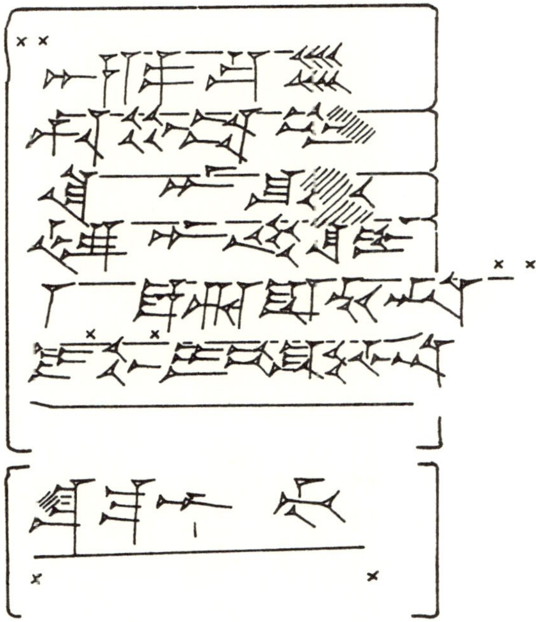

Env. Variants
1
5
6 omits SAL
7a

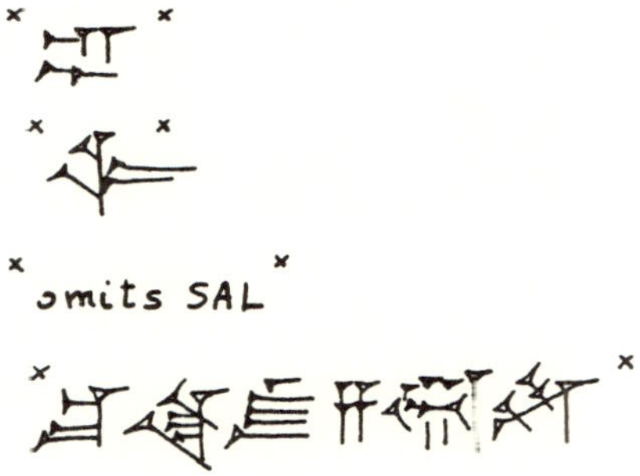

UCLMA 9/2826

Rev.
10

U.E.

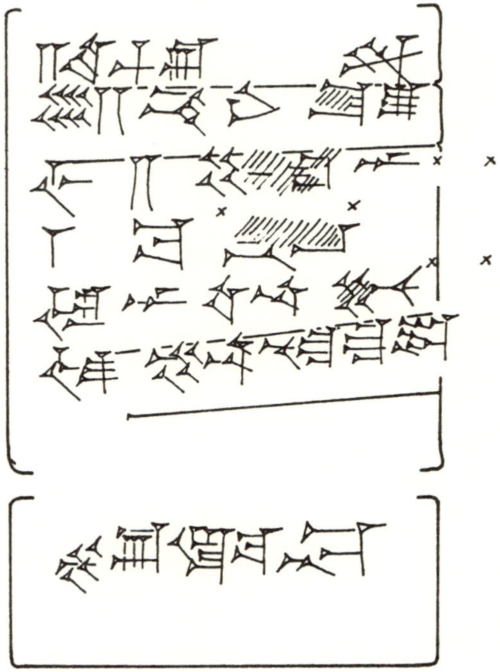

Env. Variants
10
11
12

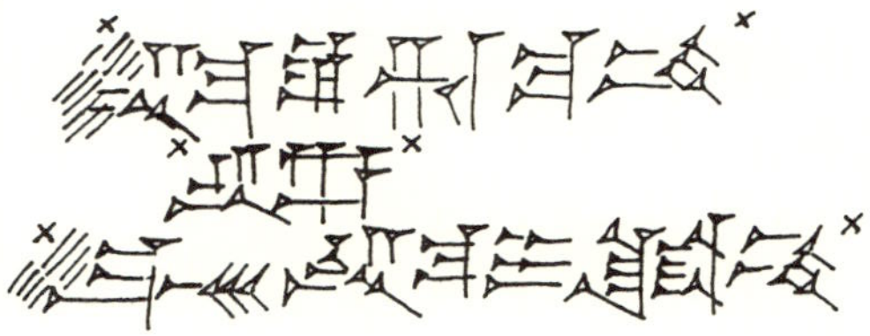

UCLMA 9/2827

71 x 15 x 21 mm.

Obv.

1

5

10

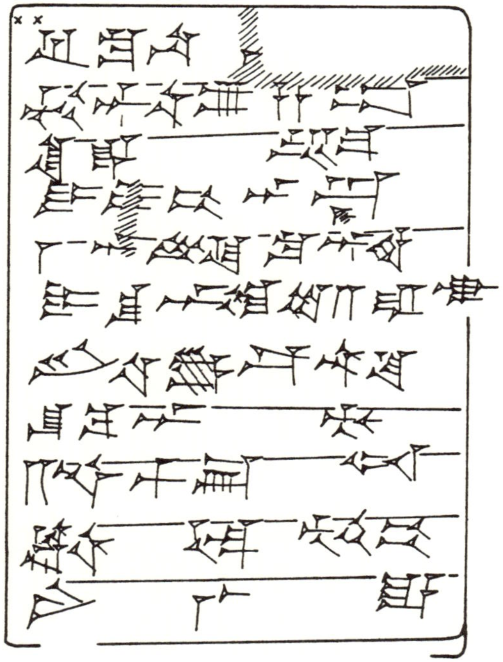

Env. Variants

1

UCLMA 9/2827

Rev.

15

20

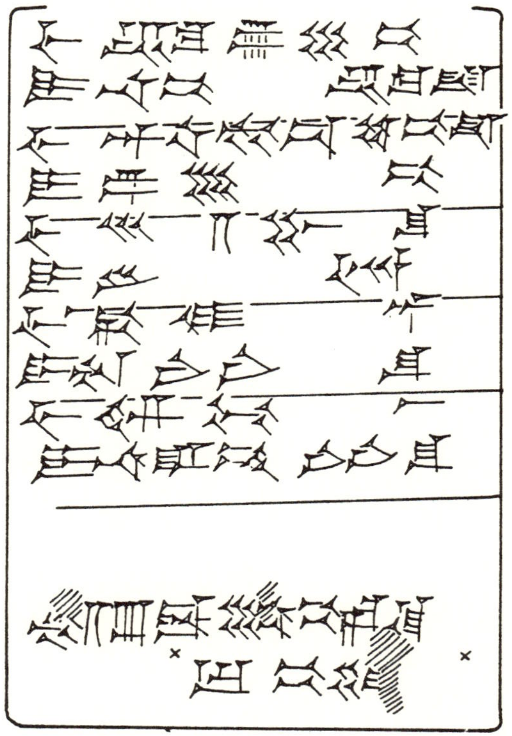

Env. Variants

22

UCLMA 9/2828

Date Formula

Envelope Variant

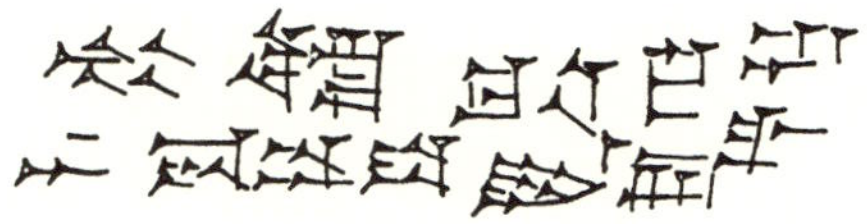

UCLMA 9/2831

46 x 37 x 18 mm.

Obv.

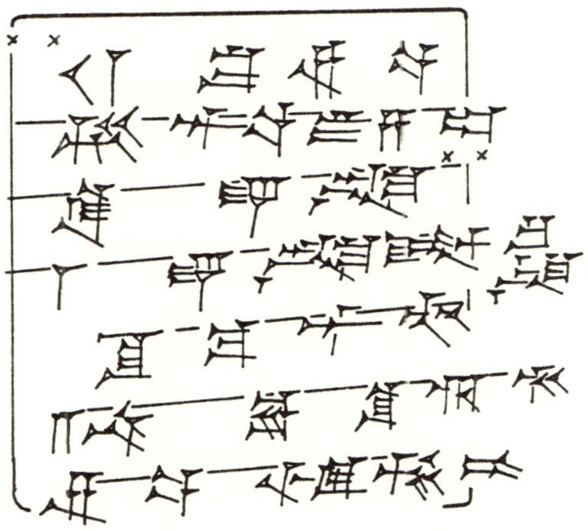

L.E.

Env. Variants

1 

3a 

8 ˣomits Eˣ

UCLMA 9/2831

Rev.

U.E.

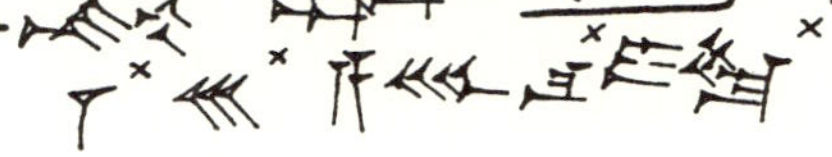

Env. Variants

12 

13 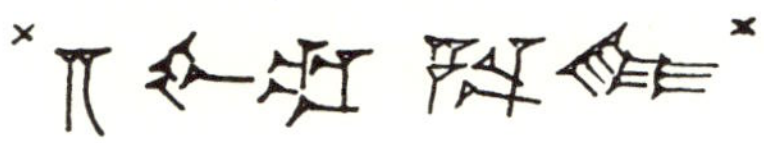

15 

16  

UCLMA 9/2858+2863

60x44x25 mm.

Obv.

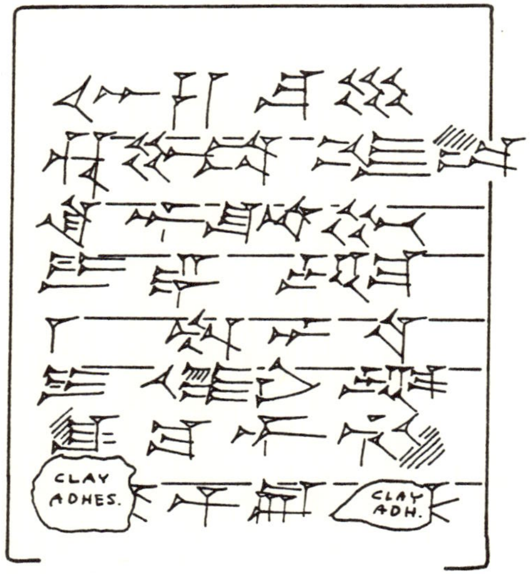

L.E.

Env. Variants

10

UCLMA 9/2858+2863

Rev.

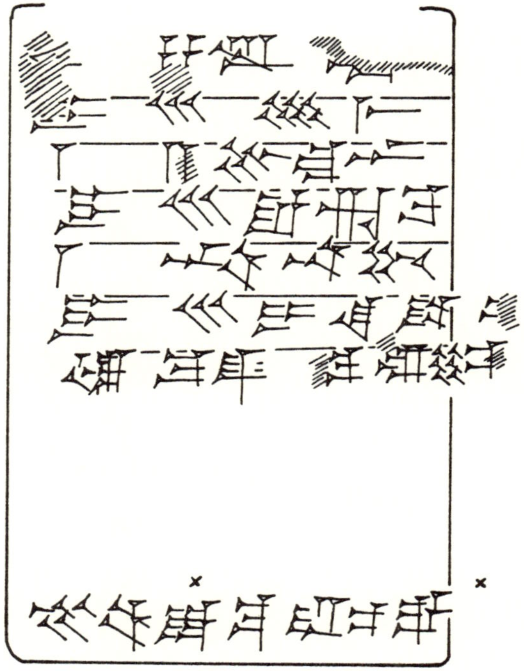

Env. Variants

18

18a

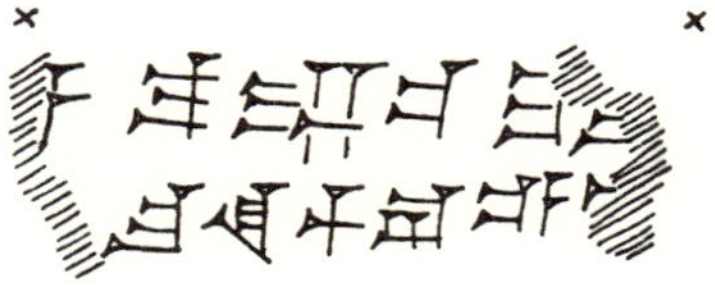

Seal Legend B

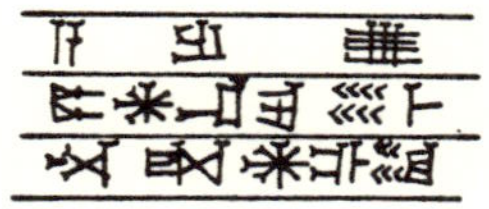

UCLMA 9/2860

39 x 36 x 22 mm.

Obv.

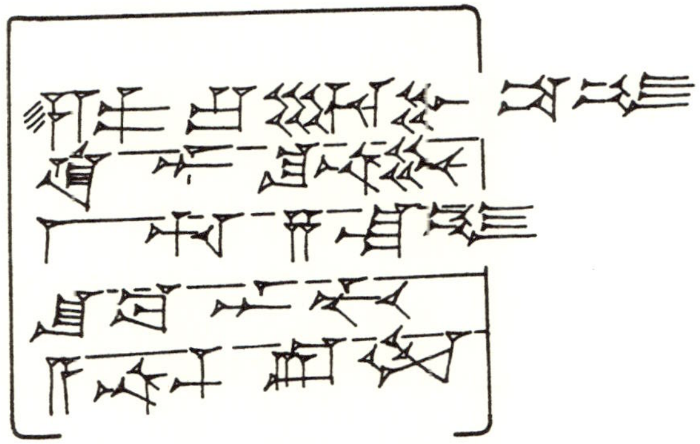

L.E.

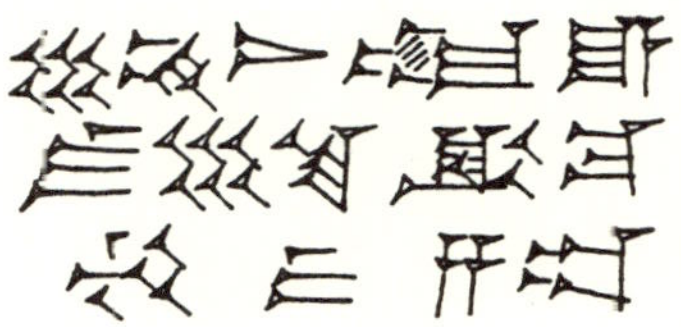

Envelope

UCLMA 9/2859

Date Formula

UCLMA 9/2860

Rev.

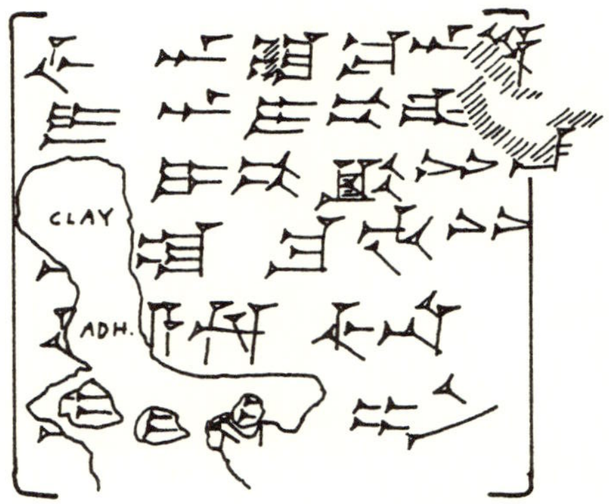

U.E.

Seal Legend

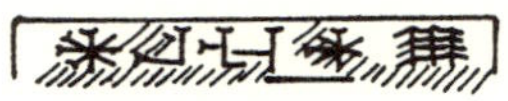

UCLMA 9/2862

53x40x22

Obv.

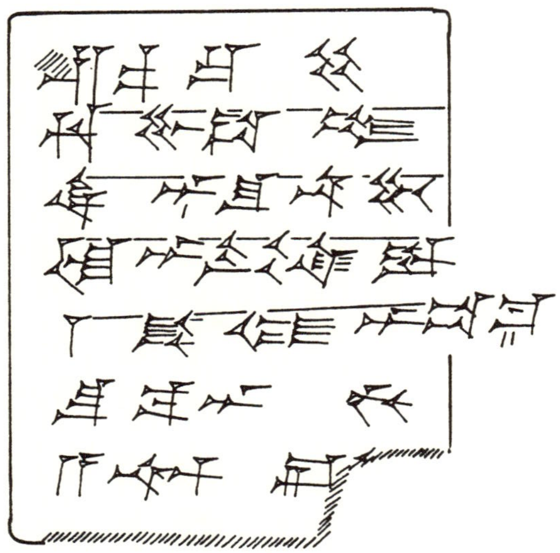

UCLMA 9/2862

Rev.

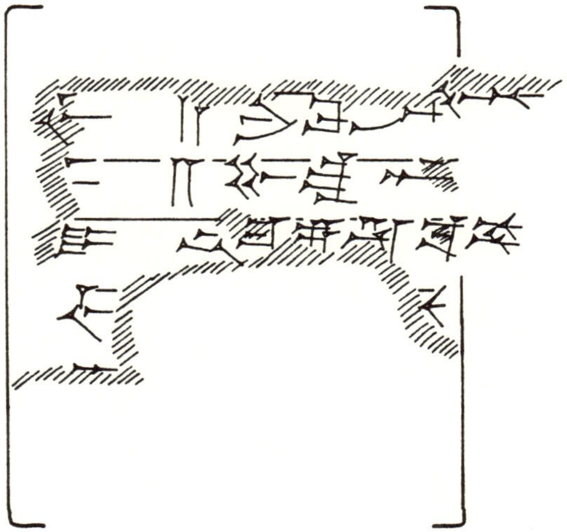

U.E.

UCLMA 9/2864

69x57x24

Obv.

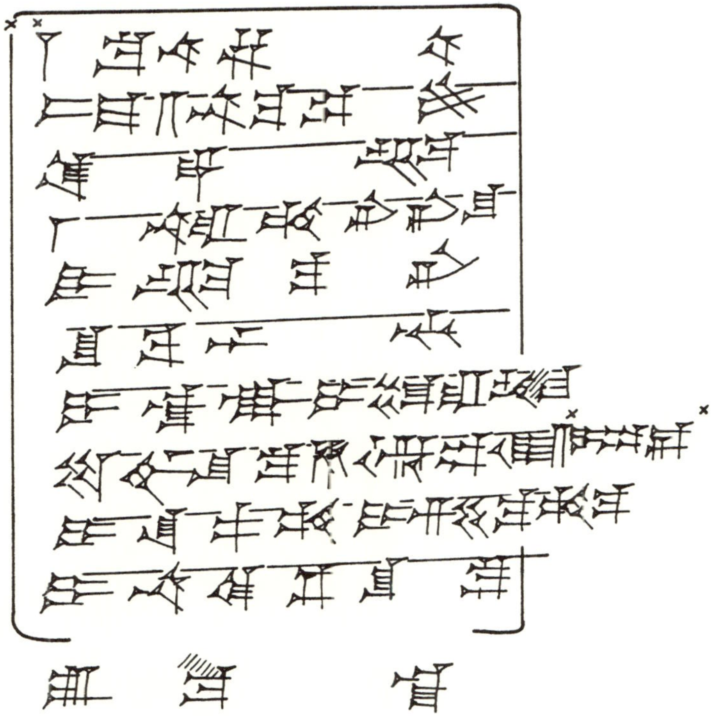

L.E.

Env. Variants

1 

8 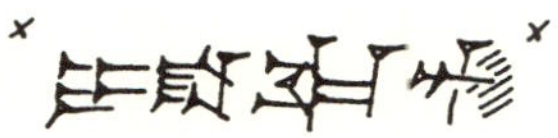

UCLMA 9/2864

Rev.

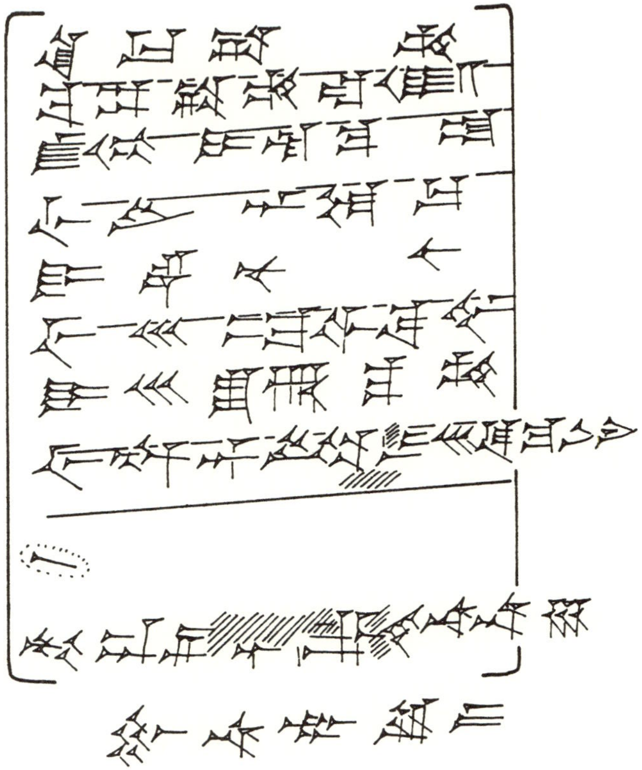

U.E.

Seal Legend

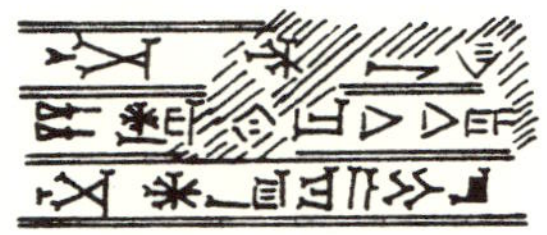

UCLMA 9/2866

52x43x28 mm.

Obv.

1

5

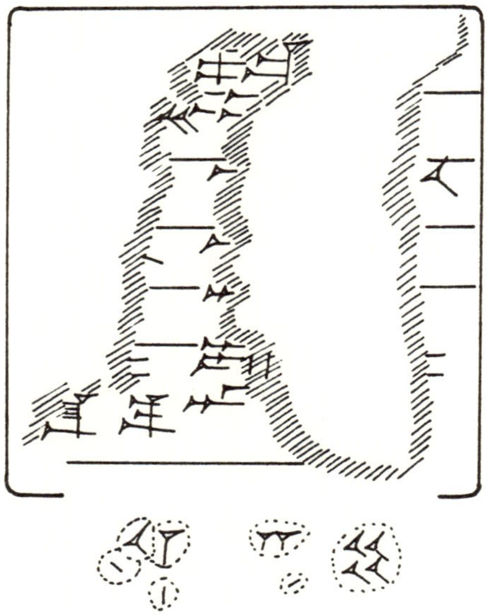

L.E.

Envelope

5

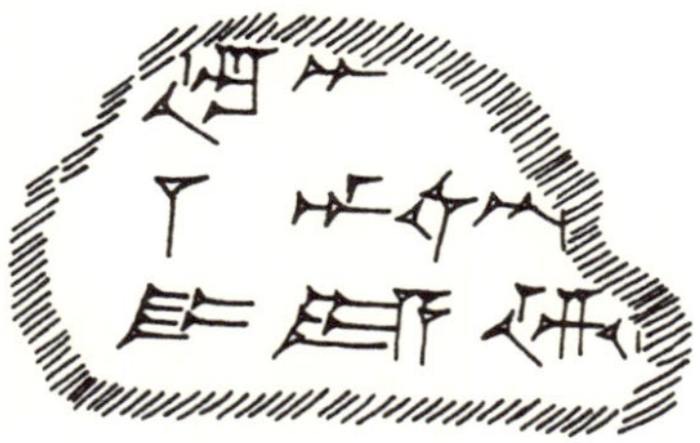

UCLMA 9/2866

Rev.

10

15

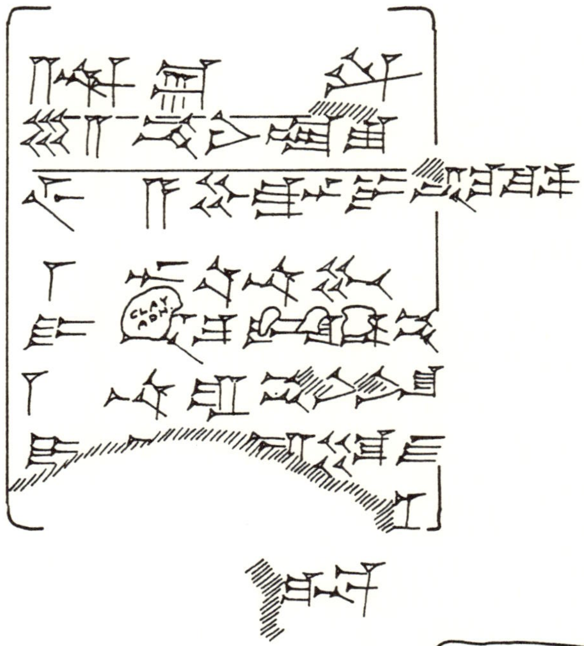

U.E.

UCLMA 9/2878

55 x 53 x 18 mm.

Rev. (?)

1'

5'

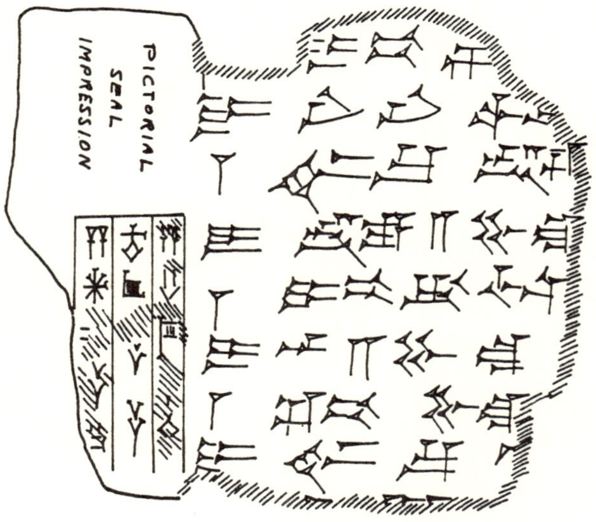

UCLMA 9/2889a

108x114x35 mm.

Obv.
col i

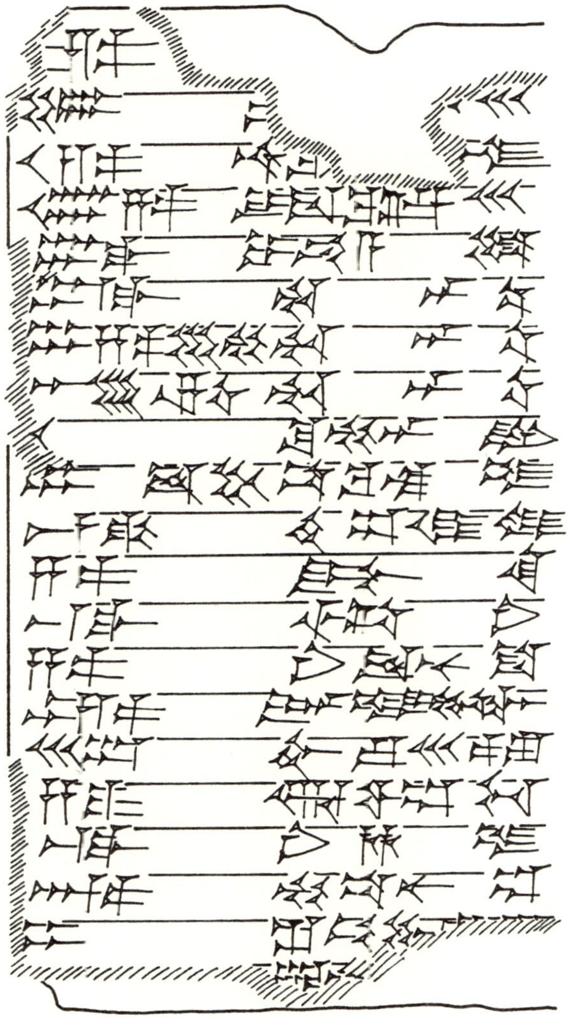

UCLMA 9/2889a

Obv.
col ii

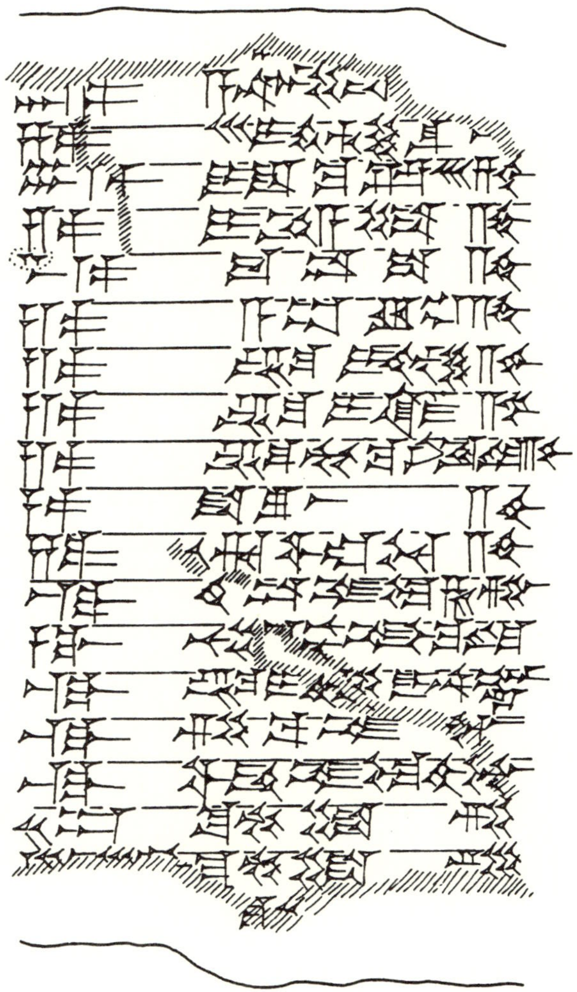

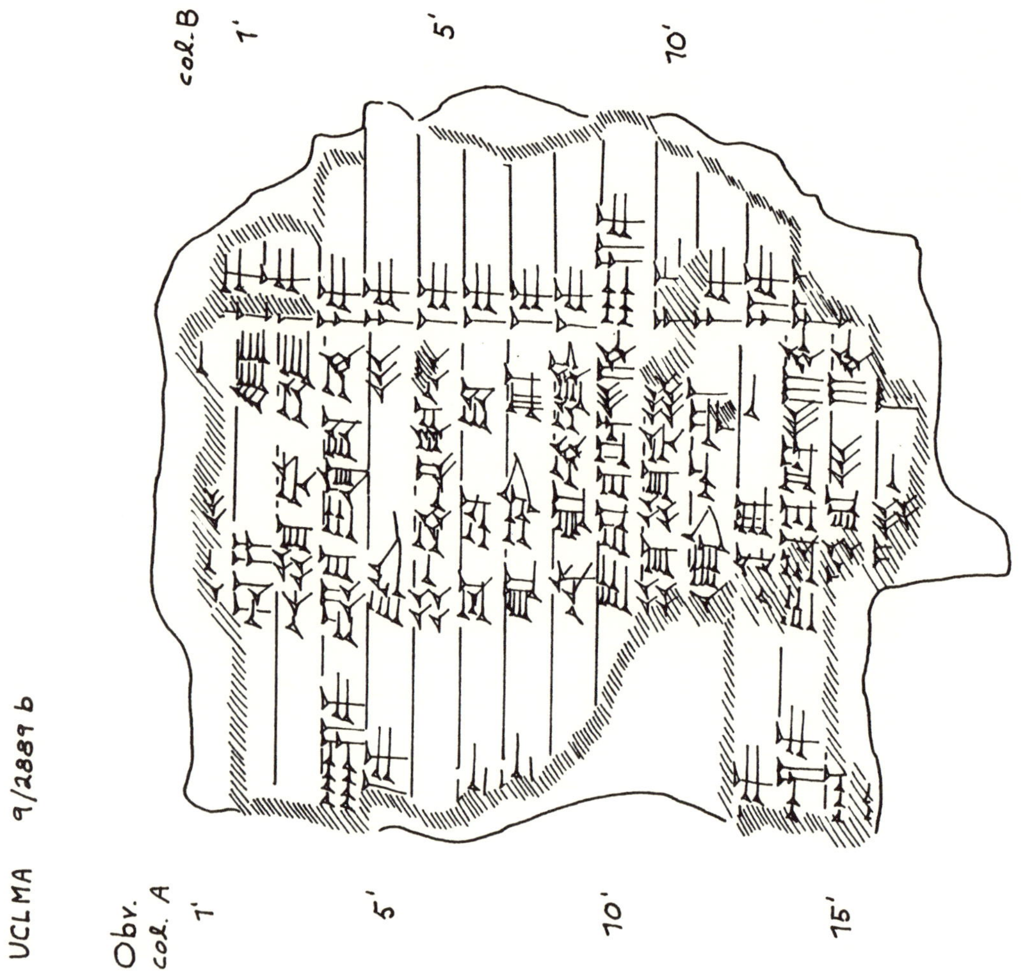
UCLMA 9/2889b
Obv.
col. A
1'
5'
10'
15'
col. B
1'
5'
10'

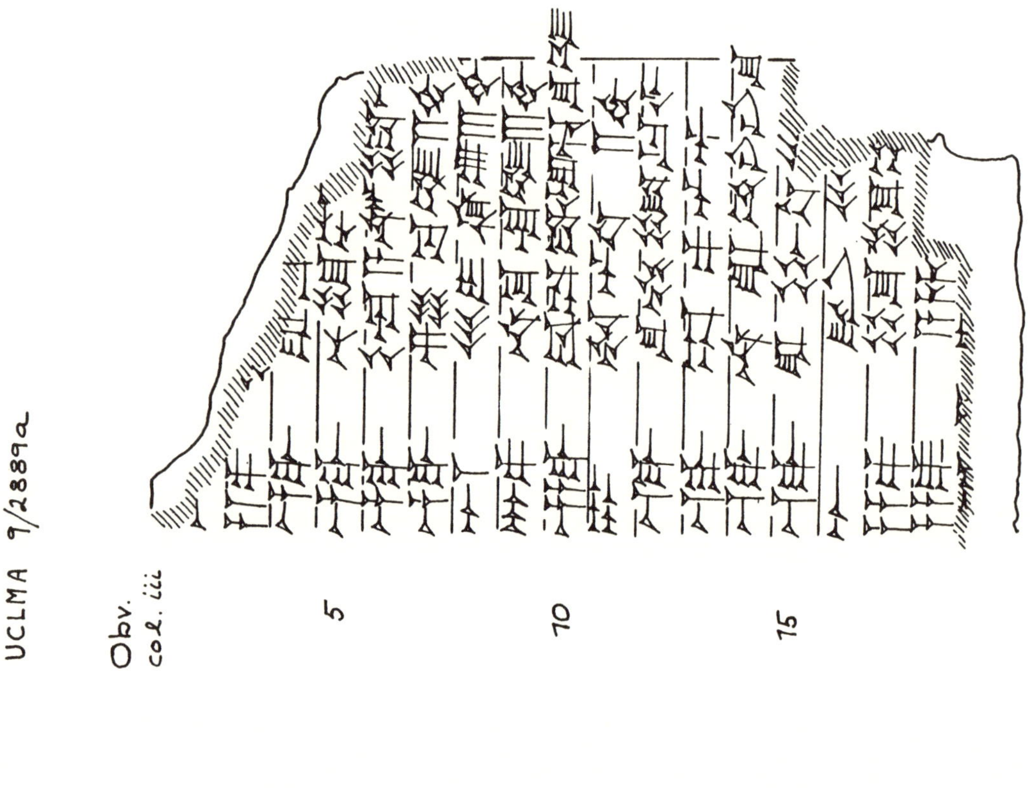
UCLMA 9/2889a
Obv.
col. iii
5
10
15

UCLMA 9/2889a

Rev.

col. v col. iv

1' 1'

5'

UCLMA 9/2889 c

47 x 58 x 72 mm.

Rev.

col. B col. A

1' 1'

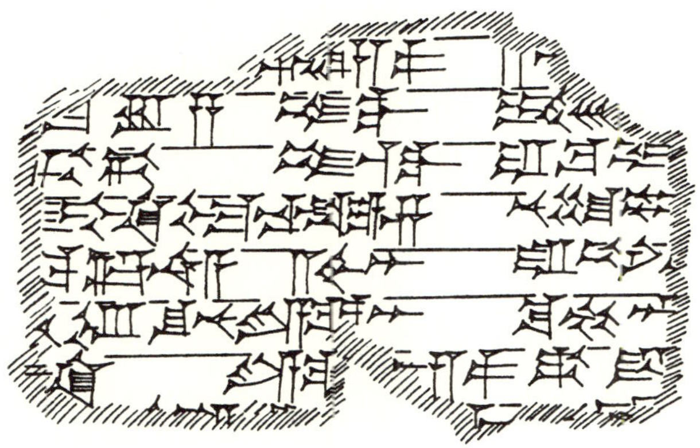

5' 5'

UCLMA 9/2892

31 x 30 x 20 mm.

Obv.

1

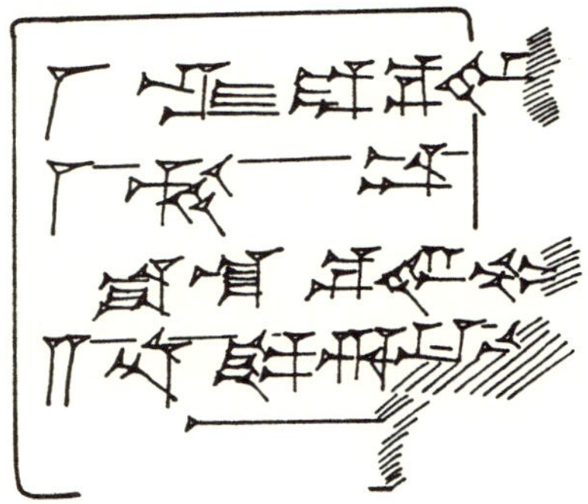

Rev.

5

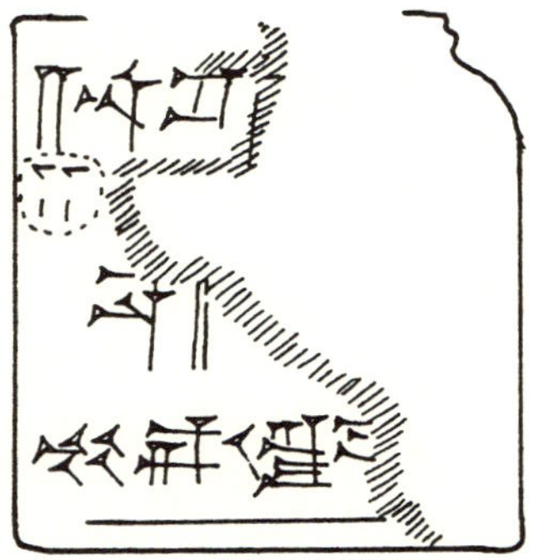

UCLMA 9/2895

59x36x23 mm.

Obv.

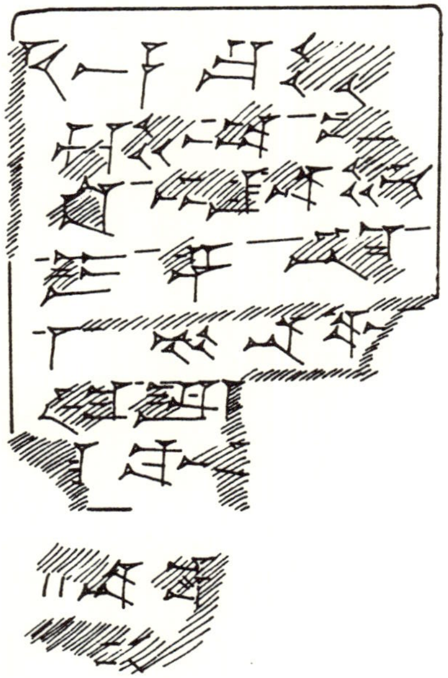

L.E.

UCLMA 9/2895

Rev.

U.E.

UCLMA 9/2906
76x47x23 mm.

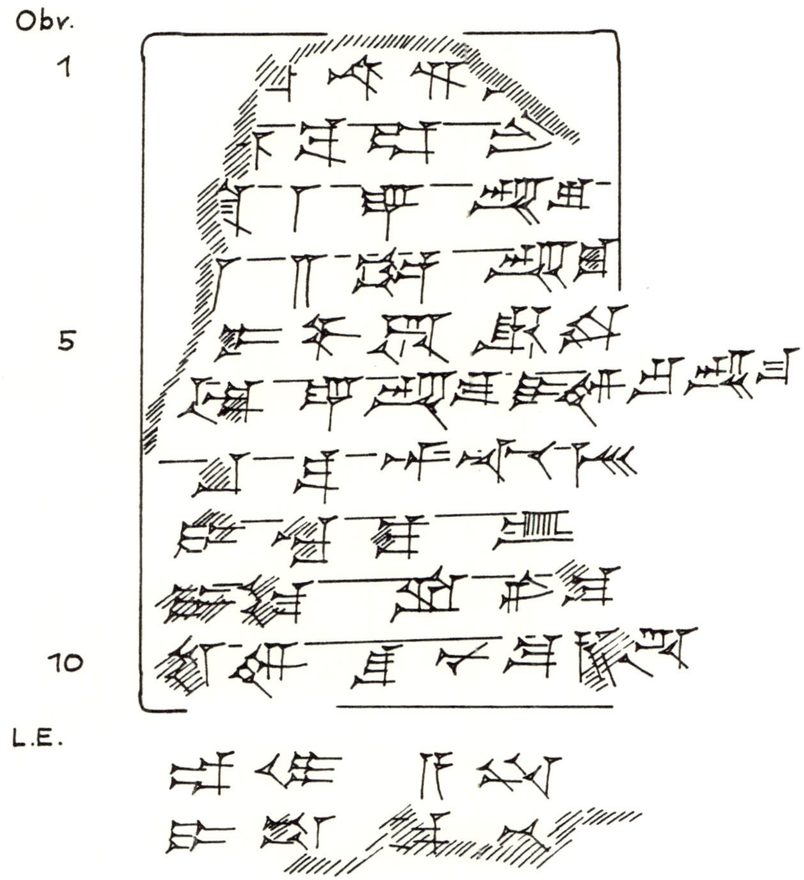

UCLMA 9/2906

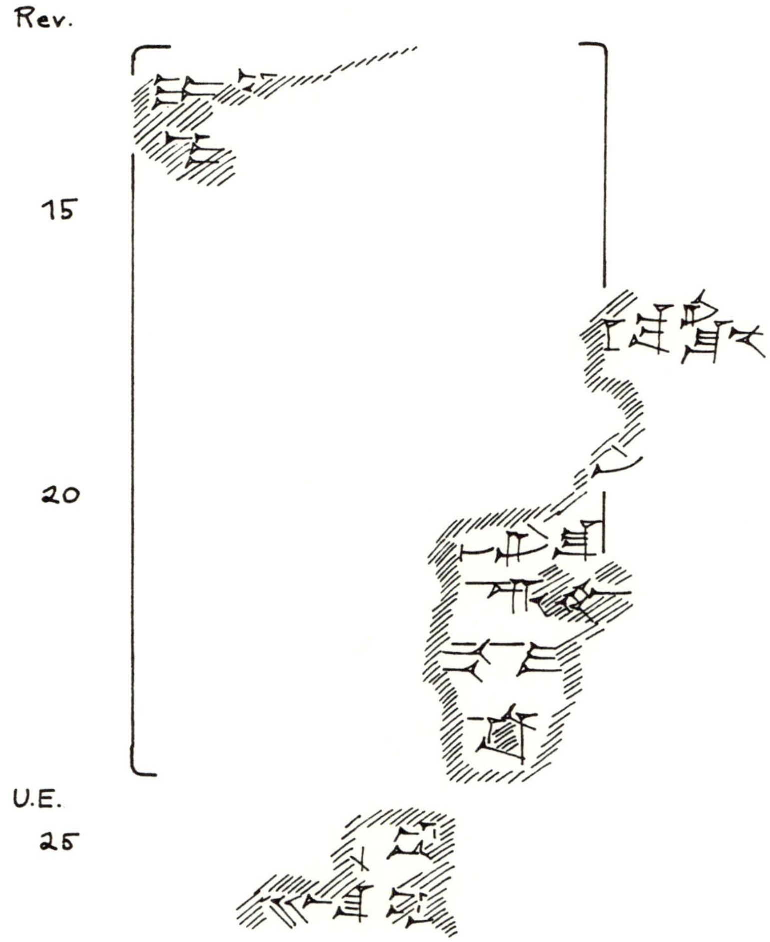

UCLMA 9/2942

26 x 18 x 19 mm.

Obv.

1

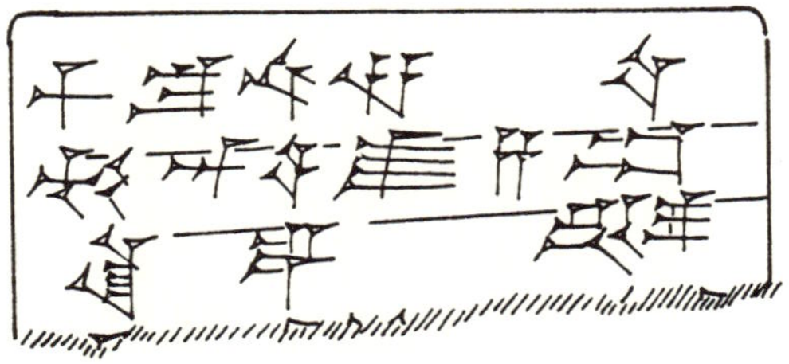

Rev.

1'

UCLMA 9/2958

37 x 35 x 18 mm.

Obv.

1

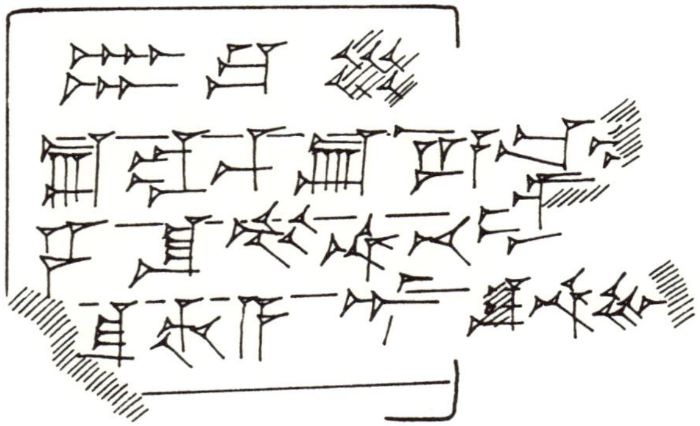

L.E.

5

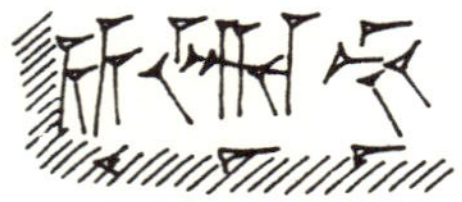

UCLMA 9/2943

33 x 31 x 23 mm.

Obv.

1

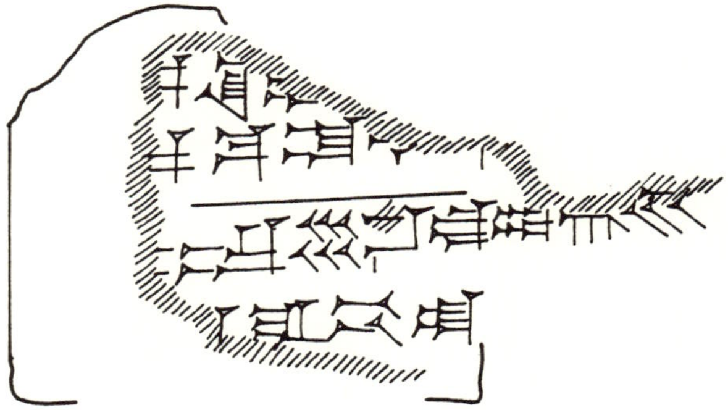

Rev.

5

UCLMA 9/2957

45 x 40 x 6 mm.

Envelope Fragment and Seal Legend

UCLMA 9/3019

90 x 50 x 26 mm.

Obv.

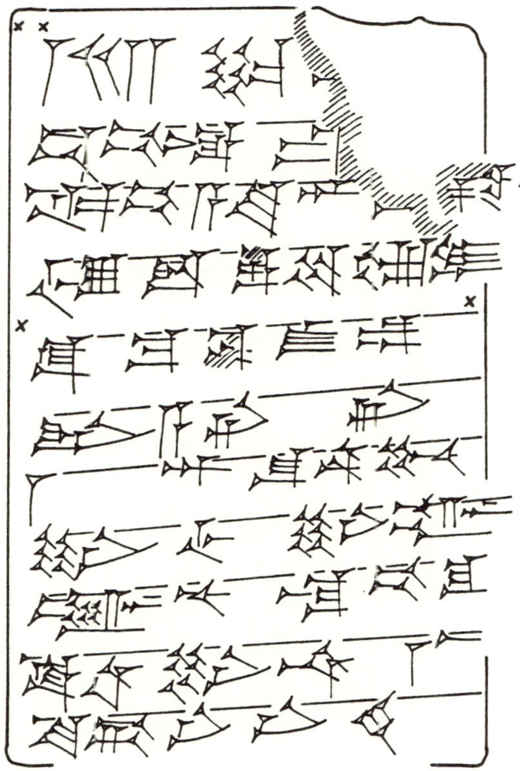

L.E.

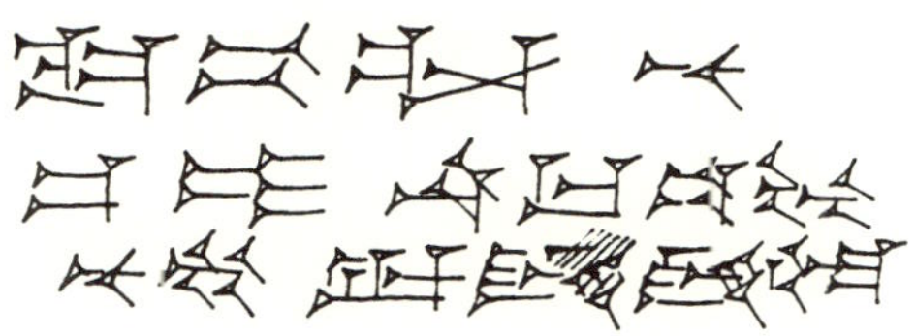

UCLMA 9/3019

Rev.

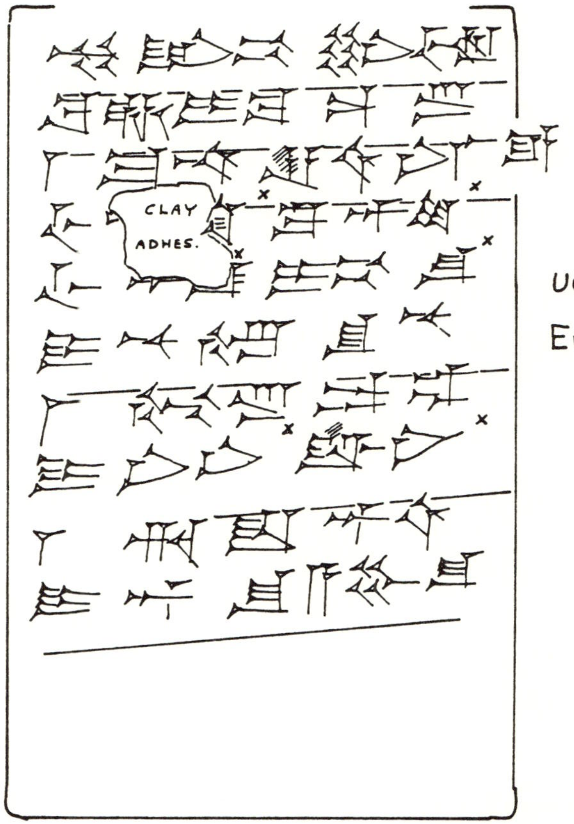

UCLMA 9/3019

Envelope Variants

1
5
18
18a
19
22

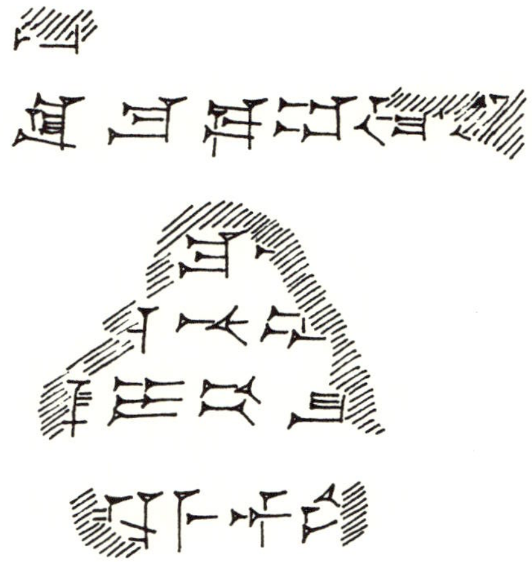

Label

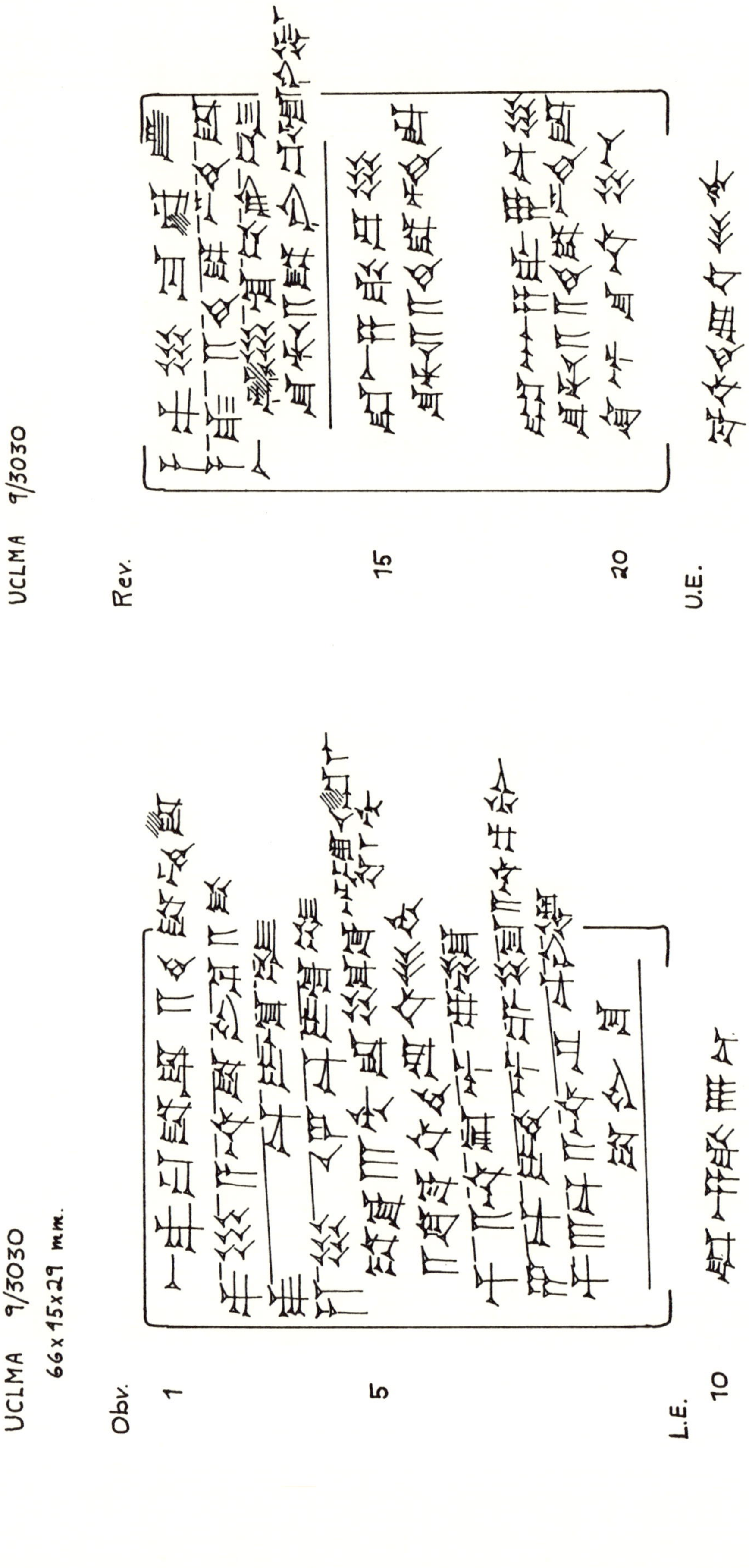
UCLMA 9/3030
66x45x29 mm.
Obv.
L.E.
UCLMA 9/3030
Rev.
U.E.